Transactions
of the
Royal Historical
Society

SIXTH SERIES

III

LONDON 1993

British Library Cataloguing in Publication Data

Transactions of the Royal Historial Society.
   —6th Series, vol. III (1993)
   1. History—Periodicals
   I. Royal Historical Society
   905   D1
ISBN 0-86193-136-X

Made and printed in Great Britain by Butler & Tanner Ltd, Frome and London

CONTENTS

	PAGE
Presidential Address: English Landed Society in the Twentieth Century: IV, Prestige without Power? F. M. L. Thompson	I
'Between the Sea Power and the Land Power': Scandinavia and the Coming of the First World War. Patrick Salmon	23
Confession before 1215. Alexander Murray	51
'Les Engleys Nées en Irlande': The English Political Identity in Medieval Ireland. Robin Frame	83
The Origins of the Gothic Revival: a Reappraisal (*The Alexander Prize Essay*). Giles Worsley	105
Providence, Protestant Union and Godly Reformation in the 1690s. (*The Alexander Prize Essay*, proxime accessit). Craig Rose	151
A Thirty Years War? The Two World Wars in Historical Perspective. (*The Prothero Lecture*). Michael Howard	171
Bristol West India Merchants in the Eighteenth Century. Kenneth Morgan	185
The Atlantic in the Eighteenth Century: a Southern Perspective on the Need to Return to the 'Big Picture'. Kenneth Maxwell	209
Economic Depression and the Making of 'Traditional' Society in Colonial India, 1820–1855. David Washbrook	237

Against Formality: One Aspect of the English Revolution.   265
    J. C. Davis

Report of Council for 1991–1992
Officers and Council 1993   289

TRANSACTIONS OF THE
ROYAL HISTORICAL SOCIETY

PRESIDENTIAL ADDRESS

By F. M. L. Thompson

ENGLISH LANDED SOCIETY
IN THE TWENTIETH CENTURY
IV. PRESTIGE WITHOUT POWER?

READ 20 NOVEMBER 1992

BY hook or by crook, sometimes by both at the same time, great landowners, and many of the not so great, have survived into the final decade of the twentieth century. Some of the survivors are, no doubt, clinging on by their fingernails, huddled over a single-bar electric fire in a damp and draughty room of a family mansion that is slowly crumbling over their heads, living on baked beans and memories in the manner of an A. S. Byatt novel.[1] Many, however, are extremely wealthy. Old-established landed families provide between a fifth and a quarter of the 200 wealthiest people in Britain in the early 1990s, a proportion which has changed very little since the 1880s.[2] But what are they for? A hundred years ago it was unnecessary to ask such a question. Meredith Townsend, who with J. L. Sanford produced two volumes on *The Great Governing Families of England*, writing in 1865 had little need of argument or evidence to support his statement that the great landowners were the governing class. He was more defensive in justifying his selection of just thirty-one families as the core of that class, but in 1865 it was not unreasonable to prophesy that 'in another hundred years these thirty one families will be the marked and ticketed families among

---

[1] The Lincolnshire Baileys in A. S. Byatt, *Possession* (1990).
[2] Calculated from *The Sunday Times: Britain's Rich, the Top 200*, 14 April 1991. For the late 19th century it can be estimated from W. D. Rubinstein, *Men of Property* (1981), tables 3.1, 3.2, and 3.3, that 43% of those dying 1880–99 worth more than £500,000 were landed, and 28% of those dying 1900–19.

two hundred millions of English-speaking men', and to argue that: 'The
redivision of property may ultimately shatter their power, but short of
that their dignity and consideration will probably for a century steadily
increase.' His conclusion that 'the political power may depart ...
but the social power must increase; and, unless we greatly mistake, a
hundred and thirty years hence a popular journalist will still find in
this series materials which will interest a far larger and more widely-
scattered audience', neatly anticipated the rise of the tabloid press.[3]
    The particular bets placed by Sanford and Townsend have in fact
turned out remarkably well. No more than two or three of their thirty-
one families—Clintons, Osbornes, Grenvilles, and perhaps the senior
line of the Montagus—have failed to stay the course as landed grandees;
although it is true that all the rest, with the exception of the Grosvenors
have experienced the effects of some 'redivision of property'.[4] Few
analysts nowadays, however, are ready to risk committing themselves
to the proposition that there is such a thing as a governing class in
Britain. Even if they were brash enough to do so they would not be so
simplistic as to identify it with a mere handful of families, let alone
with any of the thirty-one of 1865. If the idea that Britain possessed a
ruling class was still fashionable among sociologists and political scientists
in the 1960s and 1970s, the notion that it was essentially a hereditary
ruling class had been in retreat for a long time, since the First World
War if not before.[5] Power no longer resides with the thirty-one: but
then it is doubtful whether it ever did. A moderately well-informed
Victorian would have known something about the exploits of half a
dozen names from the list: a Grey, a Stanley, a Cavendish, a Manners,
a Spencer, a Russell, or a Cecil were each prominent at one time or
another in the nineteenth century, and a Petty-Fitzmaurice had has
Edwardian day, but the remainder of the families lived comfortably
through the century without making any striking contributions to public
life. In a public recognition test today the present members of these
thirty-one families might well achieve a higher score, with perhaps a
Lowther, a Grosvenor, a Somerset, a Lennox, or a Howard being as
familiar to the public as the ever-present Cecils, Spencers, or Russells.
The recognition, however, would spring from the sporting world, almost

[3]J. L. Sanford and M. Townsend, *The Great Governing Families of England* (2 vols. 1865),
I, 18–20.
[4]The 31 families in Sanford and Townsend, *Great Governing Families*, were: Percies,
Greys, Lowthers, Vanes, Stanleys, Grosvenors, Fitzwilliams, Cavendishes, Bentincks,
Clintons, Stanhopes, Talbots, Leveson-Gowers, Pagets, Manners, Montagus, Osbornes,
Fitzroys, Spencers, Grenvilles, Russells, Cecils, Villiers, Barings, Petty-Fitzmaurices,
Herberts, Somersets, Berkeleys, Seymours, Lennoxes, and Howards. Oddly, there were
no Churchills in the list.
[5]W. Guttsmann, *The British Political Elite* (1963), 356–7.

literally from the turf, or from royal marriages, not from the seats of power: not one, since the death of the 5th Marquess of Salisbury in 1972, has made a name primarily in politics or government.

This suggests that there may be something to be said for a hypothesis that the prestige and power of landed families have moved inversely, the one rising as the other has declined and vanished, rather than the charisma simply deriving from the clout. Such a view fits the evidence of our own times, when respect and veneration for the heritage and its principal custodians has swollen almost exactly in step with the process of elbowing aside the last representatives of the old order from positions of authority and influence. The trouble is that the view can equally well be made to fit the evidence of earlier centuries. For example, the rise of Thackeray's nation of snobs and of Cobden's manufacturers who 'prostrate[d] themselves at the feet of feudalism' could plausibly be linked to the immediately preceding downfall of the *ancien regime* in 1832 and anti-Corn Law agitation, when much of the landed aristocracy had been deeply unpopular.[6] Similarly, Cannadine has argued that at the civic level the decline and eclipse of aristocratic control and interference, after a period of frequently bitter confrontation with the urban middle classes, was followed in the 1890s by a great flowering of ornamental mayors and provincial university chancellors drawn from the top layer of the old nobility, who conferred civic dignity and ceremonial splendour while remaining safely impotent politically.[7] If the theory of power engendering conflict and confrontation, defeat or decline followed by dignified and ornamental, if powerless, social superiority, is a cyclical theory, then it implies intervening phases of resurgent power in order to link the cycles together: no evidence from the post-Napoleonic period could be made to fit that. If the theory is linear and cumulative, with successive surrenders of facets of power—which seems plausible—it implies successive increments in esteem and respect, until by the 1990s the surviving landed aristocracy ought to have reached their lowest ever recorded level of power and their highest ever recorded level of prestige—which seems highly implausible.

Should the formula 'less power, more prestige' be regarded as more than an arresting paradox it requires reformulation to accommodate the intricacies and changing characters of those two variables. The power element in the equation is well enough recognised to need little definition: it means control and influence over the use of resources—people, land, and capital—and is manifested in such things as command

[6] Cobden to Hargreaves, April 1863, in J. Morley, *The Life of Richard Cobden* (1920 edn.), 946.

[7] D. Cannadine, *Lords and Landlords: the Aristocracy and the Towns, 1774–1967* (Leicester, 1979), 50–9.

over armies, taxes, and laws, and influence over votes, policies, legislation, opinion, beliefs, and manners. The prestige element is more
problematic. In some respects the concept rests on a tautology: prestige
is the esteem and respect accorded by the rest of society to those
individuals or groups who exercise some form of power. People without
power of any sort cannot enjoy prestige. In a complex and pluralistic
society the influence of prestigious people may be narrowly confined,
perhaps to a small community of fellow specialists, perhaps merely to
a self-serving and self-recruiting coterie of admirers. Any broadly based
and more widely acknowledged prestige depends on the successful use
of power, that is, on the exercise of influence in ways which some
substantial sections of the general public believe to be desirable and
admirable. The public, in other words, admires success. It may be
somewhat unreliable in its recognition of literary, artistic, or intellectual
distinction, but fortunately for the landed classes those are not fields in
which they have ever aspired to shine, except obliquely and often
inadvertently as patrons. The public is more certain to recognise success
in government, war, and sport; here, while they have been eased out
of government because their presence and their performance were
unacceptable, the landed classes have remained well placed to attract
notice over the last hundred years. Above all, however, the public likes
money, and old money better than new, because inherited wealth is
comfortably distanced from association with the unscrupulous, devious,
and avaricious practices which may have lain behind its accumulation.
The preservation of their wealth is the key not only to the survival of
the landowners but also to the type and quality of their prestige at the
end of the twentieth century, when they have convinced much of the
public that their wealth is part of the national heritage. It has been a
case not so much of 'less power, more prestige', as of different forms
of power, different kinds of prestige; and while different layers of what
may be termed public-service power have been peeled away, the bottom
line for the landed classes has remained wealth and the shifts and
stratagems for preserving it.

Attitudes to inherited wealth have swung to and fro on the barometer
of informed opinion, and these oscillations have strongly influenced
perceptions of the landed classes. It would be idle to generalise about
so subjective a matter which is not susceptible to any agreed rules of
measurement, but broadly, liberal Victorian opinion, shared by political
Tories and Liberals alike as well as by political economists, approved
of inequalities of wealth including inherited wealth as necessary for
economic efficiency, rewarding enterprise, and protecting property.
The long-standing radical tradition, which by contrast championed
economic equality and attacked inequality particularly in the ownership
of property, became increasingly influential in intellectual circles in the

interwar years, and dominant among the political classes after 1945, sometimes in a watered down form. More recently, in the last twenty years a radicalised form of conservatism has regained confidence in the virtues of inequality and proclaimed a vision of wealth cascading down the generations, in somewhat inauspicious economic circumstances.[8] In this jungle, once their pre-eminence in politics and society had vanished, the landed classes have steered a tortuous course, first stressing the similarities between their kind of wealth and business wealth, and then emphasising the differences. This was less a matter of distinct and successive phases than a case of mastering the difficult trick of facing both ways without losing credibility, arguing on the one hand that owning land was a business like any other which it was unfair to penalise, and on the other hand that land and country houses formed a special case deserving of preferential treatment.

Latterly the two faces have become institutionalised, with the Country Landowners Association presenting the business front, and the Historic Houses Association adroitly playing the heritage market, although there is a complete overlap of membership between the second body and the first. It was not until the 1930s that the landed classes, stripped of political importance, shorn of part of their estates, and reduced in numbers as they were, made the fortunate discovery that they were part of the national heritage and an essential ingredient in the national identity. Since then the preservationist card has been played with enormous effect, particularly from the 1960s onwards, and landed families have found that their buildings, their furniture, their parks, and their farms have provided surprisingly robust protection for their wealth. The way in which landed possessions have become detached from other forms of inherited wealth and acquired a special aura of their own would have astonished Henry George and the armies of land taxers and land reformers, for whom inherited landed wealth had been the prime example of unjustifiable and privileged inequality. Some insiders are astonished, and sceptical. Nicholas Ridley, when Secretary of State for the Environment, told the annual meeting of the Historic Houses Association in 1988 that the government was in favour of the survival of country houses as real family homes, not as National Trust type museums, adding: 'But we cannot provide a permanent guarantee to a particular family. Many families who pride themselves on having always lived in a house in fact married into it, bought it or stole it at some point in their murky history, when they were robber barons, property speculators, or simply won the pools.'[9] Ridley was a younger

---

[8] Political and theoretical attitudes to inequality are summarised by W. D. Rubinstein, *Wealth and Inequality in Britain* (1986), esp. 12–43.

[9] *The Times*, 22 Nov. 1988, speech by Nicholas Ridley to the Historic Houses Association.

son, projecting on to the national stage the frustration and bitterness of a younger son when the entire family patrimony passes to an older brother, and most of his audience no doubt discounted his views for that reason. The Ridley position, that there ought to be a free market in country houses and estates with no favours or handouts for existing or hereditary owners, is not one shared either by the existing families themselves or by the wider public—predominantly middle class, no doubt, but far from exclusively so—which in its millions visits these houses each year. For one thing, the free-market experience, leading to untoward developments like the sale of Heveningham Hall in the 1980s to a millionaire who vanished, did not always do much for conservation or public access. Mainly, however, the public liked the idea of old houses passing down from generation to generation, and embraced the concept that old families, like the contents of their homes, were essential elements of the treasures of Britain.

This may seem an ill-chosen moment to maintain that the landed aristocracy, widely perceived as a dying breed of privileged parasites little more than half a century ago, have become admired and publicly-assisted national treasures. 1991, after all, was the year in which the obituary of a hereditary peer opened with the sentence: 'His chief occupations were bongo-drummer, confidence trickster, brothel-keeper, drug-smuggler, and police informer'; and 1992 is the year when the press in unison referred to the heir to the 6th Marquess of Bath as 'the loins of Longleat', a pun whose thrust took in the lions, 'his Kama Sutra bedroom bedecked with many [pictures of] copulating couples', and Lord Weymouth's notorious promiscuity.[10] The debauched, sleazy, criminal, and probably bigamous career of the 3rd Lord Moynihan, the bongo-drummer, can be shrugged off as nothing to do with the old landed aristocracy, since although the 3rd Lord's half-brother is a respectable politician and rather unlucky Minister for Sport, the title is of 1920s origin and records the fashionable eminence of a surgeon. The loins are another matter. Longleat is definitely one of the top treasures, and the Thynnes are a leading landed family, whose conduct might well affect the image of the order as a whole. Possibly it does, but not in the direction of tarnishing it. The status of the custodians of tradition is impervious to the dissolute or disreputable behaviour of individuals, and may even be enhanced by outrageous conduct and its attendant publicity. Lest it be thought that such a conclusion is specific to the late twentieth century because of the peculiar interests of the popular press and the prevailing openness and curiosity about sexuality, particularly hyperactive sexuality, it should be recalled that some members

[10] The *Daily Telegraph*, 26 Nov. 1991, obituary of 3rd Lord Moynihan; The *Independent*, 1 July 1992, obituary of 6th Marquess of Bath.

of the aristocracy have always been at it and that it is certainly well over a century since their indiscretions were kept from public knowledge and remained known only to an inner circle of society gossips and diarists. For example, the Marquess of Blandford, later 8th Duke of Marlborough, was a notorious adulterer in the 1870s and 1880s, and details of his private life were common knowledge to readers of *The Times*, the *Morning Post*, and many other newspapers. Somehow his own marriage to one of the Duke of Abercorn's daughters, in 1869, lasted for 14 years, but during that time he was in and out of the beds of a wide selection of his peeresses. Some of these affairs led to the divorce courts, as with Lady Aylesford, or Lady Colin Campbell; others, as with Lady Brooke, did not, since casual adultery was a widely tolerated part of the aristocratic way of life, 'what everybody does' as Lady Harriet Mordaunt said in a different case.[11] If contemporary journalists had been addicted to alliterative puns on the lines of the 'loins of Longleat' generation they would have had a field day with Blandford and Blenheim.

The Pagets (marquesses of Anglesey), the Beresfords (marquesses of Waterford), the Tollemaches (earls Dysart), or the Pellews (viscounts Exmouth), were not far behind in Victorian wife-swapping games, and from time to time bumped into the Marlborough set.[12] It is true that in the moral climate of the 1880s the behaviour of the Marlborough set was condemned as scandalous, and that it was impossible to challenge the rules of society which peremptorily ostracised for the remainder of their lives all the women publicly tainted in these affairs, innocent or not, while the men had to show barely a flicker of repentance before continuing without a blemish on their characters. This gross injustice permitted society to pretend that the standing and acceptability of the principal male actors were scarcely affected, and they certainly had little noticeable effect on the prestige or reputation of the aristocracy as a whole. If that was the case when high Victorian codes of sexual and marital behaviour were supposed to be in force it follows, *a fortiori*, that untold quantities of sex, except of the most deviant kind, are unlikely to make a dent in aristocratic prestige in the 1990s. Indeed, 'Junkie Jamie', as the present Marquess of Blandford is known in the popular press, may well have done more damage to aristocratic prestige, with his cocaine and his seemingly endless string of convictions and imprisonments, than his predecessor ever did.[13]

[11] A. Horstman, *Victorian Divorce* (1985), 118, 135–7. G. H. Fleming, *Victorian 'Sex Goddess': Lady Colin Campbell* (Oxford, 1990), 25–8, 212–16; Lord Colin, youngest son of 8th Duke of Argyll, already separated from his wife, in the end failed to obtain a divorce (1886), as did Lady Colin in her counter-petition.

[12] Curious family trees of 'notorious affairs' and divorces, Horstman, *Victorian Divorce*, 119–33.

[13] The *Observer, Magazine*, 8 March 1992, 'The Battle of Blenheim'. His marriage to

Whether modern society is more censorious of aristocratic drugs than Victorian society was of aristocratic sex will never be known with any certainty, since society has ceased to exist. That is a statement of fact, not an endorsement of one of the dottier Thatcherite opinions. The end of society is customarily placed in 1958, when the Court Circular announcing the abolition of the ritual presentations of debutantes at court explained that 'Since the last war "Society" in the sense in which it was known even in 1939 has almost died.'[14] Presentations had been the centrepiece, if not the whole *raison d'etre*, of the London season, and furnished the organising principle of high society, the sanction legitimising the filter operated by the aristocracy to determine who was and who was not a member of the upper class, and the symbolic source of the authority to regulate the morals and manners, and much of the culture, of the class. Bereft of presentations and the central presence of Buckingham Palace the social organisation of the upper class disintegrated. Several attempts at self-regulation were made, not relying on the approval or power of the court, but in the manner of self-regulatory bodies these have been largely ineffectual and tend to impress no one except themselves. Queen Charlotte's Ball without royal patronage was not an enduring social authority for validating desirable debutantes. The *Tatler's* annual list of about 150 debutantes has not made it the arbiter of entry into anything much except the list itself. True, a kind of social calendar survives, mainly tied to sporting events like the Derby, Ascot, Henley, and Cowes, but possibly also including the Chelsea Flower Show, and each of these has its own form of exclusive enclosure and its own set of royals; but they have all been so penetrated by corporate hospitality that to be seen there has no special social significance and at most signals membership of a clique, not of a governing class. The apparatus of aristocratic control of the upper reaches of society, and the cohesion of those reaches have disappeared almost without trace, and with them have gone the chief form of what may be termed the metropolitan social power of the landed families, their power over their own *mores* and over the non-landed and non-hereditary rich and influential. The decentralised, rural, social power survives in the heartlands in whose protection the energies of the surviving landed families have been concentrated.

The Queen's decision in 1958 merely recognised a state of affairs which already existed, it was not a lethal blow to a still vibrant social institution. Not that the old order surrendered the rituals of the Season

---

Rebecca Few Brown, called by his father 'a filthy little scrubber', may have improved Blandford's public image.

[14]J. Scott, *The Upper Classes: Property and Privilege in Britain* (1982), 177. D. Cannadine, *The Decline and Fall of the British Aristocracy* (1990), 689.

without resistance; but soon after 1945 it was obvious that continued defence was pointless, since old blood and old money had retired from the fray, thus nullifying the object of the exercise. Arguably between the wars, however, the old families had diverted a great deal of money and effort to maintaining the rituals, which might have been more constructively employed in preserving their basic resources, precisely because it was still felt that these rituals were the vital mechanism by which they, the landed aristocracy, reproduced themselves and determined the eligibility and compatibility of necessary transfusions of new blood. That was what the Season was designed to do, providing a carefully controlled and monitored setting for marriageable daughters of old-established and some selected new families to come out into the social limelight, to display their talents and meet partners or make contacts, and to obtain the seal of approval of presentation at the Palace. The essential part of the machinery lay in the lists drawn up by the acknowledged Society hostesses of the day, lists of the debutantes and lists of suitable young men. The arbiters of the lists emerged from a process of succession and inner-group consultation which was the female counterpart of the traditional method of finding a leader of the Conservative party. No mother, however wealthy or ambitious, could launch her daughter into Society unless she could get her on to a list, and unless she had a friend on another list, the Lord Chamberlain's list of women who had already been presented at court, for court etiquette required that every newcomer had to be introduced by an old hand. The action of the Season was then played out in a myriad of parties and receptions, breakfasts, lunches, and dinners, dances and balls, which could occupy a well-connected young person of stamina pretty well every day and every night from May to July, or if they were so inclined from January onwards, when the unofficial 'little season' or 'pre-season', developed in the interwar years, was under way. What have now become the sole events of the social calendar, like Ascot, were relaxing diversions for young men and women who had become bored to tears with each other's company and conversation after remorselessly repeated encounters night after night.

The interwar Seasons are notorious for their inconsequential, frenzied, frivolity, particularly those of the 1920s, captured by Evelyn Waugh in *Vile Bodies*: there were 'Masked parties, Savage parties, Victorian parties, Greek parties, Wild West parties, Circus parties ... almost naked parties in St John's Wood, parties in flats and studios and houses and ships and hotels and night clubs, in windmills and swimming baths.'[15] The 1930s were a little more serious and sedate, and more

---

[15] E. Waugh, *Vile Bodies* (Penguin ed., 1938), 123. See P. Balfour, *Society Racket* (1932), 170–1 for the actual antics of the 'bright young things', which were even stranger than

expensive: it was nothing to spend more than £1,000 in an evening on a grand ball, more than a year's income of a senior civil servant and twice the salary of a professor.[16] The old families ran into trouble from the expense, and found it hard to compete with the inexhaustible chic of the American-born Lady Cunard, the most successful society hostess of the 1920s. They ran into more serious trouble from the disposal of their own town houses, which deprived them of the special prestige of staging the grandest scenes of the seasonal charades in their own private theatres. Stafford House had been the first to go, sold by the Duke of Sutherland before 1914 and reborn as the jewel in the crown of official conference and reception centres, Lancaster House, after an interval in the hands of Lord Leverhulme. After 1918 the majority of these town centres of the territorial nobility were swept away, several like Grosvenor House and Dorchester House being demolished and replaced by luxury hotels; by 1939 only Londonderry House, Bridgwater House, and Holland House remained as private residences, and the latter had begun life as a semi-suburban retreat rather than a proper town palace.[17] Motives for these disposals were mixed, and the impoverishment of falling incomes squeezed by rising costs of upkeep no doubt played a part. But few would suspect the 2nd Duke of Westminster of being driven by poverty when he sold Grosvenor House in 1924.[18]

The common factor in the passing of the town houses was more likely a dawning realization that it was no longer sensible to go on sterilising large amounts of capital in assets that had ceased to produce the dividends for which they were originally intended, social leadership and control over aristocratic reproduction. Ballrooms and picture galleries, tapestries and chandeliers, butlers and footmen ceased to earn their keep when they ceased to generate the social power that had once determined who was admitted to the governing circle and who was permitted to meet, and possibly marry, the owners' daughters. It is true that in the 1920s Ramsay MacDonald could often be seen dining along with Lady Londonderry, the chief Tory society hostess, but significantly this was at Boulestin's, not at Londonderry House; while it was widely remarked that Neville Chamberlain never dreamt of moving in Society

---

fiction and included Russian, Mozart, baby, and pyjama parties as well as those noticed by Evelyn Waugh.

[16] Balfour, *Society Racket*, 127–8.

[17] F. M. L. Thompson, *English Landed Society in the Nineteenth Century* (1963), 335–6, 339–40; Balfour, *Society Racket*, 53; Cannadine, *Decline and Fall*, 116–18, 643. The casualties also included Breadalbane, Chandos, Chesterfield, Devonshire, Hertford, Montagu, Lansdowne, Norfolk, Spencer, and Wimborne Houses. Northumberland House had vanished in a street improvement scheme in the 1870s (Northumberland Avenue) and significantly had not been replaced by the dukes. Apsley House survived, and was given to the nation by the 7th Duke of Wellington after 1945.

[18] *Estates Gazette*, 27 Dec. 1924, 892.

at all.[19] Thus front-bench Tories could neglect the aristocratic embrace, if they wished, without doing themselves any harm. Aristocratic daughters could not exactly ignore the social round, but they had been liberated from close confinement to the shuttle between country house and town house, partly by the experience of the War but perhaps mainly by the motor car, which vastly increased personal mobility and the possibilities of casual visits, undermining tight parental control over their contacts.

There were two main responses to the disappearance of the large private houses, both of which served to prolong the Season but both of which also in the longer run destroyed it by handing it over to the monied men and their wives. On the one hand, the homeless borrowed or hired for an evening one of the surviving palaces, for the cachet of appearing to give a private dance in a private ballroom remained great. Holland House was much in demand in this way until the end of the 1930s, conferring much prestige on the Ilchesters; and the swansong of Dorchester House in private hands was its loan for the dazzling reception when Lord Vivian's daughter Daphne married Lord Weymouth (later 6th Marquess of Bath) in 1927.[20] The difficulty with this tactic was that it inexorably sanctioned the hiring of commercial premises for top-ranking social events, clearing the way for the domination of the Season by wealth rather than blood: indeed, when the Dorchester reopened as an hotel it quickly became the uncrowned social centre. On the other hand, in an inspired stroke Lady Howard de Walden invented the tradition of the Queen Charlotte's Ball, designed as a strictly regulated but semi-public substitute for the dwindling number of genuinely private parades of debutantes. In name an invitation-only charity dance to raise money for Queen Charlotte's Maternity Hospital, the Ball was launched by her in 1927 as an extremely exclusive social event and was quickly established as an annual fixture with a prestige equal to or surpassing that of Ascot and a considerably more bizarre ritual, continuing under Lady Howard de Walden's personal direction until the 1950s. The ritual was absurd, a debutante's parody of Trooping the Colour, but already by the mid-1930s it had the air of a venerable tradition: a gigantic cake, donated by fashionable caterers, decorated with a candle for each year since Queen Charlotte's birth in 1744, maids-in-waiting recruited from debut-

[19] Balfour, *Society Racket*, 124–5.

[20] Balfour, *Society Racket*, 63. There is some mystery about the ownership of Dorchester House, but it appears to have been the residence of the Holfords of Weston Birt, Glos., untitled aristocracy with an estate of 14,596 acres worth £20,145 p.a. in 1878: J. Bateman, *The Great Landowners of Great Britain and Ireland* (1878 edn.), 205. Father and son resided there: Walford, *County Families* (1888 edn.), 526, (1904 edn.), 497. The son, George Lindsay Holford, was a courtier, equerry in turn to the Duke of Clarence and George V.

antes of previous years, guards of honour selected from current debutantes for the honour of dragging the cake into the Dorchester ballroom, and maids of honour, the rest of the current debutantes, who were drilled to sweep in pairs down converging twin staircases for a synchronised arrival in front of the cake, to which and to the royal guest of honour they curtsied. Eventually, in the 1960s, the debutantes ended up by curtseying to nothing but the cake. Still, the strange ceremonial had a purpose, the authentication of membership of a social elite, and it continued until 1976, many years after presentations at court had stopped.[21]

From the aristocratic point of view the trouble with Queen Charlotte, despite Lady Howard de Walden's initial intentions of preserving exclusiveness, was that the Ball in its search for charitable donations actually encouraged the penetration of society by the wealthy, and was transformed into an instrument for socialising the rich rather than transmitting blue blood. The commercialisation of high society and the season was further aided by the enterprise of well-connected but needy ladies who offered their services for introducing the daughters of the nouveaux riches to the court and to the necessary preliminary social encounters. Minnie Stevens, the American who married Lord Arthur Paget (a grandson of the 1st Marquess of Anglesey) in 1878, was probably the first society lady to act as a semi-professional social sponsor, but although spiteful rumour held that she did it as a business she very likely only used her influential position as a member of the Marlborough House set to help fellow-Americans, out of kindness, on their way to introductions to court.[22] In the interwar period this definitely became a trade, and it was dominated by a couple of dowagers, the Countess of Clancarty and Lady St John of Bletso. For a fee of around £2,000 one of these would provide a fully inclusive coming-out service for the season—chaperonage, lodging in moderately smart South Kensington, guidance in getting the right clothes, placement on one or two good lists (for invitations), lessons in how to behave at lunches, teas, dinners, and dances, arrangement of a modest coming out dance, and the vital presentation at court; expenses, presumably, were extra. Business was acquired through discreet advertisements in The Times that simply said: 'Peeress would chaperone debutante, every advantage'. It seems to have been brisk. Whether the generations of Clancarty and Bletso girls received value for money, in the form of good marriages, is difficult to determine, but they clearly received social

[21] Angela Lambert, 1939: The Last Season of Peace (1989), 88–9, 214. There was talk of reviving the Ball in 1989.

[22] Maureen E. Montgomery, Gilded Prostitution: Status, Money, and Transatlantic Marriages, 1870–1914 (1989), 8, 22–3.

polish and the chance to make a new set of acquaintances. Paid presenters certainly did not outnumber the traditional aristocratic family friends before 1939, in providing access to society; and the debutantes of the last season of peace were dominated by a classic figure like Elizabeth Leveson-Gower, the Duke of Sutherland's heiress, not by any of the daughters of bankers, press barons, diamond magnates, home and colonial politicians, and other upper middle-class parents, who formed a clear majority of the two to three hundred who 'did the season'.[23] Nevertheless, the permeation of the core process of high society by new money, and the commercialisation of its machinery, had gone far enough by 1939 to make the surviving aristocratic veneer distinctly thin.

Surprisingly, Queen Charlotte's Balls kept going through much of the War, although presentations at court were suspended. When both resumed after 1945 the upper middle-class and new money elements were in complete charge, in numbers, in style, in resources, and in manners that had been acquired rather than inherited. In 1958 royalty declined to continue serving their social pretensions. Lady Bletso, however, continued for a few more years, plying her trade of making social introductions and rounding off a career of making a living out of the carrion of a system which, perhaps inadvertently, she had helped to kill off.[24] The old families had not so much surrendered control of the commanding heights of society as retreated from them, and in retreating had in effect abolished them and razed them to the ground: it was not that the glittering prizes were now won by other people, by a plutocracy or a meritocracy, but that there were no longer any glittering prizes of the old sort. Withdrawal meant that old landed families no longer had that particular kind of social power and prestige, and that created a major breach in their privileged position and in the machinery for their publicly visible perpetuation and renewal as a class. Perceptions of their significance and viability were, therefore, lowered.

[23] Lambert, *Last Season*, 4–5, 173–4. Lambert estimates that in 1939 there were 900 to 1,000 debs 'coming out', i.e. being presented, of whom 200 to 400 took a full part in the London season: 8–9. These figures may be compared with the 800 to 1,000 who were presented annually in the 1890s, of whom about 45% or 350 to 450 were debs: Nancy W. Ellenberger, 'The Transformation of London Society at the End of Victoria's Reign,' *Albion*, XX (1990), 641, 653.

[24] Lambert, *Last Season*, 5: the Bletso treatment did occasionally produce striking results, recalled by one ex-deb 50 years later.

> There were perhaps half a dozen mamas each Season who were rich (very rich) *nouveaux riches*, and were on the prowl to find very eligible but perhaps impecunious husbands for their daughters. One very aggressive one had two daughters and a son for whom she, triumphantly, found members of the aristocracy. One is now a countess, another married a baronet of long lineage, and one of her grand-daughters is married to a duke.

What they withdrew to was the land, the foundation of their existence. Here was the base on which the whole superstructure of political and social pre-eminence, power, and prestige had rested. The dissolution and collapse of the superstructure was regretted by the old landed families as they saw themselves ceasing to be a governing class, but after 1914 it was not seriously resisted. The land itself was a different matter. Unlucky or incompetent owners might lose their estates, and others might part with large portions, but it was on the land that a stand was made. The less frivolous and irresponsible landowners buckled down to do what they could to preserve the estates-system and their own stake in it. They have been far more successful than the pessimists and alarmists of the 1920s would have thought possible.

The best-known interwar link between sex, marriage, and the land was *Cold Comfort Farm*, the still hilarious satire on the sentimental cult of rural virtue and simplicity nourished by Mary Webb's enormously successful novels. This was serious, and seriously misleading, material. Stanley Baldwin probably believed his own rhetoric when he referred to 'the soil as the great womb of the true self'. Edward Wood, briefly Baldwin's Minister of Agriculture in 1924 although better known as Chamberlain's Foreign Secretary, Lord Halifax, definitely did when he identified smallholdings with 'one of the primitive instincts of man ... the call of the soil from which we spring, and to which we are, therefore, so to speak, permanently enchained in our instincts.'[25] Those were not the kind of sentiments landowners wished to hear: or rather, they did not mind hearing them as long as governments did not act on them too vigorously. To the landowners a modest number of smallholdings was unobjectionable, maybe even should be encouraged because a widening of the private ownership of agricultural land could create a barrier or smokescreen of small owners behind which the great estates would be more secure from confiscatory attacks. Wholehearted pandering to 'the primitive instincts', however, was most alarming for it implied overturning the great estates and the whole agrarian structure, and replacing it with a countryside of small farms and a rural society of peasants. This was the position articulated by Conservative landowners before 1914, sustained in the 1920s, and re-affirmed in the 1970s. This was not the sole reason, probably not even one of the major reasons, why the British estates-system has not been pulverised by some variant of those twentieth-century land reforms which much of the rest of Europe has experienced: it was, on the other hand, the main way in which the landowners helped to protect themselves. A 'Statement

[25] Both cited in A. F. Cooper, *British Agricultural Policy, 1912–36: A Study in Conservative Politics* (Manchester, 1989), 71.

on the Future of Landownership' in 1976 summarised the position admirably:

General opinion as to what degree of private landownership is acceptable is probably based more on an emotional view than on the understanding of the activities of different types of landowners [it stated] ... At one end of the spectrum the small working farmer, whether owner-occupier or tenant, attracts sympathy ... At the other end of the spectrum, absentee landlords and those who have benefited from massive increases in development land values are vilified. In between come the resident landlord and the owner of large farming businesses. There is an enormous range, but the closer the owner of land, whether owner-occupier or resident landlord, is identified with the smaller working farmer, the less likelihood that he will have to bear the brunt of political attack arising from envy. Efficiency in food production would appear as yet only a small counter to the attack on farmers and landowners who run their enterprises as a business.[26]

That statement was issued by the Country Landowners Association, and allowing for the gradual replacement of the 'virtuous smallholder' by the 'virtuous small farmer' as the representative figure in the forward defences of landownership, it was a statement that might have been made at any time in the previous fifty years. Founded in 1907 as the Central Land Association, and aiming to represent all the agricultural classes and to rise above party politics, the CLA did not make much of an impression before 1914. By then it mustered no more than 648 members, not a large proportion of the total number of agricultural landowners in the country, and insignificant in relation to the farmers and labourers unless it had an undeclared belief in eighteenth-century concepts of 'virtual representation'.[27] True, it had enlisted the most active agriculturalists among Conservative politicians: Walter Long, Wiltshire landowner, and the Earl of Onslow, Surrey landowner, both former cabinet ministers, were the first president and the first chairman, Charles Bathurst, Gloucestershire squire and prominent man of the land in the Commons, was its first secretary, while Christopher Turnor, one of the untitled aristocracy with a 20,000 acre Lincolnshire estate, was a rising agricultural spokesman as well as an active member of the CLA council. The trouble was that they were all Tories, and lent no

[26] CLA papers [for period since c.1960], CLA office, 16, Belgrave Square, London SW1 (hereafter CLA London), 'The Future of Landownership—a CLA Discussion Paper', 6 Jan. 1976.
[27] CLA papers [for period 1907–60], Institute of Agricultural History, University of Reading (hereafter CLA Reading), Executive Committee Minutes, 13 Feb. 1930, membership figures, 1908–29.

colour to the pretence that the CLA was above party. As far as the Liberal Government or the wider public could tell, the CLA was no more than a faction within the Conservative party, a reincarnation of the Liberty and Property Defence League, and a minor element in the array of property associations which got together in the Land Conference to resist Liberal taxes and Liberal policies.[28]

The 1914–18 War changed the landscape. Farmers had a good war: protected status, fat profits, and a union, the NFU, swept into prominence by prosperity and public importance. Farm workers had a mixed war, falling behind in the first half in real wages and in organised strength, but recovering ground in the second half with the aid of the statutory agricultural wages boards set up in 1917, so that they ended the war much more strongly unionised than before. Landowners had an unequivocally bad time: far from being inflation-proof their incomes were positively deflated by the rent restricting clauses of the 1917 Corn Production Act, and the CLA languished while individual landowners drifted off to serve in county agricultural executive committees administering the food production policy presided over by the Duke of Bedford's former land agent, Lord Ernle, a policy which certainly helped to feed the nation, but which also appeared to feed the farmers at the landlords' expense.[29] A reasonable reading of the agricultural landscape in 1919 was that the farmers were strong, the workers were strong, and the landowners were dangerously weak, marginalised as never before in membership of the Commons, without a recognised public voice, and starting to contract out altogether with the beginning of the huge land sales. Charles Bathurst, became Lord Bledisloe during service with the wartime Ministry of Food, made such an analysis and then used his position as President of the CLA to push through a virtual re-launch of that body as an association of landowners explicitly intended to balance the unions of the other two parties in the tripartite system, the NFU and the National Union of Agricultural Workers. Bledisloe provided landowners with what would now be called a mission statement: they should concentrate on the efficient management of their estates, in the interests of agriculture and themselves, giving up outworn and unrealistic ideas of influencing public affairs in general, and acting through their association, renamed the Central Landowners Association to mark the change of direction, should focus their political activities on protecting the legitimate interests of agricultural landowners and promoting the agricultural industry. Thus was the CLA reborn as the avowed landowners' lobby, and easily assumed the stance of being

[28] M. Fforde, *Conservatism and Collectivism, 1886–1914* (Edinburgh, 1990), 104, 153–6.

[29] P. E. Dewey, *British Agriculture in the First World War* (1989), esp. chap. 16. A. Armstrong, *Farmworkers: A Social and Economic History, 1770–1980* (1988), chap. 7.

above, or unconnected with, party, since it was obvious with the quiet abandonment of Lloyd George's land taxes and the attenuation of Liberal land reform crusades that the only surviving serious enemies of landed estates were the socialists, who were not a party which came within any landowner's ken.[30]

Not all landowners took Bledisloe's message to heart; but those who did not take themselves off to Kenya or Rhodesia in search of less harsh climates, or were not forced by debts to shut up their country houses and go to live in seaside lodgings in Hastings or Eastbourne, possibly did turn to estate management with a new seriousness from this time, and visibly gave up appearances on the national political stage except when issues directly affecting landed property were on the agenda. The new course had a more striking effect on the CLA itself. A comprehensive structure of county branches was quickly developed, 45 in all, where previously there had been none; and membership built up steadily through the 1920s, topping 10,000 by the early 1930s. All the great and the good from the landowner's world took their turns in serving on its Council and Executive Committee; in 1928, for example, its parliamentary committee in the House of Lords mustered one duke, nine earls, and eleven barons. It was embarrassed by its own chief publicists. Christopher Turnor, its leading MP once Bathurst had gone to the Lords, had to be disavowed in 1923 when he lectured a Departmental Committee on 60 years of neglect of agriculture by successive governments and rounded on 'rich and complacent land-owners', concluding passionately, and woundingly:

If at the beginning of the Great Depression landowners had refused to lower rents, but rather had devoted the money they then gave to individual farmers to the organization of the industry and the building up of co-operation, our agriculture would have been far more firmly established than it is today.'[31]

Even more wounding, Bledisloe himself seemed to have gone native when he wrote to the press about the sorry plight of British farming, and advocated what his peers saw as cutting their own throats, as the sole remedy:

[30] CLA Reading, Council Minutes, 30 Dec. 1922. Bledisloe had views on postwar agricultural policy as well as on landowners' organization, and these were separately published as *The Proper Position of the Landowner in Relation to the Agricultural Industry* (1922). In the event while the NFU remained large and representative, growing from about 80,000 members to well over 100,000 in the 1930s, the NUAW collapsed after 1921, from 93,000 members to 22,000 in 1924, and remained at no more than 6 to 10% of the total number of agricultural workers throughout the interwar period: Armstrong, *Farmworkers*, 169, 185.

[31] CLA Reading, Exec. Cttee. Mins. 22 Feb. 1923.

The most urgent need [he wrote] is the removal of the fundamental theoretical objection to all government aid to agriculture, that the benefit can pass to the landlord, who is not the wealth producer or the employer. The sole solution, apart from government ownership, is the permanent fixation of farm rents on a fair valuation.'[32]

That was a home truth, in 1929 and since, which the CLA certainly did not wish to hear. If taxpayers' money is spent on agriculture, then part of it goes to enrich landowners. The best the CLA can ever hope to do is to convince people that landowners, too, are wealth producers.

The CLA has also taken up some extraordinary positions of its own in its time, as when it put forward the demand as a main plank in its 1928 statement on agricultural policy that the government should not impose costly hygiene regulations on British dairy farmers because their competitors producing imported tinned skimmed milk did not have to comply with any similar rules.[33] That, however, was designed as an olive branch to the farmers, who were concerned about tinned milk. The CLA has always aimed at being on good terms with the farmers and the NFU, while pursuing its core concerns of getting reductions in death duties, protecting the legal status of landowners' avoidance devices, safeguarding or restoring landowners' powers to fix farm rents, and limiting statutory interference in the landlord-tenant relationship. There have been moments, when the NFU has seemed particularly ineffective or unpopular, when it has been tempted to move on to a larger and more public stage and pose as the farming lobby as well as the landowning lobby. This happened in the early 1930s, when the NFU's inbred hostility to Whitehall interference made its coolness alike towards Labour's Agricultural Marketing Bill (1930–1) and the National Government's agricultural policy (1932) seem like pigheaded short-sightedness. It happened most recently in 1967 when a large farming conference at Oxford suggested that 'the CLA should take over from the NFU' by 'increasing its grip on the more intelligent, and generally larger-scale, owner-occupiers, who seem particularly disenchanted with the NFU because they feel the Union serves the small farmer, and not always very well at that.'[34] Such temptations were resisted and the CLA prudently stayed within the narrower fields of taxation and tenure, content to play second fiddle to the NFU rather than to challenge it.

[32] CLA Reading, Exec. Cttee. Mins. 31 Jan. 1929, quoting Bledisloe to *Morning Post*, 21 Jan. 1929, and recording regrets that he had made proposals, 'quite unacceptable to landowners generally'.

[33] CLA Reading, Exec. Cttee. Mins. 22 March 1928, 'Statement on Agricultural Policy Supplementary to Statement issued in 1925'.

[34] Cooper, *British Agricultural Policy*, 128–31, 169–72. CLA London, Exec. Cttee. Mins. 13 July 1967, preliminary consideration of 'The case of the farmer's seed drill' and the question of the CLA 'taking on agriculture'.

Insofar as agricultural organisations have influenced the making of agricultural policy, legislation, and subsidies, it is the NFU which has, indeed, made the running since 1933, becoming the industry's arm in the agricultural version of the corporate state which even the post-1979 reaction has not attempted to demolish. First through running the marketing boards in the 1930s—no less than three-quarters of the NFU's 120,000 members were milk producers—then through making the Ministry of Agriculture into the Whitehall branch of the farmers during the Second World War, and finally through becoming the statutory negotiators in the annual price reviews under the 1947 Agriculture Act, the NFU moved from being a critic sniping at governments into a privileged part of the state apparatus.[35] Landowners benefited from all this, as Bledisloe had pointed out: more stable prices, and higher prices, for farm produce inexorably filtered through into higher rents, or if rents were held down by legislation then into higher land values, especially for land that could be sold with vacant possession. The landowners have gratefully pocketed these gains, doubly grateful that they do not have to appear in the public firing line in order to secure them. This may seem ignominious in comparison with the glory days of pre-1914 political prominence, but it is a more comfortable, if less exciting, life. To be paid for doing nothing is generally agreeable, although lately that has not prevented farmers from grumbling over the amounts they are paid for agreeing not to produce anything at all from some of their fields. Recently, landowners have also discovered a new slant on the public purse through riding on the coat-tails of the conservation lobby, getting large sums, sometimes in millions, for condescending not to desecrate areas of special scientific interest with far-fetched development schemes of dubious rationality. So far the authorities have been too scared of the conservation and ecology interest to dare to call the landowners' bluff; but this kind of money can only be won by individuals claiming compensation, running the gauntlet of public enquiries and the risk of bringing down unwelcome bad publicity on landowners in general, something the CLA has always dreaded.[36]

[35] On the transformation of the role of the NFU see Cooper, *British Agricultural Policy*, 177–8, 216–18; B. A. Holderness, *British Agriculture since 1945* (Manchester, 1985), 10, 16–21, 155.

[36] Large landowners also benefit handsomely from the 'set aside' system: the *Sunday Times*, 1 Dec. 1991, listed the Dukes of Atholl and of Buccleuch, the Marquess of Northampton, Earl Spencer, and Lords Beaverbrook and Belstead, among the 'land-owners reap[ing] rich harvest from EC set-aside scheme'. The Wildlife and Countryside Act 1981 entitles landowners to compensation for loss of profits on SSSIs they are not allowed to develop: some cases were reported in *Estates Gazette*, 22 Feb. 1992, and the *Observer*, 14 June 1992. Something for nothing of a more benign kind has also been available to landowners who obtain exemption from death duties in return for allowing

Exercising gentlemanly control over the conduct of landowners, discreetly dissuading mavericks from anti-social behaviour, and if all else failed, sweeping their misdemeanours under the carpet, was one of the enduring functions of the CLA and perhaps its major contribution to survival. The machinery of county branches and its personal contacts with individual members was ideal for making displeasure known at unreasonable treatment of tenants or unjustified refusal to permit a widow or offspring to 'succeed' to a farm on the death of the sitting tenant.[37] Explaining to the outside world, and not simply to governments or Parliament, what landowners did and why was one of its important tasks. Equally important, and occupying much of its time from the 1930s onwards, has been the task of explaining landlords to farmers, more particularly to the NFU, since although the two organisations are always agreed on the primacy of arguing the case for the prosperity of agriculture they are not always agreed on the division of the spoils. Tenant farmers are congenitally obtuse over understanding why they should pay rents, and particularly since the doctrine of free open market value was restored to the statute book as the definition of fair rent in 1958, after years of virtual abeyance, the CLA has engaged in vigorous public relations exercises to convince farmers that landlords are not extortionate.[38]

At this point exactly which landowners the CLA speaks for becomes somewhat obscure, and deliberately so given the aim of sheltering under the skirts of small farmers and small owners. Already by 1929 about 60 per cent of the members owned less than 250 acres apiece, and were mainly owner-farmers; by the end of the 1970s 90 per cent of the 45,000 members were owner-farmers with estates of less than 500 acres. Looked at the other way, the most recent figures show that in 1989 precisely 421 members, less than one per cent of the total, owned estates of 3,000 acres and upwards, accounting for around half of the 15 million acres which in aggregate the CLA claimed to represent.[39] In this the CLA mirrors the structure of British land-ownership, a pyramid of acres and a pyramid of wealth, in which the largest landowners, many of whom have themselves become owner-

---

public access, often purely theoretical, to their land or their works of art: the *Observer*, 14 June 1992, 'Estate owners told to end tax-for-footpaths secrecy'; 5 July 1992, 'Tax deals with wealthy cost nation £1 billion'.

[37] For example, CLA London, Exec. Cttee. Mins. 4 Dec. 1969, on 'inheritance' of tenancies, urging branch secretaries to use their local influence to avoid cases of undue hardship in denial of succession to widows or sons.

[38] CLA London, Exec. Cttee. Mins. 2 April 1964, Observations on NFU Report on Tenure of Farm Land.

[39] CLA Reading, Exec. Cttee. Mins. 31 Dec. 1929, 13 Feb. 1930; CLA London, Exec. Cttee. Mins. 26 July 1967, 11 July 1968, 11 May 1978, Council Mins. 26 Oct. 1989.

farmers on a considerable scale because of the tax and tenurial advantages, have been largely hidden from the public gaze.[40] So well hidden, they have sometimes felt, that the dilution of the CLA with small owners and farmers has led to neglect of the special interests of the traditional landowners. Thus, splinter groups, or perhaps more accurately, dedicated cells, have been formed to lobby for the more specialised aristocratic interests: the Historic Houses Association in 1975, for one, and the Moorland Association in 1985, for another. The 150 members of the latter reputedly own about 90 per cent of the open moorland in England and Wales, and under cover of the claim that they are protecting 'the only area of semi-natural wilderness left where ground-nesting birds can find a bit of peace and quiet and bring up their young', they have campaigned with some success to keep the moors closed to public access so that they can in proper season deal with the ground-nesting birds at their pleasure.[41]

The returning self-confidence of the landed elite, daring once more to stand up and be counted in public in praise of their own special interests, owes much to changes in the general political and social outlook in the 1970s and 1980s, which made great wealth respectable, and inherited wealth, especially if it took the form of country houses or works of art, positively revered. It owed something, too, to the CLA and its generally defensive stance, which saw the landowners through the bleak economic climate of the 1920s and 1930s, winning a few victories like the 1925 exemption of agricultural land from the increase in death duty rates, and which more or less hitched the landowners to the ascendant star of the NFU in the better economic but more hostile or indifferent political climate of the 30 years after 1945.[42] The CLA has not, on the whole, ever exercised more than a restraining influence on governments and public policies, and in that sense has not provided

[40] The tenurial attraction of owner-farming is chiefly that of avoiding the 'dual ownership' of a farm with a tenant effectively entrenched for life (1947 Act) or for life plus two succeeding generations (1976 Act): CLA London, Council papers 22 Jan. 1969, Succession to Agricultural Tenancies by close relatives', Council working papers 22 July 1980, negotiations with NFU on tenancies.

[41] The *Independent*, 27 July 1990, 'Ramblers lose battle over grouse moors', 9 Aug. 1990, 'Temperatures rise on the grouse moors', 4 Feb. 1992, 'Ramblers step up pressure on access rights'. Pressure by the Moorland Association led to the shelving of the Conservative 1987 Manifesto promise to legislate on access to the 1.4 million acres of common land in England and Wales. In 1930 the CLA had a policy for public access to open country through easements, to be so directed as not to damage sporting rights: CLA Reading, Exec. Cttee. Mins. 1 May 1930. In 1949 the President of the CLA had taken up the cause of historic houses, pressing for exactly the kind of tax concessions achieved only 30 years later by the Historic Houses Association: CLA Reading, Exec. Cttee. Mins. 30 April 1949.

[42] CLA Reading, Exec. Cttee. Mins. 22 Feb. 1928, claiming credit, with the Land Union, for the 1925 death duty concession.

the landowners with a substitute for the lost prestige of their former political ascendancy. What it has done is to provide the landowners with a sense of identity, of cohesion, and of purpose: the purpose being, in a much used phrase, 'that the essential function of landownership is that of a business.'[43] The carefully cultivated image of the landowner as a conscientious, socially responsible, fair-minded businessman, caring for his tenantry, for the health of his land, for his inheritance, and acting as an almost selfless and underpaid steward of the nation's treasures, is a myth. In it, it is easier to recognise members of the Historic Houses Association than those of the Moorland group, owners who keep well groomed parks than those who fiddle the tax laws and milk the public purse, landlords who plant shelter belts and care for hedges than owner-farmers who join the barley barons in agribusiness. Landowners who live largely to spend their money on horse-racing, deer-stalking, pheasant-shooting, or highly complicated matrimonial affairs, in the manner of the traditional leisure class, do not seem to fit this business image at all. Frequently, an individual landowner may be all of these things. The beauty of a myth is that it transcends discordant realities. What is not a myth is the concept of a highly professional organisation looking after the business interests of landowners and persuading the public that the landowners themselves are equally serious and professional. The degree of its success in transforming the image of the ownership of land from privileged amateurism to managerial efficiency is the best measure of the type of prestige enjoyed by the surviving landowners of the 1990s. It is a prestige rooted in the continuing control of a great deal of land, not a form of consolation prize for the loss of former pre-eminence. Certainly, not all of them deserve it. Many of them have feet of clay. These four addresses may have shown that the clay is stiff enough and strong enough to carry the twentieth-century landowners of England into another century.

[43] CLA London, Exec. Cttee. Report, 28 Jan. 1976, 'The Future of Landownership'.

'BETWEEN THE SEA POWER AND THE LAND POWER': SCANDINAVIA AND THE COMING OF THE FIRST WORLD WAR

By Patrick Salmon

READ 24 JANUARY 1992

AMONG the voluminous papers produced at the Admiralty during the Fisher era in anticipation of a war against Germany there is one entitled 'Preparation of War Plans'.[1] It is unsigned and undated, but was printed for internal circulation on 24 June 1908 and may thus form part of the work undertaken by the Naval Intelligence Division and the Naval War College in 1908–9 rather than the better-known deliberations of the 'Ballard Committee' of 1906–7.[2] Its authorship must remain a matter for speculation, and it may be the product of more than one hand, but the memorandum's breadth of historical understanding suggests that the influence of two men who played a leading part in Admiralty planning at this time: Rear-Admiral Edmond Slade, the Director of Naval Intelligence, and Julian Corbett, the eminent naval historian.[3] The memorandum begins by arguing that British war plans must take into account the political dispositions and commitments of the European powers. Since 1904, it says, these have undergone a profound change, resembling the regrouping of powers which occurred in the mid-eighteenth century. 'The result on the peace strategy of this country has been tremendous; it has necessitated a complete reorganisation of the whole of our arrangements, and it has forced us to face east, instead of south and west.' Even though Germany must now be reckoned Britain's chief potential enemy, the situation is

---

[1] Public Record Office (PRO), ADM 116/1043B, Part i, fos. 639–43. Another copy is in ADM 116/1043B, Part ii, fos. 275–9, where it appears under 'War Plans 1907–1908'.

[2] Neil W. Summerton, 'The development of British military planning for a war against Germany, 1904–1914' (unpublished PhD thesis, University of London, 1970), 265–78, 281; Paul Haggie, 'The Royal Navy and war planning in the Fisher era', in *The War Plans of the Great Powers 1880–1914*, ed. Paul Kennedy (1979), 120–5. The plans produced by the Bollard committee are printed in their entirety in *The Papers of Admiral Sir John Fisher*, ed. P. K. Kemp, II (1964), 316–468.

[3] The two men were close friends and shared an interest in eighteenth-century naval history: Summerton, 'British military planning, 221, 227. See also D. M. Schurman, *Julian S. Corbett: Historian of British Maritime Policy from Drake to Jellicoe* (Woodbridge, 1981).

still extremely fluid, and the area of greatest uncertainty lies in northern Europe. The memorandum goes on:

> Before 1904 Russia was considered dangerous in Asia only; Japan was not counted; Denmark and Sweden were not thought of; Germany was only looked on as a comparatively unimportant Sea Power; and France was accepted as our most dangerous foe. The Dual Alliance and the Triple Alliance were the governing factors of European politics, and we were more or less isolated. Now we find ourselves in close agreement with France, more or less in agreement with Russia, and in alliance with Japan. Denmark and Sweden are hovering *between the Sea Power and the Land Power* [my emphasis], uncertain with which to throw in their lot, most anxious to remain free from all complications, but, from their geographical position, almost certain to be drawn into the struggle in certain eventualities; and, lastly, Germany, more or less isolated, threatens this country almost more seriously than she has been threatened by France since the Napoleonic era.

> Now it is obvious from this that no plan of campaign can be formulated which does not take some count of all these factors. A precipitate line of action on our part may throw Denmark and Sweden into the arms of Germany, or may alienate either France or Russia at the critical moment.

To someone with an interest in Scandinavian history the most striking aspect of this discussion is the prominent position occupied by Denmark and Sweden. Not only are they mentioned in the same breath as Japan and the leading European powers, but these two countries are deemed to *matter*. It is as important for Britain to prevent them from falling into the arms of Germany as it is to avoid alienating France or Russia. Secondly, the paper assumes that Denmark and Sweden are 'almost certain' to be drawn into war 'in certain eventualities'—in other words into a struggle between the sea power and the land power: between Great Britain and Germany. Both of these assumptions are surprising in view of the obscurity that usually envelops the Scandinavian countries when viewed from the perspective of European international relations in the twentieth century.

Was the Admiralty memorandum wrong, in 1908, to attach such prominence to Sweden and Denmark? Some aspects of the analysis are certainly odd. There is, for example, no mention of Norway even though that country had been independent since 1905, following the break-up of the union with Sweden. Is the omission accidental? Does it reflect an assumption that Norway was unimportant, or so firmly under British influence that it was not a matter of concern, or perhaps that it had been removed from the arena of great-power rivalry by the

Norwegian integrity treaty, signed by Britain, Germany, Russia and France in November 1907? Secondly 'the Sea Power and the Land Power' clearly refers to Britain and Germany. But of course for Denmark, and especially for Sweden, there was a second land power—Russia—which had to be taken very seriously despite its temporary weakening at the hands of the Japanese in 1904. By 1907 Britain was, as the author says, 'more or less in agreement with Russia', but this is not seen as having any bearing on the attitude that Denmark and Sweden might adopt.

Despite these reservations, the ideas expressed in the Admiralty memorandum should not be dismissed as an aberration. They are an authentic expression of the diplomatic and strategic uncertainty that surrounded the Scandinavian countries in the first years of the twentieth century. These were years in which the alignments of the European great powers were, as the author of the memorandum emphasised, undergoing radical changes. Even an ostensibly peripheral region like Scandinavia might tip the balance if it came down on one side rather than another. Nor was Scandinavia merely passive in this period. The European balance was shaken by the crisis of 1905 between Norway and Sweden and its aftermath. In these years Scandinavia did indeed matter. And even though it was out of the limelight following the signature of the Baltic and North Sea status quo agreements of 1908, the region was not allowed to relapse into obscurity. Diplomats, sailors and soldiers all assigned a substantial role to Scandinavia in their strategic calculations. Most of their projections were of course to be overturned by the actual course of war that broke out in 1914. The war did not begin with a daring British assault on the Danish coast or the Kiel Canal; an Anglo-French expeditionary force did not land in the Baltic and advance on Berlin; the Swedes and Germans did not invade Finland and attack St Petersburg across the Karelian Isthmus. That such notions were entertained at all is, however, a matter of some significance. The first part of this paper explores the reasons for the heightened interest in Scandinavia on the part of the great powers before the war. The second part considers the strategic plans of the great powers and asks why, contrary to expectations, the Scandinavian states were not forced to make an explicit choice between the sea power and the land power but were able to preserve their neutrality throughout the First World War.

A second reason for taking the memorandum seriously is that its author was not entirely wrong when he suggested that the Scandinavian countries would be drawn into a great-power conflict. Although their territories did not become a theatre of war, many Scandinavians died: among them, two thousand Norwegian merchant seamen. And their economies were subjected to great-power pressures of a kind not experienced since the Napoleonic wars. To a large extent economic warfare—in the form of the British blockade and the German U-boat campaign—was improvised after the outbreak of war once it was evident that neither side was going to win a quick victory. However, on the British side at least, economic warfare was also planned for, notably by Maurice Hankey, secretary to the Ballard Committee in 1906–7 and, from 1912, secretary to the Committee of Imperial Defence.[4] Hankey's vision of the war of the future was shaped decisively by his experience of planning at the Admiralty. He wrote of the work of the Ballard Committee: 'We were greatly impressed as a result of our studies with the importance of the susceptibility of Germany to economic pressure, though we could not judge whether it would be possible to squeeze her into submission, or how long it would take, particularly in view of the assistance she could obtain from her continental neighbours.'[5] The weight brought to bear on the Scandinavian countries by both sides after 1914 was an acknowledgement of their vital economic importance in an era of industrialised warfare. A generation earlier this would not have been the case: the nature of warfare had changed, but so had the economic role of the Scandinavian countries themselves. The final part of the paper examines how the change occurred: how the process of economic modernisation brought prosperity to Scandinavia but at the same time made it more dependent on the outside world and more exposed to great-power pressures.

Scandinavia and European diplomacy 1902–8

Each of the great powers principally concerned with northern Europe— Great Britain, Germany and Russia—was interested primarily in stability. As long as the Scandinavian states remained neutral and non-aligned, there was little reason to intervene actively in their affairs. When the European powers started to pay closer attention to Scandinavia towards the end of the nineteenth century, they did so not because they wished to disturb the status quo but in order to prevent

---

[4] Hankey's key role is emphasised in Avner Offer, *The First World War: An Agrarian Interpretation* (Oxford, 1989), 246–9, 294–5, as well as in the official history of the blockade, A. C. Bell, *A History of the Blockade of Germany* (1937, declassified 1961), 20–2. On the inadequacy of German economic preparations for war see Lothar Burchardt, *Friedenswirtschaft und Kriegsvorsorge. Deutschlands wirtschaftliche Rüstungsbestrebungen vor 1914* (Boppard am Rhein, 1968) and Bernd Stegemann, *Die Deutsche Marinepolitik 1916–1918* (Berlin, 1970), 20–2.

[5] Lord Hankey, *The Supreme Command 1914–1918*, I (1961), 40.

others from doing so. Changes in military technology and in the European balance of power after 1890 heightened the strategic importance of the Scandinavian states and at the same time raised doubts about their capacity to preserve their neutrality. The deepening crisis between Sweden and Norway posed a threat to the balance of power within northern Europe itself.[6]

With the lapse of the Reinsurance Treaty in 1890 Denmark acquired strategic importance as a potential link between Russia and France and a sensitive point on Germany's northern flank. In 1893 the German chancellor Caprivi delivered a speech in which he reckoned as a matter of course that Denmark would be ranked alongside Russia and France as Germany's adversary in wartime.[7] The completion of the Kiel Canal in 1895, followed by the construction of a German ocean-going fleet, opened for the first time the prospect of an Anglo-German war in which both Denmark and Norway would be in the front line. The German naval staff was planning as early as 1899 for an occupation of Denmark, combined with a battle with the British fleet in the Baltic approaches, though it was not until 1904 that the British Admiralty made its first plans for war against Germany.[8] The building of strategic railways by Russia in Finland, coinciding with railway construction in the far north of Sweden and Norway, awoke Swedish fears of Russian aggression and revived British anxieties, dormant since the days of Palmerston, about Russian designs on the warm-water ports of the north Norwegian coast.[9]

Uncertainty about Scandinavian alignments in this increasingly unstable situation had two aspects. One concerned the sympathies and allegiances of influential groups in Scandinavian society. Dynastic links, such as those between the Danish and Russian, British and Norwegian

[6] For general discussions of the diplomatic position of the Scandinavian states before the First World War see Paul Herre, *Die Kleinen Staaten Europas und die Entstehung des Weltkrieges* (Munich, 1937), 104–55; Folke Lindberg, *Scandinavia in Great Power Politics 1905–1908* (Stockholm, 1958); David W. Sweet, 'The Baltic in British Diplomacy before the First World War', *Historical Journal*, XIII (1970), 451–90; Pertti Luntinen, *The Baltic Question 1903–1908* (Helsinki, 1975).

[7] Troels Fink, *Ustabil balance. Dansk udenrigs- og forsvarspolitik 1894–1905* (Aarhus, 1969), 13.

[8] Paul Kennedy, 'The development of German naval plans against England, 1896–1914', in *War Plans of the Great Powers*, 177; Carl-Axel Gemzell, *Organization, Conflict, and Innovation: A Study of German Naval Strategic Planning, 1888–1940* (Lund, 1973), 69–70; Arthur J. Marder, *British Naval Policy 1880–1905: The Anatomy of British Sea Power* (1940), 463–5, 479–82.

[9] Tuomo Polvinen, *Die finnischen Eisenbahnen in den militärischen und politischen Plänen Russlands vor dem ersten Weltkrieg* (Helsinki, 1962); Paul Knaplund, 'Finmark in British Diplomacy, 1836–1855', *American Historical Review*, XXX (1925), 478–502; C. F. Palmstierna, 'Sweden and the Russian Bogey: A new light on Palmerston's foreign policy', *Nineteenth Century and After*, CXII (1933), 739–54.

or Swedish and German royal houses; presumed identities of interest, as between Sweden and Germany in the face of a supposed Russian threat; unofficial or semi-official contacts between high-ranking officers: all of these might, in certain circumstances, lead the Scandinavian states to abandon neutrality and align themselves with one or other of the emerging power blocs. More importantly, there were serious doubts about Scandinavian military capacity in an era of rapid technological change which naturally favoured the largest and most industrially advanced states. There was, first, no realistic prospect of Scandinavian cooperation on matters of defence and foreign policy. Not only were Sweden and Norway at loggerheads up to 1905 and estranged for some years thereafter, but the limitations of 'Scandinavianism', despite a tentative revival around the turn of the century, had been painfully demonstrated by Sweden's failure to support Denmark in the war of 1864.[10] The strategic situations, capabilities and perceptions of the three Scandinavian states differed radically. Sweden enjoyed the most favoured strategic position and had a long military tradition. Influenced by the Prussian example and prompted by fear of Russia, a series of military reforms was carried out between 1885 and 1901. The Swedish armed forces were the largest and best equipped in northern Europe, but defence was nevertheless an issue of fierce party political controversy in the years before 1914.[11] Norway's defences were considerably improved between 1895 and 1905, particularly at sea. But they were directed primarily against a Swedish attempt to preserve the union by force: no serious thought was given to defence against a major European power. As a member of the British Foreign Office commented in 1911, 'The whole population is, I believe, something under three millions. How can she build and man a fleet to withstand Germany?'[12] However, the Norwegians believed that no power except Britain had the capacity to launch an attack on Norway, and that the Royal Navy could be relied on to defend Norway in all circumstances.[13] Denmark's strategic position was weaker and more exposed than that of either Sweden or Norway. Although its armed forces and land defences were by no means neglected in the decades following the war of 1864, Denmark could offer no serious resistance to a determined attack. As in Sweden,

---

[10] Folke Lindberg, *Den svenska utrikespolitikens historia*, III, part 4, *1872–1914* (Stockholm, 1958), 137–45.

[11] Douglas V. Verney, *Parliamentary Reform in Sweden 1866–1921* (Oxford, 1957), ch. ix; Leif Lewin, *Ideology and Strategy: A Century of Swedish Politics* (Cambridge, 1988), ch. 4.

[12] Undated minute by Eyre Crowe on despatch by Findlay (Christiania) of 8 February 1911, PRO, FO 371/1174, No. 5957.

[13] Roald Berg '"Det land vi venter hjaelp af"'. England som Norges beskytter 1905–1908', *Forsvarsstudier IV. Årbok for Forsvarshistorisk forskningssenter, Forsvarets högskole 1985*, Oslo 1985, 111–68.

defence was the subject of deep party political controversy. It was also linked to perceptions of threat and the likelihood of external assistance.[14] Expert opinion was polarised between the view of the army, which favoured the traditional policy of reliance on Great Britain and a relatively strong land defence, and that of the navy, which held that the growth of German naval power had placed Denmark wholly within the German sphere of influence. If Germany was to be prevented from occupying Danish territory in time of war, it must be convinced that Denmark was capable of repelling any violation of its territory by Britain. This meant strengthening the country's sea defences, particularly those of Esbjerg and Copenhagen. Politicians of the liberal and radical liberal parties who held power for much of the period after 1901 favoured a policy of minimal defence—and this too implied a tacit admission that Denmark must never be counted among Germany's enemies.

The inadequacy of the Danish defences was crucial since Denmark stood at the entrance to the Baltic. It controlled not only the southern shores of the Sound but also the Great Belt—the only route, until the widening of the German-controlled Kiel Canal in 1914, navigable by the largest modern warships.[15]The question whether the Baltic Sea could be kept open to the warships of all nations in time of war was the one issue vital to Britain, Germany and Russia alike. Free access to the Baltic was one of the cardinal principles of British naval strategy and foreign policy. Between the seventeenth century and the Napoleonic wars, when the Royal Navy had been dependent on Baltic supplies, it had been a matter of life and death. In the modern age—an age not only of steam and ironclads, but of dreadnoughts, mines and torpedoes—the principle was becoming unenforceable, but it was one upon which Britain continued to insist with the utmost vigour. German and Russian views were less consistent. The two powers hankered after a Baltic closed to foreign warships—a *mare clausum*—but Russia was uncomfortably aware that in practice this meant conceding mastery of the Baltic

---

[14]Troels Fink, *Fem foredrag om Dansk udenrigspolitik efter 1864* (Aarhus, 1958); Nikolaj Petersen, 'International power and foreign policy behavior: the formulation of Danish security policy in the 1870–1914 period', in *Power, Capabilities, Interdependence: Problems in the study of international influence* eds. Kjell Goldmann and Gunnar Sjöstedt, (London and Beverly Hills, 1979), 235–69; Carsten Due-Nielsen, 'Luck and calculation. Danish neutrality policy before 1914', in *Proceedings of the Seventh Biennial Conference of Teachers of Scandinavian Studies in Great Britain and Northern Ireland* eds. R. D. S. Allen and M. P. Barnes (1987), 18–32.

[15]For an analysis of the strategic significance of the various Baltic entrances see the despatch of 6 March 1907 by Captain Dumas, the naval attaché in Berlin, printed in *British Documents on the Origins of the War 1898–1914* eds. G. P. Gooch and Harold Temperley (11 vols. in 13, London, 1927 et. seq.) [hereafter BD], VIII, 122–9. For a description of some of the technical aspects of navigating the seaways see Gunnar Alexandersson, *The Baltic Straits* (The Hague, 1982), 63–9.

to Germany, especially after the destruction of the Russian Baltic Fleet at the hands of Japan in 1904. Within the narrow confines prescribed by British naval supremacy in the approaches to the North Sea, Germany enjoyed a uniquely favourable strategic position. The German navy was able both to dominate Danish waters and to shift its vessels quickly between the North Sea and the Baltic through the Kiel Canal. But it remained undecided whether to keep the Baltic entrances open and risk a British incursion, or to close them and gain security at the expense of its freedom of manoeuvre—the course it ultimately adopted in August 1914.

Denmark's weakness was of greatest international concern when relations between Britain, Germany and Russia were at their most uncertain—between 1902 and 1907—and when, in addition, the break-up of the Scandinavian union in 1905 created a power vacuum in northern Europe which none of the great powers could ignore. Norway's declaration of independence from Sweden in June 1905 did not lead to war between the two states—although for a time there was a risk that it might do so—but nevertheless it raised a number of questions of pressing international concern. One was whether the new nation should be a republic or a monarchy and, if the latter, what dynasty should rule there. This was an issue in which the royal houses of England, Germany and Russia all took a lively interest. In the end the Norwegians shrewdly chose a Danish prince with an English wife, who came to the throne as King Haakon VII, in order to 'strengthen the British self-interest in the welfare and security of Norway.'[16] More seriously, the union crisis set the European powers the diplomatic task of finding a replacement for the treaty of 1855 by which Britain and France had guaranteed the territorial integrity of Sweden and Norway against Russia. That replacement was ultimately to take the form of three international agreements: the Norwegian integrity treaty of 1907 and the Baltic and North Sea agreements of 1908. Because the negotiations for these treaties took place at a time when diplomatic relations among the European powers were unusually fluid, solutions to Scandinavian problems became an expression of wider European preoccupations.

After 1902 Great Britain was hesitantly abandoning isolation. One of the initial effects of this process was to set Britain against both Russia and Germany and to open up the prospect of a Russo-German rapprochement. The Anglo-Japanese alliance of 1902 made Russia more interested in good relations with Germany and provided Germany with an opportunity to drive a wedge between Russia and France. The Anglo-French entente of 1904 gave implicit support to France against Germany as the price for settling colonial rivalries in Africa. In 1905

---

[16] Berg ' "Det land vi venter hjaelp af" ', 166.

Germany sought to exploit the first Moroccan crisis and the weakening of Russia by war and revolution in order to accomplish a diplomatic revolution which would break the entente, restore the close relations with Russia that had been broken in 1890 and ultimately coerce France into joining a continental bloc directed against Great Britain.[17]
Much of the diplomatic skirmishing between Germany, Russia and Britain took place on the shores of the Baltic, as monarchs and their ministers met at Copenhagen, Swinemünde or Reval. It reached a climax at Björkö off the Finnish coast in July 1905, when Kaiser Wilhelm II and Tsar Nicholas II signed a defensive treaty which for a few months led the kaiser, his chancellor Bernhard von Bülow, and Friedrich von Holstein at the Wilhelmstrasse to believe that a continental alliance was within their grasp. Scandinavia was a key element in the attempt to achieve a Russo-German rapprochement. The two emperors had shown their concern for the strategic position of Denmark as early as 1903. They had then tried to reach a secret agreement with King Christian IX by which Germany and Russia would guarantee Danish neutrality and, if necessary, 'help to defend it by force'.[18] The Björkö discussions reflected their continuing preoccupation with guaranteeing Denmark as a means of keeping the Royal Navy out of the Baltic, as well as with the new crisis between Sweden and Norway. Wilhelm II sought to exploit the crisis by playing on the tsar's fears of British designs on Norway. Arriving at Björkö immediately after meeting the king of Sweden at Gävle, he reported a remark of King Oskar to the effect that if Norway became independent Germany would be free to occupy Bergen, after which England might seize Christiansand.[19] 'Emperor Nicholas was visibly disturbed at the prospect of a partition of Norway and the possibility of an English occupation, and said that in that case his harbours on the Murman coast would lose all value and there was an immediate danger that the Kattegat would be closed to Russia.'[20] The kaiser also hinted that British influence might be extended over Norway by other means. An opening had been created by Oskar II's refusal to agree to the Norwegian request for a Bernadotte

[17] Barbara Vogel, *Deutsche Russlandspolitik. Das Scheitern der deutschen Weltpolitik unter Bülow 1900–1906* (Düsseldorf, 1973), 8–11, 44–8; Peter Winzen, *Bülows Weltmachtkonzept* (Boppard am Rhein, 1977); idem, 'Prince Bülow's *Weltmachtpolitik*', *Australian Journal of Politics and History*, XXII (1976), 227–42; Katharine A. Lerman, 'Bismarck's heir: Chancellor Bernhard von Bülow and the national idea 1890–1918', in *The State of Germany* ed. John Breuilly (1992), 103–27.
[18] *Die grosse Politik der europäischen Kabinette 1871–1914* eds. J. Lepsius, A. Mendelssohn-Bartholdy and F. Thimme (40 vols. in 54, Berlin, 1922 et. seq.) [hereafter GP] XIX, part 1, 71 [English in original].
[19] On this meeting see Lindberg, *Scandinavia*, 32–4. Luntinen, *Baltic Question*, 57, suggests that the kaiser probably made up the story himself.
[20] GP 19, 2, 454–6.

prince as king of Norway. The alternative favoured by the Norwegians, Prince Carl of Denmark, happened to be the son-in-law of Edward VII. Merely to mention the latter's interest in Prince Carl's candidature was sufficient to revive all of the tsar's apprehensions about British intrigues.

Björkö was expected to have far-reaching ramifications. The kaiser wrote to the tsar:

> Holland, Belgium, Denmark, Sweden, will all be attracted to this new great centre of gravity ... They will revolve in the orbit of the great block of Powers (Russia, Germany, France, Austria, Italy) and feel confidence in leaning on and revolving around this mass.[21]

Even within the narrower confines of the Scandinavian region, the implications of Russo-German rapprochement were far-reaching. They amounted to nothing less than the exclusion of British political influence and naval power from the Baltic. Acting in concert, the two continental powers could dominate the Danish Straits and close them to the Royal Navy at will. British naval mastery in the North Sea could be outflanked by a Russian or German naval presence on the Norwegian coast. The Scandinavian states would be wholly under the influence of Germany and Russia.

These hopes were not to be fulfilled. By early 1906, with the Russian repudiation of the Björkö treaty and Germany's diplomatic defeat at the Algeçiras conference, the German strategy had failed. In August 1907 Britain concluded an agreement with Russia on Central Asia and the Near East. Nevertheless, it could be argued that despite the collapse of the kaiser's more spectacular efforts in 1905–6 and the conclusion of the Anglo-Russian entente, the net effect of the diplomatic manoeuvring of the period 1905–8 was greatly to diminish Britain's position in northern Europe. Admittedly Norwegian independence was achieved under British auspices, and the Norwegian integrity treaty of 1907 (which omitted any commitment to the preservation of Norway's neutrality) preserved Britain's freedom of manoeuvre in and around Norway in time of war. But the possibility of a German-Russian combination in the Baltic had not been precluded by the Anglo-Russian entente. Indeed it was given a new lease of life by the protracted negotiations over Norway. In his initiative at Swinemünde in August 1907 which led to the conclusion of a secret Baltic treaty between Germany and Russia in October,[22] the Russian foreign minister Isvolsky

---

[21] *The Willy-Nicky Correspondence: Being the secret and intimate Telegrams exchanged between the Kaiser and the Tsar* ed. Herman Bernstein (New York, 1918), 191; alternative version in Lindberg, *Scandinavia*, 35.

[22] Text in GP 23, 2, 483–5.

was hoping to create 'a counterweight to the Asian agreement to secure Russia against surprises in Europe'.[23] Even though Isvolsky's proposal was watered down, the Baltic and North Sea agreements of April 1908 to which it led marked the formal exclusion of Britain from a position of influence in the Baltic region. Britain and France were signatories of the North Sea agreement but not of its Baltic counterpart. They now possessed only the convention of 1856 on the demilitarisation of the Åland Islands (which Isvolsky had tried but failed to have set aside) as the juridical base for their claim to a voice in Baltic affairs. The agreements were thus the diplomatic equivalent of the changes in naval strategy which were to keep the Royal Navy (apart from a few submarines) out of the Baltic for the duration of the First World War.

Sir Edward Grey, British Foreign Secretary at the time, wrote of the Baltic and North Sea negotiations:

> It is not worthwhile to explain these negotiations. What result they had at the time has been superseded by the war and its consequences. Nor did they have any important influence on the course of events before the war; but the records about them show how suspicious everyone was.[24]

Their very blandness, however, is the key to their significance. The fact that they did little more than affirm the territorial status quo on the shores on the North Sea and the Baltic showed how difficult it was to achieve great-power consensus. It could be done only by shelving the really contentious issues. As Pertti Luntinen has pointed out, the agreements of 1907–8 contained no reference to Norwegian neutrality or to the legal status of the Danish Straits, nor even a definition of where the North Sea ended and the Baltic Sea began.[25] The negotiations formed, in Folke Lindberg's words, 'part of the silent, hard struggle for influence in the Northern countries and for control of the Baltic, above all the entrances to this sea.'[26]

Scandinavia and the approach of war 1908–14

After the conclusion of the Baltic and North Sea agreements, Scandinavia became less a matter of concern in its own right and more a

[23] Luntinen, *Baltic Question*, 81.
[24] *Twenty-five Years* (2 vols., 1925), I, 143.
[25] Luntinen, *Baltic Question*, 240.
[26] Lindberg, *Scandinavia*, 37.

reflection of the polarisation of relations between the great powers in the Balkans, North Africa and the Near East. In the course of 1908 relations between Britain and Germany deteriorated while Anglo-Russian friendship was demonstrated by the meeting between the tsar and King Edward VII at Reval. Towards the end of 1908 the Bosnian crisis dealt a decisive blow to relations between Germany and Russia. The fluidity which had characterised the international situation up to 1907 gave way to a situation of increasing tension and hardening alignments marked by the second Moroccan crisis and war between Italy and Turkey in 1911, followed by the two Balkan wars of 1912 and 1913. Scandinavia and the Baltic may have become less interesting to the great powers diplomatically, but the growing prospect of a major European war heightened their strategic importance in the eyes of Germany and Russia, if not of Great Britain.

A Liberal government which was preoccupied with its domestic programme and knew little of the increasingly close collaboration between the general staffs of Great Britain and France was unlikely to take much interest in more distant parts of Europe. In February 1908 'the cabinet passed hastily over the Baltic and North Sea agreements ... to consider a Licensing bill.'[27] In the Foreign Office the conclusion of the agreements was viewed as marking an end to a temporary period of instability: the main priority was now to maintain the new status quo and keep Scandinavia out of the arena of great-power conflict. To the extent that there was any significant British diplomatic activity, it focused on Sweden. Swedish policy after 1908 underwent a crisis of confidence:

> The powers on which she has been accustomed to lean for protection against the threatening power of Russia are both now in intimate relations of friendship with their former enemy. Force appears to be on the side of the central European Powers, who have imposed their will on Europe; and the impression prevails here that a conflict between the Great European Powers is inevitable in the now distant future, and that, if such a conflict occurs, Sweden may be forced to take one side or the other.[28]

It was the task of British diplomacy to demonstrate that Britain and Sweden had important interests in common, notably an open Baltic; to encourage dialogue between Sweden and Russia on the Åland Islands and other issues; and to reconcile the Swedes to the loss of Norway.[29] The visits of King Edward VII to Sweden and of King

---

[27] Zara S. Steiner, *The Foreign Office and Foreign Policy 1898–1914* (Cambridge, 1969), 86.

[28] Sir C. Spring-Rice (Stockholm) to FO, 27 April 1909, FO 371/745, No. 16381.

[29] Spring-Rice: Annual Report on Sweden for 1908, 1 January 1909, ibid, No. 1293, 2–3.

Gustav V to England in 1908 did much to restore Swedish trust in Britain. In a speech delivered on the latter occasion Grey declared that 'the relations between Great Britain and Sweden are as smooth, easy and natural as it is possible for relations between two countries to be.'[30] However, although Anglo-Swedish relations remained amicable in the years before 1914, Britain could do little to allay Swedish fears of Russia or to arrest the growing influence of Germany which fed on those fears.

Norway caused Britain much less anxiety. The regular presence of the High Seas Fleet in Norwegian waters led some Norwegians to question their country's axiomatic faith in British naval supremacy, but the British Admiralty felt no such fears. Mansfeldt Findley, appointed minister to Norway in 1912, repeatedly warned of the dangers of closer relations between Norway and Sweden, since it was 'obvious that, by an *entente* with Sweden, Norway might gradually be drawn into the German orbit', but the Foreign Office does not appear to have taken much notice of his advice.[31] The situation with regard to Denmark was entirely different. By 1914 both the Admiralty and the Foreign Office had virtually written Denmark off as being wholly within the German sphere of influence.

Much of the strategic planning for a war with Germany that was conducted under the leadership of Sir John Fisher at the Admiralty after 1904 revolved around ideas of a naval offensive in the Baltic and amphibious operations on German or Danish territory.[32] As the War Office was in the habit of pointing out, the Admiralty's schemes had a strong sense of unreality about them. The logistical problems of sending large naval forces and thousands of troops into an area where Germany enjoyed complete naval supremacy were overwhelming. By 1911 the general staff had effectively won its case for a continental commitment in France. In 1912 the Admiralty tacitly acknowledged the impossibility of operations close to the German coast when it adopted a strategy of 'open' blockade based on control of the approaches to the North Sea in the Channel and between Scotland and the Norwegian coast. Nevertheless plans for operations against German North Sea islands

---

[30] Speech of 19 November 1908, quoted in Tom Kristensen, 'Mellom landmakter og sjömakter. Norges plass i britisk forsvars- og utenrikspolitikk, 1905–1914' (Hovedoppgave i historie, University of Oslo, 1988), 155.

[31] Annual Report on Norway for 1911, 19 March 1912, FO 371/1415, 15.

[32] See, in addition to Haggie and Summerton (note 2 above), Hans Branner, 'Östersöen og de danske straeder i engelsk krigsplanlaegning 1904–14', *Historie. Jyske Samlinger*, Nye Raekke, IX (1972), 493–535; idem, *Småstat mellem stormagt* (Aarhus, 1972), 108–130; Paul Hayes, 'Britain, Germany, and the Admiralty's plans for attacking German territory, 1906–1915', in *War, Strategy and International Politics: Essays in Honour of Sir Michael Howard* eds. Laurence Freedman, Paul Hayes and Robert O'Neill (Oxford, 1992), 95–116.

and the seizure of bases in Holland, Denmark, Norway and Sweden, were still under consideration at the Admiralty in 1913–14, on the initiative of Winston Churchill, the First Lord; and after the outbreak of war the Baltic rather than the Dardanelles was Churchill's first choice for a flanking strategy against the Central Powers.[33]

The Foreign Office saw more clearly than the Admiralty the limitations of British power at the entrances to the Baltic and drew the appropriate conclusions. The growth of German influence in Denmark was overwhelming and irresistible. Denmark could not defend itself against Germany; British assistance, if it were given, would arrive too late to prevent the country from being completely overrun. Britain must not encourage the Danes to entertain false hopes. The position was made absolutely clear by Grey in conversation with the Danish foreign minister Erik Scavenius (who had no such hopes) in May 1914, when he 'took the opportunity of saying that we were aware of the delicate position of Denmark, that we should never be the first to violate her neutrality, and that we always desired to avoid placing her in an embarrassing position.'[34] The same attitude was revealed in the unexpectedly mild British response to the Danish mining of the Great Belt, at Germany's request (to guard against a naval assault on the Baltic which the British had no intention of mounting), at the beginning of August 1914.[35]

Both Germany and Russia reassessed their policies in northern Europe after 1908. Conscious of their naval weakness in relation to Germany, the Russians shifted towards the British position on an open Baltic. It was not until 1912 that it was made clear to Sazonov by Grey that Britain could not take the risk of affording Russia any naval support in a sea whose entrances were effectively controlled by Germany.[36] They also recast their plans for the defence of St Petersburg. As a result Finland became for the first time central to the security of the capital. Russia's activities in Finland, though prompted by defensive considerations, still looked threatening to the Swedes. A renewed wave of Russification was aimed at preventing a repetition of the revolutionary upheavals of 1905; the construction of a new inland railway line from St Petersburg to Vaasa on the Gulf of Bothnia was intended to enable Russian forces to meet a combined German and Swedish invasion of Finland.[37] Both actions, however, could be construed as evidence of Russia's aggressive intentions.

[33] Tuvia Ben-Moshe, 'Churchill's strategic conception during the First World War', *Journal of Strategic Studies*, XII (1989), 7.

[34] BD 10, 743.

[35] Tage Kaarsted, *Great Britain and Denmark 1914–1920* (Odense, 1979), 42–3.

[36] Lindberg, *Den svenska utrikespolitikens historia* III, 4, 226.

[37] Polvinen, *Die finnischen Eisenbahnen.*

In some respects German policy also became more cautious. The plans drawn up by the Admiralty Staff between 1899 and 1905 (though not favoured by other members of the naval hierarchy, including Tirpitz) were dominated by the idea—a not implausible one in the light of the Admiralty plans discussed earlier—of drawing British naval forces into the Baltic and destroying them in the narrow Danish waters by torpedo-boat attacks, minefields and bombardment from the land. For this purpose an occupation of Danish territory was essential, and the kaiser ordered the general staff to cooperate with the navy in drawing up plans for an invasion of Denmark. Schlieffen, the chief of the general staff until the end of 1905, consistently opposed the idea of diverting any forces from the eastern and western fronts. When Bülow added his weight to the opposition on political grounds early in 1905, the plan for an invasion was dropped.[38] Although a number of admirals continued to hanker after operations in Danish waters, the growing predominance of the army, combined with an acknowledgement of British naval supremacy, meant that by 1912 the German navy, like the British, had come round to an essentially defensive strategy.

However, the German general staff's opposition to military operations against Denmark did not imply a lack of interest in Scandinavia. On the contrary, Schlieffen's successor, the younger Moltke, was pre-occupied with the position of Denmark in an Anglo-German war, and of Sweden in a war between Germany and Russia. Where Denmark was concerned, his chief priority was to ensure that Danish territory should not be used as a jumping-off point for an invasion of Germany. To this end Germany must be assured that Denmark would adopt a policy of benevolent neutrality and would be in a position to repel a British seaborne attack which, he believed, would be directed against Copenhagen or—more likely—the port of Esbjerg on the west coast of Jutland, close to the German frontier. If Denmark was not able or willing to resist the British, Germany would be obliged to do the job itself. This was the message conveyed by Moltke in a series of conversations with Captain L. C. F. Lütken of the Danish war ministry between 1906 and 1908.[39] Lütken was a capable and strongly pro-German Danish army officer who was also a close associate of the liberal prime minister J. C. Christensen. At one time Moltke seems to have thought of persuading the Danish government to sign a military agreement with Germany. In the end he was satisfied with an assurance that 'Denmark could in no circumstances stand on the side of Germany's

[38] Walther Hubatsch, *Der Admiralstab und die obersten Marinebehörden in Deutschland 1848–1945* (Frankfurt am Main, 1958), 118–20.

[39] Troels Fink, *Spillet om dansk neutralitet 1905–1909. L. C. F. Lütken og dansk udenrigs- og forsvarspolitik* (Aarhus, 1959).

adversaries, and that if it proved impossible to maintain Denmark's neutrality in a German-British war, it would go along with Germany.[40] Despite the fall of the Christensen government in October 1908 and a temporary reversion to a more even-handed policy, the coming to power of the radical liberals in 1909–10 and again in 1913 brought a return to a pro-German orientation. This time, under the defence minister Peter Munch and the youthful foreign minister Erik Scavenius, it was combined with a policy of minimal defence. Scavenius's calculation was that no defence, however strong, would deter the great powers from intervening in Scandinavia if they wished to do so. In practice, however, their other commitments would be so great that they would never have sufficient forces for what was, for all of them, a strictly secondary theatre.[41] Accurate as this prediction was to prove, it was still vital to give Germany no pretext for violating Danish neutrality. The lengths to which the government was prepared to go were shown by its discouragement of Danish agitation in North Schleswig and by its decision to lay mines in the Great Belt following the request made by Germany on 5 August 1914.

Moltke's second major venture, towards Sweden in 1910, was more ambitious but less successful. From the Danes an assurance of neutrality was sufficient, provided it could be guaranteed by Denmark's own efforts, supplemented if necessary by German support. The Swedes were to be persuaded to depart from neutrality in favour of an alliance with Germany against Russia. This, despite promising beginnings, was more than the Swedes could accept. Moltke's initiative, backed by the new foreign secretary Kiderlen-Wächter, reflected the deepening antagonism between Germany and Russia following the Bosnian crisis of 1908. He sought to exploit the feelings of insecurity and isolation felt by the conservative Lindman government in Sweden in the aftermath of the Baltic and North Sea negotiations. To this end the Swedes had to be convinced of the reality of the Russian threat to themselves and persuaded that they stood a good chance of success if they went to war. A pretext was provided by a report of November 1909 on the construction of the St Petersburg-Vaasa railway in Finland. Moltke did not believe for one moment that Russia had any aggressive intentions towards Sweden.[42] On the contrary, he recognised correctly that Russian railway building reflected fears that a Swedish-German invasion might

[40] Ibid, 279–82.

[41] Viggo Sjöqvist, *Erik Scavenius. Danmarks udenrigsminister under to verdenskrige. Statsminister 1942–1945*, I, *1877–1920* (Copenhagen, 1973), 60–1.

[42] Folke Lindberg, 'De svensk-tyska generalstabsförhandlingarna år 1910', *Historisk tidskrift*, LXXVII (1957), 1–28; Lindberg, *Den svenska utrikespolitikens historia* III, 4, 249–56; W. M. Carlgren, *Neutralität oder Allianz. Deutschlands Beziehungen zu Schweden in den Anfangsjahren des ersten Weltkrieges* (Stockholm, 1962), 11–12.

coincide with a revolution in Finland to threaten St Petersburg. But Germany could exploit the mistrust between the two powers. If Russia could be convinced of the danger of Swedish intervention in Finland and the likelihood that it would unleash a Finnish revolution, it would be obliged to detach considerable forces for the defence of St Petersburg. If Sweden could be persuaded that the Russian threat was a real one, it might join the Central Powers in time of war. In August 1910 the Swedish government was invited to enter into military conversations in order to coordinate joint defence measures against a Russian attack.

The Swedish response was polite but cautious. Knut Bildt, the chief of the general staff, was allowed to meet Moltke in Berlin in November 1909. He was given a completely false picture of Germany's strategic plans, designed to give the impression that a Swedish expeditionary force sent to Finland for an assault on the Russian capital would encounter little resistance. Despite his pro-German sympathies, Bildt seems to have been sceptical about the practicalities of a Swedish invasion of Finland, as well as the wider political implications of abandoning Sweden's traditional policy of neutrality.[43] This view was shared by Lindman, though not by the foreign minister Arvid Taube, for whom the German proposal meant a promise of support from 'the world's most powerful military state'. King Gustav V may also have wanted a closer alignment with Germany: certainly his wife, born a German princess, was trying to push him in this direction.[44] The Swedes did not break off contact but neither did they take any step to prolong or broaden the discussions. And if the Lindman government was non-committal, the Germans had still less to hope for from the liberals who were in power from 1911 to 1914, even though the kaiser expressed his desire in January 1914 for 'an alliance, or at least a military convention' with Sweden.[45] The ostensibly non-party government headed by Hjalmar Hammarskjöld which was brought to power by a constitutional crisis a month later was to prove strongly pro-German in the conduct of its neutrality policy after the outbreak of war.[46] It used the threat of Swedish intervention on the side of the Central Powers very effectively to extract concessions from the Entente. Nevertheless, Moltke's hope

[43] Bildt's advice to the government is unknown but he told his son in 1912 that Moltke's aim had been a military convention and that he was glad nothing had come of it: Carlgren, *Neutralität oder Allianz*, 15–16.

[44] Lewin, *Ideology and Strategy*, 94; Wilhelm M. Carlgren, 'Gustav V och utrikespolitikken', in *Studier i modern historia tillägnade Jarl Torbecke den 18. augusti 1990* (Stockholm, 1990), 41–57.

[45] Carlgren, *Neutralität oder Allianz*, 22.

[46] W. M. Carlgren, *Ministären Hammarskjöld. Tillkomst—Söndring—Fall* (Stockholm, 1967); Steven Koblik, *Sweden: The Neutral Victor. Sweden and the Western Powers 1917–1918* (Lund, 1972), ch. 1; B. J. C. McKercher, *Esme Howard: A diplomatic biography* (Cambridge, 1989), ch. 5.

of an explicit Swedish commitment to the German side remained unrealised.

Why—to return to one of the questions posed at the beginning of this paper—were the Scandinavian states able to avoid direct involvement in the war of 1914–18? The answer has two aspects. The first, and probably the more important, is the explanation arrived at by Scavenius before 1914 and concerns the extent to which any of the belligerent powers had either the means or the incentive to extend the war to Scandinavia. With the bulk of their land forces held down in France and in eastern Europe; with the Russian Baltic Fleet confined to the Gulf of Finland, the High Seas Fleet tied down at Wilhelmshaven and the Royal Navy enforcing the blockade, they had little capacity for conducting offensive operations on the northern periphery. If the will existed, as it seems to have done in the case of the Baltic naval offensive advocated by Churchill and Fisher, the means were lacking. If the belligerents possessed the capacity, as with Germany's overwhelming preponderance over Denmark or Britain's over Norway, there were always powerful political and economic arguments against a seizure of neutral territory. The belligerents were unable either to persuade or to force the Scandinavian states to depart from a neutrality which was favoured by almost the whole of their populations, and they made few attempts to do so. Only in Sweden was there a significant 'activist' element which wished to go to war with Russia. The government remained wholly unresponsive to the rather low-key proposals made by Germany in 1915 that Sweden should join the Central Powers.[47]

This leads to the second part of the answer: the conduct of the Scandinavian states themselves; in other words, the extent to which they behaved in such a way as to convince the belligerent powers that they possessed the will and capacity to maintain their neutrality. This latter aspect should not be underrated. Not only Sweden but also the other Scandinavian states possessed defensive capabilities in 1914 which could not be wholly disregarded. Those of Norway and even Denmark were greater, both relatively and absolutely than they were to be in 1939. The Scandinavian countries also enjoyed a high degree of social and political stability. Internal conflicts were at times acute, as the Swedish general strike of 1909 and the constitutional crisis of February 1914 testify.[48] At no time, however, did such tensions encourage or

[47] Torsten Gihl, *Den svenska utrikespolitikens historia*, IV, *1914–1919* (Stockholm, 1951), 141–3; Carlgren, *Neutralität oder Allianz*, passim.

[48] The crisis, provoked by King Gustav V's 'palace yard speech' of 6 February 1914 calling over the heads of his government for a strong defence force, led to rumours in the foreign press of revolution and the king's abdication (Carlgren, *Ministären Hammarskjöld*, 28–9). It was resolved by the formation of a non-party (but conservative) government under Hjalmar Hammarskjöld.

necessitate external intervention. Finally, the Scandinavian states were successful in the conduct of relations among themselves.

The competence of Scandinavian foreign policy should not be exaggerated. These were small countries whose perspectives on great-power politics were frequently distorted by lack of information and the parochialism and partiality of their foreign policy makers.[49] The latter often overrated their importance in the eyes of the great powers and favoured a pedantically legalistic approach to relations between states. Norway's reliance on Great Britain led its leaders to overlook the fact that the British were much more interested in Sweden throughout the union crisis and the integrity treaty negotiations.[50] Swedes could not imagine that Russia had anything other than aggressive intentions towards them. The Scandinavian lack of interest in the outside world and rejection of great-power politics was expressed most forcefully in Björnstjerne Björnson's dictum that the best foreign policy for Norway was to have no foreign policy, or the slogan of Denmark's 'defence nihilists', 'Hvad skal det nytte?' ('What's the use?'). Even Sweden, with its great-power heritage, had, in the view of one of its prime ministers (E. G. Boström, speaking in 1905), 'no [foreign] policy in any real sense apart from protecting its neutrality',[51] and Wilhelm Carlgren has aptly described Sweden after 1905 as being afflicted by a kind of snow-blindness towards the world at large after decades of preoccupation with the problems of the union with Norway.[52] Yet some Scandinavian policy makers were highly effective: for example, the ruthlessly clear-sighted Erik Scavenius or the wartime foreign minister of Sweden, the banker Knut Wallenberg, whose methods were unorthodox but who managed to convince both sides of his indispensability. And it was a matter of some importance that, unlike other small countries, Scandinavians were prepared to settle their differences by compromise. The separation of Norway and Sweden was accomplished peacefully in 1905. There was no Scandinavian equivalent of the Balkan wars.

---

[49] For discussions of the making of Scandinavian foreign policy and the make-up and perceptions of the foreign policy-making elites before 1914, see e.g. Carlgren, *Ministären Hammarskjöld*, 86–135; Lindberg, *Den svenska utrikespolitikens historia*, III, 4, 9–22; Viggo Sjöqvist, *Peter Vedel. Udenrigsministeriets direktör* (2 vols., Copenhagen, 1964); Reidar Omang, *Norsk utenrikstjeneste*, I, *Grunnleggende år* (Oslo, 1955); II, *Stormfulle tider 1913–28* (Oslo, 1959); Berg ' "Det land vi venter hjaelp af" '. See also the more extended discussion in the latter's unpublished dissertation with the same title (Hovedoppgave i historie, University of Bergen, 1983).

[50] Berg ' "Det land vi venter hjaelp af" ', 166.

[51] Quoted in Wilhelm M. Carlgren, *Ministären Hammarskjöld*, 91–2.

[52] W. M. Carlgren, reviewing Yvonne Maria Werner, *Svensk-tyska förbindelser kring sekelskiftet 1900* (Lund, 1989), in *Historisk tidskrift* 1990, 425–7.

The Scandinavian economies: trade, blockade and *Mitteleuropa*

In the mid-nineteenth century Scandinavia was an economic as well as a political backwater. With the application of steam power and armour plating to naval warfare, Scandinavia and the Baltic had been deprived of their traditional importance as a source of essential supplies of timber, tar and hemp for European navies, while Sweden had long since lost its near monopoly as a supplier of copper and high-quality iron products. However in the last quarter of the nineteenth century the Scandinavian countries underwent a process of rapid economic expansion. Having been among the poorest countries in Europe in terms of per capita income, on a level with other peripheral regions such as the Balkans and the Iberian peninsula, they were by 1914 on the verge of joining the select group of western European industrialised economies.

Scandinavian economic development took a variety of forms. In Denmark after 1870 agriculture underwent a complete reorientation and modernisation, directed to the production of high-quality meat and dairy products for the British market. By 1913 Britain was taking 68 per cent of Danish agricultural exports. Sweden developed its timber exports and built up a sophisticated modern manufacturing industry. In addition, the discovery of the Basic Process of steel production by Gilchrist Thomas in 1878, and its widespread adoption in Germany, made possible for the first time the economic exploitation of the high-grade phosphoric iron ores of northern Sweden. The great ore fields of Gällivare and Kiruna were opened up and linked by rail to the Baltic at Luleå in 1887 and to the Norwegian coast at Narvik in 1903. Norway's economic activities were concentrated on fishing, whaling and above all shipping. By 1875 the Norwegian merchant fleet was the third largest in the world. Industrial development, based on the exploitation of Norway's ample resources of hydro-electric power, began to take off after the turn of the century. In 1904 Birkeland and Eyde patented a method for the production of artificial nitrogen which promised a solution to the imminent world shortage of nitrates for fertilizers and explosives. The Norsk Hydro plant at Rjukan in Telemark, financed by Swedish, French and German capital, was powered by what was then one of the largest hydro-electric stations in the world. Communications between Scandinavia and the outside world also improved radically, with the expansion of existing ports such as Copenhagen and Gothenburg, the construction of new ones at Esbjerg and Narvik, the establishment of ocean-going steamer services such as the Norwegian-American and Swedish-American lines, and the introduction in 1909 of direct ferry communications between Sweden and

Germany. The Scandinavian countries thus acquired a new importance as an integral part of the world economy, supplying raw materials and semi-finished goods (as well as certain specialised manufactured products such as Swedish ball bearings) to countries like Great Britain and Germany, and buying coal and manufactured products in return.

Economic development had costs as well as benefits. Each country remained 'dangerously specialized in one or two primary commodities'[53] and their dependence on foreign trade made them highly vulnerable to fluctuations in the international economy. The influx of foreign capital investment in new industries and sources of power threatened Scandinavians with the loss of control over key sectors of the economy and reduction to a semi-colonial status. They were exposed to competition among the European great powers for control of Scandinavian resources and markets. There was also the more subtle danger of cultural dependence on those societies from which they borrowed models of technological or social development. In some respects the Scandinavian countries were fully alive—and sometimes unduly sensitive—to such threats. Foreign ownership of waterfalls provoked a fierce nationalist and anti-industrial reaction in Norway which found expression in the draconian concession laws passed in the first years of Norwegian independence.[54] In the 1880s and early 1890s the British firm which was attempting to develop the northern Swedish iron ore fields was driven out of business by protectionist agitation, and between 1902 and 1907 the leading iron ore company was taken under state control in order, in part, to prevent it from falling into the hands of the German steel industry.[55] Other forms of foreign influence were less tangible and more difficult to guard against.

The influence exerted by one country over another is difficult to define or quantify. Nevertheless it seems clear that in one way or another Germany exerted a preponderant and growing influence over the Scandinavian countries before 1914. Great Britain was by far the largest market for Scandinavian goods but between 1873 and 1913 the share of Scandinavian imports supplied by Britain fell from 32 to 22 per cent, while Germany's share rose from 29 to 38 per cent. The decline accelerated after the turn of the century and was sharpest in the goods of highest value. In Denmark, Britain's share of imports of finished metal goods, ships and machinery fell from over 33 per cent in the late 1890s to less than 16 per cent in the years 1910–13, while

---

[53] Sidney Pollard, *Peaceful Conquest: The Industrialization of Europe 1760–1970* (Oxford, 1981), 233.

[54] Fritz Hodne, *An Economic History of Norway 1815–1970* (Bergen, 1975), 311–15: Sverre Steen, *På egen hånd. Norge etter 1905* (Oslo, 1976), 34–42.

[55] B. Jonsson, *Staten och malmfälten. En studie i svensk malmfältpolitik omkring sekelskiftet* (Stockholm, 1969).

Germany's share rose from 35 to over 78 per cent.[56] British investment declined in importance after the 1870s and British capitalists were more readily deterred by Norwegian legislation than were their German counterparts.[57] British sales methods lagged behind those of their German competitors.[58]

German influence was not merely economic. Nor was it restricted to the more conservative sections of Scandinavian society. In the late nineteenth and early twentieth centuries Germany stood for progress in all fields—technical, industrial and intellectual as well as military—and as a model for social legislation and political organisation for the Left as well as the Right. German was the most commonly taught second language in the schools and many members of the educated classes acquired at least part of their higher education or training in Germany.[59] Both Swedish and Danish social democrats and trade unionists were strongly influenced by their German mentors.[60] The files of the British Foreign Office are full of anxious references to the growth of German influence in Scandinavia. The minister to Copenhagen concluded his annual report for 1910 with the reflection that

> One cannot ... help being struck by the peaceful penetration which is being carried on commercially, artistically and in a literary manner, by Germany. Young Danes who wish to push themselves commercially go to Germany and establish connections there. Danish literary people turn to Germany for appreciation ... Danish universities are shaping themselves more after German models. German shops are penetrating even into Copenhagen. Such peaceful penetration it is impossible to avoid.[61]

---

[56] B. Nüchel Thomsen and B. Thomas, *Anglo-Danish Trade 1661–1963: A Historical Survey* (Åarhus 1966), 199–200.

[57] The head of a British-owned mining company was reported as saying that 'English Capitalists are so disgusted with Norwegian legislation that they would prefer to invest their money in Morocco, Spain, or South America': A. Herbert (Christiania) to Dering (FO), 31 October 1909, FO 368/15.

[58] This was the burden of numerous consular reports of the kind used extensively in R. J. S. Hoffman, *Great Britain and the German Trade Rivalry 1875–1914* (Philadelphia, 1933; republished New York and London, 1983). The thesis of 'entrepreneurial failure' has been challenged, and Hoffman's reliance on such reports criticised, e.g. in P. L. Payne, *British Entrepreneurship in the Nineteenth Century* (1974), 53; F. Crouzet, *The Victorian Economy* (1982) 408 (note 97).

[59] Study in Germany was particularly important for the least economically advanced of the Scandinavian countries and the one with the most limited educational infrastructure, the Grand Duchy of Finland: Timo Myllyntaus, *The Gatecrashing Apprentice: Industrialising Finland as an adopter of new technology* (Helsinki, 1990), 119–22.

[60] E. F. Heckscher, 'A Survey of Economic Thought in Sweden, 1875–1950', *Scandinavian Economic History Review* I (1953), 105–25.

[61] Vaughan (Copenhagen) to FO, enclosing report by Sir Alan Johnstone, 1 January 1911, FO 371/1360.

That Scandinavia might be absorbed either formally or informally into a German-dominated economic sphere came to seem increasingly probable. The favoured model was the Zollverein. In 1902 Kaiser Wilhelm II wrote that 'a customs union must be created' in order to 'draw Sweden across to us as a federal state.'[62] Reichenau, German minister to Sweden from 1911 to 1915, told a Swedish acquaintance that he wanted Sweden to become a part of Germany in the same way as, for example, Baden or Württemberg.[63] A number of Scandinavians responded positively to such suggestions, notably those Swedes (and Finns) who became pro-German activists after the outbreak of war. They advocated a Nordic confederation or Baltic league in close association with the Central Powers, and maintained links with such figures as Heinrich Class, the leader of the Pan-German League, and Friedrich Naumann, the National Liberal advocate of *Mitteleuropa*.[64] Other Scandinavians were less sanguine. Peter Vedel, the former head of the Danish foreign ministry, wrote pessimistically in 1906 of the consequences of Denmark's growing deference towards Germany in matters of defence and economic policy. He feared a gradual penetration of German capital. leading to the disappearance of Denmark as an independent entity. The Danes would have to fight to preserve their language and nationality just as they inhabitants of North Schleswig were now doing. If the dynasty were to retain its throne at all, it would have to be satisfied, at best, with a position similar to that occupied by the king of Saxony.[65]

British diplomats emphasised that Scandinavians were by no means resigned to their fate. In the report on Denmark quoted above the British minister wrote: 'I am convinced that the Danish national feeling is as strong as ever it was. Denmark has no idea of allowing herself to be absorbed into her greater neighbour.'[66] Swedes, too, were noticeably ambivalent in their attitudes towards Germany. Sir Cecil Spring-Rice, summing up from Stockholm the events of the same year, 1910, noted:

[62] Marginal note on a despatch from Stockholm, quoted in Lindberg, *Den svenska utrikespolitikens historia* III, 4, 153.

[63] Diary of Professor Gösta Mittag-Leffler: entry for 22–25 June 1913, cited ibid, 22. The liberal foreign minister Ehrensvärd, repudiating the advocates of an alliance with Germany, told the British minister that 'To ally herself with any Great Power would be, for a small state like Sweden, equivalent to becoming the vassal of that Power, and for his own part he honoured his country too highly to wish to see it occupy a position like Wurtemberg.' Howard to Grey, 27 January 1914, FO 425/380, No. 5853.

[64] L. Torbjörn Norman, 'Right-Wing Scandinavianism and the Russian Menace', in *Contact or Isolation? Soviet-Western relations in the interwar period* eds. John Hiden and Aleksander Loit (Stockholm, 1991), 329–49.

[65] Cited in Fink, *Spillet*. 50.

[66] Vaughan (Copenhagen) to FO, enclosing report by Sir Alan Johnstone, 1 January 1911, FO 371/1360.

'Sweden is conscious of the peaceful though not benevolent penetration of Germany in the world of commerce and finance; she does not like it, but she has to accept it.'[67] Both national pride and economic self-interest made Scandinavians resentful of German power even while they learned from Germany and admired much of what it stood for. The absence of a dynamic British commercial presence meant, however, that there was no effective counterweight. Politically, too, Britain seemed remote and ineffectual.[68]

On balance the fears expressed by Peter Vedel appear to have been well founded. In a sense, peace was more dangerous to the Scandinavian countries than war. If peace had continued it seems probable that nothing could have halted the penetration of German capital and German ideas. To say this is to say nothing new. As A. J. P. Taylor put it, 'The great capitalists were winning the mastery of Europe without war.'[69] War, when it came, revealed the latent strength of Great Britain's maritime position. In strategic terms it did not matter if Britain was excluded from the Baltic as long as it controlled the North Sea. Naval power enabled Britain to throttle German trade in wartime, even if its manufacturers could not compete with German exporters under normal commercial conditions. However, as Hankey, the architect of Britain's strategy of economic warfare had come to realise, in order to control German trade Britain also had to control that of the 'adjacent neutrals'—first and foremost Holland and the Scandinavian countries—through which Germany would endeavour to obtain its overseas supplies. British strategy thus required a radical reinterpretation of neutral rights in wartime. By 1912 ministers like Lloyd George and Churchill had already arrived at the conclusion that Britain would be obliged to ration Scandinavian imports to ensure that there would be no surplus left for export to Germany.[70] This was the practice which began to be adopted within a few weeks of Britain's entry into the

---

[67] Spring-Rice to FO, 31 January 1911, FO 371/1225.

[68] Sir Conyngham Greene (Copenhagen) to FO, enclosing annual report for 1911, 1 January 1912, FO 371/1360. But it should be noted that steps were taken to strengthen Britain's diplomatic representation in Scandinavia. In 1912 a new naval attaché's post was created for the three Scandinavian countries (previously divided between the attachés at St Petersburg and Berlin) in order to reflect 'the growing significance of these countries from the naval point of view.' Admiralty to Treasury, 11 April 1912, FO 371/1360. The appointment of Esme Howard as minister to Sweden in 1913 (in succession to Spring-Rice, who had been promoted to Washington), 'derived from the Foreign Office's determination to have a seasoned diplomat in what was becoming an increasingly sensitive post.' McKercher, Esme Howard, 133.

[69] A. J. P. Taylor, The Struggle for Mastery in Europe 1848–1918 (Oxford, 1954), 519.

[70] David French, British Economic and Strategic Planning 1905–1915(1982), 29–30; Offer, First World War, 305; John W. Coogan, The End of Neutrality: The United States, Britain, and Maritime Rights, 1899–1915 (Ithaca, NY and London, 1981), 146.

war.[71] The British blockade of 1914–18 evolved into a comprehensive and sophisticated system of economic warfare. It relied not so much on physical interception as on countless bargains between the British authorities and neutral merchants and governments. Sometimes the neutrals possessed powerful negotiating weapons. This was true in particular of Sweden, which exploited the Entente's need for ball bearings and other products, Sweden's role as a vital transit route to Russia and the threat of intervention on the German side to win exceptionally favourable terms in the first two years of the war. Gradually, however, dependence on the West—especially for supplies of foodstuffs and fuel—obliged even Sweden to comply to a very large extent with the wishes of the Entente.[72] Germany had no effective response except unrestricted submarine warfare.

The logic of the confrontation between Germany and Britain, once it became actual, was that the sea power could not exist in isolation from the continent: the existence of the sea power and the land power were mutually incompatible. If Germany achieved continental domination it would become a sea power. Grey perceived this very clearly. He told the American ambassador on 4 August 1914 that

> the issue for us was that, if Germany won, she would dominate France; the independence of Belgium, Holland, Denmark, and perhaps of Norway and Sweden, would be a mere shadow: their separate existence as nations would really be a fiction; all their harbours would be at Germany's disposal; she would dominate the whole of Western Europe, and this would make our position quite impossible. We could not exist as a first-class State under such circumstances.[73]

But, as Hankey had always been aware, economic pressure could take effect only slowly. There was a danger that Britain and its allies might give way first. Ultimately British sea power, even in alliance with France and Russia, was unable to defeat Germany. It could do so only with the support of the United States. In the last year of the war America, the home of millions of Scandinavian emigrants and hitherto looked upon as the leading champion of neutral rights, was to lend its weight to the British blockade and subject the Scandinavian countries to unprecedented pressures.

[71] Ibid, ch. 8.
[72] For details see Olav Riste, *The Neutral Ally: Norway's relations with belligerent powers in the First World War* (Oslo, 1965); Koblik, *Neutral Victor*; Kaarsted, *Great Britain and Denmark 1914–1920*; B. J. C. McKercher and Keith E. Neilson, ' "The triumph of unarmed forces": Sweden and the Allied blockade of Germany, 1914–1917', *Journal of Strategic Studies*, VII (1984), 178–99.
[73] BD 11, 328.

Nevertheless, none of the three states was actually forced into the war. That the Scandinavian countries were able to preserve their neutrality between 1914 and 1918 had something to do with their diplomatic skills, the strength of their defences and strategic positions and the value of their trade and natural resources. It was also due to the fact, anticipated by Scavenius, that in many respects they were marginal and of relatively little importance to the belligerents. By 1939 the position of all but one of the Scandinavian countries (now including Finland) had changed radically. The diplomacy of Denmark, Norway and Finland may have been less skilled; their defensive positions were certainly weaker and their economic resources were more dispensable. As the first months of the Second World War were to show, they were no longer on the strategic periphery. In 1939–40 none of the leading European powers—Great Britain, France, Germany and the Soviet Union—had any pressing reason to respect the neutrality of any Scandinavian country except Sweden. In November 1939 the Red army invaded Finland; in April 1940 Germany occupied Denmark and Norway; between those dates Britain and France contemplated the despatch of an expeditionary force to Scandinavia. Sweden, however, remained outside the conflict. Swedish diplomats performed an adroit balancing act between Britain and Germany and acted as mediators between Finland and the Soviet Union. Sweden's iron ore was of greater relative importance to Germany than it had been in the First World War. Whilst Britain and France tried and failed to cut Germany's supply in the winter of 1939–40, dependence on that supply acted as a major constraint on German conduct towards Sweden. Finally, Sweden retained relatively strong armed forces and enjoyed a strong defensive position: it was more sheltered with independent Finland as a neighbour than it had been when the Russian empire reached to the shores of the Gulf of Bothnia. For all these reasons Sweden was the only Scandinavian country that managed to preserve its neutrality throughout both world wars. However, the conflict between sea power and land power did not come to an end in 1945. After the Second World War the United States succeeded Great Britain as the world's leading maritime power while, with its construction of a fleet of ocean-going nuclear submarines at Murmansk, the Soviet Union mounted a more credible challenge to its rival's global hegemony than Tirpitz had achieved. Though the Reagan administration's ideas of 'steaming into the Kola Peninsula' and fighting a major naval battle in the Norwegian Sea[74] may now have as archaic a ring as the schemes devised by naval

---

[74] US Navy Secretary John F. Lehman, Jr., cited in Steven Miller, 'The Maritime Strategy and Geopolitics in the High North', in *The Soviet Union and Northern Waters* ed. Clive Archer (1988), 205–38.

strategists before the First World War, the confrontation between the superpowers in the Nordic region was nevertheless as real as any other of the Cold War era. And it should not be forgotten that although the Soviet Union has gone, Russia and its nuclear submarines remain.

CONFESSION BEFORE 1215

By Alexander Murray

READ 28 FEBRUARY 1992 AT NEWNHAM COLLEGE, CAMBRIDGE

BECAUSE research calls for work, and work for specialisation, the study of history tends always to subdivide. The deepest of its subdivisions is that between the 'outer' and the 'inner': between things like war, politics, business and law on one side, and on the other, thoughts and emotions. 'History' *tout simple* has come thus to refer mainly to the external, things usually handled in the past by men, while from the side of this Adam have sprung separate disciplines with names like the history of ideas, or *mentalités,*—not to mention the literatures in various languages. A glance even at the buildings of a university will confirm this.

The necessity of these divisions, and of the perpetual process that creates them, makes it equally necessary to be always breaking them down. We have for one thing absolutely no assurance at all that the lines we draw on experience—on the maxim *divide et impera*—really exist. A more important reason is that we ourselves are schizoid, as an organism, to the point of danger. The deep division this time is between ideal and actual, between what human beings wish or believe should be—the Latin gerundive—and what is. If our study of history, too, is to split up, it cannot perform the most valuable function it has for us, of putting our own pieces together again; because, seen as a whole, what it teaches is that the division in each of us, between ideal and actual, corresponds to another running right down the history of cultural forms and institutions—Latin grammar and all the others— and hence, on a day-to-day basis, of politics, war and so on.

It is in the light of this consideration that I want now to consider one small section of that deep division between the outer and inner aspects of history: the church institution of 'confession'. The word is understood here in a narrow ecclesiastical sense: as a Christian's private identification of his sins to a priest, receipt of a penance, and absolution from those sins in the name of the church. On one side is the individual, critically rehearsing the memory of his private, inner life; on the other, an institutional functionary who listens and reacts according to principles laid down by his office. Thirteenth-century canon lawyers would refer to confession as the *forum internum*, the 'internal court', as distinct from the public 'external' court where most of them practised. I shall come back to that distinction—its origin and shortcomings: the very concern of lawyers with confession meant it was not, in fact, as 'internal' as they pretended; and its history is not identical with that of private consciences. But confession is as close as any institution is likely to get to those consciences, and invites the historian's attention for that reason: as an 'interface' between external and internal history, and hence able to reveal contours in both.[1]

The area is almost pitch-black. Like most medieval statements confessions were spoken, not written; and they were spoken in secret, under a seal whose breach was one of the gravest sins on the list. This has understandably frightened some researchers away altogether: too much so, since medieval confessions can in fact sometimes be overheard.[2] The bare institution, nevertheless, shorn of what was said in it, is a degree less obscure. Its trouble remains that surviving documents are mostly about principles rather than practice. But if the relationship between these is what church history is about, that only poses the more strongly the question of practice; and it is in this 'almost pitch-black' area that my present question lies. It is, when did confession begin?

At once that must be qualified: when *before 1215* did confession begin? 1215 is the date of Innocent III's decree *Omnis utriusque sexus*, twenty-first canon of the Fourth Lateran Council, enjoining annual confession on all adults.[3] Most people agree that confession began either before then, or then. It is the Reformation that gives the date this significance. That movement was partly about confession. Penances, after all, included the 'works' Luther disliked; while confession gave priests too much 'social control'; and led either to moral laxity (because you could sin as you wished and confess afterwards) or, at the other extreme, scrupulosity, through excessive examination of the conscience, especially about sex. If not all these stones could have been thrown at once by all protestants, most agreed to dislike confession. Catholics, duly, tied up the procedure—for instance, with St Charles Borromeo's confessional box—and clung to it all the more firmly.[4]

---

[1] The standard survey is still B. Poschmann, *Penance and the Anointing of The Sick*. The Herder History of Dogma. Translated and revised by T. Courtney (Freiburg-London, 1964). The early medieval phase of the story is sketched with illustrative documents (translated into French) by C. Vogel, *Le pécheur et la pénitence au moyen-age*. Chrétiens de tous les temps. (Paris, 1969) [henceforth Vogel, *Pécheur*]. New perspectives are given by H. P. Forshaw, 'The Priest-Confessor in the Early Middle Ages, 600–1100' (unpublished PhD thesis, University of London, 1976).

[2] The seal: L. Honoré, *Le secret de la confession* (Bruges, 1924). Breaches of the seal are a source and subject of A. Murray, 'Confession as a historical source in the thirteenth century', in *The Writing of History in the Middle Ages. Essays presented to Richard William Southern*, ed. R. H. C. Davis and J. M. Wallace-Hadrill (Oxford, 1981), 275–322.

[3] *Conciliorum oecumenicorum decreta*, ed. J. Alberigo and others (third edn., Bologna, 1973), 245.

[4] Evidence of these views will be found in S. E. Ozment, *The Reformation in the Cities* (New Haven and London, 1975), 17, 26–32, 50–6, 67–8, 72–6, 100, 153–60; J. Bossy, 'The

This difference has coloured the medieval history of confession. Innocent III's ringing decree had the unexpected effect of playing into protestant hands, for it could so easily be read as showing that the papal monarch had invented confession,—doubtless for the very reasons protestants held against it. As if in reaction Catholic historians insisted confession had always been there. Without our going further back the dialectic can be seen in a comparison of H. C. Lea's three-volume *History of Auricular Confession*, published in 1896[5], with O. D. Watkins' two-volume *History of Penance*, published in 1920[6]; and it survived the age of these giants. Father John Dickinson, high church Anglican and historian of the Augustinian canons, was confident in 1950 that in the twelfth century confessions in England were heard 'very rarely even in monasteries'[7]; yet in the 1930s Father Bernard Poschmann, a Catholic, had written in what is still otherwise the best textbook on the subject, that by the twelfth century (he has already said almost the same for the ninth) 'the law of confession was to all intents and purposes universally enforced'.[8] Because good partisans are industrious, their spadework, complete with its problems, survives into cooler times. Professor Barlow's *The English Church, 1066–1154* has it that 'the basic disciplinary system of the church was, as it always had been, confession and penance. Two systems, public and private, existed side by side, and *both are well documented*'.[9] Dr Margaret Gibson's *Lanfranc of Canterbury*, on the other hand, can reject a traditional attribution to Lanfranc of a treatise on confession on the grounds, among others, that 'in its assumption that the sacrament of confession is a generally accepted practice for the laity and clergy alike this text is probably no earlier than *c*.1100'.[10]

This *Sic et Non* could go on, the assurance on both sides all the more remarkable for the difficulty, almost universally admitted, of discovering

---

Social History of Confession in the Age of Reformation', in these *Transactions*, 5th series, 25 (1975), 21–38; and T. N. Tentler, *Sin and Confession on the Eve of the Reformation* (Princeton, 1977).

[5] H. C. Lea, *The History of Auricular Confession and Indulgences in the Latin Church*, 3 vols. (Philadelphia, 1986).

[6] O. D. Watkins, *A History of Penance* (2 vols., 1920); esp. II, 735–6; referring mainly to the tenth, eleventh and twelfth centuries. P. Anciaux begins his *La théologie du sacrement de pénitence au xiie siècle* (Louvain, 1949), with a similar assumption (2–3): 'jusqu' à cette époque l'Église avait simplement vécu des richesses de ses sacrements, sans chercher à en approfondir la nature ou à en déterminer les elements et leur efficacité'. The otherwise excellent documentation of Dr Forshaw's thesis (as in n. 1) deserts her when she purports to describe the regular and widespread practice of confession, esp. on 198 and 293.

[7] J. Dickinson, *The Origin of the Austin Canons and their Introduction into England* (1950),228.

[8] Poschmann (as in n. 1), 140; *cf.* 139, for the eighth and ninth centuries.

[9] F. Barlow, *The English Church, 1066–1154* (London and New York, 1979), 138 [my emphasis]; *cf.* 147, 164; *cf.* the same author's *The English Church, 1000–1066* (London and New York, 1979), 265, 268, 271.

[10] M. Gibson, *Lanfranc of Bec* (Oxford, 1978), 244.

the facts.[11] It shows how the question was born; that it is still alive; and that it is worth trying to answer. It does not imply an undertaking to answer it; only to try.

I

I must start with a brief history of the first millennium AD. *Prima facie* our problem is not one at all. 'Confession' is a synonym for 'penance' and penance is as old as the church. Indeed it is older, since John the Baptist told people to repent before Jesus came (Mt. 3:2). We come here against a paradox innate in the Christian religion. For what happens when John's listeners *have* repented, and been baptised? The new man who emerges from the font has put the world, the flesh and the devil behind him. By rights he should have done the same with penance, having nothing more to repent of.

But Christ died for sinners. So somehow, Christians must be sinners. The paradox runs like a spinal cord down the history of the church. It is there in the differences between Judaism and Christianity; and, within Christianity, it has engendered heresies and schisms as well as, among the orthodox, endless debate. The history of penance draws its tension from the same paradox. Rigorists have argued that to join the church is a *poenitentia prima* (to use Tertullian's expression). So how can there be a *poenitentia secunda*? among other things it would set a bad example

---

[11] For lists of authors for and against see *Thomas of Chobham, 'Summa confessorum'*, ed. F. Broomfield (Louvain and Paris, 1968), xli; and for an earlier period, A. Thacker, 'Monks, preaching and pastoral care in early Anglo-Saxon England', in *Pastoral Care Before the Parish*, ed. J. Blair and R. Sharpe (Leicester, 1992), 137–70, on 161. As for the difficulties inherent to the subject Professor Barlow himself, in *English Church, 1000–1066*, 259, acknowledges that 'concrete examples are hard to find' to show whether the rules were kept,—but at once goes on to assume that derelictions of other duties than confession 'must have been dealt with through the *forum internum*, the confessional'. Cautious authors include H. E. J. Cowdrey, 'Bishop Ermenfrid of Sion and the Penitential Ordinance following the Battle of Hastings', *Journal of Ecclesiastical History*, XX (1969), 225–42, on 236–7. Referring to 'the penitential discipline of the Church as it was administered between the Carolingian reform and the beginning of the Crusades' he adds that 'as far as the time of the Norman ordinance is concerned, the character of this discipline and the extent to which it was effective are not easy to ascertain.' R. Sharpe, in 'Churches and communities in early medieval Ireland', *Pastoral Care Before the Parish* (as above), 82, prudently writes that private confession 'could hardly be reported and so lies beyond the scope of our evidence'. Abbé Joseph Avril recognises similar difficulties in respect of France; 'Remarques sur un aspect de la vie religieuse paroissiale: la pratique de la confession et de la communion du xe au xive siècle', in *L'encadrement religieux des fidèles, au Moyen-Age et jusqu'au Concile de Trente. La paroisse—le clergé—la pastorale—la dévotion*. Actes du 109e congrès national des sociétés savantes, Dijon, 1984. Section d'histoire médiévale et de philologie, tome 1 (Ministère de l'éducation nationale. Comité des travaux historiques et scientifiques, Paris 1985), 347–63, on 350–1.

and weaken the 'medicine' of penance (that image is from St Augustine)[12]

This view has been represented at every stage of church history. So has its opposite. After all, the very prince of the apostles had lapsed. Was he no longer a disciple? The 'apostolic' church followed Peter's lead also in this respect, raising problems which became especially acute during the persecutions. Should those who had flinched be allowed back? This question was still alive when Constantine became a Christian. His conversion changed a limited, acute problem into a general, chronic one. For not only were Christians now to be numbered in millions, making a law about lapses necessary. The millions were no longer an élite but a moral 'mixed bag', imperfect by definition.[13] So a formal procedure for reconciling lapsed Christians could no longer be kept at bay. It duly appeared, under the title 'canonical penance'. It was directed by a bishop, could only happen once, and imposed lifelong disabilities on its beneficiary, including celibacy and a measure of disgrace.[14]

Historians can foretell the future after it has happened. So you should be able to predict what became of such a rigoristic penance. It became a death-bed ceremony—it being in the face of death that its recommendations were strongest, its drawbacks least important. The development is shown by its exception. Since soldiers know least of anyone when they will die, conditions were relaxed for them by Pope Leo I in 459.[15] In practice, soldiers apart, we also know Christians showed they were sorry in a great variety of ways, either improvised or, if canonical, then privileged (clergy, for instance, could make a temporary, semi-monastic 'conversio').[16] But general canonical penance remained strict; and this meant, in Father Poschmann's words, that 'precisely in the years when sins importuned men most strongly

---

[12] Tertullian: Poschmann, 104 (the antithesis is common in Tertullian's *De poenitentia*). Augustine: *ibid.*, 104 (from *Epist.*, 153 c. 7: 'ne medicina vilis minus utilis esset aegrotis').

[13] Poschmann, 26–35 (Hermas and the doctrine of 'one penance'); 35–52 (rigorism of the Montanists and Tertullian); 52–80 (Cyprian, Clement, Origen); 82–4 (effect of Constantine's conversion).

[14] Poschmann, 87–98, 104–6.

[15] Poschmann, 107–8. It was left to Caesarius of Arles to spell out Leo's implicit allusion to soldiers in *Epist.* 167, inq.. 13, to be repeated in Gratian, *Decretum*, II, causa 33, q. 2, cap 14, in *Corpus iuris canonici*, ed. A. Friedberg, (Leipzig, 1879), I, col. 1156.

[16] John Chrystostom (†407) drew blame for reconciling sinners more than once (Poschmann, 104–5). There was room for difference, too, on such questions as what sins were grave enough to invoke the unrepeatable procedure, or the consequences of dying unreconciled (*ibid.*, 44–5, 94–6, 100–2); while the practice of *conversio*, available to candidates for the clergy and important laity, had the slight but essential difference from *penitentia* that it was honourable, not defamatory (*ibid.*, 110–6). A wide variety of practices is illustrated in C. Vogel, 'La discipline pénitentielle en Gaule des origines au ixe siècle. Le dossier hagiographique'. *Revue des sciences religieuses*, XXX (1956), 1–26, 157–86 [hereafter Vogel, 'Discipline pénitentielle'].

[meaning the fifth and sixth centuries], there was no sacramental remedy at their disposal'.[17]

This remained the case until the acceptance of what has been called 'tariffed penance'. The new penance was repeatable, and involved a 'tariff' of sins, with penances appropriate to their gravity. We hear of it first at a council of Toledo in 589, without knowing quite where they had found it. But when we hear of it again, at a council in Chalon-sur-Sâone c.650, we do know: it is attributable to Irish missionaries and to Anglo-Saxons who had learned it from them. What sources the Irish themselves had it from is another mystery. It just may echo pre-Christian Celtic law-codes, an origin which would add colour to what I shall say of the new system's coverage of 'secular' crimes, and also help explain its analogies with the 'wergeld' system, which may have eased its acceptance.[18]

Now the Toledo council had called 'tariffed penance' an *execrabilis praesumptio*.[19] This was the old rigorism, aghast at repeatable penance. As the new procedure spread after 650, opposition was renewed by some Carolingian bishops who may also have seen episcopal authority endangered by a repeatable procedure, less amenable to control.[20] But law abhors a vacuum. Tariffed penance filled one; and its utility is declared by the very anomalies which marked its reception. For it was lodged beside the old, canonical penance in an arrangement known today as the 'Carolingian dichotomy'. By it, it was agreed that the old, once-only penance would be for public sins; the new tariffed kind, for private.[21] A recognition of its anomalies is essential to the interpretation of this formula. For it silently changed the character of both its

[17] Poschmann, 123, quoting Jonas of Bobbio, *Vita s. Columbani*, c. 11: 'poenitentiae medicamenta ... vix vel paucis in illis reperiebantur locis [Gaul, c.590]', in Migne, *Patrologia latina*, XXXVII, col. 1018A [the form *Pat. lat.* 87, 1018A will be used for references to this work].

[18] Poschmann, 124–9; Vogel, *Pécheur*, 42–5, 51–73. Forshaw (36, n. 2) suggests sources for knowledge shown at Toledo: the see of 'Britonia'; areas recently influenced by St Martin of Braga; and Byzantine settlements in southern Spain. A pre-Christian origin for Irish practice was proposed with alleged parallels from north-western India (another matter) by J. T. McNeill, 'The Celtic Penitentials', *Revue celtique*, XL (1923, 89–103, with resumé and defence in J. T. McNeill and H. M. Gamer, *Medieval Handbooks of Penance*. Records of Western Civilization (New York, 1938; reprinted 1990), 25–6. Sceptical reactions: A. J. Frantzen, *The Literature of Penance in Anglo-Saxon England* (New Brunswick, N. J., 1983), 23–6.

[19] Poschmann, 124 (the expression); Vogel, *Pécheur*, 191–2 (context).

[20] The suggestion of Franz Kerff, '*Libri paenitentiales* und kirchliche Strafgerichtsbarkeit bis zum *Decretum Gratiani*. Ein Diskussionsverschlag', *Zeitschrift der Savigny-Stiftung für Rechtsgeschichte*, 106. Kanonistische Abteilung, 75 (Vienna-Cologne-Graz 1989), 23–57.

[21] Ninth-century conciliar acts and episcopal letters, and Pseudo-Isidore, contain frequent examples; see R. Kottje, 'Bußpraxis und Bußritus', in *Segni e riti nella chiesa altomedioevale occidentale*. Settimane di studio, XXXIII (Spoleto, 1985), 369–95, on 369.

constituent parts. The old, canonical penance had been for grave, not necessarily public, sins (it included secret elements); and its adoption of a public character reflected, not its original essence, but the legal conditions of the 'shame-culture' it now entered. It simultaneously became coercive.[22] (Louis the Pious learned all this in his obligatory 'penance' at Attigny). Meanwhile tariffed penance, by being allotted to private sins, when parts of its procedure (notably the penances) had been public,[23] set off in the other direction, one which would eventually lead to the confession which is the subject of this paper.

How it did so can be learned both by reflection, and from contemporary evidence. Any voluntary penance presupposes confession, or at least acknowledgement (if only 'by deed', as Tertullian recommended) that one has done wrong. 'Canonical penance' had originally entailed confession (the secret element) to the bishop: as we learn from complaints about breaches of the secrecy.[24] But tariffed penance necessarily made the 'confession' part more important. It embodied the notion that penance be proportional to a sin's gravity. That had already been expressed by Caesarius of Arles, for instance, and by some of those improvised penitential practices.[25] But tariffed penance made it an institution, whose response to sin was graduated. Instead of acknowledging one grave sin which might, indeed, already be notorious, the penitent was thus invited to range over his memory, remembering each offence and its circumstances.[26]

Critical self-examination, of a sort proper to confession, still called for one more adjustment. The 'tariffs' listed offences, according to schemes unrelated to any other we know of, and sometimes in explicit external detail (a feature which, especially with sexual sins, was incidentally a moral danger to penitents). For the moral life to come under scrutiny as a continuum the 'tariff' idea must be attached to a scheme not of acts but of dispositions. Gregory the Great and others had developed such a scheme, round a core of classical psychology, in the idea of Cardinal Sins. The main reformers had studied this tradition and sought to feed its moral approach into penitential procedure,[27]

[22] A change noticed by Vogel, 'Discipline pénitentielle' (as in n. 16), 6; and M. Rubellin 'Vision de la société chrétienne à travers la confession et la pénitence au ixe siècle', in *Pratiques de la confession, des Pères du désert à Vatican II. Quinze études d'histoire*, by the Groupe de la Bussière [= M. Sot and others] (Paris, 1983), 52–70, on 59.

[23] Pointed out by Forshaw (as in n. 1), 141.

[24] Honoré (as in n. 2), 25–31

[25] Vogel, 'Discipline pénitentielle', 23, 26, 163. In the last example a fourth-century bishop strikes the penitent with his *pallium* with a vigour proportionate to the sin.

[26] Circumstance in the Penitentials: J. Gruendel, *Die Lehre von den Umständen der menschlichen Handlung im Mittelalter*. Beiträge zur Geschichte der Philosophie und Theologie des Mittelalters, Band 39, Heft 5 (Münster-in-Westfalen 1963), 66–84.

[27] Cardinal sins: e.g. Theodulf of Orleans, *Capitularia ad presbyteros*, c. 31, Pat. lat., 105, 201AB. Contrition: Rubellin (as in n. 22), 57.

There may be allegorical, whatever the literal, truth in the ninth-century story of a priest who 'confessed' a dumb man. The priest listed the cardinal sins and said 'squeeze my hand each time I mention one you have committed.' The man did so and his tongue was miraculously loosened. A shift of emphasis from outer penance to inner confession is appropriately witnessed, from St Boniface on, by the occasional use of the latter word as synonym for the former.[28]

The doctrine of repeatable confession, then, with its internal, moral, contritional character, was formulated by the leading Carolingian reformers. The same in principle goes for lay practice of it. Some dozen conciliar or episcopal enactments survive from between the eighth century and the tenth, enjoining regular penance and confession on the laity with a periodicity of once, twice or even three times per year.[29]

This pastoral literature and legislation has lain behind the view, mentioned earlier, that confession and penance were 'universally enforced' from the early ninth century onwards.[30] I shall now give my reasons for scepticism. They are two. One is that these documents are all of the sort which say how things should be done, not how they are. This has proved a notoriously misleading type of document in the Carologian period, a distinction between ideal and reality being, apparently, a peculiarity of that culture, not unlike the relic-cult or forgery.

This reminder is made as preparatory to my second reason for scepticism, which pertains to the realities of history, underlying the sources. This demands a longer look, because it suggests the sources may say the opposite of what they seem. Charlemagne once tried to dig a canal to join the Rhine and Danube river systems, and found eventually that the soil was too damp and kept falling back. That image of ambition and eventual failure is an image of his 'state' (the term *status regni* could actually be used of it).[31] It could not be sustained in the form in which it had been conceived. This meant, by a process not uncommon in early Christian Europe, that responsibility for public

---

[28] Dumb penitent: C. Vogel, 'Discipline pénitentielle', 15, quoting the ninth-century *Vita s. Philiberti* in *Monumenta Germaniae Historica* [henceforth *Mon. Germ. Hist.*], *Scriptores rerum Merovingicarum* [henceforth *Script. rer. Mer.*], V, 593. (My 'moral' reading of the story differs from Vogel's). The word *confessio*: Poschmann, 138, modified by M Rubellin (as in n. 22), 58.

[29] Listed by J. Avril, 'À propos du "proprius sacerdos": Quelques réflexions sur les pouvoirs du prêtre de paroisse', *Proceedings of the Fifth International Congress of Medieval Canon Law. Salamanca, 21–25 September 1976* (Città del Vaticano, 1980), 471–6 [henceforth Avril 'Sacerdos'], 474, and in the same author's 'Remarques' (as in n. 11), 350–8. The reform: R. McKitterick, *The Frankish Church and the Carolingian Reforms, 789–895*. Royal Historical Society Publications. (1977).

[30] See nn. 6, 8, 9 and 11 above.

[31] *Mon. Germ. Hist.*, *Leges*, II (ii), 270.36.

order passed increasingly to bishops. Supremely interested in preserving the 'state' they were also economically equipped by an urban revival, late fruit of the conquests. Increasingly in the ninth century public justice had a partially ecclesiastical character. Bishops would be told to investigate 'incest, patricide, fratricide, adultery' in series like that, while excommunication, the church's harshest sentence, would be regularly used to protect public peace, well into the eleventh century.[32] But the bishops were meanwhile consolidating their position on another front: in the church hierarchy. This affected priests: 'let every priest in his parish', runs the injunction of an imperial *missus* in 857, 'make a record of malefactors, that is, of robbers, rapists, adulterers, the incestuous, homicides and thieves; and let such be banned from church unless they choose to do penance; and if they refuse let them be brought before the bishop'.[33]

Now the priest who thus 'shopped' his parishioners is supposed to be the one who heard their confessions, in the pastoral manner. Of course that is just another law and we cannot gauge how far its pressure succeeded, at local level, in turning priests into policemen; and it may have been resistance to such pressure that caused the accusatory function to pass to juries (recognisable ancestors of the English 'jury of presentment').[34] But the pressure remained and ran directly counter to the demands of a *cura pastoralis*. Confession was the latter's vulnerable extreme: vulnerable both because of the high demands it made on the capacity of priests, a capacity precarious even for less delicate tasks; and vulnerable because the penitential procedure itself admitted variations. At its most spiritual it could be a reflective, contritional process; at its most material, just another tribunal for punishing people, as it clearly was seen to be by that injunction of 857. Our word 'punishment' actually draws from the same Latin stem as 'penance', down lines of

---

[32] The Aix capitularies of 802–3 tell bishops to make inquisition 'de incestu, de patricidiis, fratricidiis, adulteriis, cenodoxiis et alia mala, quae contraria sunt Deo' *Mon. Germ. Hist.*, *Capit.*, I, 170. Kerff (as in n. 20), 42; *cf.* 26–7, 41. Excommunication: J. Leclercq, 'L'interdit et l'excommunication d'après les lettres de Fulbert de Chartres', *Revue historique de droit français et étranger*, 4ᵉ série, XXII (Paris, 1944), 167–77. On later fortunes of this principle, A. Murray, *Excommunication and Conscience in the Middle Ages*. The John Coffin Memorial Lecture, University of London (1991), 30–1.

[33] *Mon. Germ. Hist.*, *Leges*, II (ii), 292, 131–4 the central expression is 'presbyter inbreviat in sua parrochia'. On bishops' authority over parishes: J. Avril, 'La "paroisse" dans la France de l'an Mil', in *Le roi de France et son royaume autour de l'an Mil*. Études réunies par M. Parisse et X. Barral. Colloque international *Hugues Capet 987–1987: La France de l'an Mil* (Paris, 1992), 203–18, esp. 206–7, 215–8; and the same author's '*Sacerdos*' (as in n. 29), 482–6.

[34] A. Esmein, *A History of Continental Criminal Procedure, with special reference to France* (English translation, Boston, 1913; from the first French edition, Paris, 1882), 47, 65–6, 79; R. C. Van Caenegem, *The Birth of the English Common Law* (Cambridge, 1973), 73–6.

legal tradition which separated after the period in question (the same is true of *crimen*, which could mean 'sin' or 'crime').[35] The reformers themselves probably acknowledged these limitations. When it came to spreading their ideas their pastoral codes see Christianity as what a recent student has called 'a rule of moral conduct and code of ritual obligations'[36]; of penance as punishment, not confession as *contritio*.

So in the absence of direct evidence of pastoral practice we must rely on indirect; and this, seen in its legal-political context, mostly tells against the fruition of the reformers' plans for the general observance of confession. There is one apparent exception. I refer to the category of document which constitutes the great bulk of our evidence for Carolingian 'tariffed penance', the *Libri penitentiales*. These survive in some three hundred manuscripts, from all over the Carolingian empire, made between about 800 and about 1000, and including our earliest copies of the Irish Penitentials from which their 'tariffed penance' was derived.[37] That is, they list offences and prescribe penances, usually in the form of periods of fast, commonly on bread and water. Some of the *Libri penitentiales* have *ordines* attached which say how a priest must conduct confession and award penance. Mention of the books is found occasionally in inventories of priests' property.[38]

I mention the *Libri penitentiales*, not because all the puzzles they raise can be solved now, but because they are another kind of document to be read 'between the lines', and if they are, illustrate precisely the collapse of the pastoral programme just described; that is, the opposite of what they seem to illustrate. Two of the books' peculiarities combine to suggest this. First, they juxtapose what we would call secular and moral offences, corresponding to that fusion of jurisdictions already mentioned. Second, their 'penances' ('punishments' would be a better translation) are severe. 'Tariffs' can run to seven, or ten, or even fifteen years' fasting[39], penances would already seem severe to Alan of Lille, Cistercian-to-be, who thought the people who used Penitential Books must have been *robustior* than his contemporaries.[40] But he had lost

---

[35] Meanings of 'penitential', Kerff, 39–41; Rubellin, 59. *Crimen*: E. Powell, *Kingship, Law and Society. Criminal Justice in the Reign of Henry V.* (Oxford, 1989), 47.

[36] G. Devailly, 'La pastorale en Gaule en ixe siècle', *Revue d'histoire de l'Église de France*, LIX (1973), 23–54, at 54.

[37] C. Vogel, *Libri penitentiales*. Typologie des sources du moyen âge occidental, 27 (Turnhout, 1978); and 27* [mise à jour par A.J. Frantzen] (Turnhout, 1985); Kottje (as in n. 21), 369–88.

[38] Kottje, 388–92; Vogel, 213–20 (examples).

[39] Examples are easily found in *Medieval Handbooks of Penance* (as in n. 18); see for instance the penitentials ascribed to Bede, VIII, c. 1, and X, c. 1, 228–9; and to Theodore, II, c. 22, 186.

[40] Alanus de Insulis, *Liber poenitentialis*, Bk. II, c. 13. Ed. J. Longère. Analecta mediaevalia Namurcensia, 17. (Louvain-Lille, 1965), II, 55.

touch with the way the books were used. Some penances were impossible even to the robust. An Anglo-Saxon council in 747 had heard of a man who had accumulated three hundred years' of fasting for a number of offences; and it is, and was, easy to calculate other such impossible accumulations.[41]

Laws too harsh for observance produce two effects. One is that the policeman becomes legislator, having to decide, since all break the law, on when to inflict punishment. The second effect is commutation. Commutation was coeval with the Penitential Books, and took many forms.[42] But the commonest came to be money, which has among other advantages that of flexibility, and it is not too much to say that, through monasticism (which provided for vicarious performance of bodily penances), and in due course indulgences (used to finance crusades, cathedral-building and much else), many of the famous embodiments of medieval religion were financed by the commutation of penance.[43] But the same applied also to its less famous embodiments. Ninth-century complaints at the rapacity of ecclesiastical judges feed a suspicion, built out recently into a bold hypothesis by Dr Franz Kerff, that the Penitential Books were, in fact, largely used by them as a basis for penal amercements, easily calculated from their arithmetical penances.[44] The word 'amercement' there intentionally anticipates the Anglo-Norman euphemism, used when royal judges (this time) enforced a law similarly impossible of perfect observance by offering 'mercy' to most offenders, in return for payment. Dr Kerff backs his hypothesis by reference to both the content of the books and their manuscript context. Their main users, he suggests, were the itinerant synodal inquisitions, representing bishops.[45] The number and distribution of manuscripts, after all, even allowing for massive losses, would, at less than one per two thousand square miles of Europe, serve bishops better than priests. That pastoral statutes stop mentioning Penitential Books about mid-century would also fit with this reading.[46]

Like a dilatory crusader I have, perhaps, paused too long to 'demolish an enemy' in the conviction that it served my greater purpose. For my contention will be this: that it was precisely the separation of secular

---

[41] Clovesho (747), cap. 27, in *Councils and Ecclesiastical Documents relating to Great Britain and Ireland*, ed., A. W. Haddan and W. Stubbs (Oxford 1869–72), III, 373.

[42] Commutation: Vogel, *Pécheur*, 119–28, 200–2. Early alternatives: 'lying on nutshells', Forshaw, 317. Payment in *ancillae*: Poschmann, 127, n. 7.

[43] Poschmann, 210–32.

[44] Kerff (as in n. 20). It is Kerff who also underlines the ambivalence of the priest's role, 44–5. Complaints at rapacity: Kerff, 53; Rubellin (as in n. 22), 69.

[45] Kerff, 42–50.

[46] Devailly (as in n. 36), 41. Devailly speaks of the 'abandonment' of the rural clergy, 37.

and ecclesiastical jurisdictions, with the genesis of 'feudal monarchy' after the millennium, that left churchmen free to specialise, whether on outward lay observance in the *forum externum*, or on the consciences of the *forum internum*. Confession, on this interpretation, would be part of a bigger story. In dark-age culture a shift, broadly dateable to the eleventh century, has been noticed from supernatural to natural means for guarding public order. Miracles worked by relics, for instance, hitherto frequently designed to defend monastic property, come to leave such 'dirty work' to secular courts, freeing themselves for a humanitarian function[47]; excommunications went the same way, simultaneously losing their maledictory tone as their purpose became more strictly ecclesiastical.[48]

The nature of confession exposed it to a corresponding metamorphosis. The first sign of its occurrence is to be found in evidence for penitential procedure. Before old, external 'penance' could emerge fully as new, internal 'confession', three adjustments were needed. First, the 'tariffed' procedure had envisaged two interviews with the priest: one to confess and receive penance; and another, after the penance, to be absolved. This arrangement was less suited to 'mass production' than one in which absolution immediately followed the award of penance. The elision cannot be dated with certainty, but the weight of opinion for its presence in Burchard of Worms at the beginning of the century.[49] If that is right it would help explain a second change, easier to date. If the whole procedure is concentrated in one interview, its centre-of-gravity moves from the penitent's outer penance, to his inner disposition: he must be 'contrite'. That word, used by the Carolingian reformers, reappeared in the vocabulary of confession in the late eleventh century[50], and soon went to its centre. This is the third change. For contrition now *became* the penance. Around 1060 a book on 'True and False Penance', destined for wide professional readership in the twelfth century, says we earn mercy 'by spiritual labour', that is *erubescentia*: for *verecundia magna est poena*, and so on.[51] A later story makes the point more graphically. A man had raped his own daughter, and in confession asked for the maximum penance. 'Seven years' said the priest. 'That is not enough', said the man, and asked him to increase

[47] B. De Gaiffier, 'Les revendications de biens dans quelques documents hagiographiques du xie siècle', *Analecta Bollandiana*, L (1932), 123–38.

[48] Lester K. Little, 'La morphologie des malédictions monastiques', *Annales E.S.C.*, XXXIV (1979), 43–60.

[49] Poschmann, 145, sees the elision as already complete in Burchard of Worms, but the position is less clear for Kerff, 29 and n. 17, and Kottje, 391.

[50] Poschmann, 163; but see Rubellin, 57 (for earlier use of the term by Jonas of Orleans and Hrabanus Maurus).

[51] *Pat. lat.*, 40, 1113–30; the passage quoted is from c. X, §25 [col. 1122].

it. The priest *reduced* the penance. The exchanges went on until the penance was down to one Paternoster. The man was by then so ashamed that he died on the spot and went straight to Heaven. That inverse proportion between outer penance and inward contrition would indeed be recognised by canon law.[52]

A study of its legal environment, therefore, and of shifts in the literature of penance, points to the period when confession should come of age as a widespread pastoral practice for the laity: after the millennium, say between then and 1215. Let us now look at the evidence for this period.

II

The period in question will end well *before* 1215, and that calls for explanation. One of many things the conciliar fathers of the Fourth Lateran Council shared with their Carolingian predecessors was a lack of any guarantee that their canons would be enacted. The extent to which they were, in the various regions, is still under scholarly scrutiny, and one general lesson is that the decrees of 1215, before they could reach the millions for whose welfare they were intended, had to pass down several layers of the church hierarchy, each with its own priorities and measure of obedience. The extent to which any canon was realised cannot therefore be deduced just from its inclusions in the proceedings.[53]

Now we happen to know, from other sources, that the canon *Omnis utriusque sexus*, did have considerable effect.[54] This fact has helped deceive the unwary into thinking that a pope like Innocent III only had to decree something, and it was done. For the effect would have been less, perhaps absent, if it had depended only on the council. Indeed the council and the spread of lay confession were in some degree joint effects of the same cause: the growth over the previous two or three generations of the Paris moral theology school. At what has some claim to be dubbed the school's golden age (around 1180) the

---

[52] Thomas of Chantimpré, *Bonum universale de apibus* (Douai, 1627), II, c. 51, §7. The priest was Peter of Corbeil. Canon law: *Decretalia*, Bk. V, tit. xxxvii, c. 8; Friedberg (as in n. 15), II, 886.

[53] The council and its background: Tillmann, *Innocenz III* (Bonn, 1954); R. Foreville, *Latran I, II, III et Latran IV* in *Histoire des conciles oecuméniques*, ed. G. Dumeige (Paris, 1965); J. W. Baldwin, *Masters, Princes and Merchants: the Social Views of Peter Chanter and his Circle* (Princeton, 1970). Execution: M. Gibbs and J. Lang, *Bishops and Reform, 1215–72* Oxford, 1934). See n. 101.

[54] Entry to the large literature can be gained through R. Rusconi, 'Ordinate confiteri: la confessione dei peccati nelle "Summae de casibus" e nei manuali per i confessori (metá xii—inizi xiv secolo)', in *L'Aveu: Antiquité et moyen âge*. Collection de l'École française de Rome, LXXXVIII (Rome, 1986), 298–313.

future Innocent III had attended it; and his council was the mouth of a conduit, through which the pastoral theology developed in Paris could flow down the innumerable capillaries of the church.

This interpretation of the council would suggest that, if the 'conduit' is followed back, emphasis on regular lay confession, strong enough to yield signs of its practice, will be found. In fact for at least fifty years before the Fourth Lateran Council such signs survive, in and near Paris and in areas influenced by its school. It could be argued, though will not be here, that the lively theological debate on confession, a debate coeval with the theology school itself, is indirect evidence of practice.[55] But the theologians give us direct evidence, in the form of complaints that people do *not* confess, or confess badly or dishonestly. A leading authority has even suggested that practice was declining just before the Lateran Council, an idea backed by a remark of Alan of Lille that 'hardly anyone, clerk or lay, nowadays makes his annual confession'.[56] Whether that implicit praise of past times betrays another of Alan's historical misconceptions is the question to be addressed in a moment. But at least half a dozen more such complaints could easily be assembled from his late-twelfth-century contemporaries to indicate what theologians' and preachers' expectations were; and if expectations, then surely some grounds for them.[57]

Independent confirmation of the theologians' views also exists. I do not wish to delay the story by rehearsing this evidence now, since I hope enough has been said to give provisional assurance, at least, that *Omnis utriusque sexus* was to this extent anticipated. This is not to say older habits—of neglect, or irregular types of penance—were not still alive in the half-century before 1215, as they would be long after. But it is to say that by then at the latest anyone acquainted with theology, however briefly, knew of this corollary of the 'cure of souls'. The

[55] Murray, 'Confession as a historical source' (as in n. 2), 280. Further suggestive material in Anciaux (as in n. 6), 71, 86–7, 149–50, 183–4, 266.

[56] Avril, 'Remarques' (as in n. 11), 355–6f; Alanus de Insulis, *De arte praedicatoria, Pat. lat.*, 210, 171; quoted by Poschmann, 140.

[57] Remarks with this implication from theologians are quoted by Anciaux, 167 ('Eadmer'), 168, 174, 179–80 (Honorius of Autun), 184, 186, 187, 188, 189, 197, 217, 221, 224, 227, 262, 265–6 (Pseudo-Eadmer and Honorius are probably the earliest of these); and O. Lottin, *La psychologie et la morale au xiie et au xiiie siècles*, 6 vols. (Louvain and Gembloux, 1942–60), II, 408, and III, 674–5 (both passages from Peter Chanter). For such allusions in sermons see P. Tibber, 'The Origins of the Scholastic Sermon, *c.*1130–*c.*1210' (unpublished D.Phil. thesis, Oxford 1983), 197 (Stephen Langton); 212 (Prevostin, many of whose sermons echo this theme). For Laon see below, n. 140. The 'independent confirmation' referred to in the next paragraph will be found in *Vitae* written in or after the late twelfth-century. Regular lay confession is implied for instance in *Vita beati Bernardi Poenitentis, AS* (see n. 72 below) April II (Antwerp, 1675), 674–97, at 685A, 689E; *Vita b Alpaidis, AS* Nov. II (Brussels, 1894), 174–209, at 192CD; *Miracula s. Frideswidae, AS* Oct. VIII (Brussels, 1853), 533–90, at 567.

Lateran decree thus gave universal, authoritative stamp to a duty such people were well aware of. That was why the canon was included. That was why it had effect. It confirmed an existing momentum.

So it will be profitable to concentrate our review of evidence where matters are more in doubt, that is, on the century-and-a-half before 1150, with corroborative glances even earlier. You should now have a proper awe of the obscurity of the area of search. It is 'almost pitch-black'. Such documents as there are are not only uneven: in the century-and-a-half under review, for instance, Penitential Books end and theology begins. They leave us unsure whether it is the imaginary or the real that they describe. There remains one genre, however, so far untouched, that is proof against these flaws. I refer to miracle-stories, of the kind put in or after saints' Lives, and in special collections to boost a shrine. Miraculous literature runs the whole length of the medieval period, surviving even from centuries otherwise silent. Paradoxically at first glance, *miracula* are also more 'realistic' than other types of medieval literature. I am tempted to say 'despite their supernatural message'. But it is a case rather of 'because'. A miracle served its didactic purpose by the verisimilitude of the material. Listeners must recognise the situations described. So *miracula* often describe to us otherwise inaccessible areas of social history. This applies especially to the practice of confession. For confession served the same purpose as miracles: to alert sinners to their condition. They throve in the same milieu, working as alternatives or in co-operation; rendering likely, in either case, that confession will be found in the literary vicinity of miracle; where, that is, there is any to find.

So far two essays have explored miraculous literature for this purpose: one by Ludwig Hertling in 1931[58], and one by Cyrille Vogel in 1956.[59] Both were exclusive in the field searched but inclusive in what was sought. That is, they looked only at saints' Lives, but took from them any kind of penitential act or confession. Both concentrated on Lives written between the fifth and early eleventh centuries, though Hertling went on from then till the late twelfth. Hertling's result was just over a hundred references from the *Acta sanctorum*; Vogel's, a more systematic

---

[58] Ludwig Hertling, S.J., 'Hagiographische Texte zur frühmittelalterlichen Bußge-schichte', *Zeitschrift für katholische theologie*, IV (1932), 109–22; and 'Hagiographische Texte zur Bußhgeschiche des frühesten Mittelalters', *ibid.*, 274–387.

[59] As in n. 16. To avoid prejudice to my own sample I have avoided borrowing material from those of Hertling or Vogel. Those of their cases which appear most to challenge my present thesis in fact are in harmony with it, namely (1) *Vita Gamalberti presbyteri Michaelsbuchensis*, Mon. Germ. Hist., *Script. rer. Merov.*, VII (i), 183–91 (Vogel, 161), a Life of doubtful Merovingian relevance, and certainly written no earlier than the late tenth century, probably later (see W. Levison's introduction); and (2) the case of Godfrey of Amiens (†1115) (Hertling, 121), whose insistence on lay confession before communion is exemplified only from a leper-hospital, where patients were quasi-prisoners.

harvest of all two hundred and thirty edited Lives of Merovingian saints. My own search has been independent of theirs despite a slight overlap in chronological bracket (mine being later), and I have sought to keep it so. My field has been more inclusive (taking in *Miracula* and *Translationes* as well as *Vitae*), but my quarry more exclusive, namely, signs of regular lay confession to a priest. That has meant attention also to negative evidence, in which some of the main forms of alternative have crept back in.

My sample of sources totals twenty-one, and I shall list them. They start with three, and part of a fourth, from the ninth century: Einhard's account of the translation of the relics of saints Marcellinus and Peter, written around 830[60]; Rudolf of Fulda's record of the miracles linked with his abbey's relics between 842 and 847[61]: and Wolfrad of Eichstätt's 'Miracles of St Walpurgis', written between 894 and 899[62], while the famous Fleury miracle-book, *Miracula sancti Benedicti*, was written in stages from the late ninth century to the early twelfth.[63] The tenth century is represented by a share in two miracle books begun towards the end of it, also finished in the twelfth century, namely a short one from St Maximin in Trier[64], and a second 'classic', the *Miracula sanctae Fidis* from Conques.[65] From the second half of the eleventh century are three short miracle-books, from St Bertin[66] and St Amand[67] in Flanders, and the *Miracula sancti Nicholai* by a monk of Bec[68]; from the early twelfth, two longer ones, Peter the Venerable's *De miraculis*[69], and the first two books of 'The Miracles of St Mary of Laon'.[70] The rest of the

[60] *Mon. Germ. Hist., Script.,* XV (i), 238–64 [henceforth *Transl. ss.Petri et Marc.*]. Written *c.*830, the work contains about forty *miracula*.

[61] *Miracula sanctorum in Fuldenses ecclesias translatorum auctore Rudolfo, Mon. Germ. Hist., Script.,* XV (i), 328–41 [henceforth *Mir. Fulden.*]. There are some seventeen *miracula*.

[62] Ed. A. Bauch, *Ein bayerisches Mirakelbuch aus der Karolingerzeit. Die Monheimer Walpurgis-Wunder des Priesters Wolfhard* Eichstätter Studien, N. F., Band XII (Regensburg, 1979) [henceforth *De mir. s. Waldburgae*].

[63] Ed. E. de Certain, Société pour l'histoire de France, 54 (Paris, 1858) [henceforth *Mir. s. Maxim. Trev.*].

[64] *Miracula sancti Maximini Treverensis, Pat. lat.* 133, 967–78 [henceforth *Mir. s. Maxim. Trev.*].

[65] Ed. A. Bouillet, Collection de Textes pour servir à l'étude et à l'enseignement de l'histoire (Paris, 1897) [henceforth *Mir. s. Fidis*].

[66] Fulcard of St Bertin, *Miracula sancti Bertini, Pat. lat.,* 147, 1098–1140 [henceforth *Mir. s. Bertini*].

[67] *Historia miraculorum sancti Amandi, Pat. lat.,* 150, 1435–48 [henceforth *Hist. mir. s. Amandi*].

[68] *Miracula sancti Nicholai* in *Catalogus codicum hagiographicorum latinorum Bibliothecae nationalis Parisiensis,* Analecta Bollandiana, Subsidia hagiographica, No. 2, II (Brussels, 1890), 405–32; [henceforth *Mir. s. Nich.*]. Date: *ibid.,* No. 22, 417 (a miracle of December 1111). The work has about forty stories and was written between 1095 and 1129.

[69] *Libri duo de miraculis* ed. D. Bouthillier, *Corpus christianorum, Continuatio mediaevalis,* LXXXIII (Turnhout, 1988) [henceforth Petr. Ven., *De mir.*].

[70] *Pat. lat.,* 156, 961–87 [henceforth *De mir. s. Mariae Laudun.*]. The dating by G.

sample are Lives of saints, mostly of saintly bishops: from Gregorian
Italy, Anselm II of Lucca[71], Peter of Anagni[72], Bruno of Segni[73] and
Berard of Marses[74]; from south-eastern France, Peter of Chevenon (an
Augustinian canon and parish priest)[75], and Hugh of Grenoble[76]; from
western, Abbot Gerard of Angers[77]; and from north-eastern, Wazo of
Liège[78] and John of Thérouanne.[79] From England, finally, I have in-
cluded the Lives of Wulfric of Haselbury[80] and Christina of Markyate.[81]

How much, then, do these sources say of the regular practice of lay
confession? With a number of well-defined exceptions, which will be
considered separately in a moment, the answer is, 'almost nothing'.
The books tell of plenty of wrongdoers, many of whom repent. But

---

Niemeyer, 'Die *Miracula s. Mariae Laudunensis* des Abts Hermann von Tournai. Verfaßer
und Entstehungszeit', *Deutsches Archiv*, XXVII (1971), 135–74, esp. 163–74, is mainly
concerned with the Norbertine material in Bk. III. She convincingly assigns this to
Hermann, former abbot of St Martin's in Tournai, who lived in St Vincent's in Laon
*c.*1143–6. But the anomalies she notes in Bks. I and II, written as if by a participant, (172)
imply that Hermann was using an earlier account for these two books, doubtless one
related to that used by Guibert of Nogent when, before 1121, he put a shorter version of
the two journeys in his *De vita sua*, III, xii–xiii, ed. E-R. Labande, Les Classiques de
l'Histoire de France au moyen âge (Paris, 1981), 378–92 (date, xv). The account in *De
mir. s. Mariae Laudun.* must be after 1123, when William or Corbeil became archbishop,
see 78–9 below.

[71] *Vita sancti Anselmi episcopi lucensis, auctore Bardone presbytero, Mon. Germ. Hist., Script.,* XII,
13–35 [henceforth *Vita s. Anselmi luc.*].

[72] *Vita sancti Petri episcopi Anagniae.* Acta Sanctorum [abbreviated *AS*], Aug., I (Antwerp,
1733), 230–42 [henceforth *Vita s. Pet. Anagn.*]. On the significance of this and the next two
Lives as portraits of the Gregorian 'model' bishop: P. Toubert, *Les structures du Latium
médiévale* (Paris and Rome, 1973), 43–7, 803–40.

[73] *Vita sancti Brunonis episcopi Signiae,* in *AS,* July, IV (Antwerp, 1725), 471–84 [henceforth
Vita s. Brun. Signiae].

[74] *Vita sancti Berardi. AS.* Nov., II (Brussels, 1894), 128–35 [henceforth *Vita s. Berardi*].

[75] *Vita et miracula sancti Petri de Chavanon* in *Spicilegium,* ed. L. d'Achéry, II (Paris, 1723),
155–9 [henceforth *Vita s. Petri Chav.*]

[76] *Vita sancti Hugonis episcopi Gratianopolitani, auctore Guigone priore Carthusiensi, Pat. lat.,* 153,
759–84 [henceforth *Vita s. Hugon. Grat.*]. I have commented on this Life in 'The
Temptation of St Hugh of Grenoble', in *Intellectual Life in the Middle Ages: Essays presented
to Margaret Gibson,* ed. L. Smith and B. Ward (London and Rio Grande, 1992), 81–101,
on 84–9 (the *Life*), and 92–3 (confession).

[77] *Vita sancti Giraldi Andagavensis, AS* Nov., II (i) (Brussels, 1894), 493–509 [henceforth *Vita
s. Gir. Andag.*]. Approximate date: §24, 499EF (a vision dateable to 25 Nov. 1120). *Cf.*
Hertling (as in n. 58), 122.

[78] I have used the section on Wazo in *Anselmi Gesta episcoporum pontificum Tungrensis,
Traiextensis sive is aecclesiae Leodiensium, Mon Germ. Hist., Script.,* VII, 189–34 [henceforth
Gesta episc. ... Leod.].

[79] *Vita Johannis Morinensis episcopi* (by Walter, his archdeacon, writing in 1130), *Mon Germ.
Hist., Script.,* XV (ii), 1138–50 [henceforth *Vita Joh. Morin. episc.*].

[80] *Vita beati Wulfrici anchoretae Haselbergiae* (by John, abbot of Ford), ed. M. Bell, Somerset
Record Society, XLVII (1933) [henceforth *Vita b. Wulfrici*].

[81] *The life of Christina of Markyate. A Twelfth Century Recluse,* ed. C. H. Talbot (Oxford,
1959) [henceforth *Life of Christina*].

outside the well-defined exceptions the repentance never expressly includes confession to a priest. In Einhard's book, for instance, a man defrauds Einhard and later falls at his feet, weeping.[82] Again, he tells of a demoniac who eventually 'publicised his malice by confessing it in front of everyone'.[83] But that is as near as the book gets to confession. The Eichstätt miracle book is equally vague. On some nine occasions a character repents. But the very instability of the phraseology used tells against the regular practice of one procedure.[84] The Fleury miracle book comes no nearer. It tells of would-be robbers of the Fleury church who are halted by a miracle, and who 'culpam confitentur', lying prostrate before the door, 'confessing their fault with tears'.[85] But this is public, and plural. In another story, in a part of the work added in the eleventh century, a thievish monk proclaims his guilt 'magnis vocibus'.[86] But that is all. The Trier collection tells of a nobleman who oppressed the abbey and later repented, and 'confessed' his misdeeds to the abbot.[87] But since the narrator blithely goes on that it was the abbot who told him the whole story, this is clearly not being presented as any model of sacramental confession. In the Conques miracle book, with its one hundred and fifty stories, we hear three times of wrongdoers who 'come to understand' their error of their own accord.[88] Twice they confess their sin *publicly*, and we sometimes hear of 'penitentia', without formalities.[89] But in the only cases in which people are said to 'confess'

---

[82] *Transl. ss. Petri et Marc.*, Bk. II, c. 2, 246.40–1.

[83] *Ibid.*, Bk. II, c. 16, 262.11–12. The word *confessio* is used in Bk II, c. 1 (246.18–19) but in an untechnical sense.

[84] *De mir. s. Waldburgae*, 206.7–10 ('pro commissis a primaeva viridine facinoribus universis rea tunderet pectora pugnis'); 208.3–6 ('ipsa mihi viam, quam peccata tulerunt, misericordissima ... reparavit'); 212.6–7 ('ream et miseram se intimo cordis archano clamabat'); 230.5–16 ('si me reum ac miserum corde contrito superna respexerit pietas'); 232.5–6 ('rem quae acciderat ore veridico recitavit'); 264.3–4 ('venit ... pro peccatis admissis veniae indulgentiam quesitura'); 274.17–18 ('ob culpam ... ignaviae tale in se meruisse confessa'); 286.29–30 ('contritione indulgentiam postulavit': the woman was mute, and did it with her heart); 290.25–6 ('salutifera confessione peracta': it is a question of publicly confessing to a crime). On 328–33 a man 'confesses' to a nun; parallels in Hertling (as in n. 58), 117; Vogel, 'Discipline pénitentielle' (as in n. 16), 163–6.

[85] *Mir. s. Benedicti*, Bk. I, c. 27, 62–3.

[86] *Ibid.*, Bk. VI, c. 13, 238. The absence of confession in these places is the more conspicuous for its presence in exceptional circumstances in Bk. VIII, c. 14, 294–6, where it is a question of a monk on his deathbed, urged to seek solace 'confitendo ... proprium alicui religioso commissum'.

[87] *Mir. s. Maxim. Trev.*, c. 12, col. 973B. The first story in the collection tells of a blasphemous magnate who 'ex toto corde ... dicti poenituit' but with no hint of ceremony, *ibid.*, c. 9, col. 971A.

[88] *Mir. s. Fidis*, Bk. I, c. 18, 55; Bk II, c. 11, 120; Bk. III, c. 21, 164; *cf.* Bk. III, c. 17, 157.

[89] *Ibid.*, III, c. 21, 164 ('fatens coram astancium corona'); Bk. I, c. 22, 59 ('fit palam injuriose culpę confessio'). 'Pęnitentia': Bk. II, c. 24, 64. 'Verecundię pęnas': Bk. II, c. 11, 120. *Cf.* Bk. I, c. 25, 65: 'misericordiam sepissime repetens exclamabat'.

(there are two), circumstances make clear that it is either a *public* confession, or consists merely of acknowledgement to the party wronged.[90]

So the negative findings continue. In St Bertin we have penances, and once (in the eleventh-century section), a penance formally sought and given in a church.[91] As for the St Amand *Miracula*, they mention a madman who, when healed, made the sign of the Cross and apologised if he had said anything impure in his fit; and a cripple, whose disability was due to a blasphemy not yet paid for by a suitable penance.[92] But there is still no hint of anyone's confessing his sins privately to a priest. The same is true of the Life of the Auvergnat Augustinian and parish priest, Peter of Chavanon. He is said to have preached publicly, but not to have heard private confession.[93] More remarkable still is the silence on confession in the Lives of the new model-bishops of Gregorian Italy. Anselm of Lucca's biographer, Bardo presbyter, says he himself 'often used to confer with him about my sins'. But his encomium says nothing of Anselm's gifts as confessor to other people.[94] Bruno of Segni was once accosted by robbers, who were so struck by his sanctity that 'veniam peterent'.[95] In Peter of Anagni's diocese no-one considered he had lived well, arranged his affairs prudently, or died piously, 'if he had omitted to take advice from the great bishop' [*qui consilium ... evasisset*].[96] Comparable statements in this group of Lives, only throw into relief the absence of any mention of the bishop as a confessor. The northern group are almost as bare. Wazo of Liège confessed 'to God' on his death-bed. But when his biographer compares the virtues and services of Wazo and his *alter ego* abbot Olbert, the nearest we get to confession is that Olbert was a 'consiliorum largitione prudenter dispensator'.[97] As for John of Thérouanne, with the same exception for his own death-bed, confession may be alluded to obliquely when the biographer, John's archdeacon, protests 'I cannot rule my own soul

---

[90] *Ibid.*, Bk. I, c. 18, 15; App. IV (xxx), 229.

[91] *Mir. s. Bertini*, Bk. I, c. 12, col. 1108B. Other 'penance': Bk. I, c. 3, col. 1101C; Bk. II, c. 25, col. 1137B.

[92] *Hist. mir. s. Amandi.* §8, col. 1440D; §15, col. 1443C.

[93] *Vita s. Petri Chav.*, esp. 255–6 (preaching).

[94] *Vita s. Anselmi*, §36, 23.36–41. Anselm urges 'poenitentiam' on Henry IV in §38, 24.17–18.

[95] *Vita s. Brun. Signiae*, Day 4, *lectio* iv, §22, 482F ('veniam peterent'). When John, the next bishop of Segni, visited Monte Cassino, some of its *monks* 'eidem episcopo peccatum, quod in B. Brunonem commiserant, cum magna sunt contritione cordis confessi, suppliciter rogantes, et postulantes ab eo' for a relic of Bruno; Day 5, *lectio* ii, §26, 483F.

[96] *Vita s. Pet. Anagn.*, c. 24, 238A. Note the absence of confession in c. 31, 240AB.

[97] *Gesta episc. ... Leod.*, 233.45–6; and 232.45–7: 'se peccatorem esse ... est confessus ... sese coram Deo accusaret'.

properly for a single hour, so how shall I escape judgement for having undertaken ... the provision and care of others'.[98]

Fourteen of the twenty-one texts have been considered. Seven remain: the miracle-books from Fulda and Laon, Peter the Venerable's *De miraculis*, and four saints' Lives, two French and two English. These contain the well-defined exceptions. But before turning to them I wish to draw your attention to two important distinctions, which will, I believe, help us interpret the early evidence on confession.

The first of the distinctions is that between monks and laity. It is *lay* confession we have been looking for, in the sense of 'lay' which excludes monks.[99] Private confession by monks, as one more means to spiritual perfection, has a history independent of that of the Christian sacrament of penance, or indeed of Christianity.[100] St Benedict's rule prescribes it (c. 46), and attempts would be made in 1230 to make a monthly periodicity general in the order.[101] In the eleventh or twelfth century, therefore, to find a monk confessing is not the same as finding a layman. The *Miracula sancti Nicholai* illustrate this. The monks of St Nicholas are in a boat in a storm, and all on board fear for their lives. The monks, not the seamen or other passengers, are said to have confessed their sins to each other.[102] A similar case occurs in the Laon miracle book, but in relation to cathedral clergy, some not in priest's orders: in peril at sea these confess their sins to each other, including priest to non-priest where necessary, while merchants and seamen are once more *not* said to have confessed.[103] Again, a genuine case of confession occurs in the Fleury miracle book. It is in Book VIII, a book probably written in the period *c*.1100–*c*.1122, and concerns a monk. The monk is dying and hesitates when urged to confess. The author is shocked since it behoves every Christian 'praesertim monacho' to

---

[98] *Vita Joh. Morin. episc.*, 1144. 25–7. The witness is the more interesting for its reference to pastoral reform through Austin regulars, 1143.46–1144.27, 1145.33, 1145.38–41. *Cf.* below, 78–9.

[99] G. Constable, 'Monasteries, Rural Churches and the *Cura animarum* in the Early Middle Ages', in *Christianizzazione ed organizzazione ecclesiastica delle campagne nell' alto medioevo: espansione e resistenze.* Settimane de studio del Centro italiano di studi sull'alto medioevo, 28 (Spoleto, 1982), 349–89, at 372.

[100] Vogel, *Pécheur*, 225–30.

[101] 'Attempts' because twenty years later a new-broom Franciscan archbishop of Rouen found numerous monasteries ignoring Gregory IX's statute on the subject or indeed unaware of it: *Regestrum visitationum archepiscopi Rothomagensis*, ed. T. Bonnin (Rouen, 1852, (ignoring the statute) 60, 70, 76–8, 82, 99; (not possessing the statutes as such), 45, 61, 71; (or even the Rule!), 78, 374, 636. These are a mere selection of such references which, from a bureaucratic age and monastic milieu, induce caution in the reading of earlier lay pastoral practice from canon law.

[102] *Mir. s. Nicholai*, §33, 429.31–2.

[103] *Mir. s. Mariae Laudun.*, Bk. II, c. 4, col. 976A–B.

confess his sins.[104] In the Life of Abbot Gerald of Angers the only explicit allusions to confession, by that name, are both of monks.[105] Last, but not least: of the group of miracle books under review, much the most explicit on confession is one written by the spiritual father of the biggest monastic family in Europe, Peter the Venerable. The forty-two *exempla* in *De miraculis* are mostly about monks, and where not monks, then about priests and nobles closely associated with Cluny. The work contains no fewer than nine certain confessions, of which four are by monks, two more by priests, leaving only three laymen.[106] This brings me to the second important distinction to be made. It is one, not of status this time, but of occasion: that is to say between confession in the ordinary course of life, and as a preparation for death. 'Canonical penance' has long been acknowledged to have become a death-bed ceremony. But this applied largely to penance as such, for monk or lay. The pattern of omissions and inclusions in our *miracula* illustrates this. The Fleury book contains only one case of confession. It is in the section written in the early twelfth century. The case is that of a monk, and a *dying* monk. Again, the *Miracula sancti Nicholai* contain only one case of confession, and it occurs when the person concerned is in sudden danger of death.[107] The same is true of the first case of

---

[104] *Mir. s. Benedicti.*, Bk. VIII, c. 14 [294–61]: 'admonetur quatenus, sui memor in extremis, abbati seu cui liberet seniorum propria confiteretur peccata. ... Miror nimirum quae oblivio illius insederet menti, cum id maxime studium omni fore debeat Christiano, praesertim monacho, si peccaverit, quod humanum est, ut statim currat ad medelam, confitendo scilicet proprium alicui religioso commissum'. Eventually the sick young monk confessed, received the *viaticum*, and died. The early twelfth-century author, the Fleury monk Raoul Tortaire, invokes the authority of St Benedict to recommend confession for humility's sake alone, even in the absence of sin. Earlier books in the collection refer to public confession *prostrati ante ostium ... cum lachrymis*, I, c. 27 [62]; and *magnis vocibus*: VI, c. 13 [238].

[105] *Vita s. Gir. Andeg.*, §§33, 34 [501B–E]. We learn in §21 [498EF] that Abbot Gerald nevertheless often heard confessions from the laity. A *senior*, guilty of habitual incontinence, 'lacrimis perfusus et ad genua eius prostratus, peccata sua humiliter confessus est et, promissa emendatione, a beato viro paenitentiam accepit; quam tamen ipse pro eodem dimidiam fecit'. The biographer adds 'istud miraculum pari modo multotiens de pluribus operatus est, ut frequenter audivimus, plane possumus astruere quia, quotiens illud egit, totiens mortuorum resuscitator exstitit'.

[106] The nine are Petr. Ven., *De mir.*, I, c. 2 [10.41–5]†; c. 3 [11–13]; cc. 4–6 [13–21]*; c. 23 [69.15–25]; c. 24 [73.22–5]†; II, c. 33/32 [164–6]*. I have classed the following cases as 'uncertain': I, c. 1 [8.45–8]; c. 7 [23.51–2] (a layman dies as a monk)*; c. 8 [34.324–8]*; c. 26 [81.25–6]; II, cc. 20 [133.29–33] and 22 [136.4–11] (both references to Matthew, Bishop of Albano)†. An asterisk (*) here marks cases involving monks, a dagger (†), priests. For laity see nn. 111–13 below.

[107] *Mir. s. Nicholai*, §23, 418.38 and 419.24. The other approximations to confession in this collection are in §32, 426.40–2, where a man 'confesses' publicly while under threat of the gallows; and in §27, 422.28, where an iron hoop is worn as a 'penance'.

confession in the Laon miracle book.[108] Equally striking evidence is that of Peter the Venerable's *De miraculis*. Of those nine certain confessions in this work no fewer than eight are of persons facing death. These include all three confessions by laymen.[109] A nobleman comes to Cluny when he knows he is dying, to do 'penance and confession' there.[110] A youth believes he is dying and

> invitatus est ad eum more ecclesiastico presbyter, ut ejus confessionem susciperet, et ut morienti viaticum praeberet.[111]

More ecclesiastico: it seems to be the *dying* who 'customarily' confess.

Monastic status; approaching death; both situations appear as special occasions for confession, in connection with which it occurs precociously in our sources, far outside any context where confession appears more generally. Of the two, the approach of death was the stronger influence. This transpires in, above all, Peter the Venerable's *De miraculis*. In one of Peter's stories even a monk is urged to confess *because* he is dying.[112] In another story a monk on his deathbed is urged to confess the sins of his whole life, including the part before he entered the monastery,— as if he had never confessed before.[113] In telling the story Peter defends confession, giving scriptural authorities for it and telling vivid tales of eternal rewards and punishments sanctioning these authorities.[114] It is as if confession was not yet taken as a matter of course in his monastic milieu. Only the approach of death had the force to impose it.

In the early middle ages it is always hard to prove something was not there. In the case of confession we have sought to do so by looking in likely places and finding it absent. But another way of telling when something was not there is by looking at it when it appears, as when a visitor arrives with a wet coat, and you know he has come from the rain. A new institution can betray novelty in a similar way. So let us look in our literature at those milieux where regular lay confession does appear and see if it reveals anything about its arrival.

Three sources, or groups of sources, invite this approach. The first is the collection of relic-miracles from the great Thuringian monastery of Fulda, written between 842 and 847. In one miracle a consignment of relics bound from Rome to Fulda comes to a village near St Gall in Switzerland, and a local inhabitant is threatened by an attack of demons. The local priest advises the victim 'to make confession of his

---

[108] As in n. 103.
[109] I, c. 23 [69.15–25] and the two following cases.
[110] *Ibid.*, I, c. 27 [83.24–8]: ' . . . penitentia et confessione christiana . . . Deo satisfaciens'.
[111] *Ibid.*, I, c. 3 [12.8–11].
[112] *Ibid.*, I, c. 5 [15.8–10].
[113] *Ibid.*, I, c. 6 [19.70–24 and .91–2].
[114] *Ibid.*, I, c. 6 [18.49–19.69].

sins and then to do penance ... which the devil hates'.[115] In the same place, another visitor to the consignment had his offering rejected by the relics. The same priest thereby divined that the visitor had a hidden stain on his conscience (*conscientia* is the word used here, as in two other occasions in the work). So he is told to go home and clean it by 'a pure confession and worthy works of penance'.[116] The following year another package of relics was crossing Franconia when a woman from the neighbourhood of Mainz offered them a gift of wool, which miraculously vanished. Fearfully the woman looked for a priest 'to whom she might make confession and receive counsel for her salvation'.[117] The priest suspected a hidden sin but found eventually that the woman had unwittingly received the wool of a sheep acquired by fraud.

This theme in the Fulda book stands out more sharply when compared with its absence from our other ninth-century collections: Einhard, Aldevrald of Fleury, and Wolfrad of Eichstätt. Why should the Fulda collection, alone, make such overt reference? The answer is surely that its abbot had for twenty years been Hrabanus Maurus, one of the giants of the Carolingian reformation. Hrabanus' Penitential, and numerous other writings with a pastoral purpose (the purpose also of the relic-collection) mark him as one of the two or three most effective churchmen of his century. If confession, as described in the capitularies and penitential books, was to take root anywhere, it would be in the milieu of such a man.[118]

Comparable lessons can be learned from the second area of experiment, two centuries on, in the period of the Gregorian reform. Mention was made a moment ago of the Lives of Anselm of Lucca (†1086), Berard of Marses (†1130), Bruno of Segni (†1123), and Peter of Anagni (†1105), as a group written soon after the death of their heroes and representing Gregorian episcopal ideals.[119] These Lives describe their saints' prayers, preaching, and exertions for the poor and for the recovery of church property from usurpers. But there is still no express mention of their holding confessions or moving other priests to do so. The contrast is therefore striking when we find the opposite in another Life of a 'Gregorian' bishop. It is that of Hugh, bishop of Grenoble from 1080 to 1132.[120] He was as 'Gregorian' as the others (Hugh had been consecrated by Gregory VII himself). But this time the bishop is said to have been especially wise and kind in dealing with 'peccatores ob confessionem ad eum venientes', whom he 'patientissime audiebat',

[115] *Mir. Fulden.*, 330.51‑4.
[116] *Mir. Fulden.*, 331.44‑7.
[117] *Mir. Fulden.*, 333.52‑4.
[118] McKitterick (as in n. 29), esp. 97‑104.
[119] See nn. 71‑74.
[120] See n. 76.

weeping tears to stimulate or sympathise with theirs.[121] It should be noted that people came to visit Hugh 'not only from his diocese but from others, both for confession and for countless other reasons',[122] one of his recommendations being precisely his scorn for *deargentatam penitentiam*: 'the silvered penance' which commuted austerities for pay-ments-down.[123]

Why the exception? The answer lies in a combination of two factors. Hugh had in the 1070s studied in northern French schools, probably in Rheims under Master Bruno, and was noted for his divine learning. The second factor, partial consequence of the first, was Hugh's intimate connection with the Carthusian order, founded by the former Master Bruno with Hugh's active co-operation. Hugh often shared the quasi-eremetical life of the Grande Chartreuse. Carthusian spirituality attached special importance to monastic confession and the private examination of conscience. It was a self-conscious discovery of the 'inner world'. 'Some go to Jerusalem; but let your own pilgrimage be towards humility and patience', Guigo, Hugh's Carthusian biographer, had written shortly before in his *Meditationes*; and again: 'no region is as remote or unknown as yourself, or so readily subject to false tales'.[124] A connection of Carthusian spirituality and lay confession is confirmed, in the same region (the Dauphiné), by the Life of a second-generation Carthusian (and Hugh's admirer), Anthelme, bishop of Bellay from 1163 to 1178. 'How understanding [*pius*], how merciful, he was to penitent sinners' wrote one an intimate, 'they know who confessed to him and were reconciled to God by his hand.'[125]

You will notice that both exceptions so far, from Fulda and Grenoble, involve the same pair of factors: assiduous study, especially by one or a few people; and a fervent regular community. The effect of this combination is to be seen in the area of the third exception, England.

England is least exceptional, in this respect, in the Lives of those two solitaries. The Somerset hermit St Wulfric, whose life as such stretched from the 1120s to his death in 1154, was a priest, had been a parish priest, and after his withdrawal is still said in one place to have lived a life essentially interchangeable with that of his own local parish-priest, the exemplary Brictric.[126] Of neither is it stated that he normally heard lay confessions. Wulfric once 'saw' prophetically the sinful state of three

[121] *Vita s. Hugon. Grat.*, c. 3, §14, col. 771CD.

[122] *Vita s. Hugon. Grat.*, c. 4, §16, col. 773B.

[123] *Vita s. Hugon. Grat.*, c. 5, §20, col. 776B.

[124] Guigo, *Meditationes*, Ed. par un Chartreux. Sources chrétiennes, no. 308 (Paris, 1983), 202.

[125] *Vita s. Anthelmi*, §33; ed. J. Picard, *Vie de St. Anthelme, évêque de Bellay, Chartreux, Collection de recherches et d'études cartusiennes* (Bellay, 1978), 28.

[126] *Vita b. Wulfrici.*, c. 16, 30–1.

priests who then confessed to him and were absolved.[127] He similarly 'saw' that a certain man was in bondage to the devil, through long-standing avarice and ambition *sicut postea confessus est*. That term may or may not be read technically, but the procedure was in this respect irregular that the priest knew miraculously of the man's sin first, and reprehended him for it.[128] One more allusion to Wulfric's second sight concerns a monk's impure thoughts, and omits any reference to confession.[129] Other allusions to confession depict it as public.[130]

Any ambiguity in these allusions in Wulfric's Life has gone when we turn to that of Christina of Markyate (near Huntingdon), whose life as an anchorite was roughly contemporary with Wulfric's. Her biographer tells of the many obstacles her family put in the path of Christina's vocation and of how she won through only, in the end, but the help of an abbot, pious as well as powerful. But Christina had a second champion, one roused not just to action but to indignation by her story: Ralf d'Escures, archbishop of Canterbury from 1114 to 1122. Ralf's comment was that if Christina's mother 'were to come to me in confession I would give her the penance appropriate to homicide'.[131] It reminds the reader that no word has been said of confession earlier in the book, and suggests why: that if any of the family had been required to attend confession the story would not have run as it did. We may ask who Ralf d'Escures was, that he should take for granted an institution thus ignored by a noble clan of Huntingdon? He was a former monk and abbot of the reformed Norman monastery of St Martin's Seez, *litteris admodum ... imbutus*. It is the same combination of monasticism and learning.

The combination reappears in the last book in our sample. The Laon miracle book tells of events a little earlier than those in Lives of Wulfric and Christina, and roughly contemporary with the Lives of the three last of those Gregorian bishops; specifically, of 1112 and 1113. In the town riots of the former year, rendered vivid to historians in Guibert of Nogent's autobiography, the cathedral of Laon had been burned to the ground.[132] A group of cathedral clergy took the relics of their patron,

---

[127] *Ibid.*, c. 87, 113.

[128] *Ibid.*, c. 17, 31–3.

[129] *Ibid.*, c. 69, 96.

[130] *Ibid.*, c. 71, 97–9 (the story was public knowledge in the household where it had occurred); c. 23, 42–3 (Wulfric's own public confession).

[131] *Life of Christina*, 84. The word 'confession' or a cognate is used on 108, 190 and 192, but not in the sense in question. The absence of formal confession is noticeable on 120 (where a woman acknowledges her sin to Christina;) and on 158 (where a monk receives the Eucharist on his deathbed with no mention of previous confession). The tribute to Ralf's learning, quoted below, is from Bk. VIII, c. 8 of *The Ecclesiastical History of Ordericus Vitalis*, ed. M. Chibnall, IV (Oxford, 1973), 168,

[132] Guibert de Nogent, *De vita sua*, III cc. vii–xi (as in n. 66), 317–76.

the Virgin Mary, on a tour round northern France to raise money for the rebuilding of the cathedral.[133] Book I of the *Miracula sanctae Mariae Laudunensis* describes their journey. They stopped at Issoudun, Tours, Angers, le Mans, Chartres, and at some smaller places in between. The reliquary duly performed miracles in each, mostly medical cures, and enough money was raised to last the builders through the winter of 1113–14. Then they needed more. Some *sapientes* in the Laon clerical community advised that a deputation be sent to England, just then, they said, *opulens*, under the government of Henry I. So nine men were picked, as being well-educated and good singers. They included two priests, and one Englishman who was not a priest. Book II of the miracle-book duly describes their tour in southern England between Easter and Christmas 1113.

The two books of the *Miracula sanctae Mariae* present a significant contrast. In Book I confession is never mentioned.[134] The matter is only introduced at the start of the Book II, when the little party of Laon clergy is threatened by pirates in the Channel.[135] That was the occasion when the clerics, not the laity, confessed to each other. However, lay confession enters soon afterwards, and with an instructive abruptness.

The Laon delegation landed in Kent and were soon in Canterbury. There a sick woman's husband sought out the visitors, and asked if they knew anything of medicine. The leader of the group, a priest called Boso, indicated to the woman that she should send for her priest—her own priest—and make 'full confession of her sins' to him. When Boso was reliably assured that this had been done he brought his group along, with the relics, and the sick woman was cured. The account in the *Miracula* explains that the party adhered to two principles, under the guidance 'as we believe', of Our Lady: that the candidate for a cure should come from the diocese, lest they be accused of paying a stranger to feign a miracle; and secondly that

> of residents in the diocese no-one should be cured unless he had previously confessed his sins to his priest [*presbytero suo*], so long as he was of age. If he was too young his parents should be admonished to make confession [*facere confessionem*] instead.[136]

Leaving Canterbury the deputation toured southern England. We

---

[133] *De mir. s. Mariae Laudun* (see n. 71). Still useful as a general description of the work is J. S. P. Tatlock, 'The English Journey of the Laon Canons', *Speculum*, VIII (1933), 454–65; while S. Martinet, 'Le voyage des Laonnois en Angleterre en 1113', *Mémoires de la Fédération des sociétés d'histoire et d'archéologie de l'Aisne*, IX (1963), 81–92, briefly describes MS Laon, 166 and summarises the narrative.

[134] *De mirac. s. Mariae Laudun*. I cc. 3–13 [cols. 967D–72D].

[135] *De mirac. s. Mariae Laudun*. II c. 1 [col. 973AB]. The miracles performed on French soil early in Bk. II (cc. 1–3) still ignore confession.

[136] *De mirac. s. Mariae Laudun*. II c. 6 [col. 977C–8B; esp. 978AB].

are often told that a patient 'confessed his sins' before his cure. The context declares, implicitly or explicitly, that this was to the patient's subject's own priest, not to the visitors.[137] Penance is not paired with confession as in the Fulda account, though restitution is once mentioned: in Winchester a usurer was made, after confession, to return his usurious gains before he could be cured.[138] In Exeter a cripple who confessed was *not* cured; but it transpired that he belonged to the neighbouring diocese of Salisbury, whither he duly persuaded the visitors to take him, with the predictable result: then he was cured the moment he and they crossed the diocesan boundary.[139]

In the Laon miracle book the practice of lay confession stands out in sharp relief, then, in one area and time: England in 1113. Diocesan discipline is stronger than at Grenoble, where St Hugh heard confessions from outside his diocese. Confession is in higher relief than in the Fulda miracle book: there are twice as many cases, and the allusion now is not to confession and penance together but to confession alone. But the Fulda and Laon accounts share one feature: the relics' therapeutic power serves as incentive to bring laity to confession. It suggests that we are once again in the presence of a strong pastoral impulse, trying to make the laity do things they would not otherwise have done.

In the present case, as in the other two, it is easy to guess a source for the impulse: Laon itself.[140] Master Anselm of Laon was in 1113 head of the foremost theological school in western Christendom. If those upheavals of 1112 had never happened Laon might have become what Paris in the event did become; one consequence of Laon's eclipse being the currency given to the 'Paris version'—or one of them—of Anselm's teaching, in Abelard's *Historia calamitatum*. Anselm and his Laon school were in fact the principal re-founders, after the Carolingians, of systematic evangelical study. They were leading contributors in particular to the theology of confession and penance. That great engine of practical biblical study, the *Glossa ordinaria*, was once attributed to a pupil of Hrabanus. It has now been more securely attributed to Anselm

---

[137] *De mirac. s. Mariae Laudun.* II c. 7 [col. 978C]; c. 8 [col. 979A]; c. 12 [col. 982B]; c. 13 [col. 982C]; c. 17 [col. 984B]. In c. 22 [col. 986CD] a boy is cured without confessing; he was twelve years old.

[138] *De mirac. s. Mariae Laudun.* II c. 8 [col. 979A].

[139] *De mirac. s. Mariae Laudun.* II c. 12 [col. 982CD].

[140] The interest of the Laon school in penance in confession is abundantly illustrated in the *sententiae* examined by Lottin, *Psychologie et morale* (as in n. 57), vol. 5 (e.g.) 102, §128; Anciaux (as in n. 6), 149–50; and L. Hödl, *Die Geschichte der scholastischen Literatur und der Theologie der Schlüßelgewalt*, Erster Teil. Beiträge zur Geschichte der Philosophie und Theologie des Mittelalters. Texte und Untersuchungen, Band 38, Heft 4, pt. 1 (Münster-in-Westphalen, 1960); with references to further publications. Indications in theology of the practice of confession in the Laon region may be read in Guibert of Nogent, *Mor. in Genesim.* IX, *Pat. lat.*, 156, 259CD and *Opusc. de virginitate*, c. 15, *ibid.*, col. 603D–4A.

of Laon, his brother Ralf, and others of their circle. The first attribution was a mistake, but an appropriate one; and its fortunes neatly demonstrate the tradition Hrabanus and Anselm shared, across two centuries.[141]

For a doctrinal defence of regular lay confession we need look no further, then, than the school of Laon. But doctrine is not practice, and a see which could not protect its own cathedral was ill-placed to vindicate its own pastoral doctrines. It lay nevertheless on the edge of a polity which could. Whatever the penitential traditions of pre-Conquest England, Lanfranc and Anselm of Canterbury had set in motion a reform whose object was realisation of canon law. 'Normans', meanwhile, who came in fact from the entire length of the French northern coast, opened the way to England from the old Carolingian capital of Laon. The way was all the easier because Laon *alumni* and Laon books had access also to Normandy. Orderic Vitalis may have had some in mind when he spoke of the 'mature and religious priests' who 'discussed confession and other useful subjects' while other clergy were rioting in Rouen cathedral; and he certainly, or almost certainly, copied in St Évroult a Laon commentary on St Matthew.[142]

It was England that reaped the harvest. It abounded in Laon *alumni*. The miracle book has Master Anselm's pupils holding high church office in Canterbury, Exeter, Salisbury, and Bodmin[143], and the canon's welcome in these places betrays that it was they, the *alumni*, who had arranged the fund-raising itinerary; no doubt through those *sapientes* of the Laon chapter who had originally proposed the journey.[144]

These signs of lay confession in early twelfth-century England, then, can easily be linked to an appropriate academic centre. What of a link to a monastery or regular community? Here the answer must be sought in the early and pre-history of the English Augustinian canons.[145] Our miracle-book says the archbishop who welcomed the delegation to Canterbury was William of Corbeil. The mistake is instructive. William would in fact only become archbishop, after Ralf d'Escures, in 1123. In 1113 the see was vacant. But William had by then been an active

---

[141] B. Smalley, *The Study of the Bible in the Middle Ages* (Oxford, 1941), 35–45.

[142] Orderic Vitalis, *Hist. eccles.* (as in n. 131), Bk. XII, c. 25, Vol. VI (1978), 292. Orderic's autograph MS of this commentary is MS Alençon 25; see M. Chibnall, *The World of Orderic Vitalis* (Oxford, 1984), 95–6.

[143] *Mir. s. Mariae Laudun.* II, c. 6 [col. 977B] (William of Corbeil on the assumption that he was present in Canterbury though not archbishop, see below); c. 12 [col. 982A] (Archdeacon Robert); c. 13 [col. 983A] (Alexander and Nigel le Poore); c. 15 [col. 983BC] (Algar/Algard).

[144] *Mir. s. Mariae Laudun.* II, c. 1 [col. 973AB].

[145] Dickinson (as in n. 7) remains authoritative, despite assumptions about confession and related pastoral matters. For William of Corbeil see D. Bethell, 'William of Corbeil and the Canterbury-York dispute', *Journal of Ecclesiastical History*, XIX (1968), 145–59.

reformer in England for nine years and since he, too, was a Laon *alumnus* our loyal writer perhaps anticipated his elevation for that reason. But in 1113 William was also an Augustinian canon, that is, in the vanguard of a movement begun in England 1108 under yet another Laon *alumnus* ('Normannus')[146], which William would promote as archbishop, and which in the very decade between now and then, 1113–1123, would make its conquests largely by offering a workable rule to devout clergy already living in communities. Most of the first English Augustinians, that is to say, (including William and 'Normannus') had already been such clergy before adopting the Rule; and this is why, although most early Augustinian 'foundations' fall just after the tour of 1113, they belong to the same pastoral endeavour. Another look at the itinerary will confirm this: after Canterbury its main foci were Winchester, Salisbury and Exeter, and their cash-rich colonies respectively at Christchurch, Wilton and Bodmin. The bishops of all three at the time were noted benefactors of collegiate churches of reforming ambiance, some already Augustinian, some soon to be so.[147] Several, besides those mentioned in the *Miracula s. Mariae*, had their own personal links with Laon,—like the schoolmaster Roger of Salisbury had obtained for his cathedral chapter in 1107.[148]

If the patterns yielded by our sample are representative then they teach a threefold lesson. First, for the period reviewed, they suggest that regular lay confession, though prescribed, was a usage generally ignored, if often in favour of unofficial substitutes. Second and third, where such confession appears it does so regularly in the presence of two factors; one, an active study of pastoral divinity; the other, a body of clergy living under a common rule, in a monastery or regular order. If Laon is replaced by Paris, William of Corbeil by Innocent III, the Austin canons by the mendicant friars, precisely the same formula would apply to the century we know, from more abundant evidence, to have witnessed regular lay confession; a comparison which tends to

[146] Normannus: G. A. J. Hodgett, ed., *The Cartulary of Holy Trinity Aldgate*. London Record Society, VII (1971), 226: 'cum Anselmo in Gallia litterarum habuit exercicium ubi sciencia preditus ... ' The editor does not identify this Anselm with the master of Laon, doubtless reading him as Anselm of Canterbury. But the latter, frequently mentioned in the same document, is usually referred to with an expression like 'saepedictus pater Anselmus', making the Laon identification of the other doubly probable.

[147] M. Brett *The English Church Under Henry I* (Oxford, 1975), 138.

[148] T. Webber, *Scribes and Scholars at Salisbury Cathedral, c.1075–c.1125* (Oxford, 1992), 82: Guy of Étampes, first *magister scholarum*, sent to Salisbury soon after 1107, had been a pupil of Anselm of Laon (*ibid.*, 82). For the pastoral and reforming interests of the Salisbury school in general, *ibid.*, 82–139. I am grateful to Dr Webber for showing me proofs of these chapters before publication.

confirm our deductions without having had any part in making them.

This threefold lesson leads, in turn, to two final conclusions, relating respectively to 'external' and 'internal' history. In proposing that the diocesan church in early twelfth-century England was precocious I may have relied too much on one document. But the hypothesis fits with much else that we know of that place and time; not least, for instance, that the capricious availability of itinerant relics would be replaced as a goad to lay confession, well before 1150, by the promise of indulgences.[149] The hypothesis recalls our earlier reflections on the relation of confession with civil government. For Norman England was conspicuous for other jurisdictions than that of the *forum internum*: on one hand, its tough criminal jurisdiction (for a time supervised by the same Bishop Roger who welcomed the Laon canons); on the other, its scarcely less awesome archidiaconal courts.[150] Law and order, in other words, and certain outward church observances, were well looked-after; and it was this, the configuration of evidence suggests, which left priests free to represent aspects of their function more appropriate to private consciences.

If 'external' nurtured 'internal' in that particular, then an opposite current can be traced in the relation of lay confession with monasticism. I have avoided, as broaching questions too embattled for this occasion, the matter whether monks or regular canons should, or could, or did, act as pastoral clergy.[151] But that question clearly touches ours at several points, and one of these is worth registering among present conclusions. Too strict a theological approach to confession, especially if based on distinctions still in the future in the early twelfth century, can obscure a circumstance which our sources tend rather to highlight. Confession within monasteries or regular orders, with its various forms and sacramental statuses, nourished the spread of confession among the laity. This fact, if it is that, puts the history of confession into the context of another, larger area of the history of religion and morals:

---

[149] From *c*.1140, as kindly pointed out to me in a letter from Dr N. Vincent of 9 March 1992, quoting episcopal *acta* in A. Saltman, *Theodore, Archbishop of Canterbury* 1956), 37; *Llandaff Episcopal Acta*, ed. D. Crouch (Cardiff 1988); *English Episcopal Acta*, II: *Canterbury, 1162–1190* (1986), No. 72, 53.

[150] J. Scammell, 'The Rural chapter in England from the eleventh to the fourteenth century', *English Historical Review* LXXXVI (1961), 1–21, emphasises the brisk, 'Anglo-Norman' character of the archdeacon's court. That the separation of confession from the church courts engendered that of theology and canon law is the thesis of François Russo, 'Pénitence et excommunication. Étude historique sur les rapports entre la théologie et le droit canon dans le domaine pénitentielle du ixe au xiiie siécle', *Recherches de sciences religieuses*, XXXIII (1946), 257–79, 431–61; discussed in my *Excommunication and Conscience* (as in n. 32), 15–17. A contemporary perception of the issues raised for confessors by a ramification of jurisdiction is that of Alan of Lille (as in n. 40), III, cc. 1–7, 127–31.

[151] The best modern discussion: Constable (as in n. 99), esp. 366–89.

the emanation, whether or not with uniformly felicitous results, of monastic ideals into lay society at large.

The picture that emerges from the almost-blackness, then, emerges free from the restrictions of mere 'church history'. Whatever the optical illusions in the documents, traps to contemporaries and ourselves, the history of confession was connected, distantly but surely, with the history of everything else: on one hand, with that of kings and their rough justiciars, who faced the world as it actually was; on the other, with that of monks, who prayed for the world as it should be. Each of the triad, an uncertain pastoral clergy in the middle, was parent to the others, invisibly nourishing and protecting them. Together, they made a single organism, if, to us, one of the cells too various to be gathered habitually in one thought.

'LES ENGLEYS NÉES EN IRLANDE': THE ENGLISH POLITICAL IDENTITY IN MEDIEVAL IRELAND

by Robin Frame

READ I MAY 1992

BY the fourteenth century the descendants of those who had gone from Britain to Ireland in the late twelfth and early thirteenth centuries had come to call themselves 'the English of Ireland' or 'the English born in Ireland'. Or, to be more accurate, they did so when faced by Englishmen from England: within Ireland they described themselves simply as 'the English'. From the 1340s onwards a series of disputes with agents of the king formed a context in which they collectively stressed their Englishness. By the fifteenth century this identity was from time to time problematical, both for those who claimed it and for the metropolis. Historians who work on the late medieval and early modern periods have found it equally so, and have argued about the attitudes and nationality of the settler élite. While fourteenth-century evidence has been called upon in these debates, there has been little serious consideration of the first two centuries of the lordship of Ireland.[1] In what senses were those who went to Ireland during the founding period 'English'? Why does the emphasis upon being English appear to have intensified among their successors as time went by? What does the self-proclaimed Englishness of the fourteenth century signify? How far do the complexities and tensions associated with it foreshadow the better-known difficulties of later periods? These are the matters I wish to explore.

One way of approaching them is through that most familiar of all documents emanating from the medieval lordship of Ireland, the Statutes of Kilkenny. They were enacted in 1366 in a parliament held by Edward III's lieutenant of Ireland, his son Lionel of Antwerp, duke of Clarence and earl of Ulster. Their preamble runs:

---

[1] See S. G. Ellis, 'Nationalist historiography and the English and Gaelic worlds in the late middle ages', *IHS*, XXXV (1986–7), 3, 12–13; B. Bradshaw, 'Nationalism and historical scholarship in modern Ireland', *ibid.*, XXVI (1988–9), 329–32; A. Cosgrove, 'The writing of Irish medieval history', *ibid.*, XXVII (1990–1), 104–6; S. G. Ellis, 'Representations of the past in Ireland: whose past and whose present?', *ibid.*, 299–301. I am indebted to Dr Paul Brand and Dr C. W. Brooks for reading this paper in draft and making valuable comments and criticisms.

Whereas at the conquest of the land of Ireland and for a long time afterwards the English of that land used the English tongue, manner of riding and dress, and were governed and ruled ... by English law ... ; now many English of that land, forsaking the English speech, outward appearance, manner of riding, laws and customs, live and conduct themselves according to the customs, appearance and tongue of the Irish enemies, and have also entered into many marriages and alliances between themselves and those Irish enemies; through which that land, its liege people, the English tongue, the allegiance owed to our lord the king, and the English laws there are subordinated and diminished, and the Irish enemies are exalted and raised up, contrary to right.[2]

These sonorous phrases embody the perceptions of those who shaped them, and also, we must presume, of those who assented to them. Behind them lie not merely Lionel and his English circle but also the communities of the settled heartlands of eastern and southern Ireland, whose knights and burgesses attended the parliament, and in addition the magnates and higher clergy. The Statutes echo in important respects documents drawn up six years earlier, during the administration of the second earl of Ormond, whose lands and career lay mostly within Ireland.[3]

The preamble directs our attention to the past as well as to the present. The public identity of the English of Ireland had acquired a historical aspect, as they sought to explain to others, and perhaps to themselves, who they were, and how they had come to be where they were. In a sense it matters little whether their history strikes us as historical; it was real to them, and served its purpose. But let us pose the bald question, fact or fiction? In some ways their image of the past was undoubtedly skewed. Among the newcomers of the twelfth century, French, Welsh and possibly Flemish were spoken, alongside English.[4] We might prefer to describe their horsemanship and dress as west European rather than as specifically English. And the implication that alliances and marriages with the Irish were a recent and deplorable phenomenon is richly ironic. The formation of such ties had been central to the penetration of Ireland by the first invaders: Strongbow (d.1176) married Aoife, daughter of the king of Leinster, and succeeded

[2] *Statutes and Ordinances and Acts of the Parliament of Ireland, King John to Henry V*, ed. H. F. Berry (Dublin, 1907), 430–1.

[3] C. McNeill (ed.), 'Lord Chancellor Gerrard's notes of his report on Ireland', *Analecta Hibernica*, II (1931), 266–8; *Parliaments and Councils of Mediaeval Ireland*, ed. H. G. Richardson and G. O. Sayles (Dublin, Irish MSS Commission, 1947), 19–22.

[4] A. Bliss and J. Long, 'Literature in Norman French and English', in *Medieval Ireland, 1169–1534*, ed. A. Cosgrove (Oxford, 1987), 708–15.

him; Hugh de Lacy (d.1186), granted Meath by Henry II, wed a daughter of the king of Connacht, his neighbour across the Shannon; William de Burgh (d.1205), a *curialis* who gained lands in Munster, embedded himself in regional politics by marrying a daughter of the king of Thomond.[5]

At a crucial point, however, fourteenth-century perceptions match those of modern historians. When the Statutes say that the settlers were governed by English law and custom they come close to the literal truth. Writs inaugurating key actions of the Common Law were made available in Ireland in 1204. When King John visited the lordship in 1210 he promulgated a charter making English law in general current there.[6] Such deliberate steps only gave formality to something that was implicit from the moment Henry II set foot in Ireland and began to grant lands to members of his circle, and privileges to Irish towns, through charters couched in conventional terms upon which he or a successor might be called to adjudicate. Moreover the grantees of the early period included lords who kept property in England and had in some cases served as sheriffs and even judges there; indeed almost anybody of standing who got Irish land had experience of the royal courts as a litigant or juror.[7] Those who went to Ireland may have been polyglot, but they were the people of the king of England, and some ingredients of an English political-legal identity were present in the lordship from the start. This identity was to bind the disparate newcomers (including Welsh and even Scots)[8] together, and to mark them off from the Irish, whose law left few traces in the legal system of the emerging polity.[9]

Such facts highlight the gulf that separates the conquest of Ireland from the conquest of England one hundred years before. King William was at pains to present himself as the Confessor's heir. He used the title *Rex Anglorum*; what he inherited included the rights of the Old English monarch, along with the laws and customs of the kingdom and its considerable administrative structure. A generation later, in his coronation charter of 1100, Henry I confirmed the still-dynamic 'law

[5] M. T. Flanagan, *Irish Society, Anglo-Norman Settlers, Angevin Kingship: Interactions in Ireland in the Late Twelfth Century* (Oxford, 1989), chs. 3, 4, and p. 264; G. H. Orpen, *Ireland under the Normans 1169–1333*, 4 vols. (Oxford, 1911–20), II. 148.

[6] G. J. Hand, *English Law in Ireland, 1290–1324* (Cambridge, 1967), 2; P. Brand, 'Ireland and the literature of the early Common Law', *Irish Jurist*, XVI (1981), 95–6.

[7] See Brand, 96–9, and R. Frame, *The Political Development of the British Isles, 1100–1400* (Oxford, 1990), 85–7.

[8] R. Frame, 'The immediate effect and interpretation of the 1331 ordinance *Una et eadem lex*', *Irish Jurist*, VII (1972), 109–14; G. W. S. Barrow, *The Anglo-Norman Era in Scottish History* (Oxford, 1980), 119.

[9] For the exceptions, see Hand, 172–3, 193–8, 201–4.

of Edward'.[10] Ireland was different. Henry II did not step into the shoes of a native predecessor; while existing tribute districts may have shaped local lordships, there was little at central level to be inherited. What is more, he intervened in Ireland against a background of disquiet about Irish morals and Church order that had long been voiced, with the encouragement of Irish reforming clergy, by Canterbury and Rome. Although his motive for crossing the sea was primarily to control and exploit an occupation that lords from south Wales had begun without him, he took the opportunity to patronise a reforming synod at Cashel. When Pope Alexander III congratulated him on his work, he used well-worn rhetoric—calling the Irish 'a people uncivilised and undisciplined', who 'wander through the steeps of vice', and dwelling on their habit of mutual slaughter and odious marriage customs.[11] The laws of such folk were scarcely to be preserved, let alone emulated.

If the rationales of the conquests were different, one explanation must be the lapse of time between 1066 and 1171. By the latter date the Church distinguished more sharply between acceptable and unacceptable customs and there was a growing tendency to view peoples who lay outside the political and cultural mainstream as inferior.[12] It is true that even in 1066 Irish custom might have struck a Norman observer as odder than its Anglo-Saxon counterpart, which shared the Germanic and Carolingian inheritance with northern France. Yet after the Conquest Anglo-Norman and Celtic legal systems seem to have had less difficulty in accommodating to each other in the Welsh marches than was to be the case in Ireland a century later. When the Normans came to England they brought with them their assumptions about social relations, but not a self-conscious, written body of custom that King William could have imposed on England had the notion crossed his mind. The occupation of Ireland, by contrast, coincided with the decades when the law of the king's court was crystallising and royal jurisdiction expanding dramatically. Ireland was settled, under the monarch's eye, in the age of *Glanvill*, of Magna Carta, and of *Bracton*. It is hard to imagine the Crown at any earlier time promoting the wholesale transfer of law from England to Ireland. Nor was the

---

[10] F. Liebermann, *Die Gesetze der Angelsachsen*, 3 vols. (Halle, 1903–16), I. 522; G. Garnett, ' "Franci et Angli": The legal distinctions between peoples after the Conquest', *Anglo-Norman Studies*, VIII (1986), 109–37.

[11] *Pontificia Hibernica. Medieval Papal Chancery Documents concerning Ireland, 640–1261*, ed. M. P. Sheehy (Dublin, 1962), I, no. 6; cf. nos. 2, 4, 5, 7, and *The Letters of Lanfranc, Archbishop of Canterbury*, ed. H. Clover and M. Gibson (Oxford, 1979), nos. 9, 10. See M. Richter, 'The first century of Anglo-Irish relations', *History*, LIX (1974), 195–210.

[12] See R. R. Davies, 'Buchedd a moes y Cymry [The manners and morals of the Welsh]', *Welsh Hist. Rev.*, XII (1984), 174–8; R. Bartlett, *Gerald of Wales, 1146–1223* (Oxford, 1982), esp. 29–45, 167–71.

law merely royal or common; while its content might owe little to the Anglo-Saxon past, it was regarded as English. Around 1188 *Glanvill* set out to explain *leges Anglicanas*. At almost the same moment Gerald of Wales saw the Irish church as being brought into line, not just with the universal Church, but with *ecclesia Anglicana*. When in 1216–17 the council of Henry III extended Magna Carta to Ireland, it spoke of giving the king's people there 'the same liberties as have been granted to the king's subjects of England'.[13]

Since the law was English, so in an important sense were those who used it[14]; a form of Englishness was inherent in the lordship more or less from the beginning, together with an inclination to look askance at Irish custom. But to say this is to set a crucial question aside. Was English law from the start reserved to the settlers? Did Englishness in the legal sense coincide with Englishness (or at least non-Irishness) in an ethnic sense? The evidence for the earlier thirteenth century is thin, but it suggests that the position was not so clear-cut. There are a fair number of instances of people apparently of Irish origin using the courts or serving as jurors.[15] A traditional explanation of their legal competence supposes that many specific grants of English status (of a type familiar from the time of Edward I onwards) were issued to Irishmen almost from the beginning of the lordship's history, but that these have not come down to us.[16] This seems unlikely, not least because in the 1170s the Common Law itself was only starting to achieve definition. It is significant that in Edward's reign the descendants of the Norse of Waterford claimed that Henry II himself had granted them English law, when all Henry's charter actually gave them was a general royal protection.[17] Kenneth Nicholls's suggestion, that originally distinctions were governed less by origin than by status and tenure,

---

[13] *The Treatise on the Laws and Customs of the Realm of England commonly called Glanvill*, ed. G. D. G. Hall (London, 1965), 2; *Expugnatio Hibernica*, ed. A. B. Scott and F. X. Martin (Dublin, 1978), 98, 142; T. Rymer, *Foedera* (Record Commission, 1816–69), I. 145; *Patent Rolls, 1216–25*, 31. On the significance of the late twelfth century, see P. Brand, ' "Multis vigiliis excogitatam et inventam": Henry II and the creation of English Common Law', *Haskins Society Journal*, II (1990), 197–222.

[14] On the role of the Common Law in fostering a sense of shared Englishness, see R. C. van Caenegem, *The Birth of the English Common Law* (Cambridge, 1973), ch. 4; on the general link between law and identity, S. Reynolds, *Kingdoms and Communities in Western Europe 900–1300* (Oxford, 1984), 43–4, 250, 256–61, and R. R. Davies, 'Law and national identity in medieval Wales', in *Welsh Society and Nationhood*, ed. R. R. Davies *et al.* (Cardiff, 1984), 51–69. John Gillingham has recently argued for a self-conscious and aggressive English identity even in the later twelfth century ('The beginnings of English imperialism', *Journal of Historical Sociology*, V (1992), 392–409).

[15] K. W. Nicholls, 'Anglo-French Ireland and after', *Peritia*, I (1982), 375.

[16] A. J. Otway-Ruthven, 'The native Irish and English law in medieval Ireland', *IHS*, VII (1950–1), 5–7. For the later position, see *ibid.*, 11–16; Hand, 198–205.

[17] Brand, 'Ireland and the Common Law', n. 17 and p. 103.

and that if Irishmen were accepted as holding land freely (as they sometimes were) they could use the courts, has much to commend it.[18]

Such acceptance may, however, have been rare: there are scarcely any examples of Irish laymen witnessing baronial charters.[19] A memory of the separation of the few sheep from the many goats may be preserved in a petition in 1253 of two Leinstermen that, since they and their ancestors had always been on the side of the English, they should not now be prevented from selling their lands *licet Hibernienses sint.*[20] Their need to approach Henry III on the matter hints at the development of a chillier climate of even greater selectivity. As royal government grew, justice became more centralised, and—we might add—national stereotyping was more deeply engrained, Irish origins were becoming enough on their own to create a presumption that the courts should be closed to a plaintiff. The clearer boundary between free and unfree that the rise of the Common Law created in England was being drawn in Ireland chiefly between newcomer and native.[21]

Yet even if the lines of ethnic demarcation were not so firmly institutionalised in the first decades of the lordship's history as they were to become later, there is no doubt that as early as John's reign law could serve as a denominator of nationality. At Dover in September 1215 the following letters passed the great seal: 'the King to his justiciar of Ireland. Know that we have granted, and we will, that the bearer of these present letters, Domnall Conell, shall henceforth have English law and liberty [*habeat decetero legem et libertatem Anglicanam*]'.[22] This neglected document seems to be the first surviving example of an explicit grant of English law. Though terse, it has the main features familiar in the many such letters that survive from the later middle ages.[23] Already English legal status, as distinct from royal protection or

---

[18] Nicholls, 371–6.

[19] R. Bartlett, 'Colonial aristocracies in the high middle ages', in *Medieval Frontier Societies*, ed. R. Bartlett and A. MacKay (Oxford, 1989), 27–9.

[20] *Close Rolls, 1251–3*, 458–9. In the later middle ages it was thought that the five main provincial dynasties ('Five Bloods') had been granted English law early in the lordship's history. The basis of the story remains elusive (Otway-Ruthven, 'Native Irish', 6; Hand, 205–6). The petitioners of 1253 may have been from a branch of the MacMurroughs of Leinster, one of the five (*Calendar of Documents relating to Ireland, 1252–84*, ed. H. S. Sweetman (1877), no. 1873).

[21] P. R. Hyams, *King, Lords and Peasants in Medieval England* (Oxford, 1980), esp. 221–68.

[22] *Rotuli Litterarum Patentium, 1201–16*, ed. T. D. Hardy (Record Commission, 1835), 155. The identity of the recipient is not known. He was possibly an envoy from the archbishop of Cashel or from the king of Connacht who received charters in Sept. (*Rotuli Chartarum, 1199–1216*, ed. T. D. Hardy (Record Commission, 1837), 219).

[23] See B. Murphy, 'The status of the native Irish after 1331', *Irish Jurist*, II (1967), 122–6. Its survival adds weight to the claim of Walter O'Toole, a member of a former ruling family in Kildare, in 1299 that he possessed a charter of 1208–9 in which William Marshal as lord of Leinster granted English law to his great-grandfather (*Calendar of Justiciary Rolls,*

a recognised tenure, could be encapsulated on parchment and awarded to an individual, just as English law was deliberately extended to the lordship of Ireland itself.

The appearance of such distinctions at this time is not without parallels. Division along ethnic lines is visible in the Church: 1217 saw the first of what was to be a series of attempts to exclude Irishmen from high ecclesiastical office.[24] John's reign also affords the earliest instances of royal documents that employ as defining categories English law, as against Welsh law and the law of the March.[25] Since the Common Law developed in England and Ireland at virtually the same time, it may be suggested that in Ireland too it helped to build a sense of national identity among those who had access to it. There sprang from English law a world of courts, offices, rights and duties that nurtured, and then preserved, the idea of being English. For those within the fold of English law and institutions there was an expectation of security of tenure and of royal justice; for those outside, or not unambiguously inside, these things could not be taken for granted, as the native dynasties of Connacht and Thomond, among others, were to find to their cost during the thirteenth century.[26]

Between John's reign and that of Edward III we pass from a scene where the Englishness of the settlers, in the legal and political sense, was achieving definition, to one where it was being stridently asserted and defended. This seeming intensification of the English identity can appear at odds with the assumption—naive no doubt but curiously hard to set aside—that the longer a settler population spends in its new place, the more it will be identified with it and absorbed by it. Yet the reinforcement over time of a political consciousness rooted in association with the metropolis is not unfamiliar; nor need it be irreconcilable with involvement in the politics and culture of the host society.[27]

Ireland, ed. J. Mills et al. (3 vols., Dublin, 1905–56), I. 271. Nicholls (375–6) has speculated that the charter was merely a grant of land in fee, from which Walter drew conclusions appropriate to his own time.

[24] Patent Rolls, 1216–25, 22, 23. In 1215 a grant of Penkridge, Staffs., to the archbishop of Dublin and his successors had been subject to the condition 'qui non fuerint Hibernienses' (Rot. Chart., 218).

[25] Davies, 'Law', 52–9, at 58.

[26] J. F. Lydon, 'Lordship and Crown: Llywelyn of Wales and O'Connor of Connacht', in The British Isles 1100–1500: Comparisons, Contrasts and Connections, ed. R. R. Davies (Edinburgh, 1988), 53–9. The question of the legal status of the Irish has recently been set in a wider context in R. Bartlett, The Making of Europe: Conquest, Colonization and Cultural Change 950–1350 (Harmondsworth, 1993) ch. 8 at pp. 214–20.

[27] Cf. Jack P. Greene, 'Political mimesis: a consideration of the historical and cultural roots of legislative behavior in the British colonies in the eighteenth century', American Hist. Rev., LXXV (1969), 337–60; G. Morgan, The Hegemony of the Law: Richmond County, Virginia 1692–1776 (New York and London, 1989). I am indebted to Dr D. J. Ratcliffe for drawing my attention to the north American parallels.

I wish to pick out three things—there are certainly others—that are likely to have sharpened the settlers' sense of being English during the century and a half between Magna Carta and the Statutes of Kilkenny. One is the degree to which royal government grew, affecting Ireland more extensively, regularly and densely. There is room only for the simplest of measures.[28] In 1215 there was a justiciar of Ireland, whose seal originated royal writs, a treasurer and chamberlain of the exchequer; they were soon joined by an escheator and two justices in eyre. By the early fourteenth century there were also a chancellor who kept the king's seal for Ireland; two judges attached to the court of the justiciar (now roughly equivalent to the King's Bench); three or four judges in the Dublin court of common pleas; and two or three barons, a chancellor and two chamberlains in the exchequer. These high officials had, of course, their clerks and other underlings. The spread of government at local level is perhaps more significant. In 1215 there were only three royal sheriffs in Ireland, operating from the king's towns of Dublin, Waterford with Cork, and Limerick; most of the country lay within great baronial liberties or the remains of Irish kingdoms. By 1300 the network of shires had expanded and become much more closely textured. There were eleven sheriffs, nine of them in the provinces of Leinster, Meath and Munster. Except for Ulster, which was awkward of access, the liberties were on a smaller scale and more firmly pinned within the embrace of royal government. Under and beside the sheriff were other agents of the king's authority: serjeants, sub-serjeants, coroners, and increasingly keepers (later justices) of the peace, together with judges of assize and *oyer et terminer*.[29] We may doubt whether all this meant that Ireland was more firmly held by the English than in 1240, when the Marshals still lorded it over Leinster and the Lacys over Meath. But Crown administration was no empty shell; the interaction, despite the disturbed state of Ireland, between the centre and the localities is not to be underestimated. In the third quarter of the fourteenth century revenues came in from Munster as well as Leinster. The court of the justiciar continued to hold sessions from Drogheda to Cork and Limerick. Great councils and parliaments met frequently, attracting attendance from most of the lordship.[30]

[28] See H. G. Richardson and G. O. Sayles, *The Administration of Ireland, 1172–1377* (Dublin, Irish MSS Commission, 1963), 14–48, 92–191.

[29] A. J. Otway-Ruthven, 'Anglo-Irish shire government in the thirteenth century', *IHS*, V (1946–7), 1–28; R. Frame, 'The judicial powers of the medieval Irish keepers of the peace', *Irish Jurist*, II (1967), 308–26.

[30] R. Frame, *English Lordship in Ireland 1318–1361* (Oxford, 1982), 82–3; P. Connolly, 'The financing of English expeditions to Ireland, 1361–76', in *England and Ireland in the Later Middle Ages*, ed. J. F. Lydon (Dublin, 1981), 109; *eadem*, 'Pleas held before the chief governors of Ireland, 1308–76', *Irish Jurist*, XVIII (1983), 129–31; H. G. Richardson and G. O. Sayles, *The Irish Parliament in the Middle Ages* (2nd ed. Philadelphia, 1964), 339–43.

As government and hence English institutions reached out, segments of society fed upon them. By the fourteenth century an establishment was well rooted.[31] Some offices in central government might be the preserve of newcomers from England, especially the royal clerks who manned the exchequer.[32] But there was scope for locals too, above all in the law. As Paul Brand has recently shown, the period 1250–1350 saw the emergence of a legal profession. Serjeants and attorneys, mostly recruited from settler families of eastern Ireland, served in the courts; serjeants could aspire to become judges, though not, because of appointees from England, by any means to a monopoly of the judiciary.[33] Recent incomers, such as the Prestons and Shriggelys who arrived from north-west England during the fourteenth century, might stay and dig themselves into landed and office-holding society.[34] At local level a vastly greater number of families found themselves involved. In 1375 145 men were appointed to collect subsidies granted in the seven counties and liberties of south Leinster and Munster; and in 1382 fifty-eight keepers of the peace were named in Meath and its sub-divisions.[35]

Many influences played upon the English; those moulding the minor country lord in Wexford or Limerick, who might take his turn as sheriff or keeper of the peace, differed from those that shaped the landholder in Louth or Meath, who had connections in Dublin, and aspired to a place in central as well as local government. But they had much in common besides office-holding. Both had titles to lands and rights that ultimately flowed from the Crown and might have to be upheld in the courts. They also consorted together in parliaments and councils and shared the experience of petitioning ministers, framing appeals to the king himself, and debating and apportioning taxation. As in the eighteenth century, the fact that in many parts of Ireland the lesser nobility were thinly spread may have given parliaments and great councils a special importance as a political and social meeting-place.[36]

If one result of the development of royal government was to nurture a larger, more self-consciously English, political establishment in the

[31] Cf. Greene, 344.

[32] Frame, *English Lordship*, 91–4.

[33] P. Brand, 'The early history of the legal profession of the lordship of Ireland', in *Brehons, Serjeants and Attorneys: Studies in the History of the Irish Legal Profession*, ed. D. Hogan and W. N. Osborough (Dublin, 1991), 27–36.

[34] *Calendar of the Gormanston Register*, ed. J. Mills and M. J. McEnery (Dublin, Royal Society of Antiquaries of Ireland, 1916), iv–xi; M. J. Bennett, *Community, Class and Careerism: Cheshire and Lancashire Society in the Age of Sir Gawain and the Green Knight* (Cambridge, 1983), 200; *A Roll of the Proceedings of the King's Council in Ireland, 1392–3*, ed. J. Graves (Rolls Ser. LXIX, 1877), 99–103. See now B. Smith, 'A county community in early fourteenth-century Ireland: the case of Louth', *EHR, CVIII* (1993), 561–88.

[35] *Parliaments and Councils*, 56–62; R. Frame, 'Commissions of the peace in Ireland, 1302–1461', *Analecta Hibernica*, XXXV (1992), 24–5.

[36] O. MacDonagh, *States of Mind: A Study of Anglo-Irish Conflict, 1780–1980* (1983), 16–17.

lordship, another was to draw a firmer line between the English and the Irish. Irishmen participated, but only in certain roles. The second earl of Kildare (d.1328) no doubt valued the Vincent O'Briens of the day, who looked after his horses.[37] Members of the Gaelic aristocracy might have careers as captains in royal and magnate service, as Hugh O'Toole of the Dublin mountains did in the 1350s.[38] But unless they had been granted English law, they were excluded from public office both in counties and liberties, as they were of course from central government. In this respect Ireland was a less friendly place for native leaders than was Wales. The Welsh elites continued to manage the commote, a native administrative unit which the English incorporated in a way that has no exact equivalent in Ireland. Welshmen might also aspire to be under-sheriffs and now and then even sheriffs.[39] There were no native Irish sheriffs, seneschals of liberties, serjeants, coroners, or keepers of the peace. It may also be that, just as the growth of the central courts clarified the rules about who was or was not law-worthy (to the disadvantage of the Irish), so the proliferation of county courts multiplied the points of exclusion at local level. It has been said of eighteenth-century Virginia that such courts formed 'a public forum where men and women ... were read out of the local community whose boundaries were drawn ever more narrowly during the course of the colonial period'.[40] Where Irish lords did have some claim to English tenure, as in the case of the thirteenth-century O'Briens of Thomond, suit at the county court seemed more a threat than the privilege, or mere nuisance, it might have been to an Englishman.[41] The growth of government sharpened national distinctions, magnifying the advantages the English possessed and the Irish were denied.

My second point is that this was happening at a time when the lordship of Ireland, which had on the whole been expanding down to the mid-thirteenth century, was in physical retreat. Irish legislation and other royal records of the fourteenth century betray a deep feeling of vulnerability, as the core areas of the lordship, now often referred to as the 'land of peace', were organised for defence.[42] Admittedly the

[37] *The Red Book of the Earls of Kildare*, ed. G. Mac Niocaill (Dublin, Irish MSS Commission, 1964), 104.

[38] R. Frame, 'English officials and Irish chiefs in the fourteenth century', *EHR*, XC (1975), 771-6.

[39] R. R. Davies, *Conquest, Coexistence and Change: Wales 1063–1415* (Oxford, 1987), 365, 415-17, 451-2.

[40] Morgan, v.

[41] *Close Rolls, 1251–3*, 496. In 1353, after serving the Crown in war, Cormac MacCarthy and his heirs were granted lands at a nominal rent on condition of future good behaviour and suit at the county of Cork (National Library of Ireland, MS 761, pp. 210–11). Cf. the impact of suit at county courts in Wales (Davies, *Conquest*, 380-1).

[42] R. Frame, 'War and peace in the medieval lordship of Ireland', in *The English in Medieval Ireland*, ed. J. F. Lydon (Dublin, 1984), 126-40.

English world still had a certain drawing power. Reform-minded native bishops whose dioceses lay partly within the settled regions were hostile to Irish custom; several, attending parliament by virtue of their office, assented to the Statutes of Kilkenny. More mundanely, Nicholas Mac Mael rosa, archbishop of Armagh from 1272 to 1303, brought with him into the English areas a bevy of relatives, several of whom got grants of English status, or married into the settler gentry, or both.[43] By the late fourteenth century, however, such possibilities were fading, as the beleaguered English lordship was defined and defended ever more closely; there were no native Irish primates after 1346.

In such conditions the gap between those within and beyond the legal and political frontier was emphasized. It came into clear focus on the frequent occasions when paying for defence was at issue. The lordship had no lack of fiscally-active assemblies. Its broken borders, reflecting the distribution of upland, woodland and bog, meant that communities met in county, liberty, and borough courts in order to raise money to meet local threats. At a higher level, urgency and problems of communication saw taxation granted in swiftly-summoned regional great councils. On top of that, taxes for the defence of the whole lordship became more common in parliaments from the 1340s onwards.[44] As the English assembled, and were taxed, they defined themselves against the foe whose existence justified the financial pain.

Of course there were complications. The threat often included rebel English who had crossed the political frontier; taxes could be used to hire the services of a native chief or mercenary captain; a friendly Irishman might even attend discussions of local defence, as Muiris MacMurrough, a descendant of the kings of Leinster, did at Wexford in 1312.[45] But overwhelmingly the image presented is of division along ethnic lines, as the English gathered, in the setting of their own institutions, to arrange their protection against the Irish. The language of English solidarity pervaded such occasions—though in practice solidarity might be shown as much in characteristic forms of squabbling as in common action. The writ calling a parliament to Cashel in 1371 is not untypical: the meeting was needed because the land of Ireland 'had ... suffered untold damage through the hostile incursions of [the

---

[43] J. A. Watt, *The Church and the Two Nations in Medieval Ireland* (Cambridge, 1970), 210–11; D. Maciomhair, 'Primate Mac Maoilíosa and County Louth', *Seanchas Ardmhacha*, VI (1971), 90–3; K. Simms, 'The brehons of later medieval Ireland', in *Brehons, Serjeants and Attorneys*, 54, 67–8.

[44] Richardson and Sayles, *Parliament*, 111–18; R. Frame, 'Military service in the lordship of Ireland, 1290–1360: institutions and society on the Anglo-Gaelic frontier', in *Medieval Frontier Societies*, 111–14; *Liber Primus Kilkenniensis*, ed. C. McNeill (Dublin, Irish MSS Commission, 1931), 49–50.

[45] *Cal. Just. Rolls*, II. 215–16; PRO Dublin, Just. Rolls, K.B.1/1, m.40d.

king's] Irish enemies and rebels'. Not surprisingly, the petitions of the English and the royal records present the Irish in negative terms and menacing postures.[46]

The only significant annals to survive from a local English milieu are those of the Franciscan John Clyn (d.1349), who wrote at Kilkenny. Their main interest may be in showing the complexity of relations in a mixed and turbulent region. Clyn portrays the Irish as splintered and competitive, and the English as equally riven by conflict. He makes no bones about showing cross-national alliances, or presenting some Irish lords as less wicked than others, or condemning the extended English kins of the uplands and woods whom he saw as agents of disorder. Even so, throughout his narrative the national labels are remorselessly affixed. In 1348 the *English* of Kilkenny ride in support of one candidate for the O'More chieftaincy; the *English* of Kildare come out for his rival.[47] (No doubt some of those involved were present in their county courts in the 1350s, when subsidies were granted to maintain troops against the O'Mores.[48]) In Clyn the English attract approving epithets that are the reverse of those applied to the Irish by the official documents—'the loyal English', 'the peaceful English', 'the peace-loving English'.[49] Though some were neither loyal nor peaceful, these were qualities that they, unlike the Irish, were expected to display. Practical ties with the Irish and a measure of acculturation did not stop the strengthening of a feeling of embattled Englishness among those who lived in the encircled heartlands of the lordship. The effect was similar, though drawn out longer, to that of the Glyn Dŵr rising in Wales, which fuelled the self-consciousness and exclusiveness of English communities there.[50] It has something in common with the strengthening of the British strand in the brittle self-image of Ulster Protestants during the traumatic decade 1968–78.[51]

My third point is that the reinforcement of an English identity did not take place in a vacuum. The lordship's elites were attached to England, not just by administrative links but by ties of patronage and service, and in some cases of marriage and landholding.[52] In England royal government was well able to tease practical consequences from,

[46] *Parliaments and Councils*, 38. On the terminology, see J. Lydon, 'The middle nation', in *The English in Medieval Ireland*, 19–20.

[47] *The Annals of Ireland by Friar John Clyn*, ed. R. Butler (Dublin, 1849), 37.

[48] *Rotulorum Patentium et Clausorum Cancellariae Hiberniae Calendarium*, ed. E. Tresham (Dublin, Irish Record Commission, 1828), 74 nos. 64–5, 75 nos. 92–3.

[49] *Clyn*, 17, 27, 32, 33.

[50] Davies, *Conquest*, 443, 456–9. On the Englishness of local societies in Wales and Ireland, see *idem*, 'In praise of British history', in *The British Isles*, 14.

[51] S. Wichert, *Northern Ireland since 1945* (1991), 215.

[52] Frame, *English Lordship*, 5–123.

and to exploit, national identity. At the time when the exclusion of the Irish from the courts was becoming clearer, Edward I was setting up an English administration in north Wales and giving much of Welsh law short shrift.[53] In Ireland too change was in the air. The king, encouraged by some native bishops, toyed with the idea of selling English legal status to the Irish at large; the plan foundered, probably on the opposition of the settler magnates. In 1331 Edward III did command that Irish who were personally free should have English law without needing to buy charters, but his ordinance seems to have passed quickly into oblivion.[54] Both episodes reveal the central assumption, that there was a straight choice; the boundary between the English and native worlds could not be blurred; the Irish must be outside or inside. In 1297 any English who wore the *cúlán*, the Irish warrior hairstyle, had been threatened by the Dublin parliament with the loss of their English status. When in 1333 Dermot O'Dwyer, a Gaelic lord from the south-west, was granted the king's peace and English law, he 'had the hair of his *cúlán* cut in order to hold English law'.[55] To be inside meant remaining or becoming English.

As well as being quick to employ national categories, England was infected with a ready xenophobia, partly thanks to the Scottish and French wars and the accompanying syringe of royal propaganda. It was to a metropolis where ideas of loyalty and of Englishness were closely intertwined that the inhabitants of the lordship of Ireland began to look for help in the mid-fourteenth century. At this point the English of Ireland found added to the other pressures upon them the need to catch the attention of, and prove acceptable to, a preoccupied and possibly sceptical superior authority; they had constantly to establish their patriotic credentials. One of the most quoted passages in the Latin annals kept in Dublin concerns the arrival in 1361 of Lionel of Antwerp with an army paid for by Edward III. The settlers had begged for a governor of standing, backed by troops. The annalist described the problems attendant on its arrival; his words merit close attention. Over-confident, Lionel declared that he needed no local help, and set off to fight the Irish of the hills and glens south of Dublin. To the annalist's ill-concealed glee, he lost many men and was forced to seek assistance. He then 'brought the whole people [*totum populum*], of England and of Ireland, together, and made good headway, engaging in many wars on

[53] Davies, *Conquest*, 367–70; L. B. Smith, 'The Statute of Wales, 1284', *Welsh Hist. Rev.*, X (1980), 127–54.

[54] A. J. Otway-Ruthven, 'The request of the native Irish for English law, 1277–80', *IHS*, VI (1949–50), 261–70; A. Gwynn, 'Edward I and the proposed purchase of English law for the Irish', these *Transactions*, 5th ser., X (1960), 111–27; Murphy, 120–3; Frame, '1331 Ordinance', 109–14.

[55] *Statutes, Ireland*, 210–11; *Parliaments and Councils*, 17.

all sides against the Irish, with the help of God and of the people of Ireland'. To the annalist the English of England and of Ireland formed sub-divisions of a single *populus*. The 'people of Ireland' [*populus Hibernie*] were, of course, not the Irish; they were the English of Ireland.[56]

The need of the settlers to confirm their Englishness arose at two levels, reflecting the two-stage relationship with the Crown typical of the colonial, or distant provincial, situation. The incident involving Lionel shows that an insensitive governor with a retinue from England might provoke tensions, not least over patronage and office. As in the Tudor period, the desire for help from England was accompanied by a fear of being marginalised by it.[57] Already in the 1340s the Dublin annalist had dipped his pen in gall when describing the rule of Lionel's step-father, Ralph Ufford, who, with his circle from England, had set his face against the 'indigeni', the residents.[58] Such episodes were given added dignity when described in the language of national identity. When in 1357 Edward III was about to send a new administration to the lordship, he drew up ordinances, based on petitions from Ireland, which included the following:

> although both the English born in Ireland and those born in England and dwelling in Ireland are true English, and live under our lordship and government and use the same laws, rights and customs, nevertheless various dissensions and maintenances, by reason of origin, have arisen between those born in Ireland and those born in England.[59]

Such disputes were forbidden, but that did not stop their reappearance in 1361. The Statutes of Kilkenny returned to the matter, elaborating upon the 1357 ordinance.[60] There were to be no fine shadings; if the main aim of the Statutes was to erect a wall, broken only by official crossing-points, between the English and the Irish, a second purpose was to uproot the fence that mutual jealousies were threatening to build between the settlers and those who sailed from England to their rescue.

[56] *Chartularies of St Mary's Abbey, Dublin*, ed. J. T. Gilbert (Rolls Ser. LXXX, 1884–6), II. 395. J. G. A. Pocock characterised such groups at a later period as 'subnations': 'British History: A plea for a new subject', *Journal of Modern History*, XLVII (1975), 609–10.

[57] K. S. Bottigheimer, 'Kingdom and colony: Ireland in the westward enterprise', in *The Westward Enterprise: English Activities in Ireland, the Atlantic and America 1480–1650*, ed. K. R. Andrews *et al.* (Liverpool, 1978), 46–50.

[58] *Chart. St Mary's*, II. 385; Frame, *English Lordship*, 265–6.

[59] *Statutes of the Realm*, I. 363. 'Racione nationis' is rendered as 'by reason of nationality' in *Statutes, Ireland*, 417–8; Lydon ('Middle nation', 11) prefers 'by reason of race'.

[60] *Statutes, Ireland*, 436–7.

As well as waving their Englishness in the face of unsympathetic ministers, the English of the lordship sought to reach behind them and deal with the king directly. At such times they paraded their loyalty and nationality. In 1341–2 a spectacular piece of mismanagement, in which royal grants since 1307 were to be revoked and ministers born in Ireland ejected from office, provoked a parliamentary assembly to send Edward III a long list of criticisms of his representatives. It included the declaration that:

> whereas various people of your allegiance, as of Scotland, Gascony and Wales often in time past have levied war against their liege lord, at all times your English liege people of Ireland have behaved themselves well and loyally ... holding your said land for your ancestors and yourself both against the Scots and against the Irish, your enemies.[61]

The claim was self-serving but it was not untrue. The reference to the Scots was particularly near the mark: between 1296 and the 1330s the resources of the lordship had been repeatedly mobilised for the Anglo-Scottish war, and Ireland had suffered partial occupation and extensive raids by Edward Bruce during the years after Bannockburn.[62] In seeking royal favour and protection against the Irish, the settlers could point to a record of involvement in a common English enterprise. The identity they claimed cannot be dismissed as contrived or shallow. Professions of Englishness were anchored in a past that was, like all pasts, partly invented, and also in a tangible present—in law, institutions, liberties, property, offices, and in a living tissue of political and military relationships.

What is to be made of it all? If we look for ambiguity, in the sense of admitted doubts about identity itself, we shall be disappointed. There is no trace of the way of thinking that led some Gaelic lords, petitioning the Pope in 1317, to say that the English of Ireland called themselves a 'middle nation', in between the Irish of Ireland and the English of England. The term may well have been a fabrication to allow a play on words: the settlers were, the Irish went on, 'a people, not of middling but of extreme perfidy'.[63] Yet it is hard to believe that the English of Ireland in their unbuttoned moments did not reflect along such lines. Some knew their Gerald of Wales; Gerald had meditated on the paradoxes that afflict those who settle in a new country; he has Maurice

---

[61] *Ibid.*, 342; Frame, *English Lordship*, 242–60.

[62] J. F. Lydon, in *Medieval Ireland 1169–1534*, 195–204. Cf. Linda Colley's stress on the role of the wars of 1689–1815 in generating an over-arching British identity: 'Britishness and otherness: an argument', *Journal of British Studies*, XXXI (1992), 309–29.

[63] *Scotichronicon by Walter Bower*, ed. D. E. R. Watt *et al.*, VI (Aberdeen, 1991), 392–3; comment by J. R. S. Phillips at 473–4.

fitz Gerald (in 1170!) voice the famous grumble 'we are English to the Irish, and Irish to the English'.[64] In the areas of life that I have been exploring, however, ambiguity was not an option. On the public stage one was English or nothing; earls, barons, knights, bourgeois and rural gentry had every incentive to confine brooding about identity to places where the metropolis could not eavesdrop upon them.[65]

But if radical ambiguities were absent or masked, distinctiveness was not. Even within the legal and political arena, spread before us in formulaic official documents, it is not enough, as Art Cosgrove has remarked, to view the settlers merely as 'geographically displaced English'.[66] They were indeed English—they had no other word for it— but English in their own ways. They had a particular past which shaped their perception of the present; aware of Gerald and of papal documents of the twelfth century, they could view themselves as having been placed in Ireland to bring civility to a barbarous people; *Laudabiliter*, which was quoted more than once in the early fourteenth century, had become a founding charter.[67] They had taken over St Patrick, patron of the cathedral built by Archbishops John Comyn and Henry of London, who had come to the see of Dublin from the circles of Henry II and John. That see was set, according to a petition of 1350, in 'the principal and chief city of Ireland ... where the royal seat of the king ... has been placed from ancient times'.[68] The history of the *populus Hibernie* was a distinct sub-plot to the history of the English.

Legally and constitutionally too, the English of Ireland were English after their fashion. In the thirteenth century, alongside statements that Ireland used English law, are references to 'the customs of the land of Ireland' and evidence that law on the two sides of the Irish Sea was not identical. It has been rightly said that for the most part such customs 'had ... little to do with the Gaelic world or with the special problems of conquest; they were merely older or local variations of

[64] *Expugnatio Hibernica*, 80–1; R. Flower, 'Manuscripts of Irish interest in the British Museum', *Analecta Hibernica*, II (1931), 314–17.

[65] Other contexts and evidence afford different views: Lydon, 'Middle nation', 15–17; K. Simms, 'Bards and barons', in *Medieval Frontier Societies*, 177–97; J. R. S. Phillips, 'The Remonstrance revisited: England and Ireland in the early fourteenth century', in *Men, Women and War*, ed. T. B. Fraser and K. Jeffery (Dublin, 1993), 13–16.

[66] 'Writing of Irish medieval history', 110.

[67] J. A. Watt, '*Laudabiliter* in medieval diplomacy and propaganda', *Irish Ecclesiastical Record*, 5th ser. LXXXVII (1957), 420–32; *idem*, 'Negotiations between Edward II and John XXII concerning Ireland', *IHS*, X (1956–7), 1–20; *Documents on the Affairs of Ireland before the King's Council*, ed. G. O. Sayles (Dublin, Irish MSS Commission, 1979), no. 136; *idem*, 'The legal proceedings against the first earl of Desmond', *Analecta Hibernica*. XXIII (1966), 20. On historical consciousness, see Lydon, 'Middle nation', 23, 25; R. Frame, 'England and Ireland, 1171–1399', in *England and her Neighbours 1066–1453*, ed. M. Jones and M. Vale (London, 1989), 152–3.

[68] *Documents on Ireland*, 194.

English custom brought to Ireland by the early colonists'.[69] This does not make them insignificant. To a lord in Ireland, the ability to claim, as he mostly could not in England, the wardship and marriage of his tenants by socage was an advantage worth defending. More important, the mere existence of differences gave concreteness to the idea of a custom that belonged specifically to the English of the lordship.

This notion was enlarged by the way that legislation made in England was handled. English statutes were not regarded as having force in Ireland unless they were formally sent there for publication. In the late thirteenth and fourteenth centuries this was not invariably done at once or even at all, leading a new justiciar in 1328 to advise the English council to send over recent legislation *en bloc*.[70] More than almost any other, this topic tempts us to read history backwards. In the mid-fifteenth century the application of English statutes to Ireland was to become contentious; by the seventeenth, it was the subject of a polemical literature to do with the status of the Irish parliament and of Ireland itself.[71] Such controversies should not be idly projected back to a time when practical clarity may have been the chief concern. Yet it has recently been suggested that as early as 1279 the fact that legislation was being enacted in parliaments in Ireland may have led the Crown to ask itself whether it was any longer fitting simply to order English statutes to be observed there.[72] On the other side of the sea in 1320 a parliament at Dublin, presided over by Roger Mortimer, confirmed some English statutes and agreed that:

> the other statutes made by the king and his council be read and examined before the king's council [of Ireland] between this and the next parliament and there published, and that points that are suitable for the people and the land of Ireland be from thenceforth confirmed and held, saving always the good customs and usages of the land.[73]

We may hesitate to reduce the matter to one merely of bureaucratic tidiness. By 1423 the chancellor and treasurer of Ireland could declare that English statutes were of no force unless they had been formally

---

[69] Hand, 172–86; quotation at 177.

[70] J. F. Baldwin, *The King's Council in England during the Middle Ages* (Oxford, 1913), 475.

[71] A. Cosgrove, 'Parliament and the Anglo-Irish community: the declaration of 1460', in *Parliament and Community: Historical Studies XIV*, ed. A. Cosgrove and J. I. McGuire (Belfast, 1983), 25–30.

[72] P. A. Brand, 'King, church and property: the enforcement of restrictions on alienation in mortmain in the lordship of Ireland in the later middle ages', *Peritia*, III (1984), 483–7, 500.

[73] *Statutes, Ireland*, 280–3.

transmitted to Ireland *and* published in the Irish parliament.[74] This was a selective reading of the recent past.[75] But it reminds us that the lordship was a land whose customs, while English in essence, were distinct, and might at moments be shielded by regnal institutions of a sort that the provinces of England lacked.

There is a further point that should not be overlooked. From the late 1270s onwards there survives much legislation peculiar to Ireland, promulgated in local parliaments and great councils. Legal historians have not shown much interest in this material, which was primarily practical and mostly took English legal principles for granted.[76] Typically, it dealt with matters such as military preparedness, local truce-making, trafficking with the Irish, or the duty of aristocratic heads of kins to hand felonious dependents over to the courts. Behind everything lay the Irish whose law, with its distresses in the form of cattle-raids and its provision for compensation by kin-groups, was seen as contagious and little better than the 'mutual slaughter' referred to by the Pope two centuries before. The Statutes of Kilkenny gathered up such ordinances, and went further by presenting an image of an English world under cultural as well as military siege; its defence was to involve the subjecting of contacts of all sorts, from marriage and the fostering of children to the movements of minstrels, to official monitoring.[77]

Law in Ireland, while it embodied an English identity and served as a vehicle for its preservation, also, as in colonial America, reflected the particularity of the local experience.[78] The two faces of the English of Ireland are neatly juxtaposed when in the early fifteenth century keepers of the peace were charged to observe and enforce the Statute of Winchester, and the Statutes of Kilkenny. At the same period the Statutes of Kilkenny were confirmed in parliament, along with the liberties of the Church, and on at least one occasion in the same breath as Magna Carta.[79]

By the mid-fourteenth century key elements of a differentiated form

---

[74] PRO Dublin, Calendar of Memoranda Rolls, R.C.8/39, 158–91, at 188, 190–1. The case turned upon statutes of 1 and 2 Hen. IV concerning petitions for royal grants (*Statutes of the Realm*, II. 113, 120–1).

[75] Some writs sending legislation to Ireland imply that nothing was needed save a royal order to have it enrolled and proclaimed (*Statutes, Ireland*, 296–305, 492–9, 528–59); others hint at publication in parliament or, as in 1320, selection according to perceived relevance (230–1, 506–7).

[76] Though see G.J. Hand, 'The forgotten statutes of Kilkenny: a brief survey', *Irish Jurist*, I (1966), 299–312.

[77] *Statutes, Ireland*, 194–213, 258–77, 280–91, 306–9, 374–97, 430–69.

[78] Cf. Warren M. Billings, 'The transfer of English law to Virginia, 1606–50', in *The Westward Enterprise*, 228; Morgan, esp. 2–5.

[79] *Rot. Pat.*, 209 no. 192, 221 no. 110; National Library of Ireland, Harris Collectanea, MS 4, fo. 223d; *Statutes, Ireland*, 504–7, 520–1.

of English political identity existed in Ireland. They included a sense of history, linked with a sense of place; a distinctive variant of English law and custom; facsimiles of English royal institutions, including parliament, that could at times be used for purposes other than those intended by the king or his ministers; and a clutch of preoccupations (from dealings with an omnipresent native population to relations with a far-away ruler) that amounted to a unique political agenda. Indeed the Anglo-Irish relationship already betrays several of the frictions regarded as characteristic of the early modern multiple state.[80] Moments of stress, when province and metropolis were out of step politically, had given birth to a terminology through which the identity particular to the English domiciled in Ireland could be articulated. Its appearance is no small matter. Just as the fourteenth century was influenced by twelfth-century documents and histories, so the sixteenth century copied and paraphrased the Dublin annals, with their references to disputes between the English born in Ireland and the English born in England.[81] As Steven Ellis has said, the Tudor period in Ireland 'built on the political vocabulary of an earlier age'.[82]

In emphasising these characteristics I do not for a moment mean to suggest that the English of Ireland were neatly distinguishable from the English of England, or that they formed a community with a steady self-awareness and consistent attitudes. Like all such constructs, the settler identity has a way of evaporating once exposed to the deeds of real people in specific situations. A glance at the confrontation of 1341–2, where that identity seems first to have been coherently expressed, quickly disturbs any grand assumptions. The messengers chosen to convey to Edward III the anger his subjects in Ireland felt against his agents were the new, English-born Prior of the Hospitallers in Ireland, and the heir of a recent justiciar of Ireland, whose origins lay in Pembrokeshire and who still held lands in Wales and kept up a position at court. The ministers who feared they might be ousted, and lurked beneath the phrase 'the English born in Ireland', included some whose ties with the lordship were recent.[83] As in later disputes, the quarrel may have been more between yesterday's men, whatever their origins,

---

[80] M. Perceval-Maxwell, 'Ireland and the monarchy in the early Stuart multiple kingdom', *Historical Journal*, XXXIV (1991), 279–95; J. H. Elliott, 'A Europe of composite monarchies', *Past and Present*, CXXXVII (1992), 48–71; Frame, *Political Development*, 179–87, 197.

[81] E.g. *Jacobi Grace Kilkenniensis Annales Hiberniae*, ed. R. Butler (Dublin, 1842), 132–5, 150–3; *Calendar of Carew MSS. Book of Howth*, ed. J. S. Brewer and W. Bullen (London, 1871), 162, 168; *Holinshed's Irish Chronicle 1577*, ed. L. Miller and E. Power (Dublin, 1978), 226, 230–1.

[82] 'Nationalist historiography', 12.

[83] Frame, *English Lordship*, 105–6, 246–7, 253.

and tomorrow's, than between clean-cut national sub-groups.[84]

The link between the sections of the Dublin establishment who felt threatened with removal from office and the wider settler elite is also problematical. The Dublin annals stress that the movement against royal officials included both 'the magnates of the land' and the 'mayors of the royal cities', and imply that the earl of Desmond was associated with it.[85] The emphasis on unanimity suggests that it was uncommon; it arose because the circumstances—a threatened assault on property rights, including those of the Hospital, going back more than thirty years—were themselves unprecedented. It embraced people who usually had more to separate than to unite them, and whose conduct was rarely dominated by a sense of shared Englishness. During the 1330s and 1340s juries from Limerick and other towns and counties repeatedly indicted Desmond of oppression and of treasonable collusion with the Irish.[86] It is true that the nobles of the lordship may now and then be found acting as spokesmen for the English of Ireland—as when the earl of Ormond helped to procure Lionel of Antwerp's rescue expedition in 1360–1.[87] But their value in this role (or in their function as border magnates) sprang from the very width of their ties, which might take in English aristocratic society just as they did the native Irish world: when Ormond visited one of his Surrey manors in 1358, with him were his mother, Eleanor de Bohun, a grand-daughter of King Edward I, and also Edmund O'Kennedy, a native Irish lord from north Tipperary whom he was holding in honourable captivity.[88]

Upon inspection categories blur, solidarities fragment, horizons contract within local or sectional bounds, or expand far beyond the habitat of the English of Ireland. This is no more than we should expect; it does not render the words and ideas present in the sources insignificant. In thirteenth-century England nationality was employed to interpret political events, most notably by Matthew Paris in his descriptions of the resentment the barons of England felt against the 'foreigners' who were prominent at the court of Henry III. In fact political alignments can be shown to have been much more complex than Matthew allows: in 1258 one alien group was destroyed by an alliance between some barons of England and members of another alien group, and strong cultural and familial ties continued to bind the upper classes of England

---

[84] Connolly, 'Financing of expeditions', 108; D. Johnston, 'The interim years: Richard II and Ireland, 1395–1399', in *England and Ireland*, 184–8.

[85] *Chart. St Mary's*, II. 383.

[86] Sayles, 'Legal proceedings', 5–46.

[87] Frame, *English Lordship*, 319–22.

[88] *Calendar of Ormond Deeds, 1350–1413*, ed. E. Curtis (Dublin, Irish MSS Commission, 1934), no. 46.

and France together.[89] Yet it matters that such terms and explanatory patterns made sense to the writer and to the audience he envisaged. We should not deny to medieval men the complex layers of identity and the ability to live with inconsistencies that we take for granted in ourselves.[90]

Even in the 1340s the shrill tones in which the settlers asserted their Englishness disguised an anxiety that marks them off from their complacent metropolitan cousins.[91] In the fifteenth century, when the Crown's commitment to Ireland shrank disturbingly,[92] their unease may have seemed well founded. They protested, for instance, about attempts to exclude them from the inns of court; and in 1440 a hard struggle was needed to persuade the English government to remove them from the schedule of those taxed as aliens—a nice irony since the Dublin government was still granting charters of English law and liberty to native Irishmen.[93] Yet it would be rash to jump to the conclusion that the behaviour of individuals and groups can be *explained* by reference to 'Anglo-Irish attitudes' or a 'colonial mentality' cooked up from selected ingredients by the historian. The existence of a distinctive, and increasingly problematical, 'consciousness' cannot be disregarded; but it needs to be viewed in the light of the evidence of the practical complications and contradictions of 'being'. We are faced on the one hand by overlapping outlooks and ties, among which the sense of being English in Ireland was but one; and on the other by what J. H. Hexter has called 'intractible [sic] men, and angular and resistant events'.[94] The real interest lies in the interplay between them—in its awkward incongruities, but also in the transient, yet revealing, moments of apparent symmetry.

[89] M. T. Clanchy, *England and its Rulers 1066–1272* (1983), 140–1, 185, 241–62; D. A. Carpenter, 'What happened in 1258?', in *War and Government in the Middle Ages*, ed. J. Gillingham and J. C. Holt (Woodbridge, 1984), 109–17; H. Ridgeway, 'King Henry III and the "Aliens", 1236–1272', *Thirteenth Century England*, II (1988), 81–92; M. Vale, *The Angevin Legacy and the Hundred Years War 1250–1340* (Oxford, 1990), ch. 2.

[90] Cf. Reynolds, 330–1; Colley, 314–5.

[91] Cf. M. Zuckerman, 'The fabrication of identity in early America', *William and Mary Quarterly*, XXXIV (1977), 200.

[92] E. Matthew, 'The financing of the lordship of Ireland under Henry V and Henry VI', in *Property and Politics: Essays on Later Medieval England*, ed. A. J. Pollard (Gloucester, 1984), 107–8.

[93] *Statutes, Ireland*, 574–5; Cosgrove, 'Parliament', 34; Murphy, 125.

[94] *On Historians* (1979), 242.

THE ORIGINS OF THE GOTHIC REVIVAL: A REAPPRAISAL

The Alexander Prize Essay

By Giles Worsley

READ 29 MAY 1992

FOR the past 40 years the dominant influence over architectural history, and in particular over stylistic analysis, has been the Modern Movement. Sometimes deliberately, sometimes unconsciously, architectural history has been seen through the teleological spectacles of the Modernists who viewed architecture as a progressive force leading inevitably towards the ultimate triumph of Modernism. At its most obvious this can be seen in studies of late-nineteenth- and early-twentieth-century architecture which concentrated on those strands that could be said to have been the precursors of Modernism, while ignoring powerful contemporary factors which do not fit in with the Modernist thesis, like the strength of Classical architecture in the 1930s. But even when discussing earlier periods the same basic assumption has prevailed, that architectural style should be seen as progressive. Thus what became important was identifying new fashions and tracing the precedents. As architectural style always moved on, anything that was not innovative or seemed to be regressive was assumed to be old fashioned and the result of ignorance or lack of skill, and consequently of little interest. With the collapse of Modernism, or at least of the assumption that Modernism is the only acceptable way in which to build, and with the revival of older styles which 10 years ago were thought to be dead and buried, this teleological approach to architectural history needs revision. The study of Gothic Revival architecture in England is one area that is revolutionised by the removal of Modernist assumptions.

The incidence of Gothic Revival architecture in England has generally been marginalised by architectural historians. Examples in the seventeenth century are usually seen as 'Gothic Survival', the assumption being that the designer knew no better, while the standard account of the Gothic Revival in the eighteenth century commonly starts with Horace Walpole and Strawberry Hill—indeed the style is often described as 'Strawberry Hill Gothic'—with perhaps a nod at William Kent's Gothic designs. The Gothic work of Sir Christopher Wren and the Office of Works is acknowledged but seen to be without issue.[1] However, once the teleological spectacles of Modernism are removed it is possible to see the Gothic Revival in a very different light. Instead of being a brief, rather frivolous, episode of the 1750s it can be seen as a continuous undercurrent in English architecture from the sixteenth century. It ceases to be a stylistic footnote and becomes a document of antiquarian ideals and aspirations. Indeed, one could question the very concept of the Gothic Revival and argue that one should instead be talking of the continuing Gothic tradition.

During the middle years of the sixteenth century English builders and patrons began to demonstrate a firm grasp of Classical architecture at places like Lacock Abbey, Wiltshire (1540), Somerset House, London (1547), Kirby Hall, Northamptonshire (1570), and Longleat, Wiltshire (1573) (Fig 1), but this incipient Renaissance appears to have petered out in the 1570s, leading John Aubrey to complain a century later that 'under Elizabeth architecture made no progress but rather went backwards.'[2] This relatively pure Classicism was superseded by a style inspired more by late-Perpendicular buildings, particularly those associated with the court of Henry VII and the young Henry VIII. But as Mark Girouard suggested in an important early article,[3] this should not be seen as regression but as a deliberate stylistic choice. Three examples illustrate the point: Burghley House, Northamptonshire, Snape Castle, Yorkshire, and Wardour Castle, Wiltshire.

William Cecil, who began building Burghley House in 1556, would have been quite capable of obtaining a Classical scheme had he wanted one. Created lord Burghley in 1571 and lord high treasurer in 1572, he was the most powerful man in Elizabethan England. The early work at Burghley has strong Classical elements; in particular the chapel staircase dated 1560 is one of the most important early Classical interiors in the country (Fig 2). However, the later work, especially the west front of 1577 with its great central gatehouse (Fig 3), deliberately harks back to pre-Classical, early-Tudor and even medieval buildings. This is particularly clear in the impressively-large hammer-beamed great hall (Fig 4), and in the kitchen which is probably modelled on the monastic kitchen at Ely. It was not only through architecture that lord

---

[1] The standard account of British architectural history of this period remains *Architecture in Britain 1530–1830* by Sir John Summerson, first published in 1953 but extensively revised since. The most recent study of the Gothic Revival is *The Origins of the Gothic Revival* by Michael McCarthy (1987). This sets out to shift attention away from Horace Walpole but in the end concentrates primarily on Walpole and his circle.

[2] Quoted by Mark Girouard, 'Elizabethan Architecture and the Gothic Tradition', *Architectural History*, VI (1963), 30. Figures referred to in the text are printed after the text, beginning on page 122. Copyright in these illustrations belongs to *Country Life*.

[3] Mark Girouard, *Robert Smythson and the Elizabethan Country House*, 1983, 30–35.

Burghley tried to present an image of respectable antiquity. An elaborate but spurious pedigree commissioned by Burghley from the heralds survives at Hatfield House, 'proving' that his ancestry stretched back into the mists of time. Illustrating this is a scene of two armoured knights fighting, one a putative Cecil ancestor. All this makes sense of Burghley's lavish tomb in St Martin's Church, Stamford, which depicts him clad in full armour, an incongruous image for a statesman, but not for a man trying to stress his family's medieval origins. In fact Burghley's origins were relatively humble, to which he remained sensitive, despite holding the highest offices of state. Thus the earl of Northumberland's suggestion that Burghley's line would benefit if it 'were planted in some stocke of honour' fell on receptive ears, and Burghley quickly agreed to a proposed marriage between his eldest son Thomas and Northumberland's sister-in-law Dorothy Neville. The marriage took place in 1564, and in 1577 the young couple inherited the manor house at Snape in Yorkshire. As if to stress this link with one of England's oldest families, Thomas Cecil transformed the substantial but unfortified manor house into a sham castle, complete with crenellations and towers, although surviving fragments show that the internal decoration was carried out in an advanced Classical manner (Fig 5).[4]

Cecil's remodelling of Snape Castle makes an interesting comparison with Robert Smythson's luxurious remodelling of fourteenth-century Wardour Castle for Sir Matthew Arundell in the 1570s. Smythson would have had no difficulty working in a purely Classical manner. Longleat was being erected to his designs at the same time, while many of the details at Wardour such as the doorcases are accurately Classical, as they were at Snape (Fig 6). But when he came to rewindow the castle he deliberately kept the two-storey Gothic windows lighting the great hall, and used arched lights separated by mullions only for the new windows—a clear Gothic form which contrasted with the fashion of the 1570s for square-headed mullion and transom openings (Fig 7).[5] Arundell's medievalising attitude towards Wardour can probably be explained by his parentage. His father had risen to considerable wealth from a humble gentry background before being attainted on the disgrace of the duke of Somerset in 1554, while he himself had so increased his fortune that by 1588 he was one of twelve knights listed as being of 'great possessions' and rich enough to support a peerage. Such a dizzy rise would inevitably have brought accusations that he was an upstart, and it is not surprising that Arundell would have wanted to associate himself with the middle ages.

[4] Giles Worsley, 'Snape Castle, Yorkshire,' *Country Life*, 6 Mar. 1986.
[5] Mark Girouard, 'Wardour Castle, Wiltshire–I', *Country Life*, 14 Feb. 1991.

As Dr Girouard has shown, this Gothic Revival in architecture was part of a wider revival of interest in the middle ages to be found among courtiers in the latter part of Queen Elizabeth's reign. This expressed itself in such medieval obsessions as heraldry, pedigrees, elaborate tournaments and a chivalric cult concentrated on the queen. It was a fascination which spilled over into the next reign where it can be seen in the Jacobean sham castles of Lulworth, Dorset (1608), Bolsover, Derbyshire (1612) and Ruperra, Glamorgan (1626). Bolsover in particular, which was built on the site of a genuine castle, has a markedly medieval feel with its extensive use of vaulting and its Gothic-leaning chimney pieces.

However, although Elizabethan architecture is marked by a deliberate move away from Classicism in form if not always in detail, and a return to earlier, essentially Gothic styles, the clash between Classical and Gothic is less marked than it was to be in the seventeenth and eighteenth centuries. Houses like Longleat show that Classicism had been understood in England, but as the Gothic tradition was still very recent it was not difficult to revive it during Elizabeth's reign. Indeed it could almost be seen as a natural continuation of an earlier style. The firm establishment of a Classical tradition by Inigo Jones in the years leading up to the civil war changed this perspective. Classicism became accepted as the 'correct' style, the only style in which it was respectable to build, while Gothic architecture was dismissed, in John Evelyn's words, as 'heavy, dark, melancholy and Monkish Piles, without any just Proportion, Use or Beauty compared with the truly Ancient'.[6] For the rest of the seventeenth century and for nearly all the eighteenth century the undisputed preeminence of Classical architecture was accepted by all educated men. During these years anyone who chose to use Gothic designs did so as a deliberate reaction against Classicism.

Inigo Jones had no time for Gothic architecture, and no qualms about encasing the nave of St Paul's Cathedral in Classical dress. His contemporary Palladian enthusiast Henry Wotton was outspoken in his contempt, arguing that pointed arches 'both for the natural imbecility of the sharp angle itself, and likewise for their very uncomeliness, ought to be exiled from judicious eyes, and left to their first inventors, the Goths or Lombards, amongst other relics of that barbarous age'.[7] But this did not prevent the fellows of Oxford and Cambridge deliberately commissioning buildings incorporating Gothic elements. During the first half of the seventeenth century, and particularly during the 1630s, Oxford saw a whole sequence of Gothic buildings including the chapel windows and hammer-beam roof of the hall at Wadham (1608–10), the

[6] John Evelyn, *An Account of Architects and Architecture*, 1723, 9.
[7] Henry Wotton, *The Elements of Architecture*, 1624, 51.

purely Perpendicular chapel of Lincoln (1629–31) (Fig 8), the chapel
windows of Jesus (1621 and 1636) and the hall and chapel of St Mary
Hall (1637–42).[8] It has been questioned whether this was the result of
Gothic Survival—that is Gothic was the only style known to the fellows
and their craftsmen—or Revival—that is the fellows deliberately chose
Gothic rather than Classical. It seems clear that the latter is the case.
Members of the university were certainly aware of alternative styles, as
can be seen from a proposed plan for University College of about 1634
which would have produced a Classical quadrangle with three projecting
porticos. It was rejected in favour of the executed scheme which is
essentially Gothic in inspiration.[9] But, as Sir Nikolaus Pevsner has
pointed out, it is the example of St John's College, Cambridge, which
proves the point. Here the new library, built in 1624, was deliberately
given traceried Gothic windows on the grounds that 'some men of
judgement liked the best the old fashion of church window, holding it
most meet for such a building'. The statement was made by the donor
of the library, Bishop Williams of Lincoln, who also paid for the pure
Perpendicular chapel of Lincoln College, Oxford. The strength of the
Gothic tradition in Oxford and Cambridge probably arises from
antiquarian leanings, but also from dislike of radical changes.

However, it is with the Commonwealth that one first finds a positive
rejection of Classicism. Few people could have been as exposed to
Jonesian Classicism as Lady Anne Clifford whose second husband, the
4th earl of Pembroke, was the builder of Wilton, the greatest of the
Caroline Classical houses. And yet, when she retired on his death to
her ancestral Clifford estates in Yorkshire and Westmorland during the
Commonwealth, she deliberately put that Classicism behind her. In a
positive orgy of building intended to reassert Clifford influence in the
area, Lady Anne set about restoring the family castles of Skipton,
Brough, Brougham, Appleby, Pendragon and Barden Tower, at the
same time rebuilding or repairing the associated churches of St Lawren-
ce's and St Michael's, Appleby; Outhgill, Mallerstang; St Ninian's near
Penrith; St Michael's Brough; and St Wilfred's, Brougham (Fig 9). New
work on both the castles and the churches was in a suitably medieval
manner. At Skipton Castle, for instance, she restored the towers, which
had been slighted at the end of the civil war, to their original height,
while at Brough the windows were restored to match the existing
Norman windows in the keep (Fig 10). All the churches were executed
in a Gothic manner without a trace of the Classicism which she would
have been quite capable of imposing on her workmen had she so

---

[8] Jennifer Sherwood and Nikolaus Pevsner, *The Buildings of England, Oxfordshire*, 1974, 35.
[9] Howard Colvin, *Unbuilt Oxford*, 1983, 10–12.

wanted.[10] Instead she wished to stress the antiquity of the Clifford line and its connections with the great families of medieval England, the Lucys, Berkeleys, Nevilles and Percys, something which she did through an obsessive use of heraldry—there are seventeen shields of arms on her father's tomb, twenty-four on her own. This could best be done by using the Gothic style and ignoring Classicism.

An equally overt statement was made by Sir Robert Shirley when he built an almost pure Perpendicular church at Staunton Harold, Leicestershire, from 1653 (Fig 11). Shirley succeeded to the baronetcy and his estate on the death of his brother in 1646 when he was only seventeen, and shortly afterwards inherited substantial sums on the death of his uncle the earl of Essex. He soon proved himself a devoted Royalist who continued to conspire even after the king's execution. The result was a succession of spells in the Tower of London where he died in 1656.[11] Shirley's motivation in building such a church is made clear on an inscription over the west entrance: 'In the yeare: 1653 when all things sacred were throughout ye nation Either demolisht or profaned Sr Richard Shirley Barronet Founded this Church whose singular praise it is to have done the best of things in ye worst times And hoped them in the most callamitous. The Righteous shall be had in everlasting remembrance.' For a Royalist to build a church during these years was clearly an act of defiance, but that defiance was made even more overt by the choice of Gothic when it would have been possible to find craftsmen who could have built the church in a Classical manner, as happened at the contemporary church at Berwick-upon-Tweed.

It is not surprising that Shirley should have chosen an Anglican church as his symbol of defiance, for under the Commonwealth the Church of England suffered severely, and this was particularly true of the bishops whose offices were abolished and estates and palaces sold. Those returning at the Restoration often found their palaces badly neglected or partly demolished, and as a result the bishops were among the most active builders in the early 1660s. The most noteworthy example of this was the rebuilding of the great hall at Lambeth Palace, the archbishop of Canterbury's London seat, by Archbishop Juxon in 1660–63 (Fig 12). The use of Gothic traceried windows and a hammer-beam roof has led some commentators to assume that Juxon was unable to find an architect capable of designing a pure Classical building.[12] But contemporary work in a similar vein by other bishops suggests that

[10] John Charlton, 'The Lady Anne Clifford (1590–1676)' *Ancient Monuments and their Interpretation*. ed. M. R. Apted *et al.*, 1977, 303–14; Thomas Cocke, 'Repairer of the Breach', *Country Life*, 25 Oct. 1990.

[11] *Dictionary of the National Biography*, XVIII, 137–38.

[12] Richard Haslam, 'Lambeth Palace, London–II', *Country Life*, 25 Oct. 1990.

Juxon deliberately chose this style. At Durham Cathedral Bishop Cosin installed new woodwork in 1663–65 that is Gothic in form with some renaissance detail, the finest surviving example being the great font (Fig 13).[13] In the castle at Durham Cosin restored the great hall in 1662–63 and specifically ordered that the windows of his new staircase tower should match those of the tower at the other end of the north front with their pre-Classical hoodmoulds, mullions and arched lights.[14] At his other palace of Bishop Auckland, County Durham, Cosin had to make good the damage done by Sir Arthur Haselrigg, including the demolition of the chapel. Cosin converted the twelfth-century hall into a chapel, refacing the exterior, adding the clerestory (Fig 14) and commissioning new woodwork (Fig 15), all in a markedly Gothic manner. He also turned the presence chamber into his great hall.[15] At Bishopthorpe Palace, Yorkshire, the archbishop of York, Accepted Frewen, found the thirteenth-century great hall and chapel in ruins. He could have abandoned them and lived in the extensive north wing or rebuilt the palace to a Classical plan. Instead, like Cosin, he maintained the archaic medieval plan, restored the chapel and rebuilt the great hall.[16] Similarly, the cathedral at Lichfield, Staffordshire, had been extensively damaged during the civil war losing its spire and much of its roof. Between 1662 and 1669 it was restored by Bishop Hacket in a Gothic manner, with even the spire being rebuilt.[17]

Had these bishops wanted to build in a Classical manner there would have been no shortage of craftsmen capable of doing so, for knowledge of Classicism was widely distributed by the 1660s, even if the understanding may have been limited. Indeed, the combination of Gothic forms with quite pure Classical elements, which had been anticipated in the chapel and library at Brasenose College, Oxford, built in 1656–66, makes it clear that this mixed style was deliberate. The bishops must have chosen to maintain medieval models, in particular the great hall which secular peers were abandoning, and use Gothic forms, to emphasise the antiquity of their buildings and so reassert episcopal continuity after the unfortunate break forced by the Commonwealth.[18]

[13] Nikolaus Pevsner, *The Buildings of England, County Durham*, 1983, 195–99.

[14] *Ibid.*, 213–17; Marcus Binney, 'Durham Castle, Co. Durham', *Country Life*, 28 Sept. 1991.

[15] John Cornforth, 'Auckland Castle, Co. Durham I and II', *Country Life*, 27 Jan. and 3 Feb. 1972.

[16] Giles Worsley, 'Bishopthorpe Palace, York', *Country Life*, 18 July 1991.

[17] *Victoria County History, Stafford* XIV, 1990, 52.

[18] This mixed style was not confined to England. An interesting parallel can be found in contemporary Italian projects for completing the facades of Gothic churches, as in the designs of Girolamo Rainaldi for S. Petronio, Bologna (1626), and those of Francesco Castelli and Carlo Buzzi for the Duomo in Milana of 1648 and 1653. (Rudolf Wittkower, *Gothic vs Classic*, New York, 1974, figs. 60–67, 111.) John Onians also sheds valuable light

By the time the new Bishop's Palace at Lichfield was built in 1685–89 this sensitivity had worn off, and the design is unambiguously Classical.

For the rest of the seventeenth century the stream of the Gothic Revival runs thin but does not dry up.[19] These decades saw the final triumph of Classicism as it spread to all levels of building across the whole country, but the Gothic Revival continued in two branches, in domestic architecture, where the antiquarian interests of a number of aristocrats were expressed in medievalising references, and in public buildings, especially ecclesiastical architecture, where respect for existing fabric meant that alterations were carried out in a sympathetic style.

Henry Mordaunt, 2nd earl of Peterborough, was fascinated by his ancestors, and in 1685 published *Succinct Genealogies*, a genealogical study of them under the pseudonym 'Robert Halstead'. This included a series of plates of horsemen in armour (Fig 16) which were repeated as overdoors at Drayton House, Peterborough's medieval Northamptonshire seat which he refers several times to in *Succinct Genealogies* as 'the old castle at Drayton'. It was in fact a fortified manor house, but Peterborough emphasised its castle-air by adding a new castellated gatehouse between 1660 and 1676 (Fig 17).[20] A similar antiquarian impulse but on a much more massive scale lay behind Hugh May's remodelling of Windsor Castle for Charles II between 1675 and 1684. This is chiefly famed for its elaborate baroque interiors which contrasted markedly with May's gaunt exteriors (Fig 18). There was no stylistic or financial reason—£200,000 was spent on Windsor—why May should not have also designed elaborate baroque facades, at least to the upper ward.[21] Instead he chose to emphasise their castle-like feel by designing round-headed windows with a deliberately neo-Norman feel. There was probably more to this than respect for the antiquity of the castle. Windsor's particular significance was that it was the seat of the Order of the Garter, the oldest of Europe's chivalric orders. Charles II's remodelling was intended to stress this, as can be seen from the fact that the largest and most lavish of the interiors was St George's Hall, scene of the annual festivities of the order. On the outside the one decorative feature was the monumental gilt Garter star on the north front. May's medieval air emphasised this chivalric association.

---

on the use of combined Classical and Gothic schemes in Renaissance Italy in *Bearers of Meaning*, Cambridge, 1988.

[19] It could be argued that the towers added to Westwood Park, Worcestershire, by Sir John Packington in the 10 years after the Civil War in a manner which accurately follows the form of the original design of about 1598 follows this inspiration. Packington like Shirley was a determined Royalist, and Westwood was the home of numerous High Church Anglicans during the Civil War.

[20] John Cornforth, 'Drayton House, Northamptonshire–II', *Country Life*, 20 May 1965.

[21] Kerry Downes, *English Baroque Architecture*, 1966, 16.

On a smaller scale Hampton Court, Herefordshire, was given a symmetrical castellated north front between 1706 and 1717 by Lord Coningsby, who was similarly obsessed with the middle ages and his forebears (Fig 19).[22] This can be compared with the 1st earl of Macclesfield's rebuilding of Shirburn Castle, Oxfordshire, between 1716 and 1725 (Fig 20). A symmetrical moated castle with four corner turrets, Shirburn is built around a medieval core, but most of one tower and all of two others, together with the walls that link them, are Macclesfield's work.[23] All these examples are based on medieval work, unlike Clearwell Castle, Gloucestershire, which was designed in a similar vein for Thomas Wyndham in 1728, but on a virgin site.[24]

The other Gothic strand was dominated by the Office of Works. Sir Christopher Wren was the first English Classical architect to argue that Gothic buildings should be completed or repaired in a manner sympathetic to the original. The Sheldonian Theatre in Oxford, built in 1663–69, is one of Wren's earliest works. It is designed in a firm Classical manner, but opposite it is a doorway surmounted by a Gothic ogee inserted into the fifteenth-century Divinity Schools in 1669, almost certainly by Wren. This is the first sign of a principle which Wren was later to enunciate when asked to complete Tom Tower at Christ Church, Oxford in 1681 (Fig 21), that it 'ought to be Gothick to agree with the Founders worke'.[25]

The Divinity School door was the first in a long series of Gothic works, often of remarkable ambition, carried out by Wren and his colleagues at the Office of Works, Nicholas Hawksmoor and William Dickinson, together with John James who, while never holding an Office of Works position, was closely connected with both Wren and Hawksmoor. One of the earliest and most ambitious of these was St Mary Aldermary in the City of London (1681), with shallow domes intended to look like fan vaulting (Fig 22). Here Wren's Gothic design was at the specific request of the donor who specified that the new church be an exact imitation of what had stood before. This was followed by St Alban, Wood Street, City of London (1682); designs for rebuilding St Mary's, Warwick, after the fire of 1694 (these were not executed but the church as rebuilt by Sir William Wilson was Gothic); St Dunstan-in-the-East, City of London, which was 'new beautified' with windows and steeple 'of modern Gothic' in 1698; extensive repairs,

[22] John Cornforth, 'Hampton Court, Herefordshire', *Country Life*, 20 and 29 Feb. 1973.
[23] Timothy Mowl and Brian Earnshaw, 'The Origins of 18th Century Neo-Medievalism in a Georgian Norman Castle', *Journal of the Society of Architectural Historians*, XL:4, D639, Dec. 1981, 289–94.
[24] Alistair Rowan, 'Clearwell Castle, Gloucestershire', in *The Country Seat*, ed. H. M. Colvin and J. Harris, 1970, 145–49.
[25] Wren Society, Oxford, 1928, V, 17.

including rebuilding the front of the north transept, at Westminster Abbey between 1698 and 1722 (Fig 23); the tower of St Christopher-le-Stocks, City of London (1712); the tower of St Michael, Cornhill, City of London, begun by Wren in 1715 but completed by Hawksmoor in 1718–22; Hawksmoor's north quadrangle of All Souls' College, Oxford, 1716–35 (Fig 24); the west towers at Westminster Abbey begun by Hawksmoor in 1735 and completed by James in 1745; and the repair, recasing and raising of the tower of St Margaret's, Westminster, by James in 1735.

Like most architects throughout the eighteenth century, neither Wren nor his colleagues had any doubts about the superiority of Classical architecture. Indeed it was Wren's Classical belief in the need for a building to be uniform that lay behind his acceptance of Gothic, as he explained when putting forward plans for the restoration of Westminster Abbey in 1713: 'I have made a Design, which will not be very expensive but light, and still in the Gothick Form, and of a Style with the rest of the Structure, which I would strictly adhere to, throughout the whole Intention: to deviate from the old Form, would be to run into a disagreeable Mixture, which no Person of a good Taste could relish ... For all these new Additions I have prepared perfect Draughts and Models, such as I conceive may agree with the original Scheme of the old Architect, without any modern Mixtures to shew my own inventions.'[26]

John James's comments on Lincoln Cathedral show a similar desire to remain in keeping. Called in at the same time as James Gibbs in 1726, he suggested 'making the heads of all the apertures ... with the pointed angular arch ... after the Gothick manner in which the whole Church is built [rather] than the semicircular arch as drawn by Mr Gibbs, and consequently the ornaments about them of the same style. For structural reasons both James and Gibbs suggested removing the spires on the west towers, but James thought that Gibbs's proposed cupolas would not 'add any beauty, [and] may do great mischief', suggesting instead 'thin peramidal acroteria [in the corners], after the Gothick manner'.[27]

However, when Wren stated that Tom Tower should be Gothic 'to agree with the Founder's work'[28] he was revealing a secondary motiv-ation on top of the Classical idea of congruity, which fits closely with the antiquarian attitude discussed above, a historical respect for the founder of the college. Hawksmoor repeated the point in his explanation of the designs for All Souls' in 1715: 'I must ask Leave to Say Somthing

[26] Christopher Wren, *Parentalia*, 1750, 302.

[27] Quoted by Terry Friedman, *James Gibbs*, 1984, 199–200.

[28] Wren Society, Oxford, 1928, V, 17.

in favour of ye Old Quadrangle, built by your most Revd founder, for altho this may have Some faults yet it is not without its virtues. This building is Strong and durable much more firm than any of Your New buildings, because they have not ye Substance nor Workmanship, and I am Confident that much Conveniency and beauty, may be added to it, wheras utterly destroying or barbarously altering or mangleing it, wou'd be useing ye founder Cruelly, and a Loss to ye present possessours.'[29] In an age when respect for an institution or a family was significantly enhanced by its antiquity, it is not surprising that the importance of preserving and enhancing buildings which demonstrated that antiquity was to be an important element in the use of Gothic architecture in the eighteenth century as it seems to have been in the seventeenth century.

This Office of Works Gothic tradition is often seen as a self-contained episode,[30] but William Kent's early Gothic work needs to be placed firmly within it. Though Kent's use of Gothic detail may differ from that of Wren, Hawksmoor, Dickinson and James—as they do from each other—the spirit remains the same.

Kent, who returned to England in 1719 and joined the Office of Works that year, would have been well aware of the extensive Gothic work, particularly that in Westminster, of Hawksmoor and James in the 1720s and 1730s. His own Gothic work—a gateway in the Clock Court at Hampton Court (1732), a screen enclosing the Courts of Chancery and the King's Bench in Westminster Hall (1739), a pulpit and choir furniture in York Minster (1741), a choir screen in Gloucester Cathedral (1741)—shows a similar pattern of alterations in a sympathetic manner to ancient royal or ecclesiastical buildings. Indeed Juliet Allan's account of Kent's work at Hampton Court stresses his debt to Wren's Tom Tower and suggests that Hawksmoor's influence may also have been significant.[31]

While Kent's role in the mid-eighteenth-century Gothic Revival has never been doubted, Hawksmoor's Gothic has always been seen to be too idiosyncratic to have had much impact. Kent's influence was in the main direct, through the effect of his work on followers like Garrett, Vardy and Paine, but was partly based on the publication of a number of his Gothic schemes in John Vardy's *Some Designs of Mr Inigo Jones and Mr William Kent* (1744). However, Dr Eileen Harris's reassessment of Batty Langley, author of *Ancient Architecture Restored and Improved by a Great*

---

[29] *Explanation of Designs for All Souls by Nicholas Hawksmoor*, Oxford, 1960, 5.

[30] John Summerson, *Architecture in Britain 1530–1830*, 1977, 396; Michael McCarthy's *The Origins of the Gothic Revival*, 1987, ignores the Office of Works Gothic tradition.

[31] Juliet Allan, 'New Light on William Kent at Hampton Court Palace', *Architectural History*, XXVII (1984), 52–3.

Variety of Grand and Usefull Designs, entirely new in the Gothick Mode for ornamenting of Buildings and Gardens (1742), the first book on Gothic architecture and one which was to be a major source for Gothic designers in the early-eighteenth century, suggests that Langley was inspired to write the book by Hawksmoor's work at Westminster Abbey.[32]

Kent's real significance lay in the way that he differed from Wren and Hawksmoor by extending the use of Gothic architecture from ecclesiastical and collegiate buildings to domestic architecture. His work at Hampton Court, Middlesex, which Wren had largely remodelled in the 1690s without concern for the Tudor fabric, was the first evidence of this. Kent was called to rebuild the Clock Court range in 1731, and, according to Horace Walpole, he too initially considered a Classical design, only to be prevailed upon by Sir Robert Walpole to work instead in a Gothic manner.[33] At about the same time Henry Pelham, an intimate of Sir Robert Walpole's, approached Kent to design a house for him at Esher Place, Surrey, which he had bought with its isolated fifteenth-century tower in 1729. Again Kent at first considered a Classical solution, proposing a Palladian house on top of the hill looking down at the tower (Fig 25). He soon changed his mind and in 1733 produced plans in which Gothic wings were added to the tower (Fig 26).[34] Kent followed his domestic work at Esher with an ambitious plan for remodelling Honingham Hall, Norfolk, in 1737 for Walpole's nephew William Townshend, but this was prevented by Townshend's death the following year.[35] In 1738 Kent was able to begin the slightly less thorough-going Gothic remodelling of Rousham Hall, Oxfordshire.

But perhaps the most significant development of the Gothic Revival during the 1730s and 1740s was the fashion for informally laid out gardens and parks ornamented with occasional buildings. As such buildings were relatively cheap and not restricted by the need to be functional they encouraged architectural invention, and it was chiefly through this medium that the use of Gothic began to spread and become a fashion that was not restricted to alterations of old buildings.

Vanbrugh was a pioneer of this style of gardening, and made repeated use of towers and castellations at Castle Howard, Yorkshire (Fig 27), Claremont, Surrey (1715), and his own estate at Greenwich (1718 and 1721). Vanbrugh's appreciation of antiquarian feeling is well known from his defence of the old ruins of Woodstock Palace, and is spelled

---

[32] Eileen Harris, *British Architectural Books and Writers*, Cambridge, 1990, 267.

[33] Allen, 1984, 51.

[34] John Harris, 'William Kent and Esher Place', in *The Fashioning and Functioning of the British Country House*, ed. Gervase Jackson-Stops, Hanover, 1989, 14.

[35] John Harris, *The Palladians*, 1981, 82.

out in a letter he wrote to the earl of Manchester in 1707 about his designs for Kimbolton Castle: 'As to the Outside, I thought 'twas absolutely best, to give it Something of the Castle Air, tho' at the Same time to make it regular ... This method was practic'd at Windsor in King Charles's time, And has been universally Approv'd ... to have built a Front with Pillasters, and what the Orders require cou'd never have been born with the Rest of the Castle: I'm sure this will make a very Noble and Masculine Shew; and is of as Warrantable a kind of building as Any.'[36]

The belvedere at Claremont was probably the first in a series of Gothic towers built with increasing frequency during the eighteenth century, principally on hill tops. Sometimes these gave the impression of being complete castles. Stainborough Castle built by the 3rd earl of Strafford in 1728–30 at Wentworth Castle, Yorkshire, with a keep and bailey is one of the most important early examples. Freestanding towers, like that at Whitton Place, Middlesex—probably built in the 1730s and certainly before 1748—were more common. These were principally inspired by medieval castles and perhaps by Tudor hunting towers. At least nine examples can be found before 1750. Parallel with these towers were a series of buildings which looked rather to ecclesiastical architecture for their models. Perhaps the earliest example is John Freeman's ruin at Fawley Court, Oxfordshire, finished in 1732 (Fig 28), while the grandest is James Gibbs's Gothic Temple at Stowe, Buckinghamshire (1741).

By the 1740s Gothic garden buildings were becoming common, but this decade also saw increased antiquarian interest in the use of Gothic. The rebuilding of Welbeck Abbey, Nottinghamshire, by Henrietta Howard, countess of Oxford, from 1742 was a key example of this. Like lady Anne Clifford, lady Oxford was profoundly aware of her descent, as Horace Walpole noted after her death: 'The poor woman who is just dead passed her whole widowhood ... in collecting and monumenting the portraits and reliquies of all the great families from which she is descended, and which centred in her.' Widowed in 1742, she retired to her family's ancient seat, which she found 'in allmost Ruines', and dedicated the remaining years of her life to restoring it, principally in the Gothic manner. Her description of the new dining room in 1744 reveals the impression she was trying to create: 'ye ceiling is to be painted with ye armes of my family, and ye marriages into it in proper colours to be hung with full length pictures in cedar frames those you saw in the dining room here with more, a Gothick chimneypiece designed partly from a fine one at Bolsover ...' Horace Walpole was ecstatic: 'It is impossible to describe the bales of Cav-

[36] Kerry Downes, *Vanbrugh*, 1977, 48.

endishes, Harleys, Holleses, Veres and Ogles: every chamber is tape-stried with them; nay, and with 100 other fat morsels; all their institutions inscribed, all their arms, crests, devices sculpted on chimneypieces of various English marbles in ancient forms—mostly ugly. Then such a Gothic hall, with pendent fretwork in imitation of the old and with a chimneypiece like mine in the library ... so much of every thing I like, that my party thought they would never get me away again.'[37] This was the great hall, rebuilt in 1751, and a Gothic tour-de-force which at this date had no equal (Fig 29).

The countess of Oxford was not alone in her extensive use of Gothic during the 1740s. In Essex, Thomas Barrett-Lennard, a keen antiquary who inherited the ancient Dacre barony from his mother, set about repairing Tudor Belhus in 1745. Walpole visiting in 1754 declared that 'what he has done is in Gothic and very true ... the chimneypieces except one little miscarriage ... are all of a good King James the First Gothic.'[38] In Sussex, Wiston House, a great Elizabethan mansion, was reduced in the 1740s—one of the wings is dated 1747—and given new facades created out of a mixture of reused Elizabethan material and Gothic elements. Of the interior only the great hall survives, but that was given a vast Gothic chimneypiece and overmantel, together with Gothic doorcases and niches, all taken from Batty Langley.[39] In Oxfordshire, Sanderson Miller remodelled the chapel of Wroxton Abbey, an incomplete early-seventeenth-century house, in the Gothic style for lord North in 1747. In Warwickshire, Philip Yorke visiting Warwick Castle in 1748 noted that lord Brooke, who had come of age in 1740, had done substantial work to the castle and picked out particularly the windows in the state apartment 'made in the Gothic style and very pretty' and the 'chapel fitting up, the ceiling of which is Gothic and ornamented with different coats of arms belonging to the family' (Fig 30).[40] Brooke was anxious to stress the family's antiquity and in 1759, claiming collateral descent from the Beauchamp earls of Warwick, persuaded the king to create him earl of Warwick as well as earl Brooke within two months of the death of the last Rich earl of Warwick. Brooke's bank account[41] suggests this was the work of Daniel Garrett who also worked in a Gothic manner for the 2nd duke of Cleveland at Raby Castle, County Durham, from about 1745; remodelled Kippax Park, Yorkshire, for Sir John Bland, which Dr Pococke noticed in 1750;[42]

[37] *The Correspondence of Horace Walpole*, ed. W. S. Lewis, 1977, v35, 270–71.

[38] *Ibid.*, 183–84.

[39] Roger White, 'Wiston House remodelled', *Architectural History*, XXVII (1984), 241–8.

[40] Joyce Godber, 'The Marchioness Grey of Wrest Park', *Publications of the Bedfordshire Historical Record Society*, XLVII (1968), 138.

[41] Hoare's Bank S 446.

[42] J.J. Cartwright (ed.), 'The Travels through England of Dr Richard Pococke', *Camden Society*, CXXXI (1888), 62.

and was probably responsible for the Gothic chapel at Northumberland House begun by the duke of Somerset in 1748.

The work at Northumberland House was finished by Somerset's daughter and son-in-law the earl (duke from 1766) and countess of Northumberland who extensively remodelled Alnwick Castle, Northumberland, in an exclusively Gothic fashion from 1750 (Fig 31). Peter Waddell's description of the castle in 1785 shows that it was laden with heraldry. One hundred and ten escutcheons bearing the arms of the principal families allied with the house of Percy decorated the great staircase. The duchess's portrait in the dining room was set in a frame with the arms of Percy, Lucy, Poynings, Fitpayn, Bryan and Latimer, while the ceiling was ornamented with coats-of-arms. The arms of the duke were placed above the breakfast room chimneypiece and his crest encircled by the garter above that in the saloon, while the chapel was decorated with panels: 'each Pannel round the Chapel has near its Top, a Coat of Arms, shewing the several Alliances with this great and noble Family; and for the information of those unacquainted with Heraldry a Label is affixed to each, on which is inscribed the Name of the Family whose arms are above it. The Center pannels are much larger than any of the others, and on them are painted Labels shewing the Descent of this illustrious Family in direct line from Charlemaigne, and their Intermarriages with some of the most honourable and noble Houses of Europe.'

The earl and countess had good reason for this. No Percy had lived in Northumberland since the attainder of the 7th earl in 1572, and indeed the male line had died out with the death of the 11th earl in 1670. Since then the succession had twice gone through the female line to the countess whose husband, though a substantial Yorkshire baronet, was the great-grandson of a London haberdasher. By returning to Alnwick, rebuilding the castle in a Gothic manner and covering the interior with heraldry, the Northumberlands were glossing over the recent rupture and reasserting their links with the medieval Percies.[43]

Thus by the time of the building book which followed the peace of Aix-la-Chapelle in 1748, interest in Gothic architecture was spreading. It was to cash in on this that Batty Langley's *Ancient Architecture Revived* had been published in 1742. Only at this relatively late date did Horace Walpole become interested in the style, writing to his friend Horace Mann that he was going to build 'a little Gothic castle'. Mann's response in January 1750 was not sympathetic: 'Why will you make it Gothic? I know it is the taste at present, but I am really sorry for it.'[44] Thus even Mann in Italy was aware that Walpole was no prophet of a new style.

[43] Giles Worsley, 'Alnwick Castle, Northumberland–II' *Country Life*, 8 Dec. 1988.
[44] W. S. Lewis, *The Correspondence of Horace Walpole*, 1960, 119.

Nevertheless, he did help to popularise it by building the first Gothic house within easy reach of London. He also helped to develop it from being a purely antiquarian style associated with old buildings, for Strawberry Hill was effectively a new house. But Walpole was only able to get away with building a Gothic house because Strawberry Hill was a suburban villa. Sanderson Miller's suggestion that Sir George Lyttelton rebuild Hagley Hall, Worcestershire, to a Gothic design in 1752 was quickly squashed and a standard Palladian great house was built instead.[45] Gothic was not considered a suitable style for a new seat, only a Classical building would do. Similarly, when Miller designed the new shire hall at Warwick in 1754 there was no suggestion that Gothic would be an appropriate style for a public building, and a handsome Classical facade was built instead. As Walpole wrote to Mann, 'The Grecian is proper only for magnificent and public building.'[46] It would be another three decades before the work of architects like James Wyatt established Gothic as a style equal in its own right to Classicism.

But by 1748 Gothic design had been accepted as a respectable way of completing earlier ecclesiastical and collegiate buildings, partly out of architectural propriety, partly out of antiquarian respect. It was seen as an appropriate way to alter older houses, particularly by owners anxious to stress the antiquity of their line, and as a suitable style for garden buildings intended to give a frisson of romance. Did it have political overtones? This certainly seems to have been the opinion of an anonymous author in the *Gentleman's Magazine* in 1739: 'Methinks there was something Respectable in those old hospitable Gothic Halls, hung round with Helmets, Breast-Plates and Swords of our Ancestors, I entered them with a Constitutional Sort of Reverence and look'd upon those Armes with Gratitude as a Terror of former Ministers and the Check of Kings ... Our old Gothic Constitution had a noble strength and simplicity about it, which was well enough represented by the bold Arches and the solid pillars of the Edifices of those days. And I have not observed that the modern Refinements in either have in the least added to their Strength and Solidity.'[47] Similarly, viscount Molesworth observed in the preface of the 1721 edition of *Franco-Gallia: or, an Account of the Ancient Free State of France, and Most other Parts of France; before the Loss of their Liberties*: a 'real Whig is one who is exactly for keeping up to the Strictness of the true old Gothick Constitution ... A true Whig is of Opinion, that the Executive Power has as just a Title to the Allegiance and Obedience of the Subject, according to the Rules

[45] McCarthy, 1987, 116.
[46] Walpole Society XX, 127.
[47] *Gentleman's Magazine* 1739, 641. Quoted by Paul Frankl, *The Gothic: Literary Sources and Interpretations through Eight Centuries*, Princeton, 1960, 381.

of known Laws enacted by the Legislative, as the Subject has to Protection, Liberty and Property.'[48]

At first sight there might seem to be such a political connection. Gibbs's Gothic temple at Stowe was known as the Temple of Liberty, and in 1732 Gilbert West described the Saxon deities which surrounded it as 'Gods, of a Nation, valient, wise, and free,/ Who conquer'd to establish Liberty!/ To whose auspicious Care Britainnia owes/ Those Laws, on which she stands, by which she rose.' However, as Gibbs's biographer Terry Friedman notes, this associate between the Gothic style and the theme of liberty was unusual.[49] In architectural terms if there was a style which suggested liberty at this date it was Classicism— the style of Kent's proposed for the Houses of Parliament—not Gothic. The political overtones of the Gothic Revival were dynastic, not constitutional.

[48] Quoted in Friedman, 1984, 197.
[49] *Ibid.*

Fig 1—Longleat House, Wiltshire, an example of mid-16th-century Classicism

Fig 2—The Chapel staircase of 1560 at Burghley House, Northamptonshire, a markedly Classical design

Fig 3—The west front at Burghley House, harking back to early Tudor architecture

Fig 4—The Great Hall at Burghley which has strong medieval overtones

Fig 5—Snape Castle, Yorkshire, with towers and crenellations added by Lord Burghley's son Thomas Cecil marking his marriage into the Neville family

Fig 6—The courtyard of Old Wardour Castle, Wiltshire, with Robert Smythson's pure Classical door added in the 1570s

Fig 7.—The entrance front of Old Wardour Castle refenestrated in a sympathetic mediæval manner by Smythson

Fig 8—The Chapel at Lincoln College, Oxford, of 1629–31 with its Perpendicular windows

Fig 9 —St Ninian's, Ninekirk, built by Lady Anne Clifford to a Gothic design during the Commonwealth

Fig 10—The main gateway at Skipton Castle, Yorkshire, restored to its original height by Lady Anne Clifford during the Commonwealth

Fig 11—Holy Trinity, Staunton Harold, Leicestershire, built by Sir Robert Shirley as a Royalist statement in 1653

Fig 12—The Great Hall of Lambeth Palace, London, rebuilt using Gothic motifs by Archbishop Juxon in 1660–63

Fig 13—The font of Durham Cathedral, commissioned in an essentially Gothic manner by Bishop Cosin in 1663–65

Fig 14—The Chapel at Bishop Auckland, County Durham, remodelled by Bishop Cosin who added the Gothic clerestory

Fig 15—The interior of the Chapel at Bishop Auckland with Gothic woodwork added by Bishop Cosin

Fig 16—One of the overdoors showing ancestors of the Earl of Peterborough at Drayton
Hall, Northamptonshire

Fig 17—The Earl of Peterborough added the crenellated gatehouse at Drayton in the 1660s or 1670s

Fig 18—The Upper Ward of Windsor Castle, Berkshire, remodelled by Hugh May in 1675–84 using Romanesque motifs

Fig 19—Hampton Court, Herefordshire, was given a symmetrical castellated front by Lord Coningsby between 1706 and 1717

Fig 20—Shirburn Castle, Oxfordshire, rebuilt by the Earl of Macclesfield in 1716–25

Fig 21—Tom Tower, Christ Church, Oxford, completed by Sir Christopher Wren 'to agree with the Founder's work' in 1681

Fig 22—St Mary Aldermary, City of London, of 1681, one of Wren's earliest and most ambitious Gothic designs

Fig 23—Design by Wren for remodelling the north transept of Westminster Abbey in 1719

Fig 24—All Soul's College, Oxford, designed by Nicholas Hawksmoor and built from 1716 to 1735

Fig 25—William Kent's initial Classical scheme for Esher Place, Surrey, with the medieval tower below

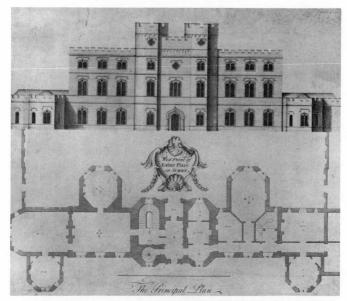

Fig 26—Kent's 1733 Gothic design for extending the 15th-century tower at Esher

Fig 27—Vanbrugh's castle walls at Castle Howard, Yorkshire

Fig 28—The Gothic ruin at Fawley Court, Oxfordshire, built before 1732 by John Freeman

Fig 29—The Great Hall at Welbeck Abbey, Nottinghamshire, built by the Countess of Oxford in 1751

Fig 30—The Gothic corridor at Warwick Castle, Warwickshire, part of a Gothic remodelling carried out by 1748

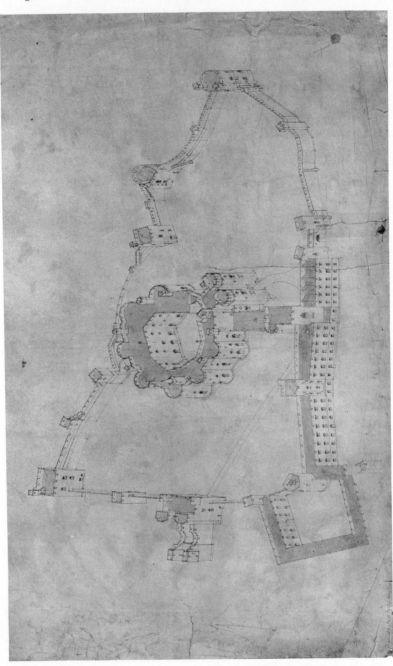

Fig 31—Alnwick Castle, Northumberland, rebuilt in a Gothic manner by the Earl and Countess of Northumberland from 1750

PROVIDENCE, PROTESTANT UNION AND GODLY REFORMATION IN THE 1690s

By Craig Rose

The Alexander Prize Essay, Proxime Accessit

THIS paper requires some justification. In what is otherwise an under-researched period, the campaign for reformation of manners in the 1690s has been a very well-ploughed furrow indeed. Since the publication in 1957 of Dudley Bahlman's *The Moral Revolution of 1688*, there have been half a dozen major essays on reformation of manners, as well as some outstanding unpublished research.[1] The work has not only been copious, but also of a very high standard. Nevertheless, there is one aspect of reformation of manners that has only been dealt with tangentially in the existing literature: the relationship between godly reformation and the cause of Protestant union. Historians have noted that the societies for reformation of manners were composed of both churchmen and dissenters, and that this stimulated high church attacks upon the societies in Anne's reign.[2] But there has been little analysis of the ways in which the ideal of Protestant union coloured some aspects of reformation of manners.[3] The second half of this paper seeks to fill that gap. But first it will be necessary to explore the providentialist context of reformation of manners ideology. We shall begin by taking a brief excursion to the island of Jamaica.

---

[1] D. W. R. Bahlman, *The Moral Revolution of 1688* (New Haven, Connecticut, 1957); T. C. Curtis and W. A. Speck, 'The Societies for the Reformation of Manners: A Case Study in the Theory and Practice of Moral Reform', *Literature and History*, III (March, 1976), 45–64; Eamon Duffy, 'Primitive Christianity Revived: Religious Renewal in Augustan England', in *Renaissance and Renewal in Christian History: Studies in Church History* 21, ed. Derek Baker (Oxford, 1977), 287–300; Tina Isaacs, 'The Anglican Hierarchy and the Reformation of Manners 1688–1738', *Journal of Ecclesiastical History*, XXXIII (1982), 391–411; David Hayton, 'Moral Reform and Country Politics in the late Seventeenth-Century House of Commons', *Past & Present*, CXXVII (1990), 48–91; John Spurr, 'The Church, the Societies and the Moral Revolution of 1688', in *From Toleration to Tractarianism: The Church of England 1689–1833*, eds, John Walsh, Colin Haydon and Stephen Taylor (Cambridge, forthcoming); A. G. Craig, 'The Movement for Reformation of Manners, 1688–1715' (University of Edinburgh PhD dissertation, 1980). Tony Claydon of London University is nearing completion of a PhD thesis on government propaganda and reformation of manners in the 1690s. For an earlier contribution, see G. V. Portus, *Caritas Anglicana* (1912).

[2] Craig, 'Movement for Reformation', 271–92; Isaacs, 'Anglican Hierarchy', 401–3.

[3] For brief discussions, see Craig, 'Movement for Reformation', 189; Bahlmann, *Moral Revolution*, 80–2.

I

On 7 June 1692 a massive earthquake struck Port Royal, metropolis of Jamaica. According to the minister of Port Royal,

> in the space of three minutes, about half-an-hour after eleven in the morning, Port Royall, the fairest town of all the English Plantations, [and] best emporium and mart of that part of the world, exceeding in its riches, plentifull in all good things, was shaken and shattered to pieces, sunk into and covered, for the greatest part by the sea, and will in a short time, be wholly eaten up by it, for few of those houses that yet stand, are left whole, and every day we hear them fall, and the sea daily encroaches upon it.

Fifteen hundred souls, he believed, had perished in the disaster.[4]

By early August news of the catastrophe had reached London. On the 10th Charles Hatton informed his brother Lord Hatton of 'very terrible news from Jamaica ... an earthquake and hurrican hath been and in less than 2 minuits destroy'd and sank ye greatest part of Port Royall with all ye factories, storehouses, and magazines.'[5] Only a month later Hatton wrote to his brother of another earthquake which, though incomparably less destructive than the Jamaican disaster, was all the more terrifying for being on his own London doorstep. 'We had here, my L^d, last Thursday [8 September] ... an earth-quake, ye effects of wch were more or less felt, not only over all London and Westminster but, it is reported, as far as Canterbury and Cambridge.'[6] Another correspondent of Lord Hatton, the physician Edmund King, had been

> at dinour in my dineing roome ... on a suddaine the table and room shakt, put us all into a strange confusion. My wife said: 'Mr King, w^{ts} this?' Her woman y^t was at dinner wth us started from the table, as pale as death, and cri'd: 'Oh! an earthquake!' I rise from the table too in the universall motion I saw and felt; it lasted about a minute and halfe. Whilst we was talking of it, a neighbour cam in and ask't if we perceivd anything of an earthquake, for a great many gentlemen came running into the coffee house, pale and frighted, out of their houses too into the street in great amazement; and it's the wholl talke now all the towne over ...[7]

The Jamaica quake and the London tremor did indeed give

---

[4] H[istorical] M[anuscripts] C[ommission] Kenyon MSS, 268.

[5] Charles Hatton to Lord Hatton, 10 Aug. 1692, Correspondence of the Family of Hatton ... 1601–1704, ed. E. M. Thompson (2 vols., Camden Society, 1878), II, 183.

[6] Same to the same, ibid., 184–5.

[7] Sir Edmund King to Lord Hatton, 8 Sept. 1692, ibid., 184.

Englishmen much food for thought. The devastation of Jamaica, affirmed the minister of Port Royal, was an unmistakable sign of the wrath of God. The citizens of Port Royal were 'a most ungodly and debauched people', and on more than one occasion the cleric had 'set before them what would be the issue of their impenitence and wickedness.' Alas, his warnings had gone unheeded,and now Port Royal had suffered 'this terrible judgment of God.'[8] The Scots presbyterian minister Robert Fleming believed that the Jamaica quake was a 'publick Beacon and Monument of Judgment in this respect, to shew how terrible a thing it is to fall immediately into the Hands of the Living God.' Thus the catastrophe was an awful warning to the people of England of God's displeasure, and the London tremor was a second divine shot across the nation's bows.[9] Fleming was not alone in believing that the London tremor bore the portentous imprint of the finger of God: ' ... o yt now Gods judgments are in the earth', wrote Abigail Harley from London on the day of the tremor, 'ye inhabitants may learn righteousness & not go on presumptuously in sin, wch will be bitterness in the end.'[10] While no family in England was more given to view the world through providentialist lenses than the Harleys of Brampton Bryan, the veteran MP Sir Thomas Clarges liked to think himself 'not in these things very superstitious'. Yet he remembered that similar tremors had preceded the outbreak of the civil war and the death of Charles II, and so 'cannot but observe they [earthquakes] have been in some places esteem'd ominous'.[11] Like the Jamaica quake then, the London tremor was seen as a warning of worse things to come. The tremor had done little damage, wrote one pamphleteer. But 'who can tell, this is not the last Warning; and that the next time he shall visit us, he will not in his Fiery Indignation utterly consume us, and swallow us up quick?'[12] 'What Controversy God intends further with us is only known to himselfe', observed Richard Lapthorne gloomily two days after the tremor in the capital.[13]

Reverses in the war against France were read by those with a providentialist frame of mind as further signs of God's anger with England. When much of the Turkey merchant fleet was captured by

[8] *HMC Kenyon MSS*, 266–8.

[9] Robert Fleming, *A Discourse of Earthquakes* (1693), 15–17.

[10] Abigail Harley to Sir Edward Harley, 8 Sept. 1692, B[ritish] L[ibrary] Add MS 70116, unfoliated bundle of Abigail Harley's letters.

[11] Sir Thomas Clarges to Robert Harley, 8 Sept. 1692, BL Add MS 70016, fols. 108–9.

[12] *A True and Faithfull Account of all the Earthquakes, and the Dreadful Effects thereof, That have happened in England since the Norman Conquest, to this Day* (1692), 1–2.

[13] Richard Lapthorne to Richard Coffin, 10 Sept. 1692, *The Portledge Papers*, ed. R.J. Kerr and Ida Coffin Duncan (1928), 147.

the French in July 1693, Robert Harley wrote to his father that 'God is pleas'd further to express his displeasure agst us in cutting us short by sea.'[14] The presbyterian minister Matthew Henry similarly believed that the loss of the Turkey fleet was 'a great token of Gods displeasure.'[15] In August 1693 Thomas Jolly, a Lancashire dissenting minister, groaned that 'the publique discouragements press sore, the Lord rebuking us, emptying us, bringing us low and into straits.' God was 'rebuking us severall wayes', he continued, 'not only as to desolation by men's hand in the warr, but by his own immediate hand in the fruits of the earth'.[16] That same month, John Evelyn confided to his diary that 'every thing [was] sadly declining; & all this for our late Injustice and disobedience, & the still reigning of sin among us.'[17]

What did Evelyn mean by 'our late Injustice and disobedience'? As a veteran Royalist, he may have been thinking back to the Great Rebellion and the Regicide. But it is equally plausible that Evelyn was alluding to the revolution of 1688. Certainly, in July 1693 he had attributed the 'ill successe in all our Concernes' to 'our folly & precipitous Change'.[18] If Evelyn did indeed see the unrighteous deposition of James II as the cause of God's controversy with England, then his views had something in common with those of unambiguous Jacobites. In 1690 Nathaniel Johnston had claimed that the revolution 'gives us nothing but the dismal prospect of all the misfortunes which can befal a nation, which hath greatly provoked God Almighty's anger'.[19] By exhorting the people to support the revolution, alleged the author of a notorious Jacobite tract of 1693, the swearing clergy were drawing down God's curse upon the nation:

> What a dishonour is this to God and religion! What a curse to the world! What an injury to men's souls! And what can it portend but vengeance, and (without a timely and extraordinary repentance) inevitable ruin? Neither can I omit putting my fellow subjects in mind of ... the never-to-be-forgotten earthquake in Jamaica, and those late monitory shakings which ran through all this island, as well as a great part of the territories of our wicked confederates. I

---

[14] Robert Harley to Sir Edward Harley, 25 July 1693, BL Add MS 70017, fol. 126.

[15] Matthew Henry to Philip Henry, 18 July 1693, D[octor] W[illiams's] L[ibrary] MS 90.7, letter 30.

[16] *The Note Book of the Rev. Thomas Jolly 1671–1693*, ed. Henry Fishwick (Manchester, Chetham Soc., 1894), 118.

[17] *The Diary of John Evelyn*, ed. E. S. de Beer (6 vols., Oxford, 1955), V, 152.

[18] *Ibid.*, 148.

[19] Nathaniel Johnston, *The Dear Bargain; or, a true Representation of the State of the English Nation under the Dutch* (1690), reprinted in Sir Walter Scott, ed., *A Collection of Scarce and Valuable Tracts ... particularly that of the late Lord Somers* (13 vols., 1813), X, 349–77, quotation at 377.

shall not pretend to divine what may be the consequence of them; but we never heard of an earthquake in this island but did certainly forerun some very remarkable calamity.

Unless the revolution was reversed England would be consumed by God's righteous anger.[20]

Needless to say, Williamites viewed matters from a rather different perspective. The revolution was a 'sudden and seasonable deliverance', preached the York priest George Halley in February 1689: 'A deliverance which argues the vigilant Eye of Providence, and the powerful Hand of God.'[21] Indeed, the revolution showed the English people to be the 'peculiar care of Heaven, to be the only Blessed Children of the Lord'. But Halley coupled this comforting thought with a worrying caveat:

> if we live not as highly sensible of God's reiterated mercies, (which sense we must demonstrate by a life conformable to his Divine Laws) then, though our Sky at the present is beautified with an Evening Redness,which speaks the Clouds thin, and the Air pure; tho' our Firmament now looks bright and serene; yet God, if provok'd by our ingratitude and impiety, can, in the twinkling of an Eye, change it from an Evening to a Morning Redness; can in a moment make the Firmament lowring, by condensing the Clouds, and veiling the Sky with darkness; will certainly bring us into worse circumstances than before, and pour upon us fiercer instances of his anger and heavy discipline.[22]

A pamphleteer in 1690 gave a similar warning: 'God can create Destruction upon a People, which he hath created Salvation and Deliverance for, that will not accept of it, nor be saved nor delivered by him.'[23]

It was the suspicion that God was about to turn away from the backsliding English people which made the military reverses of the early 1690s, not to mention the seismic shocks of 1692, so disturbing to supporters of the revolution. But to Williamites no event could have been more ominous than the premature death of Queen Mary in December 1694. 'When God deprives a People of a Wise, Good, and Pious King or Queen,' averred the Congregational minister Thomas Goodwin, 'we should tremble at such a dreadful and portentous Sign of his Displeasure, as foreboding Ruin to us, if we will yet be obstinately

---

[20] *Remarks upon the present Confederacy, and the late Revolution in England* (1693), reprinted in *Somers Tracts*, X, 491–523, quotation at 522–3.

[21] George Halley, *A Sermon Preached in the Cathedral and Metropolitical Church of St Peter in York, On Thursday the Fourteenth of February, 1688/9* (1689), 22.

[22] *Ibid.*, 27–8.

[23] *A Word of Advice unto all those that have a Right to Choose Parliament-Men* (1690), 1.

resolv'd to continue in Sin, and refuse to be reform'd.'[24] In a sermon delivered on the text of 2 Chronicles, xxxv.24, 'And all Judah and Jerusalem Mourned for Josiah', Thomas Bowber, a divine of the Church of England, suggested that the queen 'was quickly snatcht away by Death, and no doubt in Mercy, as good Josiah was, that her eyes might not see the Evil, which (we know not how soon) may befall us, without a speedy Reformation.'[25] Bowber continued his jeremiad in similar vein:

> Now that our Illustrious Princess was taken from us, soon after so great a Diliverance as this [the revolution], may strike Dread into our Hearts, and chill our Spirits! For tho She was gathered to Her Grave in Peace, yet for ought we know, it may be a sad Presage of many Miseries and Calamities ready to betide us: Mercies and Deliverances, when abused, turn into Judgments. In Josiah's days God offered the Jews Mercy, but whatever ties and Obligations lay upon them to reform and amend, they would not hearken to the voice of God, nor turn from their Evil ways, which proved their utter Ruin and Destruction.[26]

Bishop Burnet also drew an analogy between Queen Mary and Josiah, and reminded his readers that after the death of that pious king 'Jerusalem was laid in Heaps, their Temple was rased down to the Ground, and Zion became a ploughed field.'[27] The implication was devastatingly clear. Just as the death of King Josiah was swiftly followed by the fall of ancient Zion, so the demise of Queen Mary presaged the destruction of that latter-day Zion, Protestant England.

Who was responsible for England's dire predicament? The jeremiads of the 1690s tended to lay the blame squarely on the shoulders of the people. Typical were the sentiments of the presbyterian minister John Woodhouse in 1697. As 'the Sins of some Kings have had a ruining Influence upon their People; so the Sins of many a wicked People, have had a hand to weaken, disappoint (if not ruine) good Kings; Kings better than their People.' King William was just such a king, a virtuous prince whose heroic efforts were undermined by the sins of his subjects.[28] At least one commentator, however, thought that the king himself was far from blameless.

---

[24] Thomas Goodwin, *Of the Happiness of Princes led by Divine Counsel. A Sermon Occasioned by the Death Of that most Excellent Princess, Our late Sovereign Queen Mary* (1695), 24.

[25] Thomas Bowber, *A Sermon Preached in the Parish-Church of St Swithin, London, March 10th 1694/5 Upon the Much lamented Death Of our Most Gracious Queen* (1695), 2.

[26] *Ibid.*, 21–2.

[27] Gilbert Burnet, *An Essay on the Memory Of the late Queen* (1695), 38–43, quotation at 43.

[28] John Woodhouse, *A Sermon Preach'd at Salters-Hall, to the Societies for Reformation of Manners, May 31 1697* (1697), 51.

Although he had been an ardent supporter of the revolution, the barrister-turned-priest Edward Stephens soon became an astringent critic of King William and his regime. In a pamphlet written late in 1689, Stephens claimed that England's fortunes had taken a marked turn for the worse since William's accession to the throne. The revolution itself had been accomplished with an ease so miraculous that it betokened the guiding hand of providence. But in the course of 1689 there had been

> a great and unhappy Change in the Course and Progress of our Affairs, from so smooth and prosperous, that formidable Armies could give no check or interruption, but vanished like Smoke before the Wind, to so rough and disturbed, and that so universal in all, that neither Abroad nor at Home, at Sea or at Land, in Country or in Council, do we find any cheerful Face of Affairs, but everywhere Rubs, Impediments, Failures and Disappointments, and our way fenced up that we cannot pass.

These misfortunes showed unmistakably that

> Israel hath sinned and transgressed, and therefore cannot prosper. Our strength is departed from us, and we are become like other Men: Neither will it return, unless the Cursed Thing be found out and removed. This therefore is our business, which this change of Success loudly calls us to, to find out the Sin that keeps good things from us, and to dissipate the Cloud that intercepts the benign Influences of Heaven.[29]

Stephens believed that he had located the source of the nation's sin. The ease with which the revolution had been effected signified that King William was the chosen instrument of divine dispensation. However, he had been chosen by God not only to humble Popery, but also to turn back the tide of debauchery which had inundated England under the restored monarchy. Tragically, William had failed to keep his side of the bargain. Instead of pursuing God's work, the king's employment of the debauched servants of the previous monarchs showed that he had submitted himself to fleshly reasonings. In this, the king was walking in the footsteps of his great-grandfather James I. It had been the 'Unhappiness' of that king that

> after an admirable deliverance from an horrid Popish Conspiracy, ready for execution, he applied himself at first to connivance, and at last to association with Papists for his security; which, contrary to

---

[29] Edward Stephens, *Reflections upon the Occurrences of the Last Year from 5 Nov. 1688 to 5 Nov. 1689* (1689), 12–13.

expectation, proved the original of all the mischiefs which have since befallen his family: So likewise this Prince, after as great an experience of the Divine Providence over him, thought to deal wisely with them [the debauched servants of the previous two kings], and (after Hushai's advice) defer this great work [of reformation], first till the kingdom should be settled, and then when he was proclaimed King, till Ireland should be reduced, and he would have a sufficient Power (an Arm of the Flesh) to do it effectually, and in the mean time try what effect a good example and kindness, intrusting them with Offices and Employments in State, Army and Navy, would have upon such vitious People in the end, which in like manner, contrary to his expectation, hath proved the original of all the Impediments and Disappointments in his affairs.[30]

Hence King William was himself the author of the nation's sin. 'As almost all the Wickedness of the former Reigns proceeded originally from those Kings, and Judgment hath been first executed upon them; so hath likewise the Fault, whereby that great Work, whereof this King was called out to be the Glorious Instrument in these Nations, hath been hitherto interrupted, plainly proceeded from himself.'[31]

Edward Stephens was, to put it mildly, a rather eccentric figure,[32] but he was not alone in feeling that the revolution had sadly failed of its promise. Elias Pledger, a London Presbyterian tradesman, was a man much given to eschatological speculation: in 1693 he was convinced that Christ's reign on earth was imminent.[33] Before that glorious event, though, Pledger feared that England would suffer a dreadful punishment for its sins. 'I know y^t we in England & especial in y^s City have very great reason to fear such a Judgm^t', he wrote in January 1694,

For I question whether ever any nation in ye world ever enjoyed ye like means [of salvation] & yet that we have carryed o^{ur} selves worse y^n others I think is out of question we have been tryed by all means fair & foul (as we use to say) formerly by continued Judgm^{ts} Sword Plagues fire scarcity of ye word w^n our ministers w[er]e driven in to corners, & of late by a mixture of many w[onderfu]ll Judgmts &

[30] *Ibid.*, 19–23, quotation at 22–3.
[31] *Ibid.*, 32. Soon after William's landing in England, Stephens had presented him with a draft of a declaration against debauchery. It was the King's failure to implement his scheme which lay at the bottom of Stephens's animus; see *ibid.*, 21–2; *idem.*, *The True English Government, and Misgovernment Of the Four last Kings* (1689), 7–8.
[32] In the course of the 1690s, perhaps because of disillusion with King William, Stephens came to espouse fiercely anti-erastian views. In fact, he argued that the erastianism of the reformation had unchurched the Church of England. For a brief review of Stephens's ideas, see Duffy, 'Primitive Christianity', 297–8.
[33] DWL MS 28.4, fol. 59.

Mercys, a wonderful & miraculous revolution in our governmt, taking ye crown from the head of one that endeavrd to enslave us body & soul & placing another on ye throne whome we thought w^d have promoted a reformation in church & state & all y^s wth very little if any bloud spilt, & yet notwithstanding we have not behavd our selves as we ought we have not obeyd ye call of providence, but y^r has been too much use made of ye same ministers & tools of ye last raigne that helpd to enslave & debash us we are now engaged in a bloudy war wth a potent enemy who we know not but god reservd [?] him to be a scorge to ys nation, as he has been to many others we have had strange rebukes of providence we have gone many steps back to egipt after we thought we had been upon our march out of it . . .

What, then, had prevented the people of England from attaining the Promised Land? As we have seen, Pledger had expected the revolution to usher in a reformation in both church and state. Reformation in the state had been hampered by giving office to those associated with the pre-revolution regime. Nor had reformation in the church fared much better. There were 'Great divisions among protestants', Pledger complained. 'Many too much simbolizing wth Antichrist ye greatest enemy of X[Christ] & his Church that ever was in ye world both in doctrine & worship.'[34]

Although expressed in extreme terms, Pledger's disappointment with the non-reformation of the church was shared by many dissenters and not a few churchmen. In 1689 hopes had been raised that the terms of the Church of England's communion, as well as its liturgy, would be altered in order to facilitate the re-entry of moderate dissent into the establishment. But these hopes had been dashed by the implacable hostility of the Lower House of Convocation in December 1689.[35] Thus as early as February 1690 reformation of the church was coming to be viewed as an impossible dream. 'Some will not build ye Church if they would', lamented a correspondent of Richard Baxter; 'Some would, but on many accounts can not.'[36] The sense of disappointment was probably particularly acute among those who held the union of godly Protestants to be a prerequisite for a national reformation of manners.

---

[34] *Ibid.*, fols. 61–2.

[35] D. N. Marshall, 'Protestant Dissent in England in the Reign of James II' (University of Hull PhD dissertation, 1976), 554–9.

[36] F[rancis] T[allents?] to Richard Baxter, 12 February 1690, DWL MS 59.5, fol. 125.

II

It was a common refrain of critics of the restoration religious settlement that its divisiveness had crippled the Church of England's capacity to wage war against sin. According to Edward Stephens, the 'mischievous' Act of Uniformity had excluded from the church 'many good and useful men'. In their place, the church had been filled with 'Covetous, Proud, Ambitious, Wordly Men, and Court Flatterers'.[37] This sort of churchman was far more concerned with harassing dissenters than with attacking sin. As Jean Gailhard wrote in 1694, such clerics

> are glad when they have the least colour of law to justify any of their unwarrantable practices against those who dissent from them; but they do not regard good laws for the glory of God, as those we have for due observation of the sabbath, and against swearing, drunkeness, and uncleaness, &c; these they look upon as not worth being taken notice by them. That sort of men, far from advising and promoting a necessary reformation of abuses in religion, according to the word of God (the only rule of such things) though it was their duty, they hindered and opposed it, and persecuted them that were for it, slandering them with the names of fanatics, schismatics, obstinate, factious.[38]

The supporters and opponents of godly reformation, asserted the Whig MP Thomas Papillon, equated exactly with the advocates and adversaries of reform of the church. 'Under the name of Whigs', he wrote,

> is comprehended most of the sober and religious persons of the Church of England that sincerely embrace the Doctrines of the Church, and put no such stress on the forms and ceremonies, but look on them as human institutions, and not as the Essentials of Religion, and are willing that there might be a Reformation to take away offence, and that desire that all Swearing, Drunkeness, and Ungodliness should be discountenanced and punished ...

In contrast to this flattering depiction of Whiggery, Papillon caricatured the Tories as all those

> that press the forms and ceremonies more than the Doctrines of the Church, which are sound and Scriptural; and that either in their own practice are Swearers, Drunkards, or loose in their Conversation,

---

[37] Edward Stephens, *A Caveat against Flattery and Profanation of Sacred things to Secular Ends* (1689), 24–5.

[38] J[ean] G[ailhard], *Some Observations upon the Keeping the Thirtieth of January and Twenty-ninth of May* (1694), reprinted in *Somers Tracts*, IX, 481–509, quotation at 502.

or do allow of and are unwilling such should be punished, but give them all countenance, provided they stickle for the forms and ceremonies, and rail against and endeavour to discountenance all those that are otherwise minded.[39]

It is within the context of this Whiggish prejudice that we should place Roger Morrice's comment that the Church of England 'hierarchists' had always discouraged 'practical Religion and Godlynesse which their party has an enmity against and can never bear'.[40]

This was not a charge that could be easily levelled against the post-revolution episcopate. Many of the bishops appointed after 1689 were sympathetic towards the comprehension of moderate dissent within the church, not least, perhaps, because they believed unanimity among the godly to be a spiritual imperative.[41] Although saddened by the failure of the comprehension schemes in 1689–90, the new episcopate retained a strong commitment to godly reformation. Thus in December 1691 thirteen of the bishops petitioned King William to issue a proclamation for the implementation of the laws against vice.[42] In response, a royal proclamation against vice was published in late January 1692.[43] But this was not the first royal move in favour of reformation of manners. Two years earlier, in an open letter to Bishop Compton of London, King William had promised to 'endeavour a general reformation of the lives and manners of all our subjects'.[44]

What are we to make of this court-sponsored campaign for godly reformation? In part, it represented a clever exercise in propaganda on the part of the court. From the earliest days of the reign, as Tony Claydon has shown, there was a conscious effort, inspired chiefly by Gilbert Burnet, to project William and Mary as divinely-appointed

---

[39] Quoted in A. F. W. Papillon, *Memoirs of Thomas Papillon, of London, Merchant (1623–1702)* (Reading, 1877), 374–5.

[40] DWL Morrice Ent'ring Book Q, 495. See also *The Speech of the Right Honourable Henry Earl of Warrington, Lord Delamere, to the Grand Jury at Chester, April 13 1692* (1692), printed in *A Collection of State Tracts, Publish'd during the Reign of King William III* (3 vols., 1705–7), II, 195–200, esp. 198–9.

[41] Margaret C. Jacob, *The Newtonians and the English Revolution* (Hassocks, 1976), 71.

[42] BL Add MS 70015, fol. 276. Of the thirteen signatories, at least ten were either strong supporters of comprehension or noted latitudinarians: Tillotson of Canterbury, Compton of London, Burnet of Salisbury, Patrick of Ely, Sharp of York, Hall of Bristol, Stillingfleet of Worcester, Stratford of Chester, Grove of Chichester, and Kidder of Bath and Wells. Of these ten, only Compton had sat on the bench before the revolution. The three other signatories were Mews of Winchester, Hough of Oxford and Moore of Norwich.

[43] Craig, 'Movement for Reformation', 59.

[44] *His Majesty's Letter to the Right Reverend Father in God Henry Lord Bishop of London, to be communicated to the Two Provinces of Canterbury and York, 13 February 1689/90* (1690), reprinted in *Somers Tracts*, IX, 588–90, quotation at 589.

instruments of reformation. By clothing itself in the rhetoric of godly reformation, the precarious revolution regime had at hand an effective means of ideological legitimation. The cornerstone of the Williamite propaganda effort was an unprecedented series of monthly national fasts. Called to invoke divine assistance in the war against France, the fast day services also reminded the nation that God's cause and that of King William was one and the same.[45] The propagandist aspect of the fast days is nicely captured by a ballad of March 1690:[46]

> By Brittains true Monarchs, Great William and Mary ...
> Proclamation is Issu'd, whereby to prepare you,
>   by Fasting and Prayer, their Just Cause to Advance.
>   By which you may see,
>   That all Kingdoms be,
> The Gift of God only, and no Prince's Fee:
> And learn, by true Fasting, Devoutly to Pray
> Usurpers and Rebels may ne'r get the Day.

But there was more to Crown support for reformation of manners than convenient propaganda.

No one in England was more desirous of a true reformation of manners than Queen Mary: '... I wish principally ...', she wrote in August 1691, '... to see my husband in a state to be able to reform the century and establish the church, and to advance by these means the realm of Christ and to glorify also the name of God.'[47] Nor was anyone more certain of the need for reformation. A woman of deep, even somewhat morbid, piety, the queen had been shocked by the state of the nation's religious life upon her return to England in 1689: 'The first thing that surprized me at my coming over, was to see so little devotion in a people so lately in such eminent danger.'[48] While she did what she could to promote godliness at court, the queen remained fearful of divine retribution. There was so 'universal a corruption', she groaned in 1693, 'that we seem only prepared for vengeance'.[49] As Bishop Burnet wrote after the queen's death, 'how good soever she was in Her self, she carried a heavy Load upon her Mind: The deep Sense that she had of the Guilt and Judgments that seemed to be hanging over us.'[50]

[45] Tony Claydon, 'Moral Reformation in the 1690s: Country or Court?' (paper read at the Cambridge Early Modern British History Seminar, 30 Jan. 1991).

[46] *The Pepys Ballads*, ed. Hyder Edward Rollins (8 vols., Cambridge, Massachusetts, 1929–32), V, 85.

[47] Marjorie Bowen, ed., *The Third Mary Stuart: Mary of York, Orange and England. Being a Character Study with Memoirs and Letters of Queen Mary II of England 1662–1694* (1929), 238.

[48] *Ibid.*, 156.

[49] *Ibid.*, 249.

[50] Burnet, *Essay on the Memory*, 134.

The queen was also remembered for the distinctly latitudinarian tone of her churchmanship. Burnet wrote that Queen Mary 'had a true regard to Piety where ever She saw it, in what Form or Party soever. Her Judgment tied her to our Communion, but her Charity was extended to all.'[51] 'Next to her exemplary Piety towards God,' preached the presbyterian John Howe,

> shone with a second Lustre her most amiable Benignity towards men; and peculiarly towards them whom she judg'd Pious, of whatsoever Persuasion in respect of the Circumstances of Religion ... She had divers times express'd her Acceptance, Value, and Desire of their Prayers, whom she knew in some Modes of Worship to differ from her; as one that well understood, that the kingdom of God stands not in lesser things, but in righteousness, peace &c and that they who in these things serve Christ, are acceptable to God, and are to be approved of men.[52]

Howe's fellow presbyterian William Bates stressed the queen's

> sincere Zeal for the healing our unhappy Divisions in Religious Things,and declared her Resolution upon the first Address of some [dissenting] Ministers, that she would use all Means for that Blessed End. She was so wise as to understand the Difference between Matters Doctrinal and Rituals; and so good as to allow a just Liberty for Dissenters in Things of small Moment. She was not fetter'd with Superstitious Scruples, but her clear and free Spirit was for the Union of Christians in Things essential to Christianity.[53]

The royal chaplain William Payne likewise affirmed that Queen Mary had desired to bring 'all Sober Protestants to one Communion, which would have been the greatest Blow to Popery, and Service to Religion in general'.[54] According to Burnet, 'Few things ever grieved her more, than that those Hopes [of comprehension] seemed to languish: And that the prospect of so desired an Union vanished out of sight.'[55] From Queen Mary's own account we know that she was mortified by the miscarriage of the comprehension Convocation of 1689, and that she had little love for high churchmen.[56] In contrast, she warmly applauded

---

[51] *Ibid.*, 102.

[52] John Howe, *A Discourse Relating To the Much-lamented, And Solemn Funeral Of Our Incomparable and most Gracious Queen Mary, Of most Blessed Memory* (1695), 36.

[53] William Bates, *A Sermon Preached upon the much Lamented Death Of our Late Gracious Sovereign Queen Mary* (1695), 20.

[54] William Payne, *A Sermon Upon the Death of the Queen, Preached in the Parish-Church of St Mary White-Chappel* (1695), 16.

[55] Burnet, *Essay on the Memory*, 102–3.

[56] Bowen, *Third Mary Stuart*, 161, 167, 231.

the elevation to the see of Canterbury of John Tillotson, leader of the comprehensionists within the church, and consulted closely with him in a plan for clerical reform.[57]

Small wonder, then, that the deaths of primate and queen within five weeks of each other late in 1694 were viewed as a double blow to the causes of godly reformation and Protestant union. The death of Queen Mary revived in William Bates 'the sorrowful Remembrance of the late Excellent Arch-bishop ... their Principles and Temper, their Designs and Endeavours were for Peace: And the hopes of obtaining it are weakened by the fatal Conjuncture of their Funerals'.[58] Had God prolonged the lives of the queen and the archbishop, lamented Tillotson's ex-pupil John Beardmore, 'we might have expected to have seen and experienced greater public benefits by their Conjunction and further concurrence for the establishing of the church, and reformation of the lives and manners both of the clergy and people and of procuring a greater union and charity among us.'[59] John Howe was

> persuaded, nothing did more recommend our deceased, excellent Archbishop to Her Majesty, than that She knew His Heart to be as Hers, in that Design, viz. Of a General Reformation of Manners, that must have concern'd all Parties; and without which, (leading and preparing us thereto) Union, and the Cessation of Parties, was little to have been hoped for ... And that Two such Persons should be remov'd out of them, is an Awful Umbrage to us of a Divine determination, That less gentle Methods are fitter for us.[60]

But all was not quite doom and gloom. By the time of the two lamentable deaths, a public campaign which linked the causes of reformation and union was well under way.

II

'The world with us is very unruly debauched and profane,' wrote Richard Lapthorne from London in November 1690, 'aboundance of Robberies comitted and vice very little checked by those in Authority which makes me feare God is yet providing greater scourges for the Nation which God grant our humilliation and sincere repentance may divert.'[61] Nine months later, however, Lapthorne was rather more

[57] Thomas Birch, *The life of the Most Reverend Dr John Tillotson, Lord Archbishop of Canterbury* (1752), 249, 338–9.

[58] Bates, *Sermon Preached*, 20.

[59] Quoted in Birch, *Life of Tillotson*, 432.

[60] Howe, *Discourse Relating*, 38.

[61] Richard Lapthorne to Richard Coffin, 8 Nov. 1690, *Portledge Papers*, 90.

hopeful: 'things here looke with a tendency to reformation the Queen strictly enjoyning the Laws to bee put in execution against Sabath breakers and swearers and many have since felt the penalties.'[62] The initiative on the part of the queen which Lapthorne noted was a letter of July 1691 in which she had urged the Middlesex bench to implement the laws against vice. This letter had been solicited from the queen by Bishop Stillingfleet of Worcester, although Stillingfleet himself was acting on behalf of five gentlemen who had recently formed themselves into a society based in the Strand. This was the association which later became known as the First Society for Reformation of Manners.[63]

The objective of the society was to combat sin by working for the vigorous implementation of the many laws against immorality and profanity. To this end, it encouraged informers to denounce offenders before the civil magistrate.[64] In the Autumn of 1691 alleged legal irregularities on the part of the society led to a clash with some of the Middlesex JPs and the Lords Commissioners of the Great Seal. But thanks largely to the backing of the court, these early difficulties had been weathered by the Summer of 1692.[65] Indeed, by the mid-1690s a number of subordinate reformation societies had emerged in the metropolis, which, like the parent body, sponsored the use of the informer as a weapon against sin.[66]

From the viewpoint of this essay, the most interesting feature of the societies for reformation was their ecumenism. They counted among their members not only churchmen but also moderate dissenters. The broad Protestantism of the societies was symbolised by the reformation sermons, which took place from 1697. Organised by the First Society of Reformation, the sermons were preached by conformist clergy at St Mary le Bow and by dissenting ministers at Salters Hall. At both venues the congregations consisted of churchmen and dissenters.[67]

Co-operation between godly Protestants had been a keynote of the reformation societies from very early days. Having initially approached the Church of England religious societies for assistance, towards the end of 1691 the First Society asked dissenting ministers to encourage their congregants to act as informers.[68] Such a readiness to work with dissenters becomes easily understandable when we examine the membership of the First Society. We know something of the religious

[62] Same to the same, 1 Aug. 1691, *ibid.*, 117.

[63] Craig, 'Movement for Reformation,' 25–8.

[64] *Ibid.*, 31–2.

[65] *Ibid.*, 41–63.

[66] *Ibid.*, 72–3; Bahlman, *Moral Revolution*, 37–8. A reformation society established by Edward Harley the younger in 1693 was independent of the First Society.

[67] Craig, 'Movement for Reformation', 178.

[68] *Ibid.*, 95.

sensibilities of three of the society's five founder members: the Westcountryman Maynard Colchester, the Irish gentleman Richard Bulkeley and our old friend Edward Stephens. Although Maynard Colchester was a conformist, his religious views were strongly informed by the presbyterian traditions of his grandfather Sir John Maynard. He later became a Whig MP.[69] Richard Bulkeley was a broad churchman of millenarian views who later became enamoured of the French Prophets.[70] In 1689 Edward Stephens maintained that reformation had 'been greatly disturbed and interrupted by inconsiderate affectation of Uniformity, and improper and preposterous means for that purpose'. He wanted to see the repeal of the Act of Uniformity and the scrapping of all penal laws against dissenters, since charity and unanimity among Protestants were essential in order to ward off God's judgments.[71] Writing in 1699, the author of the official *Account of the Societies for Reformation of Manners* also highlighted the importance of unity in furthering the cause of reformation:

> nothing, I think, can be reasonably supposed sufficient to remove our Guilt, than some considerable and remarkable Reformation ... such a one as may be in some measure proportioned to the Leprosie of Vice and Prophaneness that seems to have almost over-spread us. But if we do truly repent of all our Abominations, and turn from our wicked ways; if we lay aside our unnecessary Strifes, and our unchristian Contentions with one another, which we have so long felt the dismal effects of; if we express our Zeal, and unite our Strength against the Patrons of Vice, who are the Enemies of God and Goodness, more than against those that differ from us in some few things, and those of lesser moment, but agree with us, I conceive, in those that are essential; if we sincerely, and without delay set about and further all pious and proper Endeavours for a National Reformation, truly pursue the things that belong to our Peace, it still seems with us a Day of Mercy, and the Scriptures give us Encouragement to hope, that we may not perish.[72]

To those, then, who believed that reformation and Protestant union

---

[69] Draft biography of Colchester, History of Parliament Trust. I am grateful to Dr David Hayton for permitting me to consult this biography, and for enlightening me on Sir John Maynard's influence over his grandson.

[70] Hillel Schwartz, *The French Prophets: The History of a Millenarian Group in Eighteenth-Century England* (Berkeley, California, 1980), 79–80, 232, n.38.

[71] Stephens, *Caveat against Flattery*, 33, 36. Stephens's broad Protestant sympathies cast doubt on Eamon Duffy's characterisation of him as a 'high-churchman'; see Duffy, 'Primitive Christianity', 297.

[72] *An Account of the Societies for Reformation of Manners, In England and Ireland* (2nd edn, 1699), 109.

were inextricably linked, the ecumenism of the reformation societies was a wholly natural and laudable phenomenon. 'A General Conflagration calls for every Man's Bucket', declared Edmund Calamy in 1699; 'And our spreading Immoralities for all Hands to check them. And it is an hopeful Prognostick in the present Case, that those who differ in Rituals but with too much Vehemence, should unanimously join together in forming those Societies for Reformation, who aim at the Checking those Vices which threaten to over-run us, which are heartily detested by Good Men of all Perswasions.'[73] 'How soon,' the presbyterian Daniel Williams asked in 1699, 'did Divinely inspir'd Minds coalesce in this Undertaking?—And easily made it evident, That there is no such difference between Members of the Established Church, and the Dissenters, that will not be overlook'd by Serious Persons, when the undoubted Concernments of Christ and Practical Godliness are in danger.'[74]

The reformation societies had effected a sort of *de facto* union among godly Protestants, and some hoped that this would pave the way for a more formal union. By 'more Familiar Acquaintance with one another,' suggested the dissenting minister John Shower in 1697, 'you may find so many Persons, of both sorts, worthy of your Esteem and Love, as will take off many Prejudices, destroy Bitterness and Rancor, and cure the Evilspeaking and Detraction, which hath been complained of on all sides; It may tend to heal the Moroseness, and Reservedness, and Distrust of one another, which has kept us at such a Distance; And let us see, that there was no sufficient reason for such an Estrangement.'[75] According to Daniel Williams, the 'very Meeting together, and joynt Concurrence [of churchmen and dissenters] in this Laudable Employment, will Conciliate your Minds and melt them down into Moderation, which is a Temper so necessary, and upon which our Happiness so much depends, that I dare deliver this Prognostick: England can never be fixedly happy in its Religious, or Civil Concernments, but by an Union between the Moderate Churchmen and the Moderate Dissenters'.[76] In 1700 the SPCK founder member John Hooke wrote that the societies for reformation 'hath been great use, to remove the Prejudices, which many had taken up, against the Establish'd Church, and against one another; and hath laid a Foundation of that Union, which may be a probable means of putting an end to Schisms and

[73] Edmund Calamy, *A Sermon Preach'd before the Societies for Reformation of Manners, in London and Middlesex, upon Monday, Febr. 20 1698/9* (1699), epistle dedicatory (unpaginated).

[74] Daniel Williams, *A Sermon Preached at Salters-Hall, To the Societies for Reformation of Manners, May 16 1698* (1698), preface (unpaginated).

[75] John Shower, *A Sermon Preach'd to the Societies for Reformation of Manners, in the Cities of London and Westminster, Nov. 15 1697* (1698), 59–60.

[76] Williams, *A Sermon Preach'd*, 54.

Divisions, of restoring the Primitive Discipline in the Church, and of teaching England to keep the Unity of the Spirit in the bond of Peace'.[77] Samuel Bradford, the rector of St Mary le Bow, was equally sanguine. 'It seems to me a good Omen,' he mused in 1697,

> that God hath stir'd up the hearts of so many among us, to express a concern and zeal for the suppressing Impiety and Vice; and that in prosecuting this Excellent Design, many of our Dissenting Brethren are join'd with those of the Establish'd Communion. 'Tis to be hoped, that the frequent conversing upon so good an Occasion as this, may be a means of removing all Unreasonable Prejudices, and by degrees may beget a better Understanding, and a more favourable Opinion of each other. If our Zeal were but once turn'd towards the great things of Religion, in which we all agree, I am persuaded that our Differences about less Matters would soon abate, and we might perhaps come to an agreement about them before we are aware.[78]

Running through this unionist reformation rhetoric is a deep vein of 'antiformalism',[79] perhaps best expressed by John Howe in 1698:

> they who are agreed, with sincere minds, upon so great and important an End, as the serving this most comprehensive Interest, are agreed in a greater Thing than they can differ in. To differ about a Ceremony or two, or set of words, is but a Triffle, compar'd with being agreed in absolute devotedness to God, and Christ, and in a design, as far as in them lies, of doing good to all. An Agreement in Substantial Godliness and Christianity, in humility, meekness, self-denial, in singleness of heart, benignity, charity, entire love to sincere Christians, as such, in universal love to Mankind, and in a design of doing all the good we can in the world, notwithstanding such go under different denominations, and do differ in so Minute Things, is the most valuable Agreement that can be among Christians.[80]

It is fitting that the words of John Howe should bring us to the conclusion of this paper, for he reminds us of an earlier era of godly

---

[77] [John Hooke], *A Short Account of Several Kind of Societies, Set up of late Years, for the promoting of God's Worship, for the Reformation of Manners, and for the Propagation of Christian Knowledge* (1700), 2. For Hooke's authorship of this tract, see C. M. Rose, 'Politics, Religion and Charity in Augustan London c.1680–c.1720' (University of Cambridge PhD dissertation, 1989), 82.

[78] Samuel Bradford, *A Sermon Preach'd at the Church of St Mary le Bow, to the Societies for Reformation of Manners, Octob. 4 1697* (1697), 42–3.

[79] This term was coined by Colin Davis to denote a central characteristic of Cromwellian churchmanship; see Colin Davis, 'Cromwell's religion', in John Morrill, ed., *Oliver Cromwell and the English Revolution* (1990), 181–208, at 191.

[80] John Howe, *A Sermon Preach'd Febr. 14 1698. And now Publish'd at the Request of the Societies for Reformation of Manners in London and Westminster* (1698), 48.

reformation. Forty years before his sermon to the reformation societies, Howe had been household chaplain to the lord protector, Oliver Cromwell. Then, too, he was noted for stressing the insignificance of divisive religious forms when set beside the virtues of substantial godliness.[81] In this he was by no means a unique figure among Cromwellian churchmen. Recent research has shown that a rejection of religious formalism and an emphasis instead on fundamental godliness were hallmarks of Cromwellian churchmanship. By highlighting the areas of agreement between the godly of all denominations, Cromwell and his clerical supporters hoped both to further the work of reformation and to foster greater unity among godly Protestants.[82] It is in this ideological tradition that we should place many of the leading godly reformers of the 1690s. Like their mid-century predecessors, the proponents of reformation in King William's reign subscribed to a belief in the circular relationship between godly reformation and Protestant union. Unanimity among Protestants, they maintained, was a prerequisite for the transformation of England into a truly godly commonwealth. At the same time, by highlighting the fundamental godly virtues at the expense of the insignificant but divisive religious forms, reformation of manners would itself help to effect the cherished goal of Protestant union.

All this, I would contend, should make us a little wary of the fashionable notion that 1688 marks the beginning of a 'long eighteenth century'. For when we consider the related themes of godly reformation and Protestant union, the continuities between the Cromwellian and the Williamite eras are very striking. Only three decades after the death of the great lord protector, some Englishmen were again seeking to build a land meet for the eyes of God and fit for the godly to live in.

---

[81] Henry Rogers, *The Life and Character of John Howe. With an Analysis of His Writings* (1836), 30–1, 82–4; R. F. Horton, *John Howe* (1895), 37, 49–50.

[82] Davis, 'Cromwell's religion', 201–7; Blair Worden, 'Toleration and the Cromwellian Protectorate', in *Persecution and Toleration: Studies in Church History 21*, ed. W.J. Shiels (Oxford, 1984), 199–233, esp. 210–11.

A THIRTY YEARS' WAR? THE TWO WORLD WARS IN HISTORICAL PERSPECTIVE*

The Prothero Lecture

By Michael Howard

READ I JULY 1992

THE great Helmuth von Moltke, addressing the German Reichstag in May 1890 in the last year of his very long life, gave a sombre warning of wars to come:

> Gentlemen, if the war which has hung over our heads for more than ten years like a sword of Damocles—if this war were to break out, no one could foresee how long it would last nor how it would end. The greatest powers in Europe, armed as never before, would confront each other in battle. None of them could be so completely overthrown in one or two campaigns that they would have to admit defeat, accept peace on harsh terms, and not be able to revive again after a years'-long interval to renew the struggle. Gentlemen, it could be a Seven Years' War; it could be a Thirty Years' War; and woe to the man who sets Europe ablaze, who first throws the match into the powder barrel![1]

We now tend to think of the Two World Wars as discrete and separate, rather than as a Thirty Years' War divided by an interval for recovery, such as von Moltke so darkly foresaw. The image and the experience of the two wars, at least for the British, could hardly have been more different. In the twenty years that separated them, technology had transformed military techniques. The deadlock of trench warfare had been broken; mechanization, air power and radio-communications had restored mobility to the battlefield. Air power had extended destruction to the cities of the belligerents, so that the horrors of the Somme and Passchendaele were to be eclipsed by those of Coventry

---

*It was only some months after completing the text of this lecture that I came across the treatment of the 'Thirty Years War' question by Dr P. H. M. Bell in his excellent work *The Origins of the Second World War in Europe* (London and New York 1986). I am deeply ashamed of this oversight. Had I read Dr Bell's work, I would have adopted a different approach, if indeed I had tackled the problem at all. But I hope that I have provided at least a tentative answer to some of the questions he raised.

[1] Reichsarchiv, *Der Weltkrieg 1914 bis 1918: Kriegsrüstung und Kriegswirtschaft, Anlagen zum ersten band.* (Berlin 1930) 43.

and Dresden. Above all, the extension of hostilities to the Pacific set on foot a new, complex and terrible conflict in that region whose battles bore almost as little resemblance to those of the First World War as they did to the battle of Waterloo.

But were the two World Wars really one war; two acts, as it were in a single drama? This is of course a deeply controversial issue in Germany. For the Germans, the suggestion that both wars resulted from a continuous national policy pursued by both the Second and the Third Reich calls in question their entire structure of national values;[2] whether through the thesis advanced by Fritz Fischer that the Second Reich, so far from fighting a defensive war, had hegemonic intentions as grandiose as those of the Third, or, conversely, the suggestion that Hitler's ambitions were simply a continuation of German traditional statesmanship; that impish Taylorian thesis which, however often it is crushed by argument and scholarship, refuses, like those other imps Petrushka or Till Eulenspiegel, to lie down and die. In a more recent *Historikerstreit* we have seen how sensitive German historians have been to both the suggestion, put forward by Ernst Nolte, that Hitler's policy should be seen as part of some historical continuum, and to the plea from Michael Stürmer that not only the Second but perhaps even the Third Reich embodied values that should not be totally jettisoned by a Germany seeking a new identity.[3]

British historians can sympathise with the sensitivities of our German colleagues and would not wish to exacerbate their problems. Nonetheless, from the point of view of German's adversaries and victims in those wars, the continuity is more apparent that the differences; however much military methods may have been transformed in the interval between them. So far as Britain and France were concerned, 1939 simply brought a renewal of war against a Germany who presented the same kind of threat as she had in 1914, and over a very similar issue. Neither went to war simply to preserve Polish independence, any more than Britain went to war in 1914 simply to preserve Belgian independence. Both fought to check what they saw as a renewed German bid for continental if not world hegemony. In 1939, as in 1914. British participation turned what might have been purely European into a World War; and as was the case in the First World War, support for British resistance ultimately drew in the United States, thus decisively weighting the balance against a Germany who, against a purely European coalition, would almost certainly have prevailed. The crushing of Germany in 1945 was seen by Britain and her allies, at least by

---

[2] See e.g. sources cited by Karl Dietrich Erdman in *The Origins of The First World War: Great Power Rivalry and German War Aims*, ed. H. W. Koch (2nd edn., 1984) 345.

[3] For a summary of the *Historikerstreit*, see *German History*, VI (1988), 63–78.

the generation which had experience the First World War (and this, we must remember, included virtually all their military and political leaders) as the completion of business left unfinished in 1918. An interesting symptom of this attitude was the continuing identification during the Second World War of 'Prussia' as the continuing focus of German militarism, in spite of the negligible part played by Prussia, and indeed by Prussians, in the promotion of the Nazi revolution and the formulation of National Socialist ideology.[4]

For Britain indeed, as for her Continental allies, both wars were really about a single issue—what might be called 'the German Question'; and the German Question had been defined so well by Sir Eyre Crowe in the famous memorandum he wrote in January 1907 in the aftermath of the Tangier crisis, that it merits the constant quotation that it has received.[5]

No one, argued Crowe, could doubt that 'the mere existence and healthy activity of a powerful Germany is an undoubted blessing to the world' or that Germany had every right to compete for 'intellectual and moral leadership': but

> If Germany believes that greater relative preponderance of material power, wider extent of territory, inviolable frontiers and supremacy at sea are necessary and preliminary possessions without which any aspirations to such leadership must end in failure, then England must expect that Germany will surely seek to diminish the power of any rivals, to enhance her own by extending her dominion, to hinder the co-operation of other States, and ultimately to break up and supplant the British Empire.

And he posed the question, which was to be of startling relevance in 1938 for Czechoslovakia and in 1939 for Poland,

> Whether it should be right, or even prudent, for England to incur any sacrifice or see other, friendly, nations sacrificed merely in order to assist Germany in building up step by step the fabric of a universal preponderance, in the blind confidence that in the exercise of such a preponderance Germany will confer unmixed blessings on the world at large, and promote the welfare and happiness of all other peoples without doing injury to any one.

When he wrote those words in 1907, Eyre Crowe was doing no more than summarizing the *Weltpolitische* ambitions being expressed at the

---

[4] See Michael Howard, 'Prussia in German History' in *Lessons of History* (Oxford 1991), 49.
[5] In *British Documents on the Origins of the War 1898–1914*, eds. G. P. Gooch and Harold Temperley, III (1928), 397–420.

time in Germany by public figures from the kaiser downward; ambitions arising from a consciousness of capabilities denied opportunities, of huge power denied outlet—and denied outlet, it was believed, specifically by Britain. I will not weary you with the familiar quotations: Max Weber's Inaugural Lecture at Freiburg in 1895, with its declaration 'that the unification of Germany was a youthful folly ... if it should be the conclusion and not the starting point for a German *Weltpolitik*'; Hans Delbrück's statement in the *Preussische Jahrbücher* of November 1899, that, 'We want to be a World Power and pursue colonial policy in the grand manner ... the entire future of our people among the great nations depends on it'; to choose only the most moderate and respectable of the academics, and ignore the outpourings of the Pan German League.[6] These advocates of *Weltpolitik* threw down an explicit challenge to Britain. 'We can pursue this policy with England or against England', Delbrück had continued. 'With England means peace; against England means—through war.' For Admiral von Tirpitz and his followers in the Navy League, peaceful accommodation with England was to be obtained through pressures and threats of a kind indistinguishable, in the British view, from expressions of hostile intentions; and to make those pressures credible German leaders found it politic to stir up among their public opinion an *England-hass* that was almost without precedent in the history of international politics. It was to find expression when war broke out in Lissauer's notorious 'Hymn of Hate'.[7]

So in 1914 there was for Britain quite certainly a German Problem— a problem of great capabilities compounded by very evident hostile intentions. The full measure of those capabilities became clear only when war broke out, with the spectacular victories of the German armies on every front. Probably not even the Germans had appreciated the formidable extent of their military power until they saw it in action, much less realised the opportunities that their victories would present. Fritz Fischer has documented very thoroughly the full range of German ambitions that was maturing before 1914, even if he failed—as in my opinion he did fail—to prove that Germany deliberately began the war

[6] Quoted by Immanuel Geiss in *The Origins of the First World War: Great Power Rivalry and German War Aims*, ed. H. W. Koch (2nd edn., 1984) 50–2. See also Woodruff D. Smith, *The Ideological Origins of Nazi Imperialism* (Oxford, 1986) and Paul Kennedy, *The Rise of the Anglo-German Antagonism* (1980).

[7] Ernst Lissauer, *Germany's Hymn of Hate* first appeared in the Munich journal *Jugend* and was published in an English translation by Barbara Henderson in 1914 by the Central Committee for Political Organisations, Leaflet No. 112. Its refrain ran:

    We shall never forego our hate
    We have all but a single hate
    We love as one, we hate as one
    We have one foe and one alone
    ENGLAND!

in order to fulfil them. Most of them were to find a place in the famous 'September Memorandum' of 1914, and Chancellor Bethmann-Hollweg defined their overall object as being to provide

> security for the German Reich in west and east for all imaginable time. For this purpose France must be so weakened as to make her revival as a great power impossible for all time. Russia must be thrust back as far as possible from Germany's eastern frontier and her domination over the non-Russian peoples broken.[8]

To this others add their glosses: the virtual annexation of Belgium and the mineral resources of France; a great African empire; a powerful *Mittel Europa* as the basis for an expanded German economy; a vassal Poland; perhaps some German settlements to provide security in the East.

But extensive as they were, these were war aims of a traditional kind, a quest for absolute security through extension of territorial control; an objective not unusual among continental powers. But absolute security for Germany was absolute insecurity for everyone else—not least the British. hence the conclusion of the British government in 1914 that the German problem could be solved only by the destruction, not so much of German power, as of the regime and the philosophy, generally stigmatised at the time as 'Prussianism', wielding that power.[9]

That was easier said than done. German military power and military skills proved immense, and the uninterrupted course of her military victories only strengthened the determination of her military and most of her political leaders to secure objectives commensurate with those victories and the sacrifices involved in gaining them. Although the Social Democrats remained true to their objective of peace without annexations and indemnities, the growth and influence of the Fatherland Front showed that expansionist war aims were not a monopoly of the military elites—certainly not the 'Prussian' elites targeted by British propaganda.

Nor could 'Prussianism' be destroyed after the war simply through the overthrow of the monarchy that embodied it; any more than Germany's power could be destroyed by the dissolution of her armed forces and the limited occupation of her territories. Whatever the peaceful intentions of the Weimar Republic, the basis of that power remained intact in the size of German's population, in her industrial strength, in the excellence of her technology, and in a military expertise too deep-rooted to be destroyed by the abolition of her general staff.

---

[8] Fritz Fischer, *Germany's Aims in the First World War* (1967), 103ff.
[9] See e.g. Norman Angell, *Prussianism and its Destruction* (1914).

The essence of that power remained intact, and available for any government willing to develop and make use of it.

There were few illusions about this at the Paris Peace Conference in 1919. But short of the kind of total conquest, occupation, division and debellation imposed on Germany in 1945, which probably lay beyond the capacity if not the ambitions of the victorious allies in 1918, what could be done about it?

The French had the clearest idea: cripple German economic power by annexing the Rhineland, by giving the industries of Silesia to the Poles, and by imposing massive reparations on Germany; the latter, admittedly, not so much in order to weaken German economy as to justify long-term occupation of the left bank of the Rhine. But how practicable was such a policy in the long run—and how much sense did it make for the economy of Europe as a whole? In any case it was a programme unacceptable to the British; both to British conservatives who did not want to see a German domination of Europe replaced by a French or, worse, a Bolshevist one, and to British liberals whose temperamental inclination to conciliation was strengthened by the arguments of Maynard Keynes.

Once that programme proved impossible, France turned to another course of action; accepting the inevitability of German revival but trying to create a balance against it, by building alliances in eastern Europe. But these new, weak east European states could provide no serious substitute for France's traditional ally, Russia; and Russia's revolutionary intentions now alarmed many people even more than did the spectre of a revitalised Germany. In any case the French political leadership was incapable of providing an army that could implement the projects of their diplomats. Meanwhile the British were indifferent, and both the United States and the Soviet Union had ruled themselves *hors de combat*. It had taken, we must remember, the combined efforts of all these powers to defeat Germany in 1918.

It is thus not surprising that within six years of the war's ending we find all Germany's former adversaries abandoning the attempt to destroy her power, and instead pursuing the path of conciliation, whether via Rapallo or via Locarno. Within twenty years the verdict of Versailles had been effectively reversed without a shot being fired. By November 1938 the reparations question had been settled and the Germany economy was booming. All servitudes imposed on Germany with respect to her western borders had been lifted. The German rump of the old Habsburg monarchy had been peacefully absorbed into the Third Reich. The principle of national self-determination was being applied in the multi-ethnic conglomerate of Czechoslovakia. German economic power dominated central Europe.There was left only the question of Germany's borders with Poland; and given the acquiescent posture of both the British and French governments there is no reason to suppose that a tough, skilful, and above all patient German government could not have settled those in its favour as well. By 1938 Germany had regained a dominance in Europe at least comparable to that of Bismarck; and like that of Bismarck, it was exercised with the willing consent of the British government and the glum acquiescence of the French. Why, therefore did a Second World War break out in September 1939?

The short answer is that Britain decided that it should. War takes place, as Clausewitz pointed out, mainly for the defender: 'the conqueror would like to make his entry into our country unopposed'.[10] If Britain had so decided, war would have broken out a year earlier over the Sudetenland, or indeed three years earlier in 1936, when Germany re-occupied the Rhineland. As it was, by guaranteeing the independence of Poland in March 1939, the British government quite deliberately created a risk of war, and did so with overwhelming public support. It did not want war: not even Neville Chamberlain's bitterest adversaries can accuse him of war-mongering; but on the assumption that Hitler did not want war either, the creation of such a risk was the only deterrent at Britain's disposal against an extension of German power far transcending the acceptable continental dominance established by 1938.

The assumption was of course false. Hitler *did* want war, if not that particular war at that particular time; and even if he had not wanted war, he wanted objectives which, whether achieved peacefully or by violence, would have established Germany in a hegemonic position undreamed of by even the most ambitious statesmen of the Wilhelmine Reich. As was becoming increasingly clear, his adversaries were faced with the stark alternatives of resistance or surrender.

Eyre Crowe's analysis, in fact, was still valid after thirty years. A powerful Germany in itself posed no threat to British interests or international stability: after all, Bismarck had provided stability in Europe for a quarter of a century. Indeed in the 1930s a powerful Germany—especially a powerful right-wing Germany—was widely believed to provide a further advantage by acting as a bulwark against Bolshevism; and for that the possessing classes in both France and Britain were prepared to forgive Hitler a very great deal. For many of them, indeed, Hitler's Germany provided not so much a threat as a reassurance, if not indeed a model. To a Germany, however powerful,

---

[10] Karl von Clausewitz, *On War*, VI, Chapter 5.

offering real stability, Britain and France would have yielded much—
certainly not excluding the Polish Corridor.

But in the latter half of the 1930s Eyre Crowe's rhetorical question
became more relevant with almost every day that passed:

> whether it could be right, or even prudent, for England to incur any
> sacrifice or see other, friendly nations sacrificed merely in order to
> assist Germany in building up step by step the fabric of a universal
> preponderance, in the blind confidence that in the exercise of such
> a preponderance Germany will confer unmixed blessings on the
> world at large.[11]

By 1939 the answer to that question had become clear. German
power and intentions were once again threatening the structure of a
world-system on whose stability British power precariously depended.
Hitler was no Bismarck; he was not even William II; he was Hitler.

Even in 1939 few people in Britain appreciated who Hitler was, and
what he intended to do. Neville Chamberlain, broadcasting to the
nation on the outbreak of war rightly told his listeners that 'it is evil
things we shall be fighting against', and he went on to define them:
'brute force, bad faith, injustice, oppression and persecution'.[12] It was
an accurate enough description of Hitler's methods but hardly an
adequate account of his objectives. Nor did it really explain why the
British people found themselves at war. Hitler might be guilty of all
these crimes and still pose no threat to British interests. But Chamberlain
can hardly be blamed for his lack of understanding if, twenty years
later, a British historian so expert in the history of Germany and central
Europe as A. J. P. Taylor could, like Mr Chamberlain, stigmatise Hitler
as being 'wicked', but doubt whether he had any long-term objectives
at all.[13]

In their baffled and insular incomprehension of Hitler's ultimate
objectives, both Neville Chamberlain and A. J. P. Taylor were probably
typical of the bulk of their fellow countrymen. But the British were
concerned less with the details of the Nazi programme than with the
revival of the power and ambition of the German State, however
horrific that programme might be. Britain did not go to war in 1939
to destroy Fascism, or to defend democracy, much less to rescue the
Jews. Even the destruction of Poland—another far-away people, like

---

[11] See n. 5 above.
[12] Keith Feiling, *The Life of Neville Chamberlain* (1970), 416.
[13] A. J. P. Taylor, *The Origins of the Second World War* (1961), 69–71.

the Czechs, of whom the British knew nothing—would hardly have constituted a *casus belli* if it had not been seen to add an intolerable accretion to the menace of German power. Britain went to war in 1939, thus ultimately turning a central European border-dispute into a world holocaust, for the oldest, the least reputable, but the most basic of all motives—power politics; to resolve Humpty Dumpty's question 'Who will be master—that's all'. But power-politics, as a rather repent-ant pacifist Norman Angell had found himself forced to confess in the 1930s, is sometimes the politics of not being overpowered.[14]

The British decision left Hitler baffled and angry. He did not want war with England and did not see the need for it. His long-term aims are now clearer to us than they were to Neville Chamberlain and even to A.J.P. Taylor, but they had been set out in *Mein Kampf* for all to see. His policy was amazingly consistent as to ends, however flexible it may have been as to means. His object, set out in *Mein Kampf* and constantly reiterated thereafter in speech after speech, was the recreation of a new German nation, cleansed of all the cultural and racial imperfections that had resulted from the process of modernisation, and above all from the termite-like activities of those enemies of culture and cleanliness, the Jews; microbes in the body-politic that had to be eliminated, if necessary exterminated, if the Germans were ever to be restored to sanity and health.[15] Further, the industrialisation and urbanisation of Germany which had done so much to rot good, healthy German stock was to be balanced and counteracted by the preservation and extension of the German peasantry, rooted in good, healthy German soil. But since there was not enough suitable territory within the existing frontiers of Germany to provide adequate living space for such an extension, more must be acquired: much as the British, Hitler pointed out, another over-industrialised people, had acquired colonies of settlement all over the world.

But such overseas settlements, Hitler realised, were likely to break away and create new states of their own. Even if they did not, links with them had to be defended by an expensive navy, the creation of which had proved so disastrous before 1914. Germany had therefore to find its *Lebensraum* in the contiguous territories to the East; territories not only temperate and fertile, but providentially left in a state of chaos by the collapse of a Russian Empire that had in any case only been kept going by its German elites. As a superior *Kulturvolk*, the Germans had as much right, and indeed duty, to take possession of and rule these territories as the Anglo-Saxons had to extend their rule throughout

---

[14] Norman Angell, *After All* (1951), 137.

[15] Adolf Hitler, *Mein Kampf*, trsl. Karl Mannheim (1969) *passim*, esp. 126–37. On the Jews, see *Hitler's Table Talk 1941–44* (2nd edn., 1973), 332.

the extra-European world. The inferior peoples who inhabited them were to be either subordinated, as the British had subordinated the native inhabitants of their African and Asian colonies, or eliminated, as the Americans had eliminated the redskins.[16]

Hitler recognised that in order to achieve these objectives it would certainly be necessary to have a final settlement of accounts with France.[17] But why should Britain object to them? One of the principal grounds for Hitler's objections to German *Weltpolitik* before 1914 was that it had brought Germany into an entirely unnecessary conflict with England. Unlike so many *Weltpolitiker* of the Wilhelmine era, Hitler did not consider the humiliation of Britain as a necessary step in the fulfilment of Germany's destiny as a world power. Indeed, Hitler seems to have been far less concerned with German's world status than he was with her cultural integrity: unlike the imperialists of the Wilhelmine era, he wanted colonies and expansion for reasons of domestic stability and racial health rather than for global prestige, or even national security. There was much to be lost by antagonising Britain—Hitler's experiences on the western front had given him a healthy respect for her as an adversary[18]—and everything to be gained by befriending her; so long as she did not block his ambitions to the East. If the worst came to the worst he would have to fight,and, if need be, invade her; but he could never quite believe that, ultimately, good sense would not prevail and that the right-minded people in whose influence he stubbornly believed would not at the last moment mount a *coup* to overthrow the Jewish warmongers and their leader Churchill. There is indeed an interesting parallel to be drawn between the hopes he placed on such a development, and those that British optimists placed on a comparable coup against Hitler.

We know that such 'right-minded people' did exist; but the remarkable thing is not that they should have existed, but that there should have been so few of them, and that their influence should have been so slight. There was after all little affection among the British for the French,and even less for the small nations of eastern Europe. There was, at least on the right wing, endemic fear of communism and some respect for the measures Hitler had taken to eradicate it. There was, to put it mildly, less sympathy for the Jews than one would wish, although anti-semitism had not penetrated so deeply into British society as it had into French. There was an overriding concern for the security of the Empire and much suspicion of any continental commitment;

[16] Norman Rich, *Hitler's War Aims: Ideology, the Nazi State and the Course of Expansion* (1973), 212-49.
[17] *Mein Kampf*, 609, 616.
[18] *Ibid.*, 133.

and among the population as a whole, there was a deep disinclination to go to war.

But none of these considerations could override the fundamental perception that, confronting a powerful and dynamic Germany dominating the continent—and, now, commanding considerable air power—Britain was not safe, or that at best her security would depend on the whim of an unpredictable ruler in Berlin. The distinction between *Weltpolitik* and *Lebensraum* as German objectives was, for the British people, academic: what mattered was the huge accumulation of German power and the evident determination of Germany's leaders to use it to extend their dominion. Even those who most sympathised with Hitler's objectives disliked the prospect of Britain becoming a tributary kingdom within the German Reich, even if their own suzerainty still embraced half of the extra-European world. So with immense reluctance, and in full realisation of the unfavourable odds, the British government decided once again to confront German power with armed force as they had in 1914, and to overthrow the regime wielding it.

But the odds were now not only unfavourable; they were impossible. The balance of power had radically shifted since 1914. After the interval foreseen by von Moltke, Germany had remobilised her resources and the will to use them. Of her former adversaries, Russia and the United States had dropped out of the contest, France was exhausted and Britain had barely begun the remobilisation of military strength needed to turn her once more into an effective continental power. Within less than a year German domination of the continent had been converted by military conquest into a hegemony that Britain was no longer in any position to contest. Even if the subjugation of Britain herself was not immediately practicable, the British could hope to do no more than stave off defeat unless, improbably, the United States emerged from its isolation and once again came to their rescue. The ambitions listed in the September Memorandum of 1914 could now be realised. France was debellated. A protectorate was established over the Low Countries. German naval control was extended from Norway to the Pyrenees. German dominance in *Mitteleuropa* was unchallengeable. Certain aspirations in the Baltic remained unfulfilled, but if a limited war with the Soviet Union proved necessary to 'liberate' the Baltic Republics, there was no doubt who would have been the victor. *Weltpolitik*, the acquisition of an overseas Empire, still awaited the defeat of England, but few people in Germany were any longer interested; Hitler least of all. The war for the mastery of Europe that had begun in 1914 was over, and the Germans had won it.

With that victory the overwhelming majority of the German people would no doubt have been content, and sooner or later Britain would have had to accept it. Had the German military victories of 1939–40 led to the creation of a politically and economically stable Greater Germany at the centre of an acquiescent Europe, they might have been regarded as the logical continuation and fulfilment of those of 1866–70. Hitler would have established his place as the rightful successor of Bismarck and of Frederick the Great. But that was not the role in which he had cast himself. The dynamic of the Nazi revolution had not been exhausted; the objectives outlined in *Mein Kampf*, never lost to sight, had not yet been achieved. So a year later, to the astonishment of the world and not least of the Germans themselves, Hitler launched a new and apparently quite unnecessary war against the Soviet Union, in pursuit of objectives that would have amazed the German policy-makers of 1914.

To the British, of course, it did not look like a new war. They saw the German invasion of the Soviet Union as a necessary preliminary to the defeat of Britain. It fitted comfortably within their historical experience of the Napoleonic Wars from which, under the tutelage of Sir Arthur Bryant, they had been deriving much-needed comfort.[19] But German historians who claim that Hitler represented a divergence from rather than a continuation of the mainstream of German history argue that this truly was a different war, one fought for different objectives and using radically different methods from the war for European hegemony that had been fought and won in the West. In my view they are correct.

There were certainly strategic arguments for attacking and defeating the Soviet Union even before the defeat of England. There was the erroneous belief that the British were sustained by expectation of Soviet help; together with the quite correct view that since Roosevelt's America would not easily permit Britain to be destroyed, the war might be a long one. There was the realisation that the Soviet Union would continue to be a tough rival both in the Baltic and in the Balkans.[20] But none of these arguments were compelling. Stalin showed no signs of abandoning his complaisant neutrality or interrupting his substantial deliveries of war material to the Third Reich; while the lamentable performance of the Red Army in the 'Winter War' against Finland makes highly implausible the argument sometimes advanced that the Soviet Union was itself planning a surprise attack. There was no strategic compulsion for Hitler to attack the Soviet Union when he did. No: the only convincing explanation of his decision is that he was

---

[19] See Arthur Bryant, *The Years of Endurance* and *The Years of Victory* (1942 and 1944).

[20] Andreas Hillgruber, *Hitlers Strategie: Politik und Kriegsführung 1940–41* (Bernard und Graefe Verlung, Frankfurt am Main, 1965).

anxious to proceed as quickly as possible to the next and final stage of the programme he had outlined in *Mein Kampf*, for which his victories in the west had been no more than a necessary preliminary. The Soviet Union was to be destroyed; the frontiers of slavdom were to be pushed back to the furthest possible extent; the newly conquered territories were to be settled with good German peasant stock, and the native inhabitants either subjugated or exterminated. Poland had already provided a testing bed for this programme. A few months later, at the Wannsee conference in January 1942, the decision was taken to use the extermination techniques being developed on the Eastern Front to provide a final solution to the Jewish problem in Europe as a whole.[21]

Was this programme a mere extension of the German war aims of 1914? I find it hard to believe so. In 1914 the German people went enthusiastically to war for vague and splendid causes; to assert and extend the greatness of their country, to destroy encircling enemies, to show that the spirit of 1870 was not dead. Would they have marched eastward with equal enthusiasm in 1941 if they had known what Hitler's very precise war aims were? It must be said that if they did not know, it was hardly Hitler's fault; after all, he had presented a copy of *Mein Kampf* to every newly-wedded couple, and the work is by no means so turgid and unreadable as is so often depicted.But Hitler himself had repeatedly expressed his doubts as to the will and the capacity of the German people to carry out his intentions unless they had been carefully indoctrinated, and indeed bred, to do so.[22] Many of them were so indoctrinated in the short time available, and carried out Hitler's gruesome programme with enthusiasm and efficiency. But it is only fair to note that it was not only the Germans who did this: Balts, Poles, Austrians and Ukrainians all assisted in the extermination process. Even in the 'liberal' societies of western Europe the police made no difficulties when called on to round up the Jews. In France and the Netherlands they did so with exemplary efficiency.[23]

Further, Hitler's ideas were not specifically German.[24] Many of them he had absorbed in pre-war Vienna from the Austrians Karl Lüger and Georg von Schönerer. If one had to name the major focus of anti-Semitism in pre-1914 Europe, one would probably cite France, or possibly Russia, before even considering Germany. The concept of *Lebensraum*, a healthy balance between population and soil, was implicit

---

[21] Norman Rich, *Hitler's War Aims vol II: the Establishment of the New Order* (1974), 7.

[22] *Mein Kampf*, 31, 307. See also Esme Robertson, *The Origins of the Second World War* (1971), 13.

[23] See Omer Bartov, *The Eastern Front 1914–15: German Troops and the Barbarisation of Warfare* (1985). For European support for Hitler's policies see John Lukacs, *The Last European War* (1976) and Norman Rich, *op. cit.*, II, *passim*.

[24] *Mein Kampf*, 91, 109, 111.

in much British Imperialist literature in the 'eighties and 'nineties, and one of the earliest expositors was a Scandinavian scholar, Rudolph Kjellen. Hitler learned his racism from a Frenchman, Gobineau, and an Englishman, Houston Stewart Chamberlain; while the idea of compulsory sterilisation of the unfit was sufficiently respectable to have been taken up enthusiastically by the British Home Secretary in 1910: Mr Winston Churchill.[25]

None of these ideas were, in fact, peculiar to Germany. Before 1914 they were as marginal there as they were in the rest of Europe. Although they may have been germinating in the minds of a few German right-wing thinkers at the time, they certainly did not figure in the war aims of the Wilhelmine Reich. It required Hitler's malign genius, first to crystallise them into a coherent programme, and then to play on the hopes, the fears, and the resentments of the German people to gain an ascendancy over them so absolute as to make them his willing accomplices in carrying it out. Hitler was the product of a European, not specifically a German culture; certainly not that of the Germany of 1914.

Nevertheless it was only Germany's victory in the long European war foreseen by von Moltke—a twenty-five, rather than a thirty-years war—that made it possible for Hitler to implement his programme. Germany had to win the interrupted First World War before he was able to embark so disastrously on the Second.

---

[25] Paul Addison, *Churchill on the Home Front 1900–55* (1992), 124–6.

BRISTOL WEST INDIA MERCHANTS IN THE EIGHTEENTH CENTURY

By Kenneth Morgan

READ 19 SEPTEMBER 1992 AT THE UNIVERSITY OF LIVERPOOL

ON the north wall of the cloisters in Bristol Cathedral there is a small headstone 'Sacred to the Memory of Thomas Daniel Esq ... a respectable Merchant of this City who was born in Barbados on the 14th March 1730 and departed this life on the 23rd February 1802.' In the north transept, on a floor marble over the family vault, another inscription to the same man can be found. Thomas Daniel Sr, as he was known, came from a mercantile family that had settled in Barbados in the mid-seventeenth century. He spent his early career in that island and later emigrated to Bristol in 1764.[1] From then onwards he built up a substantial business as a Bristol West India merchant, and handed this down to his son, Thomas Daniel Jr, at the turn of the nineteenth century.[2] The son expanded his trade in Caribbean sugar and acquired slave plantations in Barbados, Antigua, Nevis, Montserrat, Tobago and British Guiana. After Emancipation in 1834 he and his brother, John, received £102,000 in compensation for the loss of their slaves— the second largest sum awarded to Bristol proprietors.[3] The money

---

[1] Details taken from *Caribbeana: Miscellaneous Papers relating to the History, Genealogy, Topography, and Antiquities of the British West Indies*, ed. Vere Langford Oliver, 6 vols. (1909–19), II, 80; Burke's *Landed Gentry* (1871), I, 321; and C. H. Cave, *A History of Banking in Bristol from 1750 to 1899* (Bristol, 1899), 228; which provides a pedigree of the Daniel family.

[2] Based on the sugar imports of the Daniel family listed in Society of Merchant Venturers, Bristol, wharfage books. Thomas Daniel & Sons' sugar trade with Barbados is documented in University of London Library, Newton Estate Papers, MS 523.

[3] Peter Marshall, *Bristol and the Abolition of Slavery: The Politics of Emancipation* (Bristol Branch of the Historical Association, pamphlet no. 37, Bristol, 1975), app., i–ii. The figure cited is an estimate, for the lists of compensation awards do not show the amounts awarded to particular firms or families. John Latimer gives a lower estimate of £55,178 received in compensation for slaves by T. & J. Daniel (*The Annals of Bristol in the Nineteenth Century* [Bristol, 1887], 188). For indentures and deeds concerning the Daniels' West Indian properties see B[ristol] U[niversity] L[ibrary], D. M. 78/126–8, 130–1; D. M. 89/3/14–15; D. M. 89/7/56; and D. M. 183. Thomas Daniel Jr was a member of two mercantile firms: Thomas Daniel & Sons in Bristol and Thomas Daniel & Co. in London (P[ublic] R[ecord] O[ffice], London, PROB 11/2192/477 [PCC 1854], will of Thomas Daniel Jr).

accumulated by Thomas Daniel Jr enabled him to purchase a fine town house in Berkeley Square, in a fashionable residential area, plus a pleasant country seat at Henbury, just beyond the north-western boundaries of the city.[4] Burgeoning wealth went hand in hand with civic status. From 1785 until 1835, Daniel served on the Bristol Common Council, the governing body of the city. He was an alderman from 1798 until 1835, a Bristol city councillor from 1835 until 1841, sheriff of Bristol in 1786/7, mayor in 1797/8, and master of the Society of Merchant Venturers—the most prestigious mercantile body in the city—in 1805.[5] His contribution to the civic life of Bristol was such that, long before his death in 1854, he was referred to as 'king of Bristol' because of 'his complete omnipotence in corporate affairs.'[6] He left over £200,000 in his will.[7]

Similar vignettes of the careers of Bristol West India merchants and absentee planters could be presented from the many memorial inscriptions that survive in other churches in Bristol and Clifton and at neighbouring Bath Abbey.[8] They remind us that Georgian Bristol was both an important Atlantic trading centre and a city with a significant West India interest. Sugar was the main staple product that attracted merchants and planters to the Caribbean. It was the most valuable commodity imported into Britain from anywhere in the world between 1670 and 1820, before being replaced by cotton, and it was central to the prosperity of Bristol's economy in that period.[9] Bristol's sugar imports rose from an annual average of 13,604 hogsheads in 1728–32 to 21,094 hogsheads per year between 1798 and 1800.[10] The city's distilleries and sugar refineries, near the Avon and Frome rivers, were kept busy by the influx of ever-larger quantities of sugar and its by-products, molasses and rum.[11] Even the poor in Bristol became reliant

[4] Vere Langford Oliver, *The Monumental Inscriptions in the Churches and Churchyards of the Island of Barbados, British West Indies* (1915), 25.

[5] Alfred B. Beaven, *Bristol Lists: Municipal and Miscellaneous* (Bristol, 1899), 68, 285.

[6] John Latimer, *The Annals of Bristol in the Eighteenth Century* (Bristol, 1893), 455.

[7] Graham Bush, *Bristol and its Municipal Government, 1820–1851* (Bristol Record Society Publications, XXIX, Bristol, 1976), 239.

[8] E.g. *Caribbeana*, ed. Oliver, II, 78–85, 137–42, 273–4, 371–82.

[9] The general importance of sugar is emphasised in Ralph Davis, *The Industrial Revolution and British Overseas Trade* (Leicester, 1979), 43. The significance of sugar to Bristol's economy is analysed in I. V. Hall, 'A History of the Sugar Trade in England, with special reference to the Sugar Trade of Bristol' (MA thesis, University of Bristol, 1925); C. M. MacInnes, *Bristol: A Gateway of Empire* (Bristol, 1939), ch. 11; and Kenneth Morgan, *Bristol and the Atlantic Trade in the Eighteenth Century* (Cambridge, 1993), ch. 7.

[10] Morgan, *Bristol and the Atlantic Trade*, Table 7.3, 191.

[11] Maps showing the location of Bristol's sugar refineries and distilleries are included in M. D. Lobel and E. M. Carus-Wilson, *Bristol: Historic Towns Atlas* (1975). The history of Bristol's sugar refineries has been studied, mainly from an institutional perspective, in several articles by I. V. Hall: see esp. 'Whitson Court Sugar House, Bristol, 1665–1824,'

on sugar as part of their diet, either for tea, coffee or chocolate consumption, or for cooking purposes, and it seems, to judge from trends in sugar prices, that demand usually outstripped supply.[12]

As the century progressed, however, the Bristol West India trade experienced a major transformation of scale. Several hundred individuals handled sugar cargoes in the city between 1700 and 1800, but the trade became more concentrated over time in the hands of larger merchants. Between 1728 and 1732, for instance, some 513 men imported sugar at Bristol each year, with an average of 26.5 hogsheads per firm. By 1763–67, the number of firms had fallen to an annual average of 163 and the amount of sugar imported by each had increased to 84 hogsheads. The same trend continued thereafter. By 1798–1800, an annual average of eighty-five firms handled 248 hogsheads of sugar per year.[13] Concentration was accompanied by a certain amount of specialisation. Thus by the end of the eighteenth century Bristol merchants tended to take a prime interest in the sugar trade, whereas Liverpudlians were more committed to the slave trade and Glaswegians to the tobacco trade.[14] Bristol remained the leading British outport for sugar imports for virtually all of the eighteenth century. After the American Revolution this was reflected in the presence of West India merchants in the city along with sugar brokers, sugar refineries, a West India coffee house, a West India Society, and at least one MP who directly represented the West India interest.[15]

The present essay is not concerned with the mechanics of the sugar trade per se. For a discussion of the organisation of that trade, the impact of war on commerce, and the rivalry between West India merchants and sugar refiners, the interested reader should consult chapter seven of my book *Bristol and the Atlantic Trade in the Eighteenth Century*. This paper is concerned instead with whether the careers of Bristol West India merchants followed the pattern suggested in my opening sketch of the Daniels. How many Bristol sugar merchants were born in the Caribbean? To what extent did they pass on their businesses from one generation to the next? Did their growing wealth help them to gain social status and civic eminence? And what was the role of the

---

T[ransactions of the] B[ristol and] G[loucestershire] A[rchaeological] S[ociety], LXV (1944), 1–97, and 'The Daubenys: Part 1,' *ibid.*, LXXXIV (1965), app. II, 137–40.

[12] Morgan, *Bristol and the Atlantic Trade*, 184–5, 209.

[13] *Ibid.*, Table 7.3, 191. For a similar phenomenon in the tobacco and slave trades see Jacob M. Price and Paul G. E. Clemens, 'A Revolution of Scale in Overseas Trade: British Firms in the Chesapeake Trade, 1675–1775,' *Journal of Economic History*, XLVII (1987), 1–43.

[14] Cf. Jacob M. Price, 'The Rise of Glasgow in the Chesapeake Tobacco Trade, 1707–1775,' *W[illiam and] M[ary] Q[uarterly]*, 3rd series, XI (1954), 190.

[15] Bailey's *Western and Midland Directory: Or Merchant's and Tradesman's Useful Companion for the Year 1783*; MacInnes, *Bristol: A Gateway of Empire*, 235, 363.

West India interest in the economic development of Bristol in the early industrial age? These questions have not been explored satisfactorily for this group of merchants, though there are a couple of articles available on the merchant community of eighteenth-century Bristol.[16] My answer to these questions is based on a prosopographical study of the thirty leading firms in the Bristol sugar trade during the eighteenth century. Because of partnerships, fifty individuals are covered altogether.[17] A good many of these merchants continued trading into the nineteenth century, so my analysis is not always cut off at 1800. My procedure for defining this business elite is simple, and really the only one available: it is based on the total amount of sugar imported by firms during their entire commercial history. The main source for these calculations consists of the wharfage books at the Society of Merchant Venturers in Bristol. These records contain some gaps but not enough to warrant problems. They list individual consignments of all imports into Bristol by specific firms, though they do not name the islands from which the sugar was imported. They can be supplemented for several years by the Bristol presentments, or printed customs bills of entry, in the Avon County reference library, Bristol.[18] These sources are important because they provide a fairly continuous index of sugar imports for Bristol, whereas for London and Liverpool comparable information no longer exists in a useable series.[19]

The recruitment patterns of Bristol West India merchants are a suitable starting point. They can be determined from apprenticeship lists and burgess books for Bristol plus a variety of family histories and other sources that throw light on the social and geographical origins of the fifty men in our sample group.[20] In terms of social background,

---

[16] W. E. Minchinton, 'The Merchants of Bristol in the Eighteenth Century,' in *Sociétés et groupes sociaux en Aquitaine et en Angleterre*, Fédérations Historiques du Sud-Ouest (Bordeaux, 1979), 185–200; David Richardson, *The Bristol Slave Traders: A Collective Portrait* (Bristol Branch of the Historical Association, pamphlet no. 60, Bristol, 1985).

[17] The firms are listed in the appendix.

[18] Fifty-eight years of the eighteenth century can be fully covered by these sources.

[19] Eighteenth-century Liverpool Port Books are unavailable after 1726. All post-1696 London Port Books, with one defective exception, were destroyed in the late nineteenth century (Price and Clemens, 'A Revolution of Scale in Overseas Trade,' 2, 29). The availability of customs accounts for Port Glasgow and Greenock means that, as for Bristol, a collective biography of leading West India merchants is feasible: see T. M. Devine, 'An Eighteenth-Century Business Elite: Glasgow-West India Merchants, *c.*1750–1815,' *Scottish Historical Review*, LXVII (1978), 40–67.

[20] This section on the origins of Bristol West India merchants is based primarily on the apprenticeship lists and burgess books at the B[ristol] R[ecord] O[ffice]. I have not thought it necessary to give volume and folio citations. Supplementary data has been gathered from other sources. Material on Robert Claxton, Thomas Daniel Sr and Jr, David Dehany, Richard Meyler Sr and James Tobin was taken from *Caribbeana*, ed. Oliver, II, 80, 276, III, 290, V, 2–3, VI, 42–3. Details on George Gibbs were gleaned from John Arthur Gibbs, *The History of Antony and Dorothea Gibbs and of their contemporary*

most of the sugar merchants under review were drawn from the commercial bourgeoisie and artisan classes. These groups were the backbone of an urban economy that dominated Bristol's hinterland and made the city 'the metropolis of the West' in the eighteenth century.[21] Of the thirty-one merchants whose social origins can be traced with certainty, twelve were sons of shipowners and merchants already established in the West India business at Bristol. They were Michael Becher, Mark Davis Jr, John Gordon Sr and Jr, who were father and son, William Gordon, Samuel Span Jr and John Span, who were brothers, Thomas Daniel Sr and Jr, Henry Swymmer, Christopher Devonsheir and Richard Bright. Most of these recruits served apprenticeships to their fathers or to other merchants engaged in Caribbean commerce. It is noticeable that they mainly entered trade after 1750 and came from families with at least a decade of experience in the sugar business.

Two of our sample group (George Gibbs and Richard Meyler Jr) were sons of surgeons. The father of Samuel Span Sr was a clergyman. A further eight men had fathers who were tradesmen. James Bonbonous and Thomas Deane were the sons of clothiers. William Reeve, Samuel Munckley, Richard Farr Jr, John Curtis, Thomas Harris and Isaac Hobhouse were respectively the sons of a soapmaker, a tucker, a ropemaker, a grocer, a tailor, and a mariner who also worked as a wheelwright. Six merchants were drawn from the ranks of landed gentlemen. They were Robert Gordon, John Pinney, Henry and Lowbridge Bright, James Laroche and Evan Baillie. The pedigrees of their families sometimes identify their fathers as lairds or lords of the manor. To these recruits were added two merchants (James Tobin and

---

relatives, including the History of the Origin & Early Years of the House of Antony Gibbs and Sons (1992), 4. The references to John Curtis and Samuel Munckley are based on Hall, 'Whitson Court Sugar House,' 72–3, 77. The origins of John Pinney are discussed in A. Pares, *A West-India Fortune* (1950), 63, and in J. S. Udal, 'The Story of the Bettiscombe Skull,' *Proceedings of the Dorset Natural History and Antiquarian Field Club*, XXI (1910), 188, 195. The background of Isaac Hobhouse is outlined in Henry Hobhouse, *Hobhouse Memoirs* (Taunton, 1927), 15. The origins of John and Michael Becher, Robert Gordon and James Laroche are given in Richardson, *The Bristol Slave Traders*, 19–20. Details on Henry Swymmer are taken from his father's will: PRO, PROB 11/609/108 (PCC Plymouth). Evan Baillie's origins are dealt with in Cave, *History of Banking in Bristol*, 216–17; *History of Parliament: The House of Commons, 1790–1820* (1986), ed. R. G. Thorne, III, 108; and Joseph Gaston Baillie Bulloch, *A History and Genealogy of the Family of Baillie of Dunain, Dochfour and Lamington . . .* (Green Bay, Wisconsin, 1898), 35. Data on Henry, Lowbridge and Richard Bright are taken from *Familiae Minorum Gentium*, ed. John W. Clay (Publications of the Harleian Society, XXXVII, 1894), 135–6. Details on John Span, Samuel Span Jr, William Miles and Richard Farr Jr are given in *The Trade of Bristol in the Eighteenth Century*, ed. W. E. Minchinton (Bristol Record Society's Publications, XX, 1957), 9, 50, 59.

[21] On this theme see W. E. Minchinton, 'Bristol—Metropolis of the West in the Eighteenth Century,' these *Transactions*, 5th series, IV (1954), 69–89.

Robert Claxton) who were sons of plantation owners in the West Indies. They moved to Bristol to further their mercantile careers after gaining considerable experience of conditions in the sugar islands. All in all, it seems that the social origins of Bristol West India merchants were relatively open within the gentry and commercial classes, but that nearly half of the recruits were channelled into merchant houses trading with the West Indies that their fathers had established.

The geographical origins of thirty-five of our fifty merchants can be determined. Thirteen of our sample group were, not surprisingly, born and apprenticed in Bristol itself. This was especially true of sons of men already established as sugar merchants in the city. This group comprised Michael Becher, Richard Bright, Richard Farr Jr, William Gordon, Thomas Harris, William Reeve, Henry Swymmer, John Curtis, Samuel Span Jr, John Span, Mark Davis Jr and John Gordon Sr and Jr. A further seventeen were recruited from a much wider area in the British Isles. They included men from the south-west of England drawn to the commercial orbit of Bristol from lesser centres of trade. Among them were Devonians such as Samuel Munckley and George Gibbs, both from Exeter, and John Pinney, originally named John Pretor, from Okehampton. From Somerset came Isaac Hobhouse and Christopher Devonsheir, both natives of Minehead, and Thomas Deane, who came from Chard. But the area of recruitment was not limited to south-west England: people were drawn from all over the British Isles. They included Scotsmen such as Evan Baillie and Robert Gordon; Irishmen such as John Becher, Samuel Span Sr and James Bonbonous; Richard Meyler Sr and Jr from Haverfordwest, Pembrokeshire; William Miles from Ledbury, Herefordshire; James Laroche from a Huguenot family resettled in London; Henry Bright from Colwall, on the border between Herefordshire and Worcestershire; and Lowbridge Bright from Brockbury, Worcestershire. This wide catchment area, drawing recruits from both town and countryside, reflected the consistent contribution of West India commerce to the economy and society of Georgian Bristol, and the lure of the sugar trade for those wishing to pursue profits in a mercantile firm.

At least five merchants came to Bristol after being born in the Caribbean. They included Robert Claxton, a member of a family that had lived in Basseterre, St Kitts since the first decade of the seventeenth century; David Dehany and the two Daniels mentioned above, all from Barbados; and James Tobin, son of a shipmaster and plantation owner from Nevis. Several of these men were descended from Bristol emigrants to the Caribbean in the seventeenth century; in other words, from merchants, planters, mariners and bonded servants who had chosen to live 'beyond the line'.[22] The perpetuation of a number of west country families in the West Indies from these pioneering days meant that Bristol was an obvious choice of port for any members who wished to return home.

The close links between Bristol and the Caribbean were strengthened further by Bristolians who were sent to the sugar islands during the early part of their careers. Perhaps the first of our group to follow this path was Michael Atkins. He returned to Bristol around 1720 after many years living in Jamaica, where he had succeeded to the business of another Bristolian, Harrington Gibbs, who had established commercial contacts with the Beckford, Pennant and Morant families, all extensively concerned with sugar estates. Atkins proceeded to gain exclusive control over the shipping of sugar from several Jamaican harbours to Bristol. Eventually, after consolidating his business in this way, he handed over his Jamaican trade and commercial contacts to his nephew, John Curtis.[23] Others dispatched to the West Indies in their early careers before setting up in the sugar trade at Bristol included Thomas Daniel Jr in Barbados, Evan Baillie in St Kitts and St Vincent, John Pinney in Nevis, Mark Davis Sr, Lowbridge Bright and Samuel Delpratt in Jamaica, and Henry Bright in both St Kitts and Jamaica.[24] The classic example of a Bristol sugar merchant who followed such a route was William Miles. According to a story, which may be apocryphal, he arrived in Bristol with three halfpence in his pocket, was apprenticed

---

[22] For seventeenth-century Bristol emigrants to the West Indies see *Caribbeana*, ed. Oliver, V, 301–2; Richard S. Dunn, *Sugar and Slaves: The Rise of the Planter Class in the English West Indies, 1624–1713* (Chapel Hill, N.C., 1972), 70–1; Abbot Emerson Smith, *Colonists in Bondage: White Servitude and Convict Labor in America 1607–1776* (Chapel Hill, N.C., 1947), 309; David Souden, ' "Rogues, whores and vagabonds"? Indentured Servant Emigrants to North America, and the Case of Mid-Seventeenth Century Bristol,' *Social History*, III (1978), 23–41; J. H. Lawrence-Archer, *Monumental Inscriptions of the British West Indies* (1875), 261, 401; Philip Wright, *Monumental Inscriptions of Jamaica* (1966), 190; *Miscellanea Genealogica et Heraldica*, ed. Joseph Jackson Howard, 2nd series (1886), I, 4–5. Lists of seventeenth-century Bristol emigrants to the Caribbean can be found in various books compiled by Peter W. Coldham: see esp. *The Bristol Register of Servants sent to Foreign Plantations, 1654–1686* (Baltimore, 1988); *The Complete Book of Emigrants 1607–1660* (Baltimore, 1987); and *The Complete Book of Emigrants 1661–1699* (Baltimore, 1990).

[23] Morgan, *Bristol and the Atlantic Trade*, 81–2, 185; 'Letter by an Old Man,' *Bristol Gazette*, Mar. 1787; G. E. Weare, *Edmund Burke's Connection with Bristol: with a Prefatory Memoir of Burke* (Bristol, 1894), 8.

[24] Weare, *Edmund Burke's Connection with Bristol*, 8; Pares, *West-India Fortune*, 70, 78, 101; Latimer, *Annals of Bristol in the Nineteenth Century*, 455, 473; BRO, Camplin & Smith accounts with William & John Miles in Jamaica (1759–61), Acc. 11109/15; Liverpool Public Library, Case & Southworth Sales account book (1754–60), fos. 36r, 43r, 54v, 58v (for Samuel Delpratt); U[niversity of] M[elbourne] A[rchives], Parkville, Victoria, Henry Bright letterbook (1739–48); Lowbridge Bright letterbook (1765–73); Alexander & Evan Baillie to Henry Bright, 2 Sept. 1766; and Evan Baillie to Henry Bright, 1 June, 26 July 1775; box 16A, Bright family papers.

in 1742, became a burgess in 1749, spent several years as a supercargo trading with Jamaica, resided as a merchant in that island, and amassed sufficient capital to set up as a West India merchant in Bristol. He was the leading sugar importer in the city by the 1770s, and eventually built up a substantial fortune—so much so that he was able to hand his son Philip John Miles a cheque for £100,000 when the latter married in 1796.[25]

The links between Bristol and the West Indies were also sustained by merchants who visited the Caribbean later in their careers, or who married the daughters of sugar planters. For instance, Samuel Delpratt left Bristol to deal with his Jamaican estates in 1779, became a merchant in Kingston, and died at sea returning from Jamaica to Bristol in 1783.[26] John Pinney returned twice from Bristol to his plantations in Nevis during the 1790s.[27] James Tobin travelled to the same island at least three times between 1760 and 1782 and returned there again, to oversee his business concerns, in 1808.[28] Among those who married the daughters of West India planters were Evan Baillie and Thomas Daniel Sr. Baillie married the daughter of a merchant and planter in St Vincent, while Daniel wed the daughter of an old Barbados proprietor. No doubt such marriages consolidated business connections and helped to build up capital. Certainly this was true of John Span and Samuel Delpratt. Span married Dorothea Munro, the only daughter and heiress of Hugh Munro of Carriacou, Grenada. Delpratt wed Martha Foord, youngest daughter of Edward Foord, merchant of Kingston, Jamaica, with whom he was involved in trade. In his will, Foord left £4,000 sterling upon trust to Delpratt plus the residue of his estate.[29]

Of greater importance in sustaining a Bristol-West India connection, however, was the investment of merchants in the ownership or mortgage of plantations in the West Indies. Some merchants bought sugar estates to build up capital; others took out mortgages on plantations to help with debts accumulated. All of the merchant investors were involved in mergers, sales, and changes of ownership. This creates difficulties in trying to establish the extent of the investment. Yet an overall view can

[25] Fox Bourne, *English Merchants*, II, 16–17; Morgan, *Bristol and the Atlantic Trade*, Table 7.7, 197. The poor origins of William Miles may be a legend, for he was apprenticed to a hooper at the age of thirteen and married the daughter of a substantial Bristol merchant (W. E. Minchinton, 'The Merchants of England in the Eighteenth Century,' *Explorations in Entrepreneurial History*, X [1957], 63).

[26] *Caribbeana*, ed. Oliver, III, 147; PRO, PROB 11/1114/129 (PCC 129 Rockingham), will of Samuel Delpratt, abstracted in B[ritish] L[ibrary], Add. MS 34, 181: Abstract of Wills relating to Jamaica, 1625–1792, fo. 174.

[27] MacInnes, *Bristol: A Gateway of Empire*, 313.

[28] *Caribbeana*, ed. Oliver, V, 5; Pares, *West-India Fortune*, 151.

[29] *Caribbeana*, ed. Oliver, I, 76, III, 147, 149–50; Cave, *History of Banking in Bristol*, 216–17, 228.

be gleaned from piecing together scraps of data. Though it has not been possible to research land deeds in the West Indies for this paper, various sources in British repositories provide details about the ownership of slave plantations. The main sources consulted were wills, genealogical collections and business papers (the latter being, in all cases, fragmentary).

Some twenty-nine out of our fifty merchants (58 per cent) have been identified as owners of West Indian slave plantations. The investment covered virtually all of the Caribbean, though it was heavily concentrated in Jamaica, the largest of the British sugar islands and the jewel in the crown of the first British Empire. John Curtis, John Gordon Sr and Jr, Robert and William Gordon, Thomas Harris, Samuel Delpratt, Henry, Lowbridge and Richard Bright, William Miles, Richard Meyler Sr and David Dehany all owned estates in Jamaica.[30] In some cases, they owned more than one property.[31] Robert Claxton, Philip Protheroe, William Miles, John Pinney and James Tobin owned plantations in Nevis—quite a concentration of Bristol ownership in an island that covered only fifty square miles.[32] James Laroche and Robert Tudway owned estates in Antigua.[33] Walter Jacks bought a plantation

[30] For plantations owned by the Brights and Meylers see BL, Add. MS 12, 436, fo. 12v; PRO, CO 142/31 and PROB 11/1928/390 (PCC Arden), will of Richard Bright; BRO, will of Lowbridge Bright, Bright papers, Acc. 8015(58), and genealogical notes on the Bright family, microfilm F/47. fo. 426; UMA, Richard Meyler to Jeremiah Meyler, 15 July 1762; indenture of the mortgage of Cabaritta plantation from Jeremiah Meyler to Henry Bright, 25 July 1772; Thomas Chambers and Alexander Rankin's valuation of Round Valley Estate, Jamaica, 19 June 1781; and A. E. Bright, 'Letters of the Bright Family,' I, 12, II, 5 (unpublished typescript deposited at UMA); all in boxes 8, 39, 48, Bright family papers. For plantations owned by John Curtis and Thomas Harris see PRO, PROB 11/992/419 (PCC Stevens), will of John Curtis, and CO 142/31. David Dehany's landholdings in Jamaica are referred to in *Caribbeana*, ed. Oliver, III, 289, and in BL, Add. MS 12, 434: Long Papers, fo. 5r. Samuel Delpratt's plantations are mentioned in *Caribbeana*, ed Oliver, III, 147. Documentation on the Gordons' estates is available in J. M. Bulloch, *The Making of the West Indies: The Gordons as Colonists* (priv. printed, 1915), 30; BL, Add. MS 12,435, fos. 3–4; PRO, PROB 11/1138/88 (PCC Norfolk), will of Robert Gordon; and PROB 11/1922/94 (PCC Arden), will of John Gordon Jr. William Miles's Jamaican properties are noted in *Caribbeana*, ed. Oliver, I, 211; in BRO, Records of the Miles family, Acc. 12151, nos. 41(a), 47(a), 50, 52(a); and in 'Calendar of Correspondence from William Miles, a West Indian Merchant in Bristol, to John Tharp, a Planter in Jamaica, 1770–1789,' ed. Kenneth Morgan, in *A Bristol Miscellany*, ed. Patrick McGrath (Bristol Record Society's Publications, XXXVII, 1985), 105, 107, 111 n. 70, 113.

[31] This is true of Henry, Lowbridge and Richard Bright, David Dehany, Samuel Delpratt, John Gordon Sr and Jr, Robert Gordon, William Gordon and William Miles: see the documentation in note 30 above.

[32] For Protheroe, Claxton and Miles, see *Caribbeana*, ed. Oliver, I, 211, II, 169; for Pinney and Tobin, see *ibid.*, I, 212, and Pares, *West India Fortune, passim*.

[33] *Caribbeana*, ed. Oliver, I, 351; *The History of the Island of Antigua*, ed. Vere Langford Oliver, 3 vols. (1894–9), III, 275.

in Antigua and another one in Dominica.[34] Christopher Devonsheir and David Hamilton each owned an estate in Grenada.[35] Samuel Span Sr bought 3,000 acres of a cotton and sugar estate on Union Island, in the Grenadines, which was under the jurisdiction of St Vincent, and bequeathed the property to his sons, John and Samuel Span Jr.[36] Most of these men owned plantations in only one island. However, William Reeve, a large Quaker merchant, purchased land, in conjunction with others, in St Kitts, Grenada and Nevis.[37] The Daniels, as we have seen, also owned slave plantations in various Caribbean islands.[38] So too did Evan Baillie and his sons: by the time of slave emancipation they received £110,000 in compensation for 3,100 slaves in British Guiana, Trinidad, Grenada, St Kitts and St Vincent.[39]

In addition, several West India merchants were involved in extending finance for the mortgages and annuities needed for slave estates. This was true of the Pinney family in Nevis, and also of William Miles, Lowbridge and Richard Bright, and Thomas Daniel Jr in Jamaica.[40] Nor was this the full extent of Bristol's direct investment in the Caribbean. Some Bristol merchants purchased stores and livestock pens in the sugar islands. Others held estates in trust on behalf of planters with whom they were friendly.[41] There were also some Bristol families, including the Elbridges, Woolnoughs, Smyths and Pedders, who are not among our commercial elite of Bristol West India houses, but who nonetheless acquired sugar plantations.[42] All these examples are not intended to suggest that Bristol held an unduly high proportion of land in the Caribbean, but merely to illustrate the commitment by Bristol businessmen to commercial enterprise in that region.

These merchants tended to invest in plantations in those parts of the Caribbean with which they traded; they bought land in islands to which they could earn freight money on outward voyages and from

[34] BUL, D. M. 183.

[35] PRO, C 54/6143 and PROB 11/1063/192 (PCC Collins), will of David Hamilton.

[36] PRO, PROB 11/1270/40 (PCC Harris), will of Samuel Span Sr, and PROB 11/1527/511 (PCC Crickett), will of Samuel Span Jr.

[37] *Caribbeana*, ed. Oliver, I, 28, 207, 297.

[38] See above, 185

[39] Marshall, *Bristol and the Abolition of Slavery*, app., i.

[40] Pares, *West-India Fortune*, 239–319; 'Calendar of Correspondence from Miles to Tharp,' ed. Morgan, 81–121; and the records for the Daniels and the Brights cited in notes 3 and 30 above.

[41] These activities are documented in many of the sources cited in notes 3 and 30 above.

[42] D. K. Jones, 'The Elbridge, Woolnough and Smyth Families of Bristol, in the Eighteenth Century, with special reference to the Spring Plantation, Jamaica' (MLitt thesis, University of Bristol, 1972); PRO, CO 142/31.

which they could get regular seasonal sugar consignments.[43] Since Bristol sugar merchants usually owned their own ships, and had little resort to chartered vessels, they could control business decisions in the West India trade to suit their own needs.[44] They combined ship-ownership, trade and investment in the West Indies in an ever more concentrated fashion as the eighteenth century progressed—a trend that is congruent with the growing concentration of sugar imports mentioned earlier. What is striking, in fact, is the sheer extent to which Bristol was connected with the West Indies in the eighteenth century. Out of our sample group, all of the merchants who visited the Caribbean, either early in their career or later, came to own land there. Some thirty-two of our fifty merchants had direct contact with the West Indies either through birth, marriage, residence, or landownership. They were connected with the entire range of British sugar islands in the Greater and Lesser Antilles. The extensive ownership of slave plantations suggests some modification to the usual assumption that absentee planters and sugar commission merchants were separate personnel, the one group living a genteel life of conspicuous con-sumption thousands of miles from the source of their wealth, and perhaps displaying their economic status with a fine equipage and livery, and the other group busily engaging, nose to the grindstone, in the day-to-day round of trade. The case of Georgian Bristol rather points to a business elite that fulfilled both functions; that is to say, men who were merchants and planters. This distinctive commercial group became more marked over time: out of twenty-nine merchant planters so far identified, fourteen were still active in this role in the early nineteenth century.

Our Bristol West India merchant elite was not of one accord in politics or religion. Christopher Devonsheir, Thomas Deane, Richard Farr Jr, Samuel Munckley, Robert Gordon and Evan Baillie were all active in Whig politics. But there were also prominent Tories in our group, including Thomas Daniel Jr and William Miles.[45] Religious affiliation varied. Robert Gordon, Thomas Deane, Philip Protheroe, Samuel Munckley and John Curtis were all Presbyterians; Christopher Devonsheir and William Reeve were Quakers; James Laroche was a Huguenot; Richard Bright, a Unitarian; John Fisher Weare, an

[43] Morgan, *Bristol and the Atlantic Trade*, 186, 191–2.

[44] Pares, *West-India Fortune*, 209.

[45] Bush, *Bristol and its Municipal Government*, 239; *History of Parliament: The House of Commons, 1790–1820*, ed. Thorne, III, 108; Cave, *History of Banking in Bristol*, 92; Fox Bourne, *English Merchants*, II, 16–17; Ronald H. Quilici,'Turmoil in a City and an Empire: Bristol's Factions, 1700–1775' (PhD dissertation, University of New Hampshire, 1976), 174, 247; Nicholas Rogers, *Whigs and Cities: Popular Politics in the Age of Walpole and Pitt* (Oxford, 1989), 273.

Independent; and Thomas Daniel Jr and George Gibbs were Anglicans (though Gibbs started out as a dissenter).[46] The tendency towards Whiggery and dissent among these merchants is clear, but the evidence suggests that the connection should not be over-emphasised. Yet our fifty merchants were still an exceptionally cohesive group. This is apparent in more ways than the material already discussed suggests. The most successful firms, in terms of longevity and sugar imports, passed on commercial expertise, at suitable points, by adding new partners, often taken from within the family or from another firm with which they traded. Several examples will be examined here, involving the Davis, Protheroe, Claxton, Pinney, Tobin, Bright, Meyler, Baillie, Munckley and Gibbs families.

The partnerships established by Mark Davis Sr illustrate the evolution of family dynasties over time. Davis returned to Bristol from Jamaica *c.*1740 and soon established himself as a sugar merchant.[47] He entered a partnership with his former apprentice Philip Protheroe around 1768.[48] They mainly traded with Jamaica, but also took smaller quantities of sugar from Barbados and several of the Leeward islands.[49] When the partnership expired in 1776, it was followed by another one between Mark Davis Jr and Protheroe, who began trade with a considerable capital. After the death of the elder Mark Davis in 1783, his son and Philip Protheroe took in a third partner, Robert Claxton, who had carried on business in St Kitts for many years and with whom they had traded during his residence there. The firm now became Davis, Protheroe & Claxton. The younger Mark Davis soon decided to quit business, however; he felt that his co-partners had the reputation, ability and capital to carry on trade successfully by themselves. In 1796 Edward Protheroe, the son of Philip, joined the business: the firm was known as Protheroes & Claxton. But in 1808 both Protheroes, father and son, decided to retire from trade.[50] On the part of Edward Protheroe, this

---

[46] Bush, *Bristol and its Municipal Government*, 235; Rogers, *Whigs and Cities*, 273; Gibbs, *History of Antony and Dorothea Gibbs*, 4–6; Cave, *History of Banking in Bristol*, 92; Latimer, *Annals of Bristol in the Eighteenth Century*, 285; Quilici, 'Turmoil in a City and an Empire,' 174, 247, 254; *The Trade of Bristol in the Eighteenth Century*, ed. Minchinton, 21; Ignatius Jones, *Bristol Congregationalism* (Bristol, 1947), 40–3; Hall, 'Whitson Court Sugar House,' 71–6.

[47] Weare, *Edmund Burke's Connection with Bristol*, 8. For Davis's sugar imports see Kenneth Morgan, 'Bristol Merchants and the Colonial Trades, 1748–1783' (DPhil thesis, University of Oxford, 1984), app. C, 338, 348, 359.

[48] Inferred from the fact that Philip Protheroe did not come of age until that year.

[49] Morgan, *Bristol and the Atlantic Trade*, Table 7.7, 197.

[50] Derbyshire R[ecord] O[ffice], Matlock, Mark Davis Sr to W. P. Perrin, 2 Mar. 1776; Davis & Protheroe to W. P. Perrin, 23 Aug., 24 Nov. 1783; Davis, Protheroe & Claxton to W. P. Perrin, 28 Apr. 1784, 1 May 1796; Protheroes & Claxton to W. P. Perrin, 29 Jan. 1808; all in Fitzherbert MSS: West Indian papers, 239M/E19974, 20106, 20110, 20118, 20188, 20339.

was probably because by then he represented Bristol in Parliament.[51] The firm now split into two partnerships—Robert Claxton & Son, and Protheroe and Savage.[52] Both the Protheroes and the Claxtons remained in the West India trade until the 1830s (though by then members of each family opposed each other politically on the slavery issue).[53]

A similar pattern can be discerned with other firms. Pinney & Tobin, for instance, set up a sugar commission house in Bristol in 1783. This was after John Pinney and James Tobin had spent many years dealing with trade and plantations in Nevis. In 1789 John Pinney's son Azariah substituted for his father, who nominally retired from business then. The firm was now called Tobin & Pinney. In 1796 Tobin's fourth son Harry became a new partner, and the firm styled itself Tobin, Pinney & Tobin. But Azariah Pinney and Harry Tobin both died by 1802, so a new firm of Tobins & Pinney was formed in 1803. This consisted of James Tobin, John Frederick Pinney and Pretor Pinney, a partnership that lasted until 1806, when it was dissolved. John Pinney then decided to return to business to save the firm. With some help from John Frederick, he kept the merchant house going until 1811 when John Frederick and Charles Pinney, with their brother-in-law Jeremiah Ames, entered into a new partnership called Pinney & Ames. John Frederick, Pretor and Charles Pinney were all sons of John Pinney, who helped the family business until his death in 1818. The house of Pinney continued into the era of slave amelioration and emancipation with further changes of partners.[54]

The cluster of relationships among Bristol West India merchants and their evolution over time is best illustrated, however, by examining the Bright and Meyler families, for whom rich documentation is available. Henry Bright and Richard Meyler Sr were both originally emigrants to Bristol.[55] They entered business together in the late 1730s. Meyler always conducted trade from Bristol but Bright gained commercial experience both at home and in the West Indies. Henry Bright's first visit to the Caribbean was during the period 1739–42 when he was sent as a supercargo to St Kitts, where he conducted business for Meyler and bought sugar for return voyages to Bristol. Bright then spent several years in Jamaica, interspersed with a number of trips back to Bristol. While living in Jamaica, he built up a successful trade with Meyler in sugar, slaves, provisions and dry goods.[56] In 1746 Henry

---

[51] Cave, *History of Banking in Bristol*, 126.

[52] Derbyshire RO, Protheroes & Claxton to W. P. Perrin, 29 Jan. 1808, Fitzherbert MSS: West Indian papers, 239M/E20339; Pares, *West-India Fortune*, 214–15.

[53] Marshall, *Bristol and the Abolition of Slavery*, 3–24.

[54] Pares, *West-India Fortune*, 171–4.

[55] BRO, apprenticeship lists, 1724–40, fo. 135v; *Caribbeana*, ed. Oliver, II, 276.

[56] These activities are documented in UMA, Henry Bright letterbook (1739–48). The

Bright returned to Bristol and married his partner's daughter, Sarah Meyler, the heiress to Ham Green, a fine country house on the Somerset side of the Bristol Avon.[57] Henry Bright returned to Jamaica for the period 1748–51, after which he came home for good. During this final spell in the Caribbean he arranged sugar consignments for Meyler and was active in the slave trade, especially the illegal traffic with the Spanish American market. He left a mercantile house in Jamaica with two branches, one in Kingston, the other in Savanna-la-Mar. These were run by his brother Francis until his death in 1754, and subsequently by Jeremiah Meyler, younger brother of Richard. These two men became members of various partnerships in Jamaica in the 1750s and 1760s, and acquired slave plantations there.[58]

Gradually the Bright and Meyler families went their separate ways in terms of West India trade: there were disagreements over the handling of the Jamaica end of the business by Jeremiah Meyler, who piled up large debts.[59] By 1765 the Brights felt that their Jamaican interests were flagging, so Lowbridge Bright, a nephew of Henry, was sent to Jamaica to revive their commercial interests in the island. He soon entered into a partnership there with Nathaniel Milward, who had visited Bristol and who was known by several of the city's leading West India merchants.[60] Henry Bright, ill with gout, retired from trade in 1775. But he ensured the continuity of his merchant house by putting his son Richard, recently come of age, into partnership with Lowbridge Bright, who was now recalled from Jamaica to Bristol.[61] By the time of the American Revolution, all this activity meant that the Bright family was considered in higher credit than any other house in England: the Brights were known to be men of large fortune.[62]

In 1776 the Brights decided to expand their West India concerns by forming a separate partnership with Evan Baillie, recently arrived in Bristol from St Vincent, and a man with whom they had previously

---

records left by the Brights and the Meylers are discussed in Kenneth Morgan, 'The Bright Family Papers,' *Archives* (forthcoming).

[57] Cave, *History of Banking in Bristol*, 221.

[58] UMA, Henry Bright to Richard Meyler, 25 July 1749, 10 June, 25 July 1750; Jeremiah Meyler to Richard Meyler, 29 Aug. 1761, 16 May 1763; Jeremiah Meyler to Richard Bright, 5 Nov. 1783; and Francis Bright letterbook (1752–3); boxes 8, 40, 85, Bright family papers.

[59] E.g. UMA, Richard Meyler to Meyler & Hall, 22 Nov. 1763, and Jeremiah Meyler to Richard Meyler, 7 Apr. 1759, 1 Apr. 1765, box 8, *ibid.*

[60] UMA, Lowbridge Bright to Henry Bright, 28 June, 11 Dec. 1765, Lowbridge Bright letterbook (1765–73).

[61] Bright, 'Letters of the Bright Family,' I, 14–16.

[62] George Baillie, *Interesting Letters Addressed to Evan Baillie Esq. of Bristol, Merchant, Member of Parliament for that Great City, and Colonel of the Bristol Volunteers* (1809), 56.

traded when he lived in St Kitts.[63] The firm became Bright, Baillie & Bright, and it traded mainly with the Leeward and Windward islands. Lowbridge and Richard Bright, on the other hand, kept mainly to their Jamaica business and bought property in that island, including Arthur's Seat and Inverness Pen.[64] The partnerships flourished until the early nineteenth century, when Evan Baillie eventually broke away from the Brights in an acrimonious way.[65] The Bright and Meyler interests now converged once more, albeit fortuitously. In 1818 Lowbridge Bright, a bachelor, died intestate. In the same year Richard Meyler, MP for Winchester and another bachelor, died after being accidentally thrown off his horse while out riding. This Meyler was the grandson of Jeremiah Meyler and the last surviving member of his branch of the family. Richard Bright, the second cousin once removed of this Richard Meyler, and his paternal heir at law, now inherited the Meyler estates in Jamaica, valued at £60–70,000.[66] This led to a lengthy legal suit and bickering between the Bright and Meyler families that lasted for more than a decade.[67]

One consequence of Richard Meyler's death was that until 1840 Richard Bright ended up supervising slave estates—Meylersfield, Garredhu and Beeston Springs—that he neither expected to gain nor wanted. He stayed at home in Ham Green and never visited Jamaica. But this was not the end of the Bright's West India interest. Without his deceased cousin Lowbridge to assist him, Richard Bright decided in 1818 that it was time to retire from trade. The mercantile firm devolved into the hands of Robert Bright, his fourth son, who was taken into partnership by George Gibbs & Son.[68] He joined a business that had experienced continuity in the sugar trade since the time of Michael Atkins, who had first dealt in sugar at Bristol a century before. Atkins, the largest Bristol sugar merchant in the first half of the eighteenth century, handed down his trade to his nephew John Curtis, who, on his death, arranged for the business to be divided between his executors, Samuel Munckley and William Miles.[69] From 1789 until 1802 Munckley was in partnership with his cousin George Gibbs, and with James Richards, who was married to Elizabeth Gibbs, the first cousin

[63] *Ibid.*; UMA, Alexander Baillie to Henry Bright, 12 Apr. 1766, and Evan Baillie to Henry Bright, 26 July 1775, box 16A, Bright family papers.

[64] Morgan, *Bristol and the Atlantic Trade*, Table 7.7, 197; BRO, genealogical notes on the Bright family, microfilm F/47, fo. 426.

[65] Baillie, *Interesting Letters*, 57.

[66] Bright, 'Letters of the Bright Family,' I, n.p.

[67] See the extensive legal papers scattered throughout UMA, Bright Papers and the summary in Bright, 'Letters of the Bright Family,' I, 'Law Suit,' n.p.

[68] BRO, genealogical notes on the Bright family, microfilm F/47, fo. 426.

[69] Hall, 'Whitson Court Sugar House,' 74, and the Appendix below, 207.

of George. After Munckley's death, the firm was styled Gibbs, Richards & Gibbs between 1802 and 1808, then George Gibbs & Son for the next decade, and finally Gibbs, Son & Bright from 1818 until 1839, the Bright being Robert.[70]

The interconnections of Bristol sugar merchants illustrate very well the extent to which family members frequently travelled to and from the West Indies and the importance of marriage for consolidating trade connections. They also show that sugar commission partnerships depended on other family members, who are invisible in the lists of sugar imports but who assisted in other ways, often by running mercantile branch houses in the Caribbean. The cohesion of the Bristol West India interest is also apparent. Eleven of our sample group of fifty merchants were linked to the Bright-Meyler interests in the Caribbean over the course of the century from c.1740 to 1840. Furthermore, the personnel involved in the partnerships of the three West India firms examined—Davis & Protheroe, Pinney & Tobin, the Meylers and the Brights—amount to no fewer than one third of our fifty leading firms. Many of the merchant groups discussed still dominated the Bristol West India interest at the time of slave emancipation. The Baillies, Brights, Protheroes, Claxtons, Daniels and Pinneys accordingly appear in the lists of compensation paid to slaveowners by the British government in 1837.[71] This suggests that the leading Bristol West India merchant dynasties had long antecedents. It also rebuts S. G. Checkland's remark that the links between Bristol and the Caribbean in the late eighteenth century were much less pronounced than fifty years earlier.[72] In fact, the reverse was true: the height of Bristol's connection with the West Indies came in the half century after the American Revolution.

The goals of this merchant group seem to have been familiar ones: the pursuit of wealth, respectability and comfort. Obituary notices in Bristol newspapers testify to the eminence, reputation and fortunes of these leading mercantile houses.[73] Moreover a list printed in *Felix Farley's Bristol Journal* in 1785, giving fortunes left by Bristol merchants in the previous half century, is dominated by the sugar merchants named here. Michael Atkins apparently left about £70,000, Henry Bright £50,000, John Curtis £35,000, and Richard Meyler Sr £30,000.[74] Evan Baillie left £80,000 exclusive of his Scottish property and Philip

---

[70] Gibbs, *History of Antony and Dorothea Gibbs*, 13, 456–7.

[71] Marshall, *Bristol and the Abolition of Slavery*, app., i–ii.

[72] S. G. Checkland, 'Finance for the West Indies, 1780–1815,' *Economic History Review*, 2nd series, X (1957–8), 465.

[73] E.g. F[elix] F[arley's] B[ristol] J[ournal], 26 Feb. 1763 (Isaac Hobhouse), 19 Mar. 1763 (Michael Atkins), 24 Nov. 1764 (Jeremiah Innys), and 17 Sept. 1768 (John Curtis).

[74] *FFBJ*, 8 Jan. 1785, reprinted in Latimer, *Annals of Bristol in the Eighteenth Century*, 463.

Protheroe made cash bequests of £112,000 in his will.[75] The fortunes made by Thomas Daniel Jr and William Miles have already been mentioned.[76] These substantial fortunes enabled some Bristol West India merchants to make sufficient money to retire from trade, as several examples already cited show.[77] The fruits of their commercial enterprise were poured into miscellaneous industrial investments and land. This is not the place for a full investigation of these aspects of their lives, but it is worth noting that they were extensive. Our Bristol West India elite invested in breweries, gunpowder companies, ironworks, copper companies, glasshouses, canals, and thread factories.[78] They held shares in sugar refineries, though not to the extent that one might expect.[79]. Eight of our fifty merchants were partners in the first wave of Bristol banks founded in the generation after 1750.[80] Landholdings were also widespread. Richard Bright, for instance, inherited several properties in Worcestershire as well as the Meyler estates in Pembrokeshire, Hampshire and Somerset.[81] Philip Protheroe had an estate at Overcourt, Gloucestershire.[82] Jeremiah Innys owned a manor house called South Brent Huish plus land at Newton St Loe, Corston and Stanton Prior, all in Somerset.[83] Evan Baillie succeeded to the family seat in Inverness-shire.[84] A much longer list could be supplied, with landownership identified in many counties.

Wealth and respectability brought civic status. Twenty-four of our fifty merchants served on the Bristol Common Council. They often held this position for a long period. Evan Baillie, Richard Bright and Thomas Daniel Jr served in this capacity for half a century. A further

---

[75] *History of Parliament: House of Commons, 1790–1820*, ed. Thorne, III, 109, IV, 898.

[76] See above, 186, 192.

[77] See above, 196–8.

[78] *History of Parliament: House of Commons, 1790–1820*, ed. Thorne, III, 108; B. W. E. Alford, *W. D. & H. O. Wills and the Development of the U. K. Tobacco Industry, 1786–1965* (1973), 67; PRO, PROB 11/1453/950 (PCC Pitts), will of John Maxse, and PROB 11/1301/91 (PCC Walpole), will of Thomas Deane; Hobhouse, *Memoirs of the Hobhouse Family*, xxx; Francis Buckley, 'The Early Glasshouses of Bristol,' *Journal of the Society for Glass Technology*, IX (1925), 53; Bright, 'Letters of the Bright Family,' I, 16; Barrie Trinder, *The Industrial Revolution in Shropshire*, 2nd edn. (Chichester, 1981), 272.

[79] Lowbridge and Richard Bright, Thomas Deane, and Samuel Munckley were all investors in sugar refineries (Hall, 'Whitson Court Sugar House,' 76–9; 'Letters of the Bright Family,' II, n.p.; and BRO, I. V. Hall research notes on Bristol sugar refineries, Box 14).

[80] The eight were Henry and Richard Bright, John Curtis, Thomas Daniel Jr, Thomas Deane, Samuel Munckley, Philip Protheroe and Henry Swymmer (Cave, *History of Banking in Bristol*, 85–6, 90–2, 100, 103, 110–11, 113, 126).

[81] Pamela Bright, *Dr Richard Bright 1789–1858* (1983), 15, 113.

[82] Cave, *History of Banking in Bristol*, 126.

[83] PRO, PROB 11/905/21 (PCC Rushworth).

[84] *History of Parliament: House of Commons, 1790–1820*, ed. Thorne, III, 108–9.

sixteen men in our group were councillors for at least two decades. Ten became aldermen, again often for a considerable time. Twenty became sheriffs. Eleven were elected mayor, and another six declined the offer to serve in this position. Several merchants held all four major municipal positions: they included Robert Claxton, Thomas Deane, Richard Farr Jr, Robert Gordon, Thomas Harris, James Laroche Sr, William Miles and John Becher.[85] Our group were also prominent in the Society of Merchant Venturers. Twenty-seven of them were members, fourteen served as wardens, and sixteen were elected master.[86] This means that over half of the West India merchants considered here were involved in a society closely connected with lobbying parliament on commercial issues via petitions and their MPs.[87] The cohesion of the sugar merchants was complemented by their neighbourliness. Many lived cheek-by-jowl in town houses in fashionable parts of the city, Queen Square being an especially favoured area.[88] Today one can still glimpse the comfortable residences of this group by visiting the Pinney's house at no. 7 Great George Street—the Georgian House, as it is known, which is open to the public and administered by the Bristol City Museum.[89]

The pattern of family dynasties, with connections in the Caribbean, and substantial civic status at home, was not an inevitable one for Bristol merchants, or indeed any mercantile group; it emerged rather from the success of the sugar trade and the commitment to the Caribbean at Bristol from an early stage. These points can be emphasised by brief comparison with the tobacco and slave trades at Bristol. The turnover of names in the Bristol tobacco trade suggests that merchants in that trade largely failed to perpetuate dynasties. They became just as concentrated in number over time as the sugar merchants, but their small investments in the Chesapeake meant that they lacked a crucial incentive for passing on business skills and capital

[85] Beaven, *Bristol Lists*, 275–315.

[86] *Politics and the Port of Bristol in the Eighteenth Century: The Petitions of the Society of Merchant Venturers 1698–1803*, ed. W. E. Minchinton (Bristol Record Society Publications, XXIII, 1963), 209–16; John Latimer, *The History of the Society of Merchant Venturers of the City of Bristol* (Bristol, 1903), 328–31.

[87] These aspects of the Merchant Venturers' activities are covered in Patrick McGrath, *The Merchant Venturers of Bristol; a History of the Society of Merchant Venturers of the City of Bristol from its Origin to the Present Day* (Bristol, 1975) and in *Politics and the Port of Bristol*, ed. Minchinton.

[88] Based on notices for merchants in *FFBJ*, on James Sketchley, *Bristol Directory* (Bristol, 1775; facsimile reprint, Bath, 1971), and on W. Matthews, *The New History, Survey and Description of the City of Bristol, or Complete Guide and Bristol Directory for the Year 1793–4* (Bristol, 1794).

[89] The interior of this house is described in Walter Ison, *The Georgian Buildings of Bristol* (1952), 217–20.

acquired through trade from one generation to the next. Furthermore, Bristol's inability to expand her tobacco re-exports—the major source of increasing sales in the trade—discouraged newcomers from entering the trade.[90] The city's slave merchants also became a concentrated group numerically over the course of the eighteenth century. But they too failed to perpetuate merchant dynasties on the whole. This was partly unavoidable, since eighteen of the twenty-five leading Bristol slave merchants in the 1720s and 1730s either died as bachelors, or married without leaving a direct male heir, or died before their children reached maturity. After 1750 Bristol's slave merchants were drawn more readily from the ranks of shipmasters with experience in handling black cargoes than from families already established in the Guinea trade.[91] This was partly a consequence of the demographic problems left by their earlier counterparts, but partly an indication that more secure businesses could be established in the sugar rather than in the slave trade.

There was naturally some overlap among personnel in the sugar and slave trades at Bristol, for both branches of commerce handled the same major import commodity from the Caribbean. But though twenty-one of our fifty Bristol West India merchants participated in the slave trade for part of their career, they largely pulled out of that traffic by the time of the American War of Independence.[92] By then the Bristol slave trade was very much in decline. The disease problems prevalent on the African coast, the cost of outfitting vessels for triangular voyages, and the difficulty of securing returns for slave sales all discouraged a transference of interest by Bristol's sugar merchants to the slave trade. The ad hoc nature of partnerships in the slave trade, arranged from voyage to voyage, also did not help to foster permanency.[93] By the late 1780s an anti-slave trade movement was in progress in Britain, and opprobrium soon became attached to handling black cargoes. Yet there was no attempt at that time to abolish slavery itself or the sugar plantations, and so Bristol's West India trading elite could still feel reasonably secure. The fact that their investments in the Caribbean were, so to speak, invisible in Bristol itself enabled them to avoid the risks and stigma of direct participation in the slave trade while still opposing the anti-slave trade movement.[94]

---

[90] Morgan, *Bristol and the Atlantic Trade*, 154, 156, 158–9, 161–2.

[91] Richardson, *The Bristol Slave Traders*, 24.

[92] Based on a comparison of *ibid.*, 29–30, with my list of leading sugar merchants in the appendix below, 207–8.

[93] Richardson, *The Bristol Slave Traders*, 12, 14.

[94] Thomas Clarkson, *The History of the Rise, Progress and Accomplishment of the Abolition of the African Slave Trade by the British Parliament*, 2 vols. (1808), I, 294–367; A. M. Richards, 'The Connection of Bristol with the African Slave Trade, with some account of the currents of public opinion in the city' (MA thesis, University of Bristol, 1923), 23–87;

Contemporary comments convincingly suggest, nevertheless, that the eminence and wealth of Bristol West India merchants at the end of the eighteenth century was a mixed blessing. The signs of material success were visible in the fine Georgian townhouses and country seats, but an air of complacency and conservatism in business affairs had undoubtedly crept in. Thus John Pinney, warning his partner James Tobin to be cautious in taking on new correspondents, commented in 1793 that 'you had better have a snug little business and safe than an extensive one which may produce a contrary effect.'[95] And a visitor to Bristol in 1790 found that the leading traders were 'principally rich respectable West India Merch[an]ts who do not go out of their usual line of business & averse to speculation.'[96] Even before the American Revolution the Jamaican agents of a Bristol firm had stated, in a similar vein, that 'Bristol ... is rich enough but don't care to launch out much.'[97] This conservative approach to business explains why merchants like the Brights were not keen either to re-enter the slave trade in the early 1790s or to engage in complex three-legged voyages in the search for additional freight money for their ships.[98] One of the most telling comments on Bristol's merchants at this time came from John Wesley, who had been visiting Bristol almost annually for nearly fifty years by the time he declared in 1786 that 'the chief besetting sins' of that city were love of money and love of ease.[99] These critical comments by contemporaries are markedly different from those made earlier in the century, in which the emphasis was always on the energy and bustle of the trading groups in Bristol.[100]

The concentration of Bristol's sugar merchants on their Caribbean interests naturally made much economic sense. For one thing, it generated a lot of money. By the late 1780s, the annual value of the city's ships and cargoes in the West India trade was £400–500,000, and the produce imported to Bristol from the Caribbean was worth three quarters of a million pounds.[101] For another, the sugar trade could mainly be conducted on a commission basis by the late eighteenth

---

Peter Marshall, 'The Anti-Slave Trade Movement in Bristol' in *Bristol in the Eighteenth Century*, ed. Patrick McGrath (Newton Abbot, 1972), 185–215.

[95] Quoted in Pares, *West-India Fortune*, 176.

[96] Historical Society of Pennsylvania, Philadelphia, Robert Philips to Philips, Cramond & Co., 7 Apr. 1790, Cramond, Philips & Co. correspondence.

[97] UMA, Bright & Milward to Henry Bright, 15 June 1773, box 16, Bright family papers.

[98] UMA, Lowbridge Bright to David Duncombe, 6 Apr. 1791, box 16, Bright family papers; Morgan, *Bristol and the Atlantic Trade*, 79–80.

[99] *The Journal of John Wesley*, ed. Nehemiah Curnock, 8 vols. (1909–16), VII, 209, 15 Sept. 1786.

[100] Peter T. Marcy, 'Eighteenth Century Views of Bristol and Bristolians' in *Bristol in the Eighteenth Century*, ed. McGrath, 11–40.

[101] Morgan, *Bristol and the Atlantic Trade*, 185.

century—a relatively easy commercial method—and regular seasonal consignments of the crop came home via ships, often sailing in fleets, that were more and more tied to direct, regular crossings year after year.[102] Why quit this trade if it was so lucrative? Why turn to other avenues of commerce, such as the tobacco and slave trades, which had lost ground respectively to Glasgow and Liverpool by the 1780s? Why sell slave plantations if they still made a profit, given the difficulties of repatriating one's capital because of the endemic debt situation in the Caribbean?[103] These are all questions that must have gone through the minds of merchants and planters at Bristol. Possibly they helped to engender solidarity among the West India interest there as the era of anti-slavery agitation got under way.

Yet Bristol was over-committed to the West India trade by 1800 and the cohesive nature of her sugar merchants may have taken the edge off competitive enterprise. This can only be hinted at rather than pinned down precisely. But the close connections of the merchants— in terms of family allegiances, connections in banking, and residential patterns—were so great that, as Richard Pares once remarked, it would have been lacking in gentility for such a group 'to wage war to the knife on each other by cutting freight rates or instructing their captains to snatch consignments from each others' ships.'[104] Other problems had also emerged. Much of the energy involved in direct participation in the West Indies had gone by the era after the American Revolution: most of the examples given earlier in the paper of merchants criss-crossing the Atlantic are confined to the pre-1776 era when the dynasties were being established. The sugar trade was not one in which there were significant multiplier effects in local industry. Bristol West India merchants were mainly separate in personnel from sugar bakers and grocers in the city—indeed, there was almost permanent friction between the two groups—so mercantile expertise was never fully integrated with local sugar refineries.[105] It might also be true that Bristol generally poured too much money into the Caribbean and not enough into local industrial enterprises (though naturally this is not really possible to prove).[106] One would not want to conclude that Bristol lost ground in the early industrial age simply because of the commercial

[102] *Ibid.*, 80–5, 87, 195–6.

[103] Details on the debts of John Pinney, James Tobin and William Miles are available in Pares, *West-India Fortune*, 239–319, and in 'Calendar of Correspondence from Miles to Tharp,' ed. Morgan, 93–101, 103, 105, 111, 113–16, 118–21.

[104] Pares, *West-India Fortune*, 212.

[105] Morgan, *Bristol and the Atlantic Trade*, 215–16; BRO, I. V. Hall research notes on Bristol sugar refineries.

[106] Alfred J. Pugsley, 'Some Contributions towards the Study of the Economic Development of Bristol in the Eighteenth and Nineteenth Centuries' (MA thesis, University of Bristol, 1921), ch. 5, p. 7.

attitudes and decisions of its West India elite; the better factor endowments of Liverpool, its transport connections with the midlands, its links with the cotton industry in south Lancashire, and the demographic and industrial growth of its hinterland were all, it hardly needs saying, crucial external factors in the relative commercial decline of Bristol towards the end of the eighteenth century.[107] Nevertheless the business caution, concentration and specialisation of the city's West India elite seem to have produced an air of desultory entrepreneurship that hindered the economic development of Bristol as a national trading centre and left a legacy of poor adaptability that informed the whole commercial ethos of the city by the 1830s.[108]

[107] E.g. F. E. Hyde, *Liverpool and the Mersey: An Economic History of a Port, 1700–1970* (Newton Abbot, 1971), 21, 31; John Langton, 'Liverpool and its Hinterland in the late Eighteenth Century' in *Commerce, Industry and Transport: Studies in Economic Change on Merseyside*, ed. B. L. Anderson and P. J. M. Stoney (Liverpool, 1983), 1–25.

[108] B. W. E. Alford, 'The Economic Development of Bristol in the Nineteenth Century: An Enigma?' in *Essays in Bristol and Gloucestershire History*, ed. Patrick McGrath and John Cannon (Bristol, 1976), 252–83. For an alternative view see B. J. Atkinson, 'An Early Example of the Decline of the Industrial Spirit? Bristol Enterprise in the first half of the Nineteenth Century,' *Southern History*, IX (1987), 71–89.

APPENDIX

LEADING SUGAR MERCHANTS AT BRISTOL, 1728–1800[a]

Merchants	Hogs-heads imported	Years active in the sugar trade
Michael Atkins	40,289	1730–49, 1754–63
William Miles	36,543	1764–8, 1773–80, 1785, 1788, 1791–5
Robert Gordon	35,070	1747, 1749, 1754–68, 1773–9
Protheroe & Claxton	31,897	1785, 1788, 1791–1800
Thomas Daniel & Sons	20,993	1785, 1788, 1791–1800
Evan Baillie	20,271	1785, 1788, 1791–9
John Maxse	17,126	1785, 1788, 1791–1800
John Curtis	16,342	1748–9, 1754–68
James Laroche	15,226	1728–49, 1754–68, 1773–8
Meyler & Maxse	14,445	1773–80, 1785
Mark Davis	12,043	1729–33, 1735, 1737, 1740–9, 1754–68, 1773–80
Isaac Hobhouse	11,966	1728–49, 1754–8
Lowbridge & Richard Bright	11,939	1775–80, 1785, 1788, 1791–1800
John Fisher Weare	11,733	1773–80, 1785, 1788, 1791–1800
Samuel Munckley	11,501	1743–4, 1746–8, 1754–68, 1773–80, 1785, 1788, 1799
John Gordon, Sr	11,133	1774–80, 1785, 1788, 1791–1800
Samuel Delpratt	10,501	1764–8, 1773–9
Munckley, Gibbs & Co.	10,427	1773–8, 1791–1800
Samuel Span	10,158	1762–3, 1766, 1768, 1773–80, 1785, 1788, 1791, 1793
Thomas Harris	6,914	1748–9, 1754–68, 1773–80, 1785, 1788, 1791–3, 1796–7
David Dehany	6,896	1738–47
Devonsheir & Co.	6,064	1755, 1757, 1759–66
Evan Baillie & Sons	5,867	1799–1800
William Hare & Co.	5,723	1728–30, 1732–45, 1749, 1754
W. & J. Gordon	5,513	1785, 1788, 1791
Walter Jacks	5,450	1774, 1778–80, 1785, 1788, 1791–1800
Robert Lovell	4,872	1768, 1774–80
James Laroche & Co.	4,842	1728–32, 1734, 1736, 1738, 1740–9, 1754–7, 1761–3, 1765–6
David Parris	4,778	1764–8, 1773–4
Richard Meyler, Sr	4,757	1728–49, 1754–64, 1767–8
Thomas Penington	4,726	1728–32, 1734–48, 1754, 1756–65, 1767–8, 1774
Jeremiah Innys	4,564	1736–49, 1754–9
Henry Swymmer	4,507	1749, 1754–68, 1773
William Hare	4,462	1731–49, 1754
Michael Becher	4,319	1728–49, 1754–7
Tobin & Pinney	4,318	1785, 1788, 1791–5, 1798
Henry Bright	4,246	1746–8, 1754–68, 1773–7
John Gordon, Jr	4,062	1791–4
Samuel & John Span	3,835	1791–6

David Hamilton	3,740	1766–8, 1773–9
Samuel & John		
Span & Co.	3,554	1796–1800
John Becher	3,539	1728–43
Thomas Deane	3,528	1737, 1741, 1743–9, 1754–68, 1773–8
Tudway & Smith	3,522	1754–63
James Bonbonous	3,514	1745–9, 1754–67, 1774–6, 1778–80, 1785, 1788, 1792, 1794, 1797–9
Richard Farr	3,511	1728–40, 1754–60
William Gordon	3,436	1728, 1731–49, 1754–7
Mark Davis & Co.	3,352	1742–4, 1746–8, 1755, 1759, 1761, 1763, 1773–6
Devonsheir, Reeve		
& Co.	3,154	1746–8, 1755–61
Tobin, Pinney & Tobin	2,991	1796–7, 1799–1800

Sources: Society of Merchant Venturers, Bristol, wharfage books; Avon County Reference Library, Bristol, *Bristol Presentments*.
Note: [a] only includes years where a complete record of sugar imports is available. To standardise sugar imports I converted various containers into hogsheads. I counted a tierce as three-quarters of a hogshead and a barrel as one quarter. This method follows John J. McGusker, 'The rum trade and the Balance of Payments of the Thirteen Continental Colonies, 1650–1775' (PhD dissertation, University of Pittsburgh, 1970), app. c, 795).

THE ATLANTIC IN THE EIGHTEENTH CENTURY: A SOUTHERN PERSPECTIVE ON THE NEED TO RETURN TO THE 'BIG PICTURE'

By Kenneth Maxwell

READ 19 SEPTEMBER 1992 AT THE UNIVERSITY OF LIVERPOOL

LOOKING at the Atlantic in the eighteenth century, it seems to me that we still lack a comprehensive view of what changed during this period, where we should set its boundaries, and how we might interpret the salient characteristics of the century. Perhaps, we have been both too general and too specific, simultaneously seeking with the synthesisers to explain too much and with the more specialised monographic literature to explain too little.

If we begin in the South, which is my own starting point, this is a frustrating situation. Because our historiography on the Ibero-American and Afro-American Atlantic is still in a state of development, not to say underdevelopment, we are often forced to establish context and frameworks out of thin air; to ask what must appear from the perspective of the more developed historiographies of the north Atlantic to be obvious, foolish, and even naive questions. We are obliged, I think, to look at the 'big picture' if only to see if what happens in our sphere has any resonance elsewhere. Such, at least, is my apology for the title of my paper. Perhaps a better way of explaining what I will attempt to do this afternoon, is to say that I want to hold up a mirror from the south Atlantic to see if you find any reflections of what I am talking about in the north.

I will try to tackle two themes: The first relates very broadly to economic chronologies within the Portuguese and Spanish Atlantic and whether what we see here allows one to speak sensibly of an Atlantic system in the eighteenth century, and what the dimensions and limits of such a system might be. The second theme relates more to geopolitics and questions of empire or, if you will, of imperial hegemonies and the challenges that these hegemonies faced as the century ended.

I

We are of course confined to some degree, as we must be in any historical speculation, not only by our own research but by what our colleagues have chosen to write about. And inasmuch as history writing since the Second World War has tended to de-emphasise the role of individuals, of institutions, and of events—instead plotting the longer-term trends in economic development and delineating social and economic structures—the recent decades have seen an accumulation of more information about the first theme, the economic aspects of the Portuguese and Spanish Atlantic systems, than about the second: the policies and politics of empire. While much has been achieved by the emphasis on conjunctural economic analysis and social history, it has unquestionably also led to the almost total exclusion of detailed examinations of elites, institutions, and above all intellectual life and politics and policy. Hence, today, if we look at the late colonial period of the Spanish and Portuguese empires in America, we tend to know more about slaves than their masters, more about the forced Indian labour drafts of the Andes than the attitudes of Peruvian merchants and bureaucrats in Lima, more about Mexican silver production than the political role of mining entrepreneurs. The best book on the Enlightenment in Latin America, for example, remains the collection of essays edited by the late Arthur Whitaker in the early 1940s, twice reissued in the early 1960s but long since out of print.[1]

The end of our period is also compromised by the consequences of colonial emancipation in the sense that a relatively cohesive imperial past is fragmented into a series of sometimes spurious national histories, and we can no longer rely on the well-organised archives of the Indies in Seville or of the overseas dominions in Lisbon to help reveal to us what happened—or at least what the record keepers thought happened. For the western shores of the Atlantic we thus have a division of historical output into two broad categories, one of which might be called the vertical dimension, the other the horizontal. By the vertical dimension I mean a form of history writing confined by the geographical limits of what became after independence national entities. National histories inevitably stress originality and uniqueness, rather than any common colonial background, and are sometimes hostile to a point of view that would place the new nations that emerged in the Americas within an international or comparative framework, or even within a colonial or neocolonial context. The horizontal dimension is, of course,

---

[1] *Latin America and the Enlightenment*, ed. A. P. Whitaker (Ithaca, 1961); I am drawing in this section on my chapter, 'The Impact of the American Revolution on Spain and Portugal and Their Empires,' in *The Blackwell Encyclopedia of the American Revolution*, ed. Jack P. Greene and J. R. Pole (Oxford, 1991), 528–43. Since my lecture at the Liverpool seminar was intended as an interpretive essay I have kept footnotes to a minimum. When I have based my arguments on my own work the full documentation can be found in the sources cited. In other cases I have indicated the principal contributions by other scholars rather than provide a comprehensive bibliography in each case.

the comparative one—but this is also something we still largely lack even for North America (with the possible exceptions of Canada and the Caribbean). Despite the heroic efforts of Jack Greene and J. R. Pole, most U.S. historians still seem locked within the concept of the 'singularity' of U.S. history. For Latin America the situation is no less extreme. The recently published *Cambridge History of Latin America* (Cambridge, 1984), for example, is almost totally devoid of comparative analysis, especially in its colonial and early national volumes, a factor emphasised by the ease with which the original volumes are now being subdivided and reissued as what are essentially national histories. And a final caveat: According to a popular recent textbook, *Early Latin America* by Stuart B. Schwartz and James Lockhart (Cambridge, 1980), national independence is, in any case, a shadow thing at best. As they put it, 'It has been said often and truly that the division between colonial and national periods is an artificial one, especially in the social, economic, and cultural domains where so much current scholarly interest lies.' But if this is true, the eighteenth century becomes a mere blip on a very broad canvas. It is significant that Schwartz and Lockhart have long been leading rejectionists of what they call 'institutional history', by which they appear to mean essentially Atlantic history and the history of European ('Eurocentric') colonialism, including the great works on Atlantic commerce and navigation written by their immediate predecessors, such as C. H. Haring, not to mention those of Richard Pares and Vincent Harlow on this side of the ocean. Not all revisionists, of course, have taken this narrow view. Radical comparativists like Susan Deeds and Edward Countryman ['Independence and Revolution in the Americas,' *Radical History*, XXVII (May 1983] see the political emancipation from Europe as a critical transition, which at the very least requires an inquiry into the place of north and south America within the process of industrial, political, and social transformation that flowed from the circum-Atlantic upheavals of the late eighteenth century, of which the American Revolution was, of course, the most dramatic colonial manifestation during the eighteenth century. The question they raise is one Stanley and Barbara Stein raised some time ago [Stanley J. Stein and Barbara Stein, *The Colonial Heritage of Latin America* (Oxford, 1970)]; that is, why at independence did the histories of south and north America diverge so dramatically; or to put it in Immanuel Wallerstein's terms, how was it that North America moved from the periphery to the core of the world system, while Latin America remained peripheral?[2]

Currently, of course, there are two major interpretive frameworks for examining the impact of the North Atlantic democratic revolution

[2] Immanuel Wallerstein, *The Modern World System*, 2 vols. (New York, 1980).

in Latin America. First, there is the Robert Palmer–Jacques Godechot vision of an Atlantic-based transformation, an essentially political and institutional view, which sees mutual influence in political theory, constitutional experimentation, and the politics of democratic incorporation. In this view, the Enlightenment is a positive, benign, and causative influence, essentially a progressive force.[3]

A second view is a more economic view—partly Marxian but also capable of incorporating much of classical Liberalism; that is, it is a view that sees a general crisis of the old colonial system which affects the British empire in the 1770s and the Spanish and Portuguese empires in the early nineteenth century, all of which flows from the shift from commercial to industrial capitalism. In this view, the intellectual contribution is minimal. The revolutions in America, both North and South, represent a shift from formal to informal domination, with the newly industrialising states of Europe—especially Great Britain—replacing the decaying bureaucratic and mercantilist empires of Spain and Portugal.

Brazilian historians such as Fernando Novais have also been concerned to place the late eighteenth and early nineteenth century experience of Brazil within the context of a crisis of the old regime and of the old colonial system in the face of the Atlantic and Industrial revolutions.[4] Less work of this nature has been done on Spanish America, although Tulio Halperin has long focused on the economic and political complexities of the independence period in the La Plata region and more broadly in Spanish America [*Reforma y disolución de los imperios ibéricos, 1750–1850* (Madrid, 1985)]. And Nancy Farris, in her brilliant book on the Maya, sees the impact of the reformist proto-liberal policies of the Spanish Bourbons as marking the critical divide in the history of Meso-America.[5] Much of the new economic history of late colonial Mexico is seeking some explanation for the paradox of coexisting boom and rising social tensions within the most important of Spain's colonial holdings in the Western Hemisphere. And we have the now substantial body of new writing on the Bourbon reforms in Spanish America with major contributions by John Lynch, John Fisher, and David Brading. Yet, it seems to me that mainstream economic historians remain sceptical about the significance of the Atlantic-based commercial system to the onset of industrialisation. The important

---

[3] R. R. Palmer, *The Age of Democratic Revolutions*, 2 vols. (Princeton, 1959 and 1964); Jacques Godechot, *Les revolutions, 1770–1799* (Paris, 1964) and *L'europe et l'Amerique a l'époque napolienne, 1800–1819* (Paris, 1967).

[4] Fernando Novais, *Portugal e Brasil na crise do antigo sistema colonial, 1777–1808* (São Paulo, 1978). Also see Emilia Viotti da Costa, 'Introdução ao estudo da emancipaçao política do Brasil', in *Brasil em perspectiva*, ed. Carlos Mota (São Paulo, 1969).

[5] Nancy Farris, *Maya Society Under Colonial Rule* (Princeton, 1984).

point about these disagreements is how 'scatter shot' they are and to emphasise how very little explicit discussion we have had about the broader context of some of the most critical elements in eighteenth-century Atlantic history and their implications.

Perhaps we would be better off speaking of process, which involves, in part, a rethinking of the history of ideas within their social and economic context—again, looking from the south, which is my basic perspective here. For Latin America and the Iberian powers, this involves very much a new look at the impact of the ideas of the Enlightenment, which for Spain under Charles III (1759–88) and Portugal during the predominance of the Marquês de Pombal (1750–77) led to major reforms in the management of colonial affairs. This was motivated in both cases by a decision to fortify their colonial links, retake the benefits of Atlantic commerce from their northern competitors, and re-establish their power and prosperity by adapting the techniques they believed Britain and France, in particular, had used to surpass them. These measures by Portugal and Spain in some instances served also to pre-empt and in others to mitigate the impact of the north American revolution, although neither Spanish nor Portuguese America were able to avoid the consequences of the late-eighteenth-century European upheavals. Secondly, however, it is important to look not only from south to north but also from the north to south. The issue of revolution as example and as potentiality, involving the creative articulation of new institutional mechanisms of government was a central concern to would-be anticolonialists in the late eighteenth century. In both Brazil during the late 1780s and in Spanish America in the aftermath of the wars of independence, the north American constitutional model proved attractive. Yet, thirdly, we are also dealing with colonial opposition to metropolitan powers and it is this aspect, of course, the achievement of national independence, where the ambiguity of the Iberian and Ibero-American role in the Atlantic as a whole is most apparent. Spain was an important component of the European alliance that helped the thirteen colonies in north America escape from British rule. Many would be Latin American nationalists on the other hand saw Britain, the erstwhile colonial power, as a potential ally against Spain for their own independence movements. Process, therefore, is a critical element in the period because we are dealing with a complex interaction involving the impact of the Enlightenment—both in its absolutist form, involving a reformulation of imperial policy along neo-mercantilist lines and redefining thereby the rights of the state, as well as in its more liberal form as a guide to experimentation with new forms of governance and constitution making, defining thereby the rights of the individual within the process of decolonisation. Both imply a de-linking of previously set patterns and an upsetting, changing, and resetting of the institutional context within which collectivities define themselves.

II

How do the Portuguese and Spanish Atlantic fit into this picture? The case of Portugal and Brazil is especially interesting, given the Atlantic focus of their trade, Brazil's large slave population and consequent links to Africa, and the interpenetration of the Luso-Atlantic system via Lisbon by the British-dominated commercial system of the north Atlantic. But first it is essential to establish the parameters of the system we are talking about—for, if the eighteenth century Luso-Atlantic commercial system is characterised overwhelmingly by the rise of gold production in Brazil and its subsequent fall, both cycles took place within a broader framework which changed surprisingly little between the 1660s and 1807, the year of the Napoleonic invasion of Portugal. Hence, we are here talking about what I would call the long eighteenth century. Let me look briefly at the origins of this long eighteenth century and explain why I take these origins back to the 1660s.

The Dutch assault on the Portuguese overseas possessions during the mid-seventeenth century had been transatlantic in scope. The Dutch were well aware that control of the sugar producing north-east of Brazil was useless to them unless they also controlled the source of slaves in Africa. Hence, in 1641, the Dutch seized the slave supply port of Luanda, the capital of Portuguese Angola, the slave trans-shipment depot located on the offshore island of São Tomé, as well as the sugar producing Brazilian captaincy of Pernambuco. These Dutch successes, however, were temporary. In 1648, an expeditionary force mounted by the Portuguese governor of Rio de Janeiro retook Angola, and after a long and bitter guerrilla campaign in Pernambuco the Dutch were expelled from Recife in 1654.[6]

The Portuguese victories in Africa and Brazil were not repeated in the orient. The 1650s, in fact, saw Portuguese power virtually eliminated in Asia, or at least reduced to a shadow of what it had been in the sixteenth century. The oceanic dimension of Portuguese imperial interest, therefore, from the 1660s until the early nineteenth century, came to be pre-eminently focused on the south Atlantic. As early as 1644, moreover, direct trade between Bahia and the west African coast had been authorised; Bahia exporting tobacco and importing slaves. These trading and commercial links between south America and west Africa remained important well into the nineteenth century, making Bahian

---

[6] C. R. Boxer, *Salvador de Sá and the Struggle for Brazil and Angola, 1602–1680* (1952).

merchants involved in African trade wealthy and virtually independent of Lisbon.

On the mainland of south America, the northern and southern frontiers of the Portuguese dominions were also established, or, at least, the claims to these frontiers were staked out in the seventeenth century. In 1670, for instance, the bishopric of Rio de Janeiro was created, its jurisdiction reaching in theory to the northern banks of the Rio de la Plata. In 1680, the Portuguese established a 'new colony' (*Nova Colonia do Sacramento*) opposite the Spanish port city of Buenos Aires. The reaction of the Spaniards was rapid and Nova Colonia was seized after only a few months. But, in 1681, the Portuguese re-established and fortified the outpost. The issue of the Portuguese presence on the Rio de la Plata caused continuous friction with Spain. Despite several treaties, the problem was not resolved and remained after the independence of both Spanish and Portuguese America to complicate the relations between the successor states.

In the far north, the Amazon frontier also remained subject to dispute—in this case by France, which had in 1676 established a strategic presence on the coast of south America in Cayenna. French interest in Brazil, in fact, did not abate throughout the eighteenth century, despite the fact that in 1712, following the war of Spanish Succession, France formally renounced all claims to the left bank of the Amazon.

In the late seventeenth century, therefore, the focus of Portugal's imperial interest shifted decisively westward from the trading-post thassalocracy of the Indian Ocean first established in the early sixteenth century to the plantation based colonies of the South Atlantic. The Afro-American Atlantic commercial complex which had predated the Asian empire and thrived even while overshadowed by the Asian spice trade, now came fully into its own. Within the south Atlantic system itself, integrated by the triangular interdependence of Lisbon, the slaving enclaves of the west and central African coast, and the expanding colonies of European and African settlements in Portuguese America, imperial priorities were reordered to favour support of Portugal's territorial empire in Brazil.

Portuguese America in the 1650s was also very different from the collection of small coastal enclaves it had been sixty years before at the time of the union of the crowns of Spain and Portugal. The development of a fleet system between Lisbon and Brazil in the immediate aftermath of Portugal's independence from Spain, and the imposition of heavier customs duties to support the construction of warships at mid-century as well as the newly imposed monopoly of the Brazil company, proved advantageous to the south of Brazil which had previously competed under serious disabilities in terms of access to European markets with

Bahia and Pernambuco. The sugar ships from all the Brazilian regions now arrived at Lisbon together. The escort vessels left Rio de Janeiro towards the end of March and picked up the sugar ships of Bahia in April, the fleet arriving at Lisbon during early July or August.

Between the mid-1640s and 1650, sugar prices were high in Europe, but after that date the price of Brazilian sugar plummeted on the Amsterdam market, falling constantly until the 1680s. The major cause was competition from the Caribbean. The Dutch, and later the British, were developing their own sugar trade, and in the case of the British beginning to develop a system of preferential tariffs to protect British markets for British grown Caribbean sugar. The response of the Brazilian sugar sector to this loss of markets is very imperfectly understood, and little research has been done on the second half of the seventeenth century. There are some indications of attempts by Brazil mill owners to lower costs by vertically integrating their enterprises. The Jesuit-managed Sergipe mill in Bahia, for instance, which had relied entirely on sharecropping arrangements in the early years of the century, was directly producing sixty percent of its own cane by the 1680s. Producers also managed to transfer some of their losses to salaried employees whose wages suffered a substantial real decline over the second half of the seventeenth century.[7]

The social and political consequences of the new economic situation were significant. Planters and mill owners tended to lose their dominant position in urban institutions. Certainly, merchants began to hold positions of importance in prestigious urban voluntary lay organizations, such as the *misericórdia* in the Brazilian port cities. And in the municipal governments the old planter domination was challenged by the appointment of a university trained lawyer as presiding officer (*juiz de fora*) and the appearance (at least in Bahia in 1641) of representatives of the urban artisan population, the 'people's tribune' (the *juiz do povo*).[8]

At the same time, the municipal councils in Brazil were acquiring added importance in the broader imperial context. The fact that the recovery of Pernambuco from the Dutch had resulted as much from the actions of the inhabitants themselves and their allies from São Paulo and Bahia within Brazil as from the intervention by Lisbon undoubtedly encouraged this autonomy. Indeed, the Pernambucans had been prepared at one point to seek the support of the Catholic monarch of France when the aid of Portugal for their cause had seemed problematical. The municipal councils had raised money for defence.

---

[7] Stuart B. Schwartz, *Sugar Plantations and the Formation of Brazilian Society: Bahia, 1550–1835* (Cambridge, 1985).
[8] A. J. R. Russell Wood, *Fidalgos and Philanthropists: The Santa Casa da Misericórdia of Bahia, 1550–1755* (Berkeley, 1968).

They subsequently instigated a vigorous opposition to the monopoly of the Brazil company, and with the aid of the Inquisition (which opposed the privileges granted to New Christian bankers who had invested in the Brazil company) they succeeded in destroying the company's monopolies in 1659. The fleet system which had been imposed at the time of the company's establishment, however, was retained and continued to operate under the administrative direction of a new Lisbon-based board of commerce (*junta do comércio*). The Brazilian municipal councils, however, were represented in Lisbon by procurators; and the council of Bahia acquired the right of sending two representatives to the Cortes in 1653, a privilege of some importance because the Cortes played a vital part in the years following the restoration of Portuguese independence, meeting eight times between 1641 and 1698. Peace with Spain in 1668, the treaties with the Dutch in 1661 and 1688, and with the English in 1654 and 1662 had been bought at considerable cost in terms of special privileges granted to foreign merchants and indemnities paid, including the theoretical right of British merchants to reside in Brazil, something which in practice was rigorously opposed.[9]

The weakness of Portugal undoubtedly contributed to the relative autonomy of Brazilian institutions. Portugal was well aware of the need to treat Brazilians with care and respect since Portugal's power to coerce obedience was very limited. By the 1690s Brazilian sugar no longer dominated world markets. It did not, however, disappear from circulation. Brazilian white sugar was of high quality and remained an important export (and for Lisbon re-export) item. The major positive impact of sugar's relative decline in value was to stimulate diversification and give new incentive to exploration and expansion into the vast hinterland of South America. Tobacco, for instance, became a key Brazilian export to both Portugal and Africa; the quantity of tobacco sent to Portugal doubled between 1666 and 1672. Attempts were made to introduce cloves and cinnamon from Asia and to develop a trade in cacao. The cattle frontier was also pushing inland opening up connections between the São Francisco river valley and the São Paulo plateau. With Paulista aid the long lasting complex of fugitive slave settlements known as *Palmares* in the backlands between Pernambuco and Alagoas was destroyed. Since 1670 the Crown had also used the Paulistas extensively for systematic exploration of the interior rewarding them with the titles of nobility and membership in the chivalric military orders.

[9] Carl Hansen, *Economy and Society in Baroque Portugal* (Minneapolis, 1981); also the classic works by C. R. Boxer, *The Portuguese Seaborne Empire, 1415–1825* (1969) and *The Golden Age of Brazil, 1695–1750* (Berkeley, 1962).

The most dramatic and decisive consequence of Portuguese exploration of the interior, however, was the discovery of gold. The search
for precious metals had of course brought many of the first Europeans
to the western hemisphere, and also provoked the most audacious
explorations of the vast interior of south and north America and the
Spanish had been well rewarded for their early explorations. In the
Caribbean within months of Columbus's landfall, gold had been
discovered. During the 1540s in the barren mountains of the Andes,
the Spaniards came upon a vast mountain of silver at Potosi in present-
day Bolivia, and in Mexico along the eastern slope of the Sierra Madre
they were no less successful in exploiting silver ore. The Portuguese,
on the other hand, were less fortunate. For almost two hundred years
after Portugal laid claims to the territory which became known as
Brazil, they had to make do with more prosaic products—Brazil wood
used to produce red dye, sugar, hides, cacao, and tobacco—worthy
and valuable products all, but the previous metals the early settlers
hoped for eluded them. At the end of the seventeenth century, however,
half-Indian frontiersmen from the small inland settlement of São Paulo
struck it rich. São Paulo was a resource-poor community which made
its living by capturing and selling Indian slaves and raiding the
prosperous Jesuit missions in Paraguay. The Paulistas were ever on the
lookout for booty. In the 1690s, after years of searching, they eventually
came across rich deposits of alluvial gold in the streams along the flanks
of the mountain range of Espinhaço, which runs north–south between
present-day cities of Ouro Preto and Diamantina in the state of Minas
Gerais across the great interior plateau of Brazil. Three hundred and
fifty miles inland from the port city of Rio de Janeiro, the Mantiqueira
range marked the watershed for the great north-flowing São Francisco
river, as well as for the tributaries which flowed south into the vast La
Plata river basin. As word spread, avid speculators used both river
systems to reach the gold field and within a decade of the Paulistas'
discovery, the first great gold rush of modern history was in full swing.
More than anything else, it was gold that pushed Portuguese settlements
deep into the interior of Brazil—first to Minas Gerais, later to Goias
and Mato Grosso—well beyond the traditional sphere of Portuguese
interest determined by the Treaty of Tordesillas. The issue of the
interior frontier hence became a matter of acute concern to both the
courts of Lisbon and Madrid.

As the negotiations for a treaty to establish boundaries between
Portuguese and Spanish America progressed during the 1740s, it became
generally accepted that clear topographical landmarks such as rivers
and mountains should serve to delineate frontiers. The Portuguese had
two major bargaining chips. First, they held Colonia do Sacramento
on the east bank of the Plate Estuary. Second, the westernmost

Portuguese mining region, in what is now Mato Grosso, had been integrated administratively and economically with the northern Brazilian coast by means of a fluvial transportation and communications route running along the Guaporá, Mamoré, and Madeira rivers in the western Amazonian basin. When an agreement was finally reached, these rivers constituted the northwestern border of Portuguese lands, much to the satisfaction of authorities in Lisbon.[10]

It was within these broader geographical limits that the economic characteristics of the long eighteenth-century Portuguese-Atlantic system need to be seen. They were therefore: first and foremost, marked by the flow of specie (gold and silver, the latter obtained from the contraband trade with Spanish) and the pre-eminence of colonial, mainly Brazilian, staples. Second, the growth, decline, and revival of manufacturing industry in Portugal, was inversely proportional to the rise and fall of gold production in the Brazilian interior. That is to say, Portuguese domestic manufacturing thrived prior to 1700 and again after 1777, but languished during the golden age. This had major implications for the Portuguese foreign and colonial policy. Portugal also remained throughout the eighteenth century a chronic grain importer—from northern Europe at the beginning of the century and from north America, especially Virginia and the Carolinas, towards the end. This fact during the 1780s and 1790s had a major impact on the attitudes of the new north American republic, for example, marked especially in the person of Thomas Jefferson, towards proto-nationalist republican movements in Brazil. These attitudes were ambivalent at best when Virginia's trade with Portugal was placed in the balance against support for nationalist movements for independence from Portugal of uncertain origin in Portugal's vast South American territories.

The third important characteristic of the long eighteenth century was the British presence in Portugal and indirectly within its empire, protected by treaties and exercising de facto extra-territorial rights and privileges much on the pattern later imposed during the nineteenth century on China. For example, the whole period from the late 1660s through 1807 was marked by the dominant—the Portuguese felt—domineering presence of influential British merchant communities established in Lisbon and Oporto. The British merchants in Lisbon and Oporto were organised within so-called 'factories', which were in effect legally recognised commercial corporations, their privileges guaranteed by the Cromwellian treaty of 1657, reinforced by the Methuen Treaty of 1703. Through their entrepreneurial skills and

---

[10] David Davidson, 'How the Brazilian West Was Won,' in *Colonial Roots of Modern Brazil*, ed. D. Alden (Berkeley, 1971); J. R. Amaral Lapa, *Economia Coloniol* (São Paulo, 1973).

access to capital, British merchants penetrated the whole fabric of the metropolitan and colonial economy.[11]

The need for external political and military support was at the core of the commercial concessions Portugal had made to the British and others in the seventeenth century. This need remained a basic given throughout the eighteenth century, setting the parameters within which Portuguese foreign and colonial policy had to be conducted. Political and military dependency, however, did not mean there was no room for manoeuvre in the national interest or options open to a skilful Portuguese nationalist to extract whatever benefits he could from the Anglo-Portuguese relationship. In fact a central preoccupation of Portuguese economic thinkers and diplomats throughout the eighteenth century had been precisely how to achieve balance in what had become an unequal relationship but which intrinsically need not be so if a true reciprocity could be achieved. Nor did all British economic thinkers see pure benefit in the series of treaties and tariff privileges which governed Anglo-Portuguese commerce. The issue in fact became, as the eighteenth century wore on, a central topic of debate among the leading lights of the new science of political economy engaging both Adam Smith and Ricardo.[12]

The eighteenth-century Luso-Atlantic world, finally, was caught up in the struggle between France and England, a struggle that increasingly compromised Portugal. Lisbon tried to accommodate both, but by its very Atlantic nature, and because of the central economic role of Brazil within the Luso-Atlantic commercial system, Portugal was tied inextricably to Britain and, although it always sought to remain neutral and thereby retain the prosperous entrepôt function of Lisbon for the re-export of colonial products, it was very rarely able to maintain neutrality for long.

The role of Brazil in Portuguese calculations and diplomacy, economic and institutional, thus held much higher priority than did the colonial weight of north America in British calculations. These preoccupations with the development of the Portuguese Atlantic empire on the one hand, and with Portugal's diminished stature and apparent backwardness on the other, permeated the Portuguese intellectual milieu of the age.

The most dramatic reformulation of Portugal's policy towards Brazil occurred during the long period of rule by the Marquês de Pombal, between 1750 and 1777. Pombal himself took much from classic mer-

[11] K. R. Maxwell, *Conflicts and Conspiracies: Brazil and Portugal, 1750–1808* (Cambridge, 1973) [hereafter Maxwell, *Conflicts and Conspiracies*].

[12] H. E. S. Fisher, *The Portugal Trade: A Study of Anglo-Portuguese Commerce, 1700–1770* (1971). Also, Virgílio Noya Pinto, *Ouro Brasileiro e o comércio Anglo-português* (São Paulo, 1979).

cantilist theory and practice in his policymaking, both from its British and its French or Colbertian origins, but the use of the term mercantilism to describe Pombal's policy is not entirely appropriate. Mercantilism, when defined narrowly, as we know, describes a policy whereby trade is regulated, taxed, and subsidised by the state to promote an influx of gold and silver—the objective of such state intervention being aimed more broadly at achieving a favourable balance of trade.

Pombal's policy was at once limited and more focused than this. Its objective was to use mercantilist techniques—monopoly companies, regulation, taxation, and subsidies—to facilitate capital accumulation by individual Portuguese merchants. This aid to individual Portuguese capitalists had wider objectives and consequences because it was part and parcel of a scheme to fortify the nation's bargaining power within the Atlantic commercial system.[13]

The problem for an enlightened Iberian economic nationalist, which is perhaps a more accurate way to describe Pombal, was not so much to encourage the influx of precious metals; this was rarely a problem for Iberian economic policymakers given the fact that Spain and Portugal and their empires were the principal source of the world's bullion supply in this period, gold from Brazil, and silver from Peru and Mexico. The dilemma was precisely the opposite; that is, policymakers needed to devise measures to retain capital within their own economic system and at the same time to multiply the positive and diminish the negative economic impact of being producers of precious metals. The theory and practice of mercantilism was, after all, the creation of bullion-poor north-western Europe. The application of the theory and practice of mercantilism in the bullion-rich Iberian peninsula was bound to be partial because the end of the policy was fundamentally different from that sought by mercantilism's progenitors. The Iberians aimed to retain bullion, the north-west Europeans aimed to attract it.

Pombal's methods reflected, in fact, the peculiarities of Portugal's position within the Atlantic system, and the particular impact on Portuguese entrepreneurship of the Brazilian gold boom of 1700–60. Essentially, the all-powerful minister, Pombal, placed the power of the state decisively on one side of the conflict that had developed between Portuguese entrepreneurs as a consequence of the gold boom. He chose the large established Portuguese and Brazilian merchants over their smaller competitors because he saw the small merchants as mere creatures or commission agents of the foreigners. With support from

---

[13] Maxwell, *Pombal: A Paradox of the Enlightenment* (Cambridge, forthcoming) [hereafter Maxwell, *Pombal*]; and Francisco José C. Falcón, *A época Pombalina: política, económica e monarquia ilustrada* (São Paulo, 1982).

the state he hoped the large Portuguese merchants would in time be able to challenge the foreigners at their own game. His economic policy was a logical one in view of Portugal's position within the eighteenth-century international trading system. It protected mutually beneficial trade (such as the Portuguese wine trade), but it also sought to develop a powerful national class of businessmen with the capital resources and the business skills to compete in the international and Portuguese domestic markets with their foreign, especially British, competitors. It was not an easy policy to pursue, at least overtly, because it was essential to achieve this outcome without bringing into question the political and military support that the treaties with Britain guaranteed and which was essential if Spanish ambitions were to be kept at bay.

At the same time in Brazil, in striking contrast to the Bourbon reformers in Spanish America, Pombal sought to incorporate and coopt the Brazilian oligarchy. Portugal was, after all, a small country with a large empire. It did not possess the resources of a Britain or France. It did not have the military capabilities or the economic resources to force Brazil into a subservient role. Indeed, as Pombal watched the British attempt to repress the rebellious colonists in English-speaking north America during the 1770s, he was fortified in his belief that conciliation was a more effective weapon against colonial uprisings than military force.

Portugal's colonial policy under Pombal in effect served to diffuse tensions within the colonial nexus by preventing any polarization along colonial versus metropolitan lines. The intervention of the Pombaline state had almost always been sectoral; that is, it had swung state support behind one side in a series of pre-existing conflicts which themselves bridged the metropolitan–colonial divide. Hence, Pombal supported the large entrepreneurs against their smaller competitors; he had aided the educational reformers with the church such as the Oratorians while destroying the Jesuits and their colleagues; he had crushed powerful elements among the old aristocracy while encouraging the access of businessmen to noble status. The benefits and the displeasure of the Pombaline state, in other words, helped and hindered both Brazilian and Portuguese, forging a series of alliances across the Atlantic, as well as counter-alliances that linked Portuguese and Brazilian interests at a variety of levels. Some of these results of policy were unintentional; but the conciliatory aspect of Pombal's policy towards powerful Brazilian interests was entirely explicit.

The fundamental problem for Portugal, however, arose from the logic of the Brazil-based Atlantic system within which Pombal had operated. In the final analysis, Brazil would inevitably become the dominant partner within the Portuguese-speaking empire. If the political constraints that had governed the whole period from the 1660s to the end of the eighteenth century also changed, that is, if for example Great Britain no longer saw it in its own interest to protect Portugal from her continental neighbours, then the British might opt for a direct relationship with the colony rather than with the mother country[14] Since the whole basis of Portugal's prosperity had been built on the manipulation of colonial monopolies, cash-crops exports, colonial markets, and colonial gold, such a rupture would bring fundamental change and would close an epoch. Ironically it was the French seizure of Lisbon in 1807 that forced the effective political and economic emancipation of Brazil in 1808 by neutralising the power of those in Portugal opposed to recognition of Brazil's central economic and political role within the Luso-Brazilian Atlantic system, collapsing thereby the structure of the Luso-Atlantic system as it had existed since the 1660s and replacing Lisbon as the required intermediary between south America and Europe by direct access between Europe and the ports of Brazil.[15]

[14] There had, of course, been clandestine direct trade between British merchants and Brazil, especially involving the slave trade. The rolled tobacco of Bahia, most of it from the Cachoeira and Mantiba regions, was the basic commodity of exchange on the African coast, as necessary to other European slavers as to the Portuguese.[José da Silva Lisboa to Domingos Vandelli, Bahia, 19 Oct.1781, *Anais da Biblioteca Nacional, Rio de Janeiro (ABNRJ)*, XXXII (1920), 505; J. H. Rodrigues, *Brazil and Africa* (Berkeley, 1965) and Pierre Verger, *Flux et reflux de la traite des nègres entre le golfe de Bénin et Bahia de todos os santos du dix-septième au dix-neuvième siècle* (Paris, 1968).] Some fifty vessels a year, corvettes and smaller vessels, left Bahia for Africa, four-fifths of them for the Guiné Coast and the remainder for Angola. [Luís dos Santos Vilhena, *Recopilação de noticias soteropolitanas e brasilicas (1802)*, 3 vols. (Bahia, 1922–35).] European goods and gold dust came back to Bahia with the cargoes of slaves. This clandestine commerce had outraged the secretary of state for overseas dominions, Melo e Castro, as had the degree of control that the merchants of Bahia exercised over the African commerce to the exclusion of metropolitan merchants. ['Instrucção paro o marquêz de Valença', Martinho de Melo e Castro, Queluz, 10 Sept. 1779, *ABNRJ*, XXXII (1910), 442.] The Bahians always pleaded that they were forced into accepting European goods by the other slavers who needed their tobacco. ['Officio do Desembargador Gervasio de Almeida Paes para o Governador Marquês de Valença, no qual informa a respeito da referida devassa … ', Bahia, 4 Feb. 1783, *ibid.*, 529.] The contraband manufactures, however, did underprice those imported from the metropolis, and restricted the market for metropolitan goods. [José da Silva Lisboa to Domingos Vandelli, Bahia, 19 Oct. 1781, *ibid.*, 505.] The profitable subsidiary trade which accompanied the slave and tobacco commerce contributed to the favourable balance Bahia enjoyed with the metropolis. Most of the capital obtained was sunk into the purchase of more slaves. Martinho de Melo e Castro held that the working of the Bahian–African trade was the same as 'according to the English, French and Dutch a free trade by the ports of Africa between those nations and the Portuguese dominions in Brazil without the intervention of the merchants of the metropolis.' ['Instrucção para o marquêz de Valença', Martinho de Melo e Castro, Queluz, 10 Sept. 1779, *ABNRJ*, XXXII (1910), 444.

[15] José Jobson de Andrade Arruda, *O Brasil no comércio colonial* (São Paulo, 1980); Joseph Miller, *The Way of Death: Merchant Capitalism and the Angolan Slave Trade, 1730–1830* (Madison, 1988).

III

But what of the Spanish American Atlantic world? Here the eighteenth century had seen three major processes at work. First, the old monopolistic trading connection of Atlantic convoys of protected ships sailing on a regular pattern between the Caribbean and the monopoly port of Seville (later Cádiz) had been superseded by a *de facto* diversification of trade. Some of this diversification was illegal—but like the trade through Jamaica, this had become a substantial contribution to overall Atlantic commerce. After 1715, in fact, the old fleet system was clearly limiting the growth of trade as economic and demographic expansion occurred throughout Spanish America. Spain had also eventually permitted other Spanish ports into Atlantic commerce, gradually ending the Cádiz monopoly between 1765 and 1789, and given formal administrative recognition to the peripheral coastal regions in south America away from the old highland Indian-populated core areas, where Spain's major bases in the western hemisphere had been since the time of the Conquest. Thus, while Lima and Mexico City remained important (Mexico still accounted for half the population of Spanish America in this period), new regions also developed, such as the Rio de la Plata, Caracas, and Cuba, which had previously been backwaters—good for provisions but producing very little else. These regions all became major exporters in the late eighteenth century—Buenos Aires, an exporter of salt beef, silver, hides, and grains; Caracas for cacao and hides; Cuba, especially after the revolt in Haiti, a major centre for sugar and slaves.

Second, starting at mid-century Spain had attempted to implement a series of major administrative, mercantile, and fiscal reforms aimed at the enhancement of the power of the metropolis through the more efficient exploitation of its colonies.[16] As in Portugal, there had been growing awareness in Spain that its role as a great power was severely undermined by the failure to adapt to modern conditions; which in eighteenth-century terms meant using the power of the state to increase revenues and impose a more centralised administrative system. This preoccupation with national regeneration was in the forefront of the minds of several high government officials during the first half of the eighteenth century who saw Spanish America as the means for Spain to recuperate its position in Europe if colonial resources could be more effectively utilised. The 1743 proposal of José de Campillo, minister of

---

[16] I am drawing here on the work of Stanley J. Stein and Barbara Stein in 'Concept and Realities of Spanish Economic Growth, 1759–1789', in *Historia Ibérica*, I (1973), 103–119. Also see Carlos C. Noel, 'Charles III of Spain', in *Enlightened Absolutism*, ed. H. Scott (1990), 119–43.

finance, in which he called for a 'New System of economic administration for America' [*Nuevo Sistema de Gobierno Económico para la América*]
encapsulated the intention to develop the empire as a market for
Spanish manufactures and as a source for raw materials. Campillo
wished to see a system of general inspectors [*visitas generales*], the creation
of intendancies on the French model, and the introduction of 'free
trade' into colonial administration, by which they meant the ending of
the Andalusian monopoly and the opening of Spanish American trade
to all the ports of Spain, as well as the creation of a more economically
integrated society within Spanish America by changing the way in
which the Indian communities within the New World were governed.
Campillo's proposals, however, were not published until 1789. It was
the Bourbon monarch Carlos III (1759–88) whose reign became associated with the implementation of a series of far-reaching new governmental measures for the administration of the vast Spanish territories
in the New World. The urgency of these reforms became more than
ever evident after the seizure of Havana by the British in 1762, during
the Seven Years War.[17]

Each major Spanish crisis in the eighteenth century had a colonial
component. Commercial competition between England and France for
the Spanish contract (*asiento*) to supply African slaves to Spain's colonies
in America had been a prominent issue in the War of the Spanish
Succession. At mid-century, the second crisis in 1759–62 was precipitated
by English commercial expansion in India, Canada, and the Caribbean,
gateway to Spain's colonies in middle America and northern south
America. The third crisis at the century's end came with the conflict
between England and Napoleonic France in large measure over sea-
power and trade with Spain's colonies. What defined these crises was
Spain's monopoly of American silver production, its inability to develop
a manufacturing industry to supply its colonies, and the competition
between two more developed European economies over exploiting the
Spanish empire in America.

To England and France, Spanish America represented, above all, a
market for manufactured goods and a source of silver essential for
expanding international trade and settling the imbalance of payments.
At the end of the War of Succession, however, the forms of British and
French commercial penetration in Spain diverged. Less developed
commercially and industrially than the British, and linked to Spain as
wartime ally and tied by the Bourbon dynasty, French merchants and
shippers had to expand inside the Spanish colonial trading system now

---

[17] John Fisher, *Commercial Relations Between Spain and Spanish America in the Era of Free
Trade, 1778–1796* (Liverpool, 1985); and António Garcia-Baquero González, *Cádiz y el
Atlántico, 1717–1778*, 2 vols. (Seville, 1976).

centred on Cádiz. The Utrecht settlement confirmed the concessions yielded by Madrid over the last half of the seventeenth century to foreign resident merchants and shippers at Cádiz. Such concessions included extra-territorial rights, the exemption of firms and vessels from certain customs controls, and lower duties on imports such as French linens and other select items.[18]

There were on average over the decades 1724–78 about sixty major French commercial houses established in Cádiz. Of the declared value of the Cádiz merchants, moreover, the French merchants accounted for forty-three per cent—the Spanish merchants only eighteen per cent. Until 1789, the French remained the largest foreign colony at Cádiz, always conspicuous and sensitive, like the British factory in Lisbon, to any infringement of their treaty rights. A significant percentage of French textile exports shipped to Cádiz were re-exported; and the sales of French linens, woollens, and silks at Cádiz had important repercussions for employment and earnings in France's textile producing centres.[19] French industry also absorbed appreciable quantities of Spanish primary exports—raw wool, soda ash, raw silk—along with products from Mexico and Guatemala like cochineal and indigo dyes. As little as ten per cent of colonial cargoes consisted of Spanish goods, with the balance made up by the production of Spain's French ally. Sales to the Spanish colonies generated a counter-flow of silver that fed into the private banking system centred on Paris and Lyons, which was vital for trade with India and China and for the deficit-plagued finances of the French state. Silver, in fact, continued to dominate the Spanish American traffic: between 1717 and 1778 it composed 77.6 per cent of the annual value; and 75.4 per cent of the value of the trade of New Spain. And this was still a very substantial business comparatively speaking—the value of the commerce of Spanish America being double that of the British West Indies in the 1780s.[20]

---

[18] Fernando Murillo Ribiera, *L'Amerique et le changement economique de l'espagna du XVIII siècle: administration et commerce*, 11–26; Lutgardo Garcia Fuentes, *El comércio español en America, 1650–1700* (Seville, 1980); Miguel Artola, 'América en el pensamiento español del siglo XVIII', *Revista de indias* XXIX (1969); and N. M. Sutherland, 'The Origins of the 30 Years War and the Structure of European Politics', *English Historical Review*, CVII (July 1992), 586–625.

[19] Carlos D. Malamud, 'España, Francia y el comércio directo com el espacio peruano, 1695–1730'; 'Cádiz y Saint Marlo', in *La economia española al final del antiquo regime: comércio y colonias*, III (Madrid, 1982). Also, Albert Girard, *Le commerce français à Seville et Cadix au temps de Habsbourgs: contribution à l'étude du commerce étranges en Espagna aux XVIe et XVIIe siècles* (Paris, 1932).

[20] *L'Amerique espagnole a l'epoque des lumieres: Tradition – innovation – représentation*, XV (Paris, 1987). Also the excellent overview by D. A. Brading, 'Bourbon Spain and its American Empire', in *Cambridge History of Latin America*, I, ed. L. Bethel (Cambridge, 1984), 389–439.

English merchants were less important at Cádiz. They enjoyed other channels of trade with Spain's American colonies, especially along Spain's Caribbean coasts. Between Utrecht and the outbreak of war in 1739, the British managed the slave supply contract (the *asiento*) at Havana, Veracruz, Cartagena, and Buenos Aires, where along with African slaves they introduced smuggled goods; from Jamaica the British developed an extensive smugglers' network to Havana and Santiago on the island of Cuba, to the Campeche and Belize coasts, and to New Spain's sole major Caribbean port of Veracruz. Jamaica also served as both entrepôt and naval base; there British naval forces could threaten the French sugar islands and Spanish American ports. This threat materialised, of course, in the war beginning in 1757, when English forces took Canada and occupied first Guadeloupe and later Martinique.[21]

For Spain the accession of Charles III offered an opportunity to reform traditional attitudes. And for France, which saw its colonial empire in India and Canada collapse, and for Spain, unprepared alone to withstand English assaults upon its Caribbean trading zone, the accession of Charles III was the opportunity at last to renew their dynastic alliance of mutual convenience. Charles III, and the key collaborator he brought from Naples, Esquilache, like Pombal in Portugal, wished to diminish the pressure from French commercial and manufacturing interests who had long enjoyed direct and indirect participation in Spain's transatlantic trading system. Yet, there was a paradox to the Franco-Spanish diplomatic and military collaboration not dissimilar to that within the Anglo-Portuguese alliance.

Charles revived projects of economic reform outlined earlier by men like Campillo. Charles and Esquilache's first actions were to terminate the seventeenth-century tariff concessions hampering the development of domestic industry; this was followed by standardising tariffs and procedures at all peninsular ports. Given the importance of colonial trade in Spain's aggregate external exchanges, Madrid was, in effect, shifting much of the burden of customs revenue to colonial consumers. Charles's government also attempted to reduce the illegal foreign share in Spain's colonial exchanges, in effect, attempting to increase Spain's participation and advantages in colonial trade. And, in light of Franco-Spanish diplomatic and defence collaboration symbolised in the family pact, Madrid expected French manufacturing interests to tolerate Spanish protectionism designed as Madrid saw it, to make Spain's contribution in the joint containment of English commercial and naval power more effective.

[21] Dorothy Goebel, 'British Trade to the Spanish Colonies, 1796–1823', *American Historical Review*, XLIII (1938), 288–320.

The impact of the new governmental measures within Spanish America varied considerably from region to region. One immediate consequence was that tensions were aggravated between European Spaniards and the old Latin American white Creole oligarchies, which had for several centuries, it should be remembered, found a political niche within local administrations throughout the Americas. The Bourbon reforms, especially the intendant system, were therefore first introduced in the regions where the opposition of the old Creole oligarchies was less formidable; Cuba after 1764 and the Rio de la Plata after 1776. Only in 1784 was the system introduced in Peru, and in 1786 in Mexico. The articulation of the new system owed much to the reforming visitor general of New Spain (Mexico), José de Gálvez (1765–71), who later became the long-term secretary for the Indies (1776–87). His objective in Mexico had encompassed the establishment of a tobacco monopoly (to raise revenue), the reorganisation and raising of the sales tax (the Alcabala), and the stimulation of silver production (by lowering the price of mercury).[22]

In practice, Spanish neo-mercantilism proved limited in its impact. State intervention did not create an industrial base in textile manufactures, except in Catalonia whose cotton mills were the product of private rather than state initiatives. In the mid-1780s, the colonial trade expanded, but the increase in colonial exchanges appears to have been based largely on the sustained surge in Mexican silver mining and colonial staple exports, more shipping in low-tonnage vessels, and Europe's insatiable appetite for silver and staples.[23]

Spain, Europe and the East were still linked to American (now largely Mexican) silver and transforming a bullionist into a neo-mercantilist Spanish state was no easy process. The threat to the system from north-west Europe remained. The English manufacturers and merchants in preferring their Caribbean outposts from which they participated directly (and illegally) in Spanish colonial markets to the French method of participation via Cádiz were, in effect, pointing to one of the basic flaws in the Spanish neo-mercantilist project. The inability of the Spanish state to curb smuggling from English Caribbean

[22] Allan Kuethe and Douglas Inglis, 'Absolution and Enlightened Reform Charles III and the Establishment of the Alcabala', *Past and Present*, CIX (1985), 118–143; and Jacques Barbier, 'Indies Revenues and Naval Spending: The Cost of Colonialism for the Spanish Bourbons, 1763–1805', *Jahrbüch für Geschichte von Staat, Wirtschaft und Gessellschat Latinamerikas*, XXI (1984).

[23] Jacques Barbier, 'Peninsula Finance and Colonial Trade: The Dilemma of Charles IV's Spain', *Journal of Latin American Studies*, XII (1980), 21–37; John Fisher, 'The Imperial Response to "Free Trade": Spanish Imports from Spanish America, 1778–1796', *Journal of Latin American Studies*, XVII (1985), 35–78; and A. Garcí-Baquero González, 'Comércio colonial y producción industrial en Cataloñia a fines del siglo XVIII', *Actas del I Coloquio de história economica de España* (Barcelona, 1975), 268–94.

ports or from Dutch and French islands for that matter, demonstrated clearly what the merchants well understood; that multiple charges on goods within the formal Spanish trading system—repeated duties, commissions, and insurance fees—all raised the price of legal goods in Spanish America to levels that compensated for the risks of smuggling.

French textile manufacturers were also unable to provide the Spanish colonial system with merchandise whose quantity, quality, and pricing was competitive with other European goods. To protect their deteriorating competitive position, the French defended traditional commercial privileges in Spain's colonial trade. Yet, it was precisely here that the French manufacturers faced the competition of Spain itself which was trying to reduce the privileged status of French merchants and goods in colonial trade. The fundamental premise of mercantilism was economic competition, not cooperation. Thus, ironically, both French commercial agents and their Spanish counterparts, failed to observe that by the last third of the eighteenth century both Spanish and French economic policies were being bypassed by the rapid expansion of the international economy. English industrial development was generating products whose price and quality would permit them to penetrate most mercantilist barriers.

Neither Spaniards nor Frenchmen engaged in colonial trades with Spanish America wanted to recognise that the age of mercantilism was rapidly passing. Ironically, by the end of the eighteenth century, the British had made this leap, and in their relationship with Portugal, no less; and partly because of the comparative success of Pombal's policies, not because of their failure; and it was France, or more precisely Napoleon, who forced the issue to a denouement. Let me explain.

Between 1785 and 1790 the balance of trade between Portugal and Great Britain was brought almost into equilibrium. From 1791 to 1795 for the first time during the whole eighteenth century Portuguese exports to Britain showed a surplus over British exports to Portugal. From 1783, and especially from 1788, there was rapid growth in Brazilian raw cotton re-exports from Portugal to Britain—and by the first decade of the nineteenth century, about a quarter of Lancashire's cotton wool export came from Brazil, especially Pernambuco and Maranhão. Robert Walpole, British envoy in Lisbon, looked on in astonishment as Britain remitted gold to Lisbon to pay for its now unfavourable balance of trade. 'It may be looked upon as a kind of phenomenon', he told Lord Grenville in 1791.[24]

It was now the British who clamoured for reciprocity, a reversal of

---

[24] Michael M. Edwards, *The Growth of the British Cotton Trade, 1780–1815* (Manchester, 1967); Arthur Redford, *Manchester Merchants and Foreign Trade, 1794–1858* (Manchester 1934); and [Robert Walpole] to [Lord Granville] Lisbon, 12 Oct. 1791, PRO: FO 6/14.

circumstances which would have gratified the subtle old Marquês de Pombal had he lived long enough to see it. Between 1786 and 1788, extensive investigations were conducted in London into the changed Anglo-Portuguese commercial relationship. Both the old woollen and wine industries and the new cotton manufacturing interests pressured the government and the committee of the Privy Council for Trade. The cotton spinners and the calico and muslin manufacturers of Manchester and Neighbourhood were especially vocal as were the Borough Reeve and constable of Manchester.[25] In 1801 Lord Hawkesbury instructed the British minister in Lisbon to let it be known that 'in the case of invasion, the British envoy was authorised to recommend that the court of Portugal embark for Brazil ... and the [British] were ready for their part to guarantee the security of the expedition and to combine with [the Portuguese government] the most efficacious ways to extend and consolidate [their] dominions in South America'.[26]

This was an astonishing change of policy. But its immediate implementation was not easy—the traditional commercial organisations and their lobbies remained powerful—not only in the form of the British Factories in Portugal, but also among the new Portuguese merchant industrial bourgeoisie Pombal had created. But the British government was clear on the issue. As Robert Fitzgerald, Walpole's successor in Lisbon, wrote to Lord Hawkesbury, 'the British property within these dominions forms no object of great national importance ... especially where in the opposite balance are viewed the innumerable advantages to be derived from an open, unrestrained trade with the Brazils'.[27] It took the French invasion of 1807 to neutralise the old interests. One cannot help thinking that it would have been better for the French if they had left Iberia alone when after the victories of Nelson they could not challenge British naval superiority in the Atlantic Ocean. A factor incidentally, I notice, the citizens of Liverpool well noted at the time.

IV

But if the policies of neo-mercantilism in both Spain and Portugal were thwarted, and thwarted be it noted where they succeeded as much as

[25] 'Minute of Propositions Impeding the Treaty with Portugal', Sept. 1786, Chatham Papers, PRO 30/8/342 (2) f. 59; Office of the Committee of Privy Council for Trade, 25 June 1787, PRO, BT 3/1, 102; [W. Fawkener] to [Borough Reeve] and [constable of Manchester], Office of Privy Council for Trade, 23 August 1788, PRO, BT, 3/1, 290.

[26] D. José de Almeida de Melo e Castro to Dom João, 1 Sept. 1801, Arquivo Instituto Historico e Geografico Brasileiro, Rio de Janeiro, Lata 58, doc. 17.

[27] [Robert Fitzgerald] to [Lord Hawkesbury], Lisbon, 21 Oct. 1803, PRO, FO, 63/42.

where they failed, and if Enlightened Absolutism proved incapable in the long term of preventing the inexorable rise of the British commercial and naval hegemony within the Atlantic system as a whole, what of the forces of proto-nationalism on the other side of the ocean—can we speak here of an age of Democratic Revolution as Robert Palmer proposed, or of an Atlantic Revolution in the sense Jacques Godechot used the term? Or are we indeed seeing a more economically based transformation from direct to indirect dominion, from the old formal to the new informal empire of trade and industrial power. The ferment of innovation and the difficulty of implementing reform in the Americas had certainly revealed just how complex Spanish American colonial society had become by the late eighteenth century. It also demonstrated how difficult it would be in Spanish America for a clear regional focus of proto-nationalistic sentiment to emerge, or for the creation of a cohesive social base to support any rebellion against Spain. Internal social, racial, and caste divisions permeated colonial society, and it was very difficult anywhere in Spanish America for European Spaniards living in the colonies, Creole magistrates, soldiers, and local businessmen to come together in even the embryonic independence movement that had briefly made the idea of an economically independent and Republican Minas Gerais on the north American model so pertinent in Brazil in 1788-9.

The example of the American Revolution had been particularly important in Brazil for reasons that lay in the coincidence of its anticolonial message with the severe tension between Lisbon and major segments of the local elite in the one area in Portugal's American territories that had the capacity to articulate as well as make effective an independent state, possessing as it did in the 1780s adequate revenues, military forces, administrative experience, and a close attention to international developments. That it failed despite all these elements is an indication of how difficult the achievement of colonial independence would be in Ibero-America.[28]

Movements of social protest did, of course, emerge in Spanish America, and with much more violence, bloodshed, and disruption than ever occurred in Brazil where proto-nationalist movements, however articulate, never got further than conspiracy in the eighteenth century. But the movements of social protest in Spanish America were limited in their ideological content; they did not make the leap from protest against bad government to an attack on the rule of Spain in America. The most significant of these movements of protest and rebellion, the Comunero rebellion in New Granada (present-day Colombia and Venezuela) in 1781; and the Túpac Amaru rebellion in upper Peru

---

[28] Maxwell, *Conflicts and Conspiracies*, especially 115-40.

(present-day Bolivia) in 1780–1, never projected themselves into an anti-colonial struggle and both, especially the latter, served to terrify the Creole elites and make them acutely aware of the risk of race and ethnic violence implicit in the complexity of Spanish America's social makeup.[29]

Given the heterogeneity of Spanish America in the late eighteenth century, the uneven impact of imperial reform, the diversification of the economic system, and its reorientation toward the Atlantic trading system in the new peripheral growth areas, such as Venezuela and the Rio de la Plata,as well as the limited anticolonial sentiment apparent in the rebellions of the 1780s, incipient nationalism was, when it emerged, more a characteristic of disgruntled individuals than of the masses. The latter were, on the whole, more preoccupied with immediate inequalities and exploitation than with intra-imperial injustices, and they felt more the oppression of the local oligarchies than of the crown in Madrid. The rebels in both Peru and Venezuela, in fact, had looked to the Crown for redress of grievances. The notion of independence from Spain, of a colonial emancipation from Europe,was hence confined to a very small number of the white Creole elite and developed after the putative popular revolts of the early 1780s had been repressed. These aspirations also were of a reformist rather than a revolutionary nature, and while the institutional model of the new north American nation was often an inspiration, in terms of overseas contacts and hope of assistance it was Britain to which they looked rather than to the United States.

By the turn of the century, it is true that works by John Adams, George Washington, and Thomas Jefferson were circulating in both Mexico and South America, and key leaders of the Spanish America independence movement, most notably Francisco de Miranda, visited the United States, as did Simón Bolívar, who admired Washington. Miranda, however, summed up the complex reaction of whites to the events of 1776 in North America and 1789 in France. 'We have before our eyes two great examples', he wrote in 1799, 'the American and the French Revolutions: let us prudently imitate the first and carefully shun the second.' After the revolt in French Saint-Domingue in 1792, as in Brazil, property owners throughout Spanish America became even more cautious, especially if their property included African slaves. 'I confess that as much as I desire the liberty and independence of the New World', Miranda observed, 'I fear anarchy and revolution even more.'[30]

The impact of the American Revolution would be confined mainly to the peripheries in Spanish America. Very little impact can be

[29] John Laddy Phelan, *The People and the King: The Communero Revolution in Colombia, 1781* (Madison, 1978).

[30] Peggy K. Liss, *Atlantic Empires: the Networks of Trade and Revolution, 1713–1826* (Baltimore: 1983).

discerned in the two great core regions of Spanish dominion, Peru and Mexico. In many respects, the north Americans, in terms of trade, influence, and contacts, followed the sea-lanes, and their role was most significant with the Caribbean and along the coastlines where they had long been involved in the transatlantic commercial complex as purveyors of codfish, sugar, slaves, grain, tobacco, and most recently cotton. But here it was the north American commercial role within the Atlantic commercial system as a whole that was decisive. The grain trade, in particular, found ready customers in the Iberian peninsula, among the colonial overlords of south and central America. And trade more than republican ideology would be the watchword in the United States' dealings with both Spain and Portugal. These powers, Spain in particular, had aided in very substantial ways the attainment of American independence; it was a connection that made for some caution when it came to aiding and abetting revolutionaries to the south, at least until the Napoleonic period, when for all effective purposes the United States gained direct access to Spanish American ports and Spain to all intents and purposes lost direct administrative control of its empire in America due to British control of the sea-lanes.[31]

In the case of Portugal and Brazil, it had become very evident that the impact of the American Revolution in Brazil, which was a powerful influence before 1789, was nonetheless diluted and eventually rejected by the mid-1790s. This rejection was partly due to the failure of the Nationalist and Republican conspiracy in Minas Gerais during early 1789, but it was due also to the counter influence of the French Revolution and most particularly the manifestation of the French Revolution in the Americas, the great slave revolt in the French Antilles.

The white Brazilian elite, slave owners and those opposed to slavery alike, found by the 1790s that republicanism and democracy were concepts too dangerous for experimentation within a society half slave, and where blacks outnumbered whites two to one. The consequence was that those who avidly and approvingly followed the events in north America before 1790 turned away from the north American model and, encouraged by the Portuguese government, which had learned its own lessons from the revolt of the thirteen colonies, embraced monarchy in the interest of preserving the status quo against racial and social upheaval. A similar interaction between the chronology of revolutions and elite attitudes took place in all the American states and ex-colonies where slavery was entrenched.

In mainland Spanish America, independence followed from external

---

[31] John Lynch, *The Spanish American Revolution, 1808–1826* (1973). *The North American Role in the Spanish Imperial Economy, 1760–1819*, ed. Jacques Barbier and Allan Kuethe (Manchester, 1984); also *The Economics of Mexico and Peru During the Late Colonial Period, 1700–1810*, eds. Nils Jacobson and Hans-Jürgen Puhle (Berlin, 1986).

more than internal events: the collapse of the Bourbon monarchy in Spain itself in the face of the Napoleonic onslaught in 1808. Unlike Portugal, where the French invasion brought about a denouement to the dilemmas of the metropolitan–colonial relationship with the removal of the Portuguese court to Brazil and the *de facto* (later *de jure* establishment of Rio de Janeiro as the seat of a New World monarchy, in Spain the invasion in effect cut Spanish America loose of the old metropolis for a critical six years between 1808 and 1814, with major consequences for Spanish American unity and stability. The successor Spanish American republics often took shape within the new boundaries imposed by the eighteenth-century reformers, but they all faced massive problems of social cohesion and economic and administrative dislocations. The conflicting pressure arising from unequal economic growth within the Spanish empire in America, the ambiguities of an administrative reform that was in part an attempt to respond to those changes, as well as the several social, ethnic, and racial tensions that permeated the social makeup of Spanish America had all served to limit the development of a broad-based anti-colonial sentiment prior to 1808, and fragmented the social bases of support for a nationalistic project on the north American model, limiting thereby the potential impact of the north American example. Again, as in the lowland tropical areas of the western hemisphere, the example of the great slave revolt and consequent bloody conflicts in Haiti reinforced the fears arising from the uprisings in Upper Peru in the early 1790s. Those who saw the North American model as relevant tended after 1800 to see it as the conservative option; a solution to the colonial dilemma that preserved the basic social organisation, especially the system of slavery, but brought political emancipation from Europe. For an effective partnership they more often looked to Great Britain and to trade: espousing 'liberalism' in the sense of access to world commerce rather than liberalism in the sense of democratic government.

For Latin America, especially for the areas where plantation economies and African slavery predominated, it is essential, therefore, if we are seeking to mark the end to the long eighteenth century, to look at the relationship between the three revolutions of the late eighteenth century, the American, the French, and the Haitian, and for Spanish America to look to the vicissitudes of the eighteenth-century experience with reform and rebellion. From the perspective of the Americas at the time, the great slave revolt of 1792 in French Saint-Domingue was a second 'American' revolution that seemed no less important than the first. It brought to the forefront of elite consciousness fears and tensions inherent to plantation systems throughout the New World. Within the empires of Spain and Portugal, the Haitian revolt served to stimulate both a reapproximation between local oligarchs and the more progressive elements within the metropolitan governments as in the Portuguese-speaking empire, and as in Spanish America made it inevitable that the independence movements, when eventually they came, would always find questions of race, class and social stability close to the surface. Whereas in the 1780s would-be Latin American revolutionaries had found inspiration in George Washington, by the 1790s they would recoil in fear before the example of Toussaint L'Ouverture.

The Haitian revolt also had a major impact on the attitudes of the governments of Spain, France, and Britain towards independence movements in the Americas. For Britain, in particular, Haiti brought great caution to the encouragement of colonial rebellion if such revolts threatened to bring about so much instability and violence as to destroy the very wealth which had attracted British traders and merchants to the region in the first place. Here, the British soon began to see the advantages of the Luso-Brazilian solution to the dilemmas of the epoch of the Atlantic revolutions. As John Barrow summarised the issue in 1806:

Revolutions in states where each individual has some interest in their welfare are not effected without the most serious calamities. What, then, must be the consequences in a country where the number of slaves exceeds the proprietors of the soil? In promoting revolutions. I trust England will never be concerned, being fully convinced that however much South America might gain by a quiet change of masters, she will be soon thrown back into a state of barbarianism by revolutions.[32]

From the early nineteenth-century British perspective, the reasons for this essentially conservative stance are not hard to discern. Hegemonic powers, then as now, never like to see their interests challenged or their commercial interests destroyed by radical and unpredictable change. The recently independent north Americans were the first to see through such stratagems and their implications for Spanish America and Brazil. The American secretary of state, John Quincy Adams, writing on 28 June 1818, ably summed up the British attitude towards the political emancipation of south America when he wrote:

[32] John Barrow, *A Voyage to Cochinchina in the Years 1792 and 1793* (1806), 133–4; Also see John Lynch, 'British Policies and Spanish America', *Journal of Latin American Studies*, I (1969), 1–30; Saint Dominique had been producing about 40% of the world's sugar and over half of the world's coffee, according to David Geggus, when the 1791 slave revolt occurred. The government of William Pitt and Henry Dundas sent some 15,000 soldiers to their deaths in Saint Dominique and spent some £10m trying to conquer it. Geggus calls this 'among the greatest disasters in British Imperial History. D. Geggus, 'The British Government and the Saint Dominique slave revolt 1791–1793,' *EHR*, XCVI (1981), 285–305.

The Revolutions in South America had opened a new world to her commerce, which the restoration of the Spanish colonial domination would again close against her. Her Cabinet, therefore, devised a middle term, a compromise between legitimacy and traffic ... She admits all the pretensions of legitimacy until they come in contact with her own interests, and then she becomes the patroness of liberal principle and colonial emancipation.[33]

Only two months later the British envoy in Rio de Janeiro, Henry Chamberlain, in fact, was writing secretly to Viscount Castlereagh (22 August 1818) in terms which reflected Adams's supposition exactly:

The political state of this part of the South American continent has become so changed by the establishment of the seat of the Portuguese Monarchy in the Brazils that a change in the system under which Spain formerly governed her colonies in the Plata is become necessary and unavoidable, even if they had remained faithful; they have, however, thrown off their allegiance, and have maintained a struggle of several years for Independence. ... For Brazil, having ceased to be a colony and being become an independent kingdom open to the commerce of the whole world, they cannot return to their former state. However, as I regard the re-establishment of Spanish authority as impossible, it appears to me that the real interests of His Catholic Majesty would be secured by his putting an end to the contest as soon as possible, ... such as to promise stability, revolution would cease and prosperity would be restored in these fine countries to the advantage of the whole world, and of none more than of Great Britain.[34]

John Adams and Henry Chamberlain were both right. The characteristics and options that had marked the long eighteenth century in the Spanish and Portuguese Atlantic had been permanently transformed. Yet this had occurred at least in part because the options for two very important participants in the eighteenth century South Atlantic world, Spain and Portugal, had been largely superseded and destroyed. For them, the long eighteenth century had ended.

[33] *Diplomatic Correspondence of the United States Concerning the Independence of the Latin American Nations*, ed. William R. Manning, 3 vols. (New York, 1925), I, 72.

[34] 'Britain and the Independence of Latin America, 1812–1830', in *Selected Documents from the Foreign Office Archives*, ed. Sir Charles Webster, 2 vols. (1938), I, 190–3.

ECONOMIC DEPRESSION AND THE MAKING OF 'TRADITIONAL' SOCIETY IN COLONIAL INDIA

1820–1855

By David Washbrook

READ 16 OCTOBER 1992

OVER recent years, questions concerning the character and direction of social change in colonial India have become increasingly complex.[1] Until the 1960s, it remained possible to conceive the coming of British rule as representing 'the beginnings of modernisation'[2] and to write Indian history in terms of an 'heroic' struggle to fulfil the civilising mission: 'heroic', in the British sense, because it largely failed. Except among a narrow stratum of elites, Indian society obviously refused the West's invitation to 'usher it into history'[3] and India's culture moved very little towards convergence with the West's.

In the 1960s, however, some historians began to wonder whether the West's invitation had been seriously or honestly offered; and whether India's failure to modernise was not the result of colonial intent. The works of Eric Stokes, Robert Frykenberg and Bernard Cohn emphasised the extreme caution with which British rulers had approached indigenous society and the extent to which the Raj had left large areas of its 'tradition' untouched. For Stokes, 'The First Century of British Rule in India' wrought no major societal transformation; for Frykenberg, the British state in south India remained essentially a 'Hindu Raj'; for Cohn, Benares rural society was subject to no 'structural change'.[4]

During the 1970s, the questioning started to take a new direction. Now, while it was agreed that many of the cultural and societal relations of colonial India did not conform to ideal types of the modern(-ising) or the western(-ising), it began to be doubted that they conformed

---

[1] I am grateful to Burton Stein for his comments on an earlier draft of this paper.

[2] As in *Indian Society and the Beginnings of Modernisation, c.1830–1850*, eds. C. Philips and M. Wainwright (1976).

[3] The phrase, of course, is that of Karl Marx. See K. Marx, *Surveys from Exile* [ed. D. Fernbach]. (1973), 306.

[4] See E. Stokes, 'The First Century of British Rule in India, 1757–1857' in *The Peasant and the Raj*, ed. E. Stokes (Cambridge, 1979); R. Frykenberg, 'The Silent Settlement in South India, 1793–1836' in *Land Tenure and Peasant in South Asia*, ed. R. Frykenberg (New Delhi, 1977); B. Cohn, 'Structural Change in Indian Rural Society, 1596–1885' in *Land Control and Social Structure in Indian History*, ed. R. Frykenberg (Madison, 1969).

either to the social relations which had actually existed before the colonial conquest. In the context of south India, for example, Arjun Appadurai and Nicholas Dirks found little in common between the 'official' caste system of the colonial era, with its ideological base in the *Brahmanic* theory of *varnashramadharma,* and the systems of social stratification operating in the pre-colonial era.[5] These last, which perhaps harked back to the principles of the 'segmentary' medieval state perceived by Burton Stein, drew on notions of royal and divine 'honour' to demarcate patterns of relationship which were far less rigid and hierarchic than those of the nineteenth century.[6] 'Caste' before colonialism had been imbricated in a social structure permitting high degrees of group autonomy and mobility, and fostering competition between rival sectarian traditions (of 'the right-' and 'left-hand' and of the *Thengalai* and *Vadagalai* schools of *Vaishnavism*)[7] While, no doubt, *varnashramadharmic* ideology had long existed in Sanskritic scriptural sources, its realisation in the social practices of the colonial south represented a considerable novelty which in no way could be understood as the simple continuity of 'tradition'.

Similarly, in the south no less than the north, the 1970s saw received images of 'traditional' society resting upon a base of self-contained and semi-autonomous 'village communities' beginning to take a severe historiographical battering.[8] Revisionist perspectives started to re-conceive the village as but a 'moment' in much broader and more complex systems of kinship, kingship, trade and settlement, which possessed dynamics and mobilising forces of their own.[9] As Christopher Fuller has argued with regard to the south, it may well have been the dissolution under colonial rule of many of these broader systems, which permitted the village community—or at least the image of the village community—to establish itself as the nucleus of nineteenth-century society.[10]

Or again and relatedly, it started to be questioned whether the classical *jajmani* system—as observed by the Wisers in the last colonial decades— can have reflected a structure of economic relations whose history reached far back into the 'traditional' past.[11] Set against the

---

[5] See A. Appadurai, *Worship and Conflict under Colonial Rule* (Cambridge, 1981); N. Dirks, *The Hollow Crown* (Cambridge, 1987).

[6] B. Stein, *Peasant State and Society in Medieval South India* (New Delhi, 1980).

[7] B. Stein, *Peasant State,* esp. 173–215; B. Stein, 'Social Mobility and Medieval South India Hindu Sects' in *Social Mobility in the Caste System in India,* ed. J. Silverberg (The Hague, 1969); A. Appadurai, *Worship and Conflict,* ch. 1.

[8] C. Dewey, 'Images of the Village Community', *Modern Asian Studies,* VI:3, (1972).

[9] See T. Kessinger, *Vilyatpur 1848–1968* (Berkeley, 1974); R. Fox, *Kin, Clan, Raja and Rule* (Berkeley, 1971).

[10] C. Fuller, 'British India or traditional India?', *Ethnos,* 3–4 (1977).

[11] W. H. and C. V. Wiser, *Behind Mud Walls* (Berkeley, 1969).

Wisers' observations of a 'non-market' economic system marked by ascriptive hierarchy, custom and rank must be set the findings of many historians—Chicherov, Perlin, Commander, Chaudhuri and Mizushima, to name but a few—that pre-colonial economic systems functioned around negotiated bargaining relations between independent corporate groups and were heavily inflected by competitive and market rationalities.[12]

In the light of these findings, a major concern of nineteenth-century social history became understanding how Indian 'tradition' had been re-defined and structured into society under colonial rule, apparently to a far greater extent than 'modernity' ever had been. Indeed, 'pseudo-traditionalisation' was now taken much better to describe the dominant social processes of the nineteenth century than 'modernisation'.

In pursuit of this understanding, the spotlight very quickly fell on the western ideology of modernisation itself and, in particular, on the way that it approached the question of 'tradition'. Here, the self-referentially 'radical' view of European civilisation taken by much post-Enlightenment thought would seem to have had its corollary in the production of 'conservative' caricatures of non-European civilisations: from Hegel to Marx to Weber, the dynamism, egalitarianism and individualism of 'the West' were weighed and appreciated principally against the supposed enervation, hierarchicalism and corporatism of the 'irrational' East. The Indian past became re-defined as static and mindless 'tradition' to serve as 'the other' to modern Europe's self-flattering understanding of its own history.[13]

Equally, the obsessions of 'modernity' with bureaucratic rationality and 'scientific' forms of knowledge promoted approaches to social categorisation, which froze the mutable relations of Indian society into fixed and rigid patterns and which denied them further rights to change. For administrative and anthropological purposes, castes became 'things', with definable boundaries, constituents and ranks, rather than the loose and changeable congeries of multiplex relationships, which they had been in the past.[14]

In addition to the cultural logic lying behind the modern West's encounter with the East, there was, of course, also a political logic. As

[12] K. N. Chaudhuri, 'Markets and Traders in India during the Seventeenth and Eighteenth Centuries' in *Economy and Society*, eds K. Chaudhuri and C. Dewey (New Delhi, 1979); T. Mizushima, *Nattar and Socio-Economic Changes in South India in the 18th–19th Centuries* (Tokyo, 1986); A. I. Chicherov, *India: Economic Development in the 16th–18th Centuries* (Moscow, 1971); F. Perlin, 'Proto-industrialisation and Pre-Colonial South Asia', *Past and Present*, XCVIII, 1983; S. Commander, 'The Jajmani System in North India', *Modern Asian Studies*, XVII:2 (1983).

[13] R. Inden, *Imagining India* (Oxford, 1989).

[14] B. Cohn, 'The census, social structure and objectification in South Asia' in B. Cohn, *An Anthropologist among the Historians and Other Essays* (New Delhi, 1987).

Edward Said has argued, in a political culture whose key value was progress, the image of oriental societies as backward and inherently static served as a ready justification for their colonial domination.[15] And further, as colonial rule removed from them legitimate access to political power over themselves, it was hard to see by what means they could legitimately promote change (that is, generate history) within themselves. Colonial rule required colonised societies to exist in a condition of hierarchically-ordered stasis, and so they came to be.

Or at least, so they came to appear in certain of the canonical 'representations' of 'traditional' Indian society produced by colonial 'authorities'. One major problem of treating India's 'traditionalisation' largely or exclusively as the function of Western cultural perceptions is that it does not immediately explain why these perceptions—or misperceptions—should have mattered much to Indians themselves and have become translated into concrete forms of social reality. Why should the often ill-informed and prejudiced views of a handful of extremely distant scholars and administrators, themselves usually far more concerned with audiences in London than in India, have restructured the social relations of an entire sub-continent? How did they?

And yet there cannot be much doubt that, through certain mysterious processes, somehow they did. By the end of the nineteenth century, the basic structures of Indian society—of caste and village—conformed far more to the colonial stereotype of 'what they had always been' than to what they may actually have been one hundred years earlier. Indigenous discourses of 'rank' and 'right' now focused largely on caste and village, to the exclusion of the older references of kingship, kinship and territory.[16] Indeed, by this time, a new generation of Indian intellectuals was starting to emerge, who would take the colonial definition of Indian tradition as their starting point and, perhaps most famously under Gandhi, re-interpret it as the basis of a national identity for the post-colonial twentieth century.[17] For Gandhi, adherence to caste principles (albeit highly eccentric ones!) and loyalty to the village community defined what it meant to be 'Indian' in the modern world.

In seeking to explain the remarkable power of colonial conventions to re-make Indian society, historians, first and perhaps most obviously, turned to the instrumentalities of the colonial state. Here, through various legal formulations, administrative regulations and offers of

[15] E. Said, *Orientalism* (New York, 1978).

[16] The classic exposition of the (new) discourse of caste rank and village dominance, albeit on the understanding that it represented a 'traditional' discourse, is to be found in M. N. Srinivas, *Caste in India and Other Essays* (Bombay, 1962) and *Social Change in Modern India* (Berkeley, 1966).

[17] For Gandhi's 'affirmative orientalism' see R. Fox, *Gandhi's Utopia* (Durham, 1990).

prescriptive privilege, colonial perceptions of Indian society were actu-
alised in local-level structures of political power sustained by the state.
And for a long time so it seemed to some historians (of which this
author was one), the British authorities had merely to invent any
category, any 'tradition', any privilege that they chose, no matter how
preposterous or 'inauthentic', and somebody in Indian society was
bound to leap forward to ratify its authenticity and to utilize the powers,
however minimal, offered by it.[18] The colonial state appeared to have
an almost limitless capacity to 'persuade' Indians of the rectitude of its
reasoning, even about their own characters and antecedents, and to
coerce them into subscribing to its own mistaken re-inventions of them.

In retrospect, however, this emphasis on the innate power and
authority of the colonial state, with its implied corollary of a plastic
and passive Indian society, seems inadequate. This is in part, but only
in small part, because of the tide or research unleashed in the 1980s
by the celebrated Subaltern Studies group, who reveal evidence of far
more extensive 'resistance' to colonial authority than had been thought
the case. Even admitting all of this evidence, it would be stretching the
limits of historical interpretation to breaking point to hold that it
sustains a general case that 'the masses' of Indian society existed in a
condition of near-continuous and incipient rebellion through the long
history of the British Raj; still more than this condition enabled them
to preserve the autonomy and authenticity of their culture from colonial
'hegemony'.[19]

On the one hand, for a society supposedly teetering on the edges of
mass rebellion, it must be deemed remarkable how small were the
extraneous forces of coercion which the British ever needed to hold it
'in thraldom'. Including the white army, the British never numbered
more than 90,000 (or 0.03 per cent. of the population) at any time
during the nineteenth century. Also, the case is not helped by the extent
to which so many of the representations of 'autonomous' and 'authentic'
indigenous culture, which we are offered in Subaltern Studies' literature,
turn out to reflect the neo-colonial constructed 'traditions' which we
noted above.[20] Colonialism was very much a matter of 'hegemony', not

[18] See D. A. Washbrook, 'The Development of Caste Organisation in South India' in
South India: Political Institutions and Political Change, eds C. Baker and D. Washbrook (New
Delhi, 1975); L. Carroll, 'Colonial Perceptions of Indian Society and the Emergence of
Caste(s) Associations,' *Journal of Asian Studies*, XXXVII:2 (1978).

[19] See *Subaltern Studies*, ed. R. Guha, I–VI (New Delhi, 1982–90): esp., R. Guha
'Dominance without Hegemony and its Historiography', VI; also R. Guha, *Elementary
Aspects of Peasant Insurgency in Colonial India* (New Delhi, 1982).

[20] Compare, for example, Chatterjee's treatment of Gandhi as a 'traditional' Indian
intellectual, outside the framework of western thought, with Fox's treatment of him as
an 'affirmative orientalist'. P. Chatterjee, 'Gandhi and the Critique of Civil Society' in
Subaltern Studies, III, (New Delhi, 1984); R. Fox, *Gandhi's Utopia*. And compare Chakrabarty's

just 'domination', and a large part of the Subaltern Studies *oeuvre* attests, unfortunately, to its subtlety and pervasiveness.

Rather than just the result of the revelation of resistance, the inadequacy of a 'colonial state'-centred understanding of this transformation may owe more to the implications which flow from appreciation of the Raj's very 'success' at holding down the sub-continent so cheaply and, relatively, so easily. Upon examination, the scope and apparatus of 'British' law and government, imputed here with the power to re-make society, look remarkably weak and thin. Moreover, it is not at all clear that they can simply or meaningfully be thought of as 'British'.

On the one hand, from the publication of Robert Frykenberg's pioneering study of Guntur District onwards, it has become difficult to hold that the British administration possessed anything like the levels of direct control and authority over local society to which it rhetorically pretended.[21] Its will was deflected, diffused and re-directed through a variety of the local-level power networks on which it was heavily dependent: networks which frequently saw to it that the consequences of its actions were precisely the opposite of those which it intended. As Anand Yang has put it, the colonial state in India represented an extremely 'limited raj' which, in Lord Curzon's celebrated dictum, usually succeeded in achieving 'absolutely nothing'.[22] The very real weaknesses of the supposedly 'mighty and magnificent machine' of colonial government make it hard to believe that it can be credited with directing so profound a social transformation—or anything else.

Although perhaps that very weakness suggests another way in which 'traditionalisation' came about, albeit a way which alters its cultural character. Whenever examples of the functioning of this 'limited raj' are broken open and explored, the significance of the local indigenous elite groups who ran its activities on the ground usually comes to the fore. In south India by the nineteenth century, these were predominantly *Brahmin* groups and they were in an extremely powerful position to influence the state: as translators and 'authorities' they provided it with much of its basic information about the nature of society; and as administrators and bureaucrats, they enforced its regulations. How far was the 'caste-ification' of society, which took place under specifically *Brahmanic* norms, simply the result of their ability now to realise, through the apparatuses of colonial state, aspirations for a general social

---

conception of hierarchical Indian 'tradition' with the orientalist conceptions of the same exposed by Inden. D. Chakrabarty, 'Trade Unions in a Hierarchical Culture: the Jute Workers of Calcutta 1920–50' in *Subaltern Studies*, III; R. Inden, *Imagining India*.

[21] R. Frykenberg, *Guntur District 1788–1848* (Oxford, 1965).

[22] A. Yang, *The Limited Raj* (Berkeley, 1989).

dominance, which they may long have possessed but never before been able to enforce?[23]

Equally, as David Ludden has argued, the break-up of broader 'community' forms of land tenure, and the definition of the village as the only legitimate source of private landholding rights, was pressed from below, in certain southern agrarian contexts, by richer farmers eager to slough off the social responsibilities which went with 'community' membership, at least as much as it was 'imposed from above' by the dictates of the *ryotwari* revenue system of the colonial state.[24] Looked at this way, perhaps these processes of 'traditionalisation' were not so much the direct result of the 'colonial' character of British rule, of its peculiar cultural norms. But rather, and more prosaically, of the way that the weakness of the regime permitted aspirant elites to seize and manipulate state power to their own advantage: an advantage which had the consequence of generating those processes which we have called 'traditionalisation' but which actually, and simply, represented new configurations of indigenous elite power.

Yet there may remain problems. In the first place, where did these 'aspirant elites' come from and what sustained their power? Thus far the only source of power considered has been that of the colonial state, which, by general agreement, was weak. But how could a weak state generate the forces to empower the dominance of new elites? Or, put another way, how is it that the state apparatus was 'weak' when in the hands of the British but so 'strong', when in the hands of Indians, that it could drive at least a circulation, and possibly a transformation, in the character of dominant elites?

The paradox, of course, points to the fact that the colonial state was not the only source of power in nineteenth-century Indian society. At least one further source, curiously omitted from most of the debates on 'culture and society', may be seen to have lain in the economy, which was itself undergoing a profound transformation during the colonial epoch. How far it is possible to apply the concept of 'capitalism' to the changing relations of material production and social reproduction in colonial India is a much disputed, and inherently tendentious, question—depending as it does upon a terminology about which there is little agreement. But certain points concerning the material context of the age seem less arguable. India's relations of trade and production were more deeply integrated with those of the world economy; forms

[23] N. Dirks, 'Castes of Mind', paper read at California Institute of Technology, May, 1987; C. Bayly, *Indian Society and the Making of the British Empire* (Cambridge, 1989), ch. 5.

[24] D. Ludden, 'The Terms of Ryotwari Praxis: Changing Property Relations among Mirasidars in the Tinnevelly District, 1801–1855' in *Studies of South India*, eds P. Kolenda and R. Frykenberg (New Delhi, 1985).

of proprietary right modelled on those of Britain advanced (if slowly and fitfully) at the expense of forms inherited from the pre-colonial past; the balance within the Indian economy between primary, secondary and tertiary sectors, and between pastoralism, cultivation and manufacture, underwent a considerable change.[25] The material bases of Indian civilization shifted, generating new relations of domination and subordination, which are excluded from understandings of 'social and cultural' change only at major cost and are not immediately subsumable into categories derived from the colonial state. How did the processes of class formation, taking place under the colonial regime, affect the definition and functioning of 'tradition'?

And there may be a further set of questions, too, which the historiography of 'social and cultural change' has been inclined to neglect. The social processes represented by 'traditionalisation', which rendered society more hierarchic and static, were no doubt of considerable benefit to some groups. But, reciprocally, they must therefore have been of considerable disadvantage to others. *Brahminisation* of the caste system confined the non-*Brahmin* majorities of society to the demeaned and semi-rightless status of *Sudras*; the 'village-ification' of land rights was at the expense of broader kinship and community rights. In the circumstances, it seems reasonable to expect that the imposition of this 'false' colonial tradition would have been greeted with mass resistance and social protest.

Intriguingly, however, this does not seem to have been the case. The middle decades of the nineteenth century were relatively quiet in terms of the contestation of 'tradition'—although not necessarily in terms of the contestation of other features of colonial rule. What makes this quiescence the more remarkable is that later on, towards the end of the nineteenth century, 'tradition' did indeed start to become objectionable. A major protest movement arose among 'non-*Brahmins*' to challenge the insulting *Sudra* caste-designation; and a variety of broad cultural movements arose to overcome the atomising consequences of 'village-ification'.[26] By the twentieth century, the colonial version of Indian tradition was in full retreat across the south. But why, then, was it not contested at the time of its initial imposition?

And, further, could this temporary quiescence, and perhaps acceptance, help to explain that paradox in the self-understanding of 'tradition' that we noted earlier: namely that large sections of Indian society did come to accept the 'false' colonial version as the true version of their own traditional pasts? For it is noticeable that when the non-*Brahmin*

[25] See C. Bayly, *Indian Society*, esp., ch. 4.
[26] See my 'Caste, Class and Dominance in Modern Tamilnadu' in *State Power and Dominance in Modern India*, eds F. Frankel and M. Rao (New Delhi, 1989).

movement did finally begin to contest *Brahmanic* ideology, it did so from the premise that this ideology had truly represented the historic south Indian past and was not simply a recent and 'false' colonial adumbration. The non-*Brahmin* movement internalised the colonial version of tradition even while protesting at its immorality.[27] But why should it, or rather the non-*Brahmin* society which it represented, ever have accepted as 'true' that which it knew to be 'wrong'?

II

Some clues to colonial India's 'missing' history of class formation and to the dialectics of acquiescence and resistance have started to become available in the most recent historical literature. While the notion of a serious decline, or depression, in the Indian economy has been a commonplace of the historiography since the nineteenth century, the work of Christopher Bayly is the first to spell out its full implications for the character of social change. For Bayly, the crisis, which dominated the second quarter of the nineteenth century, was manifested in consistently low prices (in the south, rarely reaching sixty per cent of their 1800–1820 levels). He sees its causes to lie partially in the deepening impact of international economic forces: the loss of India's overseas textile markets to Manchester manufactures, the general lowering of world commodity prices attendant on the rise of industrial Europe and the pumping of specie out of India to prime Britain's trade with China.

But some of its causes also derived from British political policies: a heavy and extractive revenue demand to meet escalating military expenditures and loss of domestic purchasing power due to the dismantling of Indian armies and court centres across most of the interior. With regard to this dismantling, these armies and court centres had acted as the principal foci of consumption and demand and had spun out complex networks of trading and banking connections, involving and articulating large areas of the internal economy. Their breaking-up greatly reduced the forces of demand, threw out of employment large numbers of erstwhile consumers and cut many long-established banking and trading networks. De-industrialisation and de-urbanisation took place in many areas as an increasing proportion of society was obliged to look to the land and to farming for its subsistence.[28]

Bayly takes the social consequences of the depression to have been to strengthen, or to give, Indian society many of those features of 'backwardness', which the perspectives of the later nineteenth and twentieth centuries assumed were part of its long-term character.

[27] *Ibid.*
[28] C. Bayly, *Indian Society*, esp., ch. 4.

Peasant petty commodity production, carried on with limited inputs of investment capital, became near-universalised among the work force, displacing the higher value and more capital intensive forms of production to be found widely at an earlier date. Mobile service and trading groups became fixed permanently to the land, giving society a more static appearance. Elaborate structures of finance and commerce, attached to the old courtly centres, collapsed into little more than systems of peddling. In effect, Indian economic society became simplified and 'peasantised'. This process, of course, also made it ripe for the imputation and imposition of 'tradition'[29]

In many ways, Bayly's general Indian categorisation of the 'peasantisation' and 'traditionalisation' of the period fits the particular circumstances of southern India extremely well. As Sarada Raju has seen, there was extensive de-industrialisation and de-urbanisation; and shortages of money pushed some parts of the economy towards a reversion almost to barter relations.[30] Equally, as Arun Bandopadhyay has recently described, the frontiers of peasant production pushed relentlessly forward, keeping well ahead of levels of population increase and outstripping significant investments in irrigation, which were negligible before the 1850s.[31] Erstwhile mobile groups, of peripatetic warriors, herdsmen and pastoralists, also were 'sedentarised' as a deliberate policy of the state.[32] The social structure began to develop the simplicities and rigidities required by the modern definition of tradition.

Where, however, the south's experience may have differed from that of Bayly's Indian model—or where that model may need modification—concerns the implications of these processes for social, and class, stratification. Broadly speaking, Bayly sees the social effects of the depression as 'flattening' and 'homogenising' the previously complex hierarchies of society. The polities of little kings and warriors had been sustained by alliances right down to the local level, alliances which marked out petty hierarchies and elite statuses. As those polities collapsed, and as the value of the production controlled by their local allies declined, so the once distinct levels of local society became pressed together and homogenised. Virtually everybody in rural society, in effect, became 'a peasant' and many distinctions of rank (once articulated through the terms of village officer status and dominant clan membership) were lost.[33]

In the south, it is possible to see something of this process at work

[29] *Ibid.*, ch. 5.
[30] A. Sarada Raju, *Economic Conditions in the Madras Presidency 1800–1850* (Madras, 1941).
[31] A. Bandopadhyay, *The Agrarian Economy of Tamilnadu* (Calcutta, 1991), ch. 6.
[32] C. Bayly, *Indian Society*, ch. 4.
[33] *Ibid.*, ch. 5.

in the bottom levels of peasant society, where distinctions between lineages and adjacent caste clusters, and between warriors, farmers, artisans and pastoralists, tended to break down to produce a more homogenous community of petty cultivators.[34] However, if the upper levels of rural society are examined, no such 'levelling' process would seem to have taken place. Indeed, social relations appear to have been moving in the opposite direction.

As revenue re-surveying operations from the 1850s subsequently revealed, it was during this earlier period that leading families secured control of most of the best lands in their villages. In the Madras Deccan districts, for example, prominent village *Reddis* increased their share of the highest quality 'black-soil' lands from twenty to over sixty per cent of the total.[35] Various forms of privileged revenue right also became more narrowly distributed. In Tanjore district, one family (with major representation in the local bureaucracy) acquired rights in thirty-five per cent of the villages in the district.[36] Another family, with extremely recent and tenuous claims to pre-eminence, consolidated 'interests in' into 'ownership of' 6,000 acres of highly productive wetlands.[37]

This shift in the distribution of assets also went hand in hand with an increase in the security of local notables and a strengthening of their authority over society. As Eugene Irschick has recently seen, in Chingleput district the recognition of superior claims to rights by certain *Vellala* notables terminated long-term pressures from below on their possession of the land and greatly weakened the position of 'inferior' castes in relation to them.[38] In Tanjore and Malabar districts throughout this period, high caste families who had 'run away' during the troubles of the late eighteenth century were being encouraged to return and re-take possession of their lands from the low caste families who had occupied, and cultivated, them, sometimes for as long as two generations. The 'dispossessed' were driven back into the multitude of landless and semi-landless paupers who now constituted the majorities

---

[34] It was the consequent tendency of previously 'non-landed' pastoralist and service groups to take up petty cultivation, which may be seen to have increased cultivated acreages well ahead of population. See my 'The Commercialisation of Agriculture in Colonial India: Production, Subsistence and Reproduction in the "Dry" South, c1870–1930', *Modern Asian Studies*, XXVII: 3 (1993).

[35] *Idem.*

[36] H. S. Thomas, *Report on Tanjore Remissions in Fasli 1294. (A.D. 1884–85)* (Madras, 1885). Tamilnadu Archives.

[37] This was the 'Pundi' family of Udaiyans from Vandiyar. During the disturbances of the 1780s, they had become pattucdars (revenue contractors) for an extensive tract of depopulated land. Somewhat mysteriously, these contractual rights were converted into 'mirasi' [proprietary] rights during the early years of British rule.

[38] E. Irschick, 'Order and Disorder in Colonial South India', *Modern Asian Studies*, XXIII:3 (1989).

of village society.[39] Further, all over the south large quantities of landed resources, dedicated to the gods but shared broadly by the agrarian community, were turned into the exclusionary possessions of temple 'trusts', increasingly under the control of selected local notables.[40]

The concept of 'levelling' would but very inadequately describe the social process to which the agrarian south was subject in the second quarter of the nineteenth century: the bottom segments of society may have been pounded flat, but the top segments grew taller yet. The privilege of dominant elites was greatly enhanced and, with the possession of land playing a larger part in it, the nature of elite authority itself was coming to shift towards a basis in class. These changes were also manifested in the kinds of 'tradition' which the south now developed. These evoked less a 'peasant' past of community and egalitarianism than a royal and divine past of dominance and hierarchy.[41] Privileged rights, which previously had circulated widely through society (and often had been bought and sold) now were deemed the direct 'gifts' of gods and kings, permanently and exclusively in the possession only of those families who had initially received them. The principle of heredity increased its authority over those of acquisition and achievement in the determination of elite status. Equally, as noted before, 'caste' relations became subsumed beneath the *Brahmanic* theory of *varnashramadharma*, which imposed on them the most rigid and static of hierarchies.

As southern society became 'traditionalised', so it became noticeably more stratified. The nature of its stratification, however, was extremely curious. On the one hand, deepening insertion into the world economy and the growing importance within it of the possession, or 'ownership', of land, appeared to make dominance a product of capitalism—and hence a function of class. But, on the other hand, elite status itself became increasingly defined in relation to heredity and caste, which suggests an altogether different basis to power and authority. How did the two become interwoven? And, to return to a previous issue, why did not the masses of society, who were plainly the chief victims of the new social design, not raise more protest against it while it was in the process of creation—rather than half a century later?

---

[39] See my 'The Golden Age of the Pariah' in *Labour and Dalit Movements in India* (New Delhi, forthcoming).

[40] Appadurai, *Worship and Conflict*, ch. 3.

[41] On the 'communitarian' logic of southern society, see B. Stein, 'Politics, Peasants and the Deconstruction of Feudalism in Medieval India', *Journal of Peasant Studies*, XII:2, 3, (1985).

III

To appreciate the logic of the south's 'traditionalisation', and of the peculiar kind of colonial capitalism which it reflected, it may be necessary to consider not only the economic imperatives released by the depression, but the way that they worked in relation to the institutions of the colonial state. During the second quarter of the nineteenth century, the Company state launched a major 'revenue offensive' against agrarian society.[42] The immediate reasons for this were rapidly rising military expenditures and the immediate excuse was the invocation of an (invented) theory of oriental despotism under which, supposedly, all land belonged to the state. However, given that 'the state' was also 'a Company', and heavily engaged in commercial activities, the formal reasons and excuses can be understood in a different light. The offensive served generally to increase the share of surplus extracted from the peasantry, which ultimately went as returns to capital. Indeed, as Eric Stokes and Sugata Bose have shown, in other parts of India where *zamindari* rights had been created, to constitute forms of proprietary right between the peasantry and the state, the period was marked by a 'rental offensive' which directly raised returns to landlord capital.[43]

As I have argued elsewhere, certain aspects of 'traditionalisation' may be understood as functions of the revenue offensive. The colonial state's principal concern at this time was to allocate responsibility for tax payment and to fix assets in such a way that they could easily be seized and liquidated for the redemption of debt. 'Traditional' forms of property right, which emphasised principles of heredity over market acquisition, served the state's needs nicely. The circulation of wealth within Indian society was immobilised, so that realisable assets could not disperse and disappear. And the state's claims to those assets were guaranteed by the establishment of the convention that payment of tax revenue and debt represented the first call on all private wealth, against which the prerogatives of 'traditional' right could not stand.[44]

But such a functionalist formulation of the matter may miss other aspects of the 'traditionalisation' process, several of which by no means reflected the Company state's needs and against whose implications it fought several battles. Most of these battles centred on the issues of

---

[42] See N. Mukherjee, *The Ryotwari System in Madras* (Calcutta, 1962), chs. 5, 10.

[43] S. Bose, *Agrarian Bengal* (Cambridge, 1986), ch. 2; E. Stokes, 'Agrarian society and the Pax Britannica in northern India in the early nineteenth century' in E. Stokes, *Peasant*.

[44] See my 'Law, State and Agrarian Society in Colonial India', *Modern Asian Studies*, XV:3 (1981).

privileged tenure or *inam* rights, which themselves provided the material underpinnings of 'traditional' social relations.

As the Company state had expanded across the south in the closing decades of the eighteenth century, it had encountered an agrarian structure defined in terms of extensive 'immunities' to land revenue payment. These went under a wide variety of local names but, for convenience, will hereafter be termed *inam* (after Persian and British usage). *Inams*, of one kind or another, were held by a wide variety of village officials and servants, by principal landholders and notables, by *Brahmins* and holymen, and by temples and *maths*. Their origins remain the subject of lively debate in the historiography of the medieval south. Burton Stein sees them deriving from the 'communitarian' institutions of the southern peasantry, and representing gifts or offerings to religious and secular elites.[45] Nicholas Dirks, by contrast and following more the established conventions of southern history, views them as the products of 'kingly' politics, representing the mechanisms by which pre-colonial royal states procured loyalty and support and satisfied clients and followers.[46] Whatever their origins, *inams* certainly were used as the currency of royal politics in the closing pre-colonial decades although, by then, they had also acquired another function. In the highly commercialised economy of eighteenth-century south India, certain types of *inam* were widely bought and sold as valuable properties and potential stores of wealth.

In the period from 1790 to 1810, the in-coming Company state broadly recognised the provenance of *inam*, and of privileged rights of all kinds. Its principal concerns at this time—an era marked by warfare and social disturbance—were to achieve as quick a settlement with agrarian society as possible and to restore agricultural production. To these ends, while cutting out large numbers of warriors and petty kings who were deemed 'unsettleable', it sought a ready accommodation with rural elite groups nearer to the land and to the direction of cultivation, and with 'religious' authorities. The *inam* rights of such groups were generally recognised in a 'silent settlement' which bound the interests of much local elite privilege in with those of the new state.[47]

Robert Frykenberg has seen this arrangement guaranteeing long term continuity in the relations of southern society across the divide between the pre-colonial and colonial periods. However, in one regard at least, the 'silent settlement' already presaged significant change. Definition and protection of *inam* right was passed by the Company state to the new courts of 'Anglo-Hindu' law established by Lord

[45] B. Stein, 'Politics, Peasants'.
[46] N. Dirks, *Hollow Crown*, pt. 2.
[47] R. Frykenberg, 'The Silent Settlement'.

Cornwallis. These immediately altered the character of the right by construing it, not in relation to the dynamic and contestatory processes of community, kingly-state and market formation, but in relation to the static principles of ancient precedent, hereditary succession and caste hierarchy. Most forms of *inam* were held to represent properties or trusts, bequeathed by an originatory act or 'from time immemorial' to particular persons, families and institutions, and to be 'encumbered' and inalienable.[48]

The reasons for this re-interpretation of 'right' have formed the focus of much debate. The proclivities of a judiciary drawn from the English gentry, with its own beliefs in the primacy of genealogy, the immutability of common law right and the importance of social deference undoubtedly played their part. Never was this clearer than in the way that rules for the 'proper' administration of temple endowments were drawn up in a terminology—replete with references to 'ministers' and 'congregations'—which came straight out of the Church of England.[49] Equally, 'accidents' of documentation played their part. As Bernard Cohn has argued, English culture gave precedence to written over oral forms of authority, and documentary over non-documentary sources of right.[50] *Mirasidari* elites able to produce documents outlining their 'ancient' privileges, 'gift' *inamdars* with *sanads* of appointment and *Brahmin* priests, able to cite the canons of Sanskrit scripture, found their cases carrying much more weight in the courts than those of people without the appropriate papers.[51] Further, in certain ways, there seems an elision of social perception—or at least aspiration—between a number of Tamil elite groups and their new English masters. The ideal of a peasant society meekly paying its dues and deferences and keeping 'to its station' was a property common to *Brahmin*, *mirasidar* and English gentry pretension.

The concentration of debate on the intellectual origins of the new 'colonial' version of traditional right, however, may have obscured full appreciation of the social and political effects of its construction. It was not only that certain types of *inam* and claim to right were validated and strengthened by the support of the colonial law: it was also that others were invalidated. Claims not cast in the approved forms—often claims which contested the privilege of the approved forms—were delegitimated and taken out of 'tradition'. Hosts of claims to a share in the agricultural product—especially from tenant-, labouring- and village

---

[48] See N. Dirks, 'From little king to landlord', *Comparative Studies in Society and History*, XXVIII:2 (1986); E. Irschick, 'Order and Disorder'.

[49] A. Appadurai, *Worship and Conflict*, chs. 3, 4.

[50] B. Cohn, 'The Command of Language and the Language of Command' in *Subaltern Studies*, IV (New Delhi, 1986).

[51] See my 'Law, State and Agrarian Society'.

servant groups 'below' the enfranchised *mirasidars* and 'personal' *inamdars*—were abrogated in a way which fundamentally shifted the balances of the social structure.[52]

Nor was this to be the only transformation affecting *inam* right. In the next generation, the character and purposes of the Company state changed rapidly, as did the material context in which *inam* right was set. By the 1820s, possessed of overwhelming military strength in the south and of an army which needed to be both paid and used, the Company's concerns turned from settlement and restoration to surplus extraction and expropriation. The weight of the revenue demand escalated in inverse proportion to the depression-hit south's ability to pay: rates of per acres assessment, set in the high-price years of the early nineteenth century (and, often, on the basis of inflated estimates of productivity) went unrevised.[53] The demand was enforced by military methods of coercion, which, as the *Torture Commission* of 1855 revealed, rendered the concept of the British civilising mission somewhat problematic.[54] Whatever may have been the case, both earlier and later, there can be little doubt concerning the strength of state power at this time—albeit a power very narrow in its focus and largely negative in its economic consequences. Southern society was bludgeoned and robbed with a remarkably single-minded purpose.

One effect of the 'revenue offensive' was to consolidate the village community as the basic unit of rural society and politics. Previous south Indian state systems, as they grew powerful, had sought to break down intermediary layers of warrior-clan and peasant community organisation between their treasuries and the village base. The scope and shape of peasant social institutions had long varied inversely with the power of emperors and sultans.[55] None, however, had ever succeeded in eliminating intermediary authority on the scale now achieved by the British; nor in isolating the village so completely as the central arena of 'material' politics. The *ryotwari* revenue system progressively swept aside the taxation and rental functions of clan-chiefs and *zamindars* (in many cases, even after they had been supposedly 'permanently settled') and carried its claims for a preponderant share of agricultural surplus to the village boundary.

Significantly, however, not even in these years or irresistible military

[52] For example, the courts refused to recognise the claims of labourers to share-rights in the crops that they cultivated. See D. Ludden, *Peasant History in South India* (Princeton, 1985), ch. 6; also my 'Law, State and Agrarian Society' and 'The Golden Age of the Pariah'.

[53] N. Mukherjee, *Ryotwari System*, ch. 10; A. Bandopadhyay, *Agrarian Economy*, chs. 6, 7.

[54] See Government of Madras, *Report of the Commissioners for the Investigation of Alleged Cases of Torture in the Madras Presidency* (Madras, 1855).

[55] This is a major theme of B. Stein, *Peasant State*.

power did the state get much beyond the boundary. Allocation of the demand between rural families remained very much an intra-village affair, brokered by village officers and notables. Ability to deflect or reduce the revenue burden determined the difference between wealth and poverty, sometimes between survival and starvation, and made the village arena a central focus of 'indigenous' political economy and concern over property right.[56]

It also made the village a rare field for the exercise of 'entre-preneurship' in an otherwise depressed, dislocated and 'colonised' economy. Through their ability to manipulate the revenue demand inside the village, local officers and notables were able to accumulate for themselves substantial quantities of rights and lands. The *Reddis* of the Madras Deccan, whom earlier we noted trebling their holdings of the best black-soil lands across this period, were all hereditary 'village officers' with a strong hold on the allocation of the revenue demand and the written records of local rights.[57] It was, above all, through the functioning of the revenue system, rather than the development of the economy, that rural society became increasingly stratified in this era.

But the revenue offensive did not only promote the 'village-ification' of society. It also, albeit by complex and indirect means, can be seen as responsible for its wider 'traditionalisation' as well. Needless to say, the imperatives of the offensive soon began to run up against the walls of 'immunity' represented by *inam* right and to provoke a rapid change of attitudes in certain sections of the bureaucracy. What had seemed necessary and just in the conditions of 1790 to 1810 now appeared unwarranted profligacy in the circumstances of 1825 to 1850. With political supremacy assured, population increasing and cultivation extending, the services of most classes of *inamdars* no longer were so essential to the state. Yet, across the various districts, anywhere between twenty-five per cent and fifty per cent of cultivation, usually on the best lands, were under some species of *inam* immunity and protected from the revenue demand.

The revenue offensive began to question and to probe the prerogatives of *inam*. By order of London, after 1824 no new *inam* grants were to be made. Certain types of *inam*, which depended more on the recognition of 'local custom' than documentary authority, were steadily phased out. General reductions on the revenue demanded from Brahmin holders of 'government land', for example, began to disappear in the 1830s. Equally, the privileges of *mirasidars* in wetland areas to enjoy a share of the produce of non-*mirasidari* cultivators (or of the revenue, as the bureaucracy saw it) and to control access to village lands, were

[56] See R. Frykenberg, 'Village Strength in South India' in R. Frykenberg, *Land Control*.
[57] See my 'Commercialisation of Agriculture'.

challenged.[58] Even the revenue immunities enjoyed by temple lands did not escape. Notionally, revenue and rents were collected from lands pledged to temples and used for a wide variety of purposes, from maintenance of fabric and ceremonies, to feeding the poor, to investing in joint-projects of economic development with devotees and worshippers. On the claim that the state had supervisory functions over their administration, the Company bureaucracy seized direct control of many temples. Its officers then reconstrued the notion of 'legitimate' temple expenditures in order to reduce them, particularly to reduce their contribution to welfare and economic development, and either passed back the resulting surpluses to the regular revenue account or used them for their own projects.[59]

During the 1830s, the Board of Revenue also sent out general orders to its district Collectors to scrutinise carefully all 'personal' *inam* titles with a view to uncovering as many 'false' and 'fraudulent' claims as possible. As the precise terms on which *inam* titles could be validated were by no means crystal clear anyway, this opened the door to extended investigations which challenged and 'resumed' to the revenue department considerable quantities of what had been thought of as *inam* property. In two districts in the 1840s, energetic young Collectors took the Board's instructions as a general licence to question many forms of *inam* right derived from erstwhile military service. In Cuddapah and Nellore, large numbers of *inamdars* protested that the bureaucracy, rather than seeking to disprove particular claims, had insisted that all claims were to be re-scrutinised and had to be re-proved anew—which threatened to abrogate the great majority of their rights at a single sweep.[60]

If that was the intention of the Board of Revenue, the developments in Cuddapah and Nellore soon terminated it. Major riots broke out in defence of *inam* rights and post-pacification southern society was brought to a rare condition of open revolt.[61] But the revenue offensive, in any event, had already started to be turned by resistance of a less dramatic, but no less effective, kind. In the wetland areas, *mirasidar* groups regularly organised cultivation and revenue strikes, which forced local officials into compromises and which successfully defended their privileges.[62] Further, a major rift began to develop inside the colonial state

[58] See D. Ludden, *Peasant History*, ch. 4; E. Irschick, 'Order and Disorder'.

[59] A. Appadurai, *Worship and Conflict*, ch. 3; F. Presler, *Religion Under Bureaucracy* (Cambridge, 1987), chs. 2, 3.

[60] Government of Madras, *A Collection of Papers Relating to the Inam Settlement of Madras Presidency* (Madras, 1906), 12–14.

[61] *Idem.*

[62] See, for example, D. Ludden, *Peasant History*, chs. 4, 6; E. Irschick, 'Order and Disorder.

itself over the rights of *inam* and property as opposed to those of the state.

What English courts of law have construed as a right, still more a 'sacred' property right, they are most unlikely ever to give up—and least of all to a self-styled 'despotic' regime. The courts validated and stoutly defended large numbers of *inam* claims against the attempts of the bureaucracy to abrogate them. Indeed, they frequently declared the de facto actions of Collectors and revenue bureaucrats illegal and unwarranted and handed out awards against them of compensation and restitution.[63] Relations between the judicial and executive branches of the Company service became poisonous: with the latter regularly denouncing the former in its despatches; and the former launching a pamphlet war against 'state despotism', which represented perhaps the first stirrings of a 'modern' political consciousness in Madras.[64]

The revenue department's offensive against *inam* rights plainly failed and, by the 1850s and in the context of rather different economic conditions, was brought to an unceremonious end. A general review of the revenue system was set in motion, with the specific object of reducing a weight of taxation which was generally agreed to be penal and destructive.[65] Further, an *Inam Commission* was established to 'modernise' such rights by transforming them from revenue immunities into real properties in the land.[66] The struggle over them, however, may be seen to have had lasting consequences. It generated a particular 'rhetoric of right', and sets of relations of domination and subordination, authority and defiance, and acquiescence and resistance, which go a long way to explaining the processes which 'traditionalised' southern society.

IV

The extremely distinctive ways in which the courts validated—and invalidated—*inam* rights very quickly had a general affect on the way that all claims to right and privilege came to be cast. Claims put forward in terms of the prerogatives of acquisition, achievement and 'history' failed; those in terms of antiquity and heredity at least had a chance of success. South Indian society did not take long to learn the lesson and to develop its own rhetoric of right accordingly.

[63] See my 'Law, State and Agrarian Society'; D. Ludden, *Peasant History*, ch. 6; E. Irschick, 'Order and Disorder'.

[64] See J. B. Norton, *The Administration of Justice in South India* (Madras, 1853); and *Reply to a Madras Civilian's Defence of Mofussil Courts in India* (London, 1853).

[65] See my 'Law, State and Agrarian Society'.

[66] See *A Collection of Papers ... Inam Settlement*.

In the Sri Parthasarathi temple in Madras city, for example, initial reactions to the new legal terms of temple administration, which imposed a Scriptural interpretation of caste hierarchy onto a community previously riven along the lines of *Vadagalai-Thengalai* ritual factionalism, may have been contentious. Petitions drawn up in terms of the old criteria of legitimacy continued to be presented through the early years. But, as Arjun Appadurai has seen, by the 1840s the new rhetoric of right was starting to take over. Petitioners (the very same petitioners) who previously had couched their claims in ways which denied the authenticity of a uniform *Brahmanic* caste hierarchy, now couched their claims in ways which accepted it. Their new pleas centred only on the extent to which their own given place within that hierarchy was 'mistaken' and too 'low', and should be raised to a 'higher' level which would give them greater rights.[67] Elsewhere in Madras, and around other temples, the cleavage between right-hand and left-hand castes, which had dominated social relations for centuries, similarly underwent a rapid 'disappearance'.[68] The new language of caste contention focused on disputes within the *Brahmanically*-validated hierarchy.

Similarly, petitions in defence of personal *inam* rights tended progressively to drop de-recognised criteria and to dress themselves up, however implausibly, in the language of ancient and hereditary privilege. In one particular case, the invented character of this 'tradition' stands out most clearly. Puddukottai 'state' passed into the Madras presidency in a highly unusual condition, retaining the paraphernalia of a 'princely' kingdom but with its laws subject to direct British administration. Here, in the mid-nineteenth century, the power of its royal house to redistribute *inam* grants was still etched in living memory. But members of the local 'gentry' appealed to British judges that their privileged rights were derived from hereditary kinship criteria and hence were neither resumable nor re-distributable by the state.[69]

The apparent facility of south Indian society to transform its 'tradition' and rhetoric of right along lines prompted by the colonial power may seem remarkable—and suggestive of at least 'oriental dishonesty' (as the bureaucracy tended to see it) and, at worst, unbridled opportunism.[70] However, in the economic and political context of the time, it can better be understood as an action born of 'resistance' and essential to social survival. Under the pressure of the revenue offensive and the doctrines of the despotic state, the defence of *inam* right was one of the

[67] A. Appadurai, *Worship and Conflict*, chs 4, 5.

[68] Throughout the seventeenth and eighteenth centuries, for example, Madras city was riven by repeated outbreaks of right-hand/left-hand rioting. But, from the 1840s, the rioting simply ceased. See H. D. Love, *Vestiges of Old Madras* (Madras, 1913).

[69] N. Dirks, *Hollow Crown*, 335–36; also his 'From little king to landlord'.

[70] See N. Dirks, *Hollow Crown*, 335–36; also, R. Frykenberg, 'Village Strength'.

few available means of preserving resources, property and some kind of social continuity. Had the revenue bureaucracy had its way, south Indian society would, indeed, have been 'levelled' and 'flattened' to the ground.

The division within the structure of the colonial state between judiciary and executive offered a mechanism which indigenous society could use to protect itself. Moreover this mechanism involved the use of forms of rhetoric which, if selected and reinterpreted from those found in pre-colonial society, were not wholly without precedent there: *Brahmins* and 'gentry' elites had used them in the past, if never so exclusively and authoritatively. The truly novel element in the situation was the despotic pretension of the colonial state, which had no precedent in practice (and little even in rhetoric) in the history of the south. Against the novelty of that pretension, south Indian society might better be seen as creatively using history in order to defend itself.

Moreover, the very processes by which southern Indian society was obliged to defend itself through, and in relation to, the law imposed on it also an obligation actively to participate in the construction of its new traditions. Unable to effect a general abrogation of *inam* rights, the revenue department pursued a policy of particularistic interrogation. It challenged specific rights on the grounds that they did not meet the validatory criteria of antiquity, heredity or conformity to the caste hierarchy established by the courts. If rights could be shown not to have been 'ancient' or held in unbroken hereditary succession or reflective of established caste propriety, they could be resumed by the state.[71]

This interrogation tightened the definition of 'tradition' and constructed a bizarre ontological context within which state–society relations were to be conducted. In the courts, it was now not 'modern' western intellectuals who told south Indian society that it had no history and was 'traditional'. Rather, through the legal processes of petition, it was south Indian society which had to represent itself before the tribunals of colonial 'justice' as having been, indeed, changeless, static and 'traditional'; and to convince often-sceptical bureaucrats and judges that its structures of privilege and right did, indeed, date back directly to ancient precedent and 'time immemorial'. The penalty for admitting the possibility of change—of history—was the immediate loss of rights and privileges to the revenue coffers of the state. If necessity is the mother of invention, there can have been few cases of the invention of tradition born out of a greater necessity than this.

Furthermore, it was an invention whose influence soon came to reach outside and beyond the courts and to promote a wider re-

[71] See Government of Madras, *A Collection ... Inam Settlement.*

conceptualisation of relations with colonialism and within colonial society. The Indian lawyers who were involved in its construction enjoyed a much broader role as spokesman for Indian society at large in its dealing with the British Raj; and the petitional style of politics dominated 'modernising' India's first attempts at self-liberation later in the nineteenth century. In those attempts, the prerogatives of 'tradition' were frequently invoked against the interferences and threats of the colonial state: to protect, for example, 'religious' customs, joint-property forms and certain structures of gender relations.[72] India's claims to autonomy and an important part of her sense of 'nationhood' were ultimately derived from the premises of her new tradition.

In the colonial situation of South India, then, 'resistance' proceeded much less by sacrificing effective 'domination' to the preservation from Western 'hegemony' of cultural autonomy and authenticity.[73] Rather, and taking strategic advantage of contradictions within the colonial regime and the ideology of 'modernity', autonomy and authenticity (whose historical meaning is unclear) were frequently sacrificed to limit the effects of domination. A neo-colonial constructed 'tradition' of irresumable *inam* right and Anglo-*Brahminised* 'Hinduism' preserved southern society—and economy—from the full impact of the revenue offensive and state despotism.

But just as the real historical dynamics of 'resistance' did not leave culture unchanged, so too they did not leave the structures of social relations untouched. The struggle to protect *inam* rights was, by its nature, a struggle to protect particularistic privilege. Further, it was only partially successful: some rights, which met the novel criteria of official tradition, were saved but many others were not. The economic consequences of this 'resistance' were, as we have noted, to constitute considerable concentrations of wealth and property in certain narrow sections of society—concentrations which stood out starkly in comparison to the situation of growing numbers of the now-rightless masses. Indeed, the success of the former was very directly at the expense of the latter. The price of the partial protection of *inam* right was deepening social stratification and Robert Frykenberg seems seriously mistaken in supposing that the *inam* settlement reflected a fundamental continuity between pre-colonial and colonial society.[74] But in one regard, however,

---

[72] The first attempts at 'popular' nationalist mobilisation, particularly those of B. G. Tilak in Maharashtra in the 1890s, strongly emphasised the defence of 'traditional' social relations. See R. Cashman, *The Myth of the Lokmanya* (Berkeley, 1975); also R. O'Hanlon, 'Issues of Widowhood' in *Contesting Power*, eds D. Haynes and G. Prakash (New Delhi, 1991).

[73] Pace R. Guha, 'Dominance without Hegemony'.

[74] R. Frykenberg, 'Silent Settlement'.

his interpretation does highlight a feature of the transformation, which now becomes problematic and requires explaining.

The 'masses' of society remained remarkably 'silent' while their own claims to right were dismantled and while the new configurations of elite power and prestige were established over their heads. Although there was some subsidiary litigation around the rights of *inamdari* and *mirasidari* 'tenants' and of labourers to customary shares in the crop, it was limited and almost entirely unsuccessful.[75] Yet, in the wake of its failure, there were no major uprisings of outrage and protest against the new pretensions of the privileged. Certainly, there were no uprisings on the scale of those led by the elites themselves in Cuddapah and Nellore when their rights were generally questioned; nor long-term resistances such as those mounted by *mirasidars*, through rent and cultivation strike, when their privileges were threatened. In fact, one of the ironies of the situation was that many lesser cultivators rallied to the causes of these 'greater' *inamdars* and *mirasidars*, which helped them to succeed: even though that 'success' guaranteed their own subordination.

To appreciate the reasons for this 'silence' and apparent acquiescence in intensifying elite domination, it may be necessary again to consider the material logic of depression and revenue offensive. It was not merely 'surplus' and 'profit' that were put at risk, but subsistence and social reproduction too. Official rates of assessment on 'government land' could often be higher than the depressed value of annual production. High quality lands were driven out of production in favour of lower quality lands which bore lower rates of assessment. State expenditure even on the maintenance, let alone development, of irrigation resources was negligible. Private capital investments on government land, when discovered, brought instant increases in revenue assessment to penal levels.[76] The logic of Company revenue policy spread devastation and agricultural regression in its wake. Without the immunities provided by *inam* rights, south Indian society in this era might well have faced a serious crisis of social reproduction—as some critics of the Company regime in the 1840s actually thought it was.

In this context, hardly surprisingly, cultivation and production tended to concentrate on *inam* land. Petty cultivators found it extremely difficult to survive without access, even as temporary and unprotected tenants, to 'validated' *inamdari* land; and, as high value and labour intensive cash-cropping tended to be concentrated here as well, labourers needed work on *inamdari* holdings. In effect, and as many Collectors of the

[75] As in D. Ludden, *Peasant History*, ch. 6.
[76] See A. Bandopadhyay, *Agrarian Economy*; D. Ludden, *Peasant History*, chs 4, 5; N. Mukherjee, *Ryotwari System*, ch. 10.

time ruefully admitted, *inam* land came to form the hub of local cultivating economies with government land used sparsely and often only under direct duress.[77]

The social consequence of this was, in many ways, to structure a kind of *inamdari* paternalism and hierarchy into agrarian relations on a much more extended scale than ever before. As the highly mobile and commercially-orientated rural society of the pre-colonial era gave way to the settled and more subsistence-orientated peasantry of the depression era, so the role of local elite groups in dictating and dominating regimes of material production and social reproduction tended to become enhanced. In the Madras Deccan, in the process of trebling the rich *inam* lands under their control, big *Reddis* took into their own houses the grain stores of their whole local communities—doling out wages, credit and subsidies to large numbers of tenants, clients and labourers.[78] In wetland areas, the relationship between 'dependent' and 'independent' *mirasi* tenants underwent a change, as more and more land was cultivated by peasants without implements and bullocks of their own who could provide only labour and had to borrow everything else (including pre-harvest subsistence) from their *mirasidar*.[79]

In these circumstances, where protection of *inam* right from the avaricious grasp of the state had logical priority over the internal distribution of the resources covered by that right and where an *inam*-centred economy offered the formally 'rightless' some means of livelihood and subsistence, which was better than anything that they could find outside, the apparent acquiescence of the 'dispossessed' in the new order does not seem so difficult to understand. Against the despotic revenue state, all of agrarian society shared a common interest; and elite 'paternalism' offered some rewards for abandoning claims to an economic 'independence' which now promised more risk than profit.

This paternalism, itself, began to generate its own custom of rights, in the claims of personal clientage and dependence, which displaced older conceptions of right, based on the autonomous privileges of clan, craft and occupational groups to a fixed share of the social product. And, by the mid-nineteenth century, the politics of 'poverty' were plainly coming to be played out in these terms, of insistent demands for patronage and support, rather than of independent claims to

[77] See my 'Commercialisation of Agriculture'; also, B. Stein, 'Does Culture make Practice Perfect?' in *All the Kings' Mana*, ed. B. Stein (Madras, 1984); also N. Mukherjee, *Ryotwari System*, 214.

[78] See my 'Commercialisation of Agriculture'; also my 'Economic Stratification in Rural Madras' in *The Imperial Impact*, eds A. Hopkins and C. Dewey (1978).

[79] C. Baker, *An Indian Rural Economy 1880–1955* (Oxford, 1984), 168–200.

'right'.[80] In effect, the elongated social hierarchies and exaggerated social deferences promoted by the south's new 'traditions' were underpinned by changing relations of material production and social reproduction, as much as of culture'.

V

By the middle of the nineteenth century, the economic depression, the revenue offensive and the neo-colonial reconstruction of 'tradition' had done their work. Out of a once highly mobile, commercialised and contentious society, they had created, albeit by complex means, an agrarian structure marked now by the appearance of 'feudal' hierarchy. In south India, as in many other parts of the world, the first consequence of the rise of western dominance over capitalism would seem to have been the enlargement of 'serfdom'. However, beginning also in the middle of the nineteenth century, the dynamics of international capitalism, and the responses to it of colonial states, underwent a change.

With the expansion of markets created by the building of the railways and of the Suez canal, the economic depression started to lift. The colonial state (brought now under immediate parliamentary direction) reviewed both its ideological stance and its economic priorities. The affectations of 'oriental despotism' dropped away to be replaced by a more consistent recognition of real private property rights in land, even so-called government land. Equally, economic policies moved away from the simple extraction of revenue and exploitation of Company monopoly rights and towards the promotion of a more general commercial expansion.[81] The effective weight of the revenue burden declined rapidly and, with it, the significance of *inam* immunity. During the 1860s, *inam* rights were converted into regular rights in landed property, alienable and transferable and scarcely distinguishable from ordinary rights. The colonial age of *inam* was over—and very noticeably, so too was the uncontested legitimacy of the cultural 'tradition' which had grown up with it.

While *Brahmins* and other elites, whose privileges had been enlarged by it, still clung to its tenets—and even generalised them into the bases of Indian national identity—many elements in southern society started to become more questioning. As noted previously, the south was galvanised by movements which sought to challenge the deferences and prerogatives of 'tradition'. Self-conscious 'non-*Brahmins*' disputed (once more) the authority over them of *Brahmins* and of hierarchical schema

---

[80] See my 'Country Politics: Madras 1870–1930', *Modern Asian Studies*, VII:3 (1973).
[81] C. Baker, *Rural Economy*, ch. 6.

of caste. A variety of identity movements emerged to break down the atomism caused by 'village-ification' and to create (or re-create) broader communities defined by ties of 'blood', which harked back to the clan past.[82] Very often these latter movements also contested hierarchy by claiming for all their members privileges once enjoyed only by elite families within them: *Gounder Vellala* and *Maravar* community movements, for example, expanded the prerogatives of kingship as defining characteristics of their entire blood-lines and sponsored the development of a new (or re-newed) ideology of corporate 'dominance' over the countryside.[83] A 'new' cultural tradition—or tradition of culture—asserted (or re-asserted) itself to reflect the changing context of social, political and economic relations in the later colonial age.

But in at least two regards, the experiences of the era of depression and of colonial 'despotism' continued to mark the ways in which questions of right, morality and identity were construed and to give testimony to the irreversibility of history. In the first place, those movements which now contested *Brahmanic* caste hierarchy and the particularities of privilege never doubted, as did their forebears in the pre-colonial age, that such hierarchy and privilege had a 'true' base in history. Whereas then, *Brahmin* pretension might have been swept aside or modified by the generation of alternative Hindu traditions based on *bhakti* devotionalism and popular heterodox practice, now non-*Brahminism* started from the premise that *Brahmins* had established their authority over 'all' of Hinduism. Non-*Brahminism* accepted the 'Anglo-Hindu' notions both that Hinduism existed as a single organised religion and that, for at least the last two thousand years, *Brahmins* had possessed authority over it. Its dispute was with the moral status and implications of this fact: not with its status as an historical and cultural 'fact' in the first place.[84]

And second, non-*Brahminism*'s case for altering this fact in the future centred not, as it might have done in the pre-colonial era, on the imperatives for the re-distribution of 'honour' created by changing relations of wealth and power, but on the prerogatives of 'tradition' itself. The social critique offered by the non-*Brahmin*, and many other 'caste' movements, focused on the notion that Brahmin hierarchy and privilege were the products, not of 'original tradition' but only of 'history' and 'change'. The critique argued, in a way colonial jurists would readily have understood, that a primal, pre-Aryan social condition had existed, which was the 'true' seat of rights from time immemorial and which 'history', in the form of the Aryan conquest,

[82] See my 'Caste, Class and Dominance'.

[83] B. Beck, *Peasant Society in Konku* (Vancouver, 1972); C. Baker, *Rural Economy*, 267–74.

[84] See my 'Caste, Class and Dominance'.

had illegitimately abrogated. The non-*Brahmin* movement sought a revolution 'backwards' into a past as immemorial as any English common lawyer could have conceived.[85]

In reducing the scope of claims to right almost exclusively to the provenances of 'authentic tradition', and thus in de-legitimating history, colonialism, not only immobilised, dominated and exploited Indian society, it also entrapped Indian culture and self-conception in an ontological net from which even those seeking to overturn its consequences have found escape extremely difficult.

[85] *Idem.*

AGAINST FORMALITY: ONE ASPECT OF THE ENGLISH REVOLUTION

By J. C. Davis

READ 11 DECEMBER 1992 AT THE UNIVERSITY OF BIRMINGHAM

WE live in an age (perhaps particularly apparent to those of us who work in universities) when informality is *de rigueur*; its own conventions and forms to be mastered if one is to live easily and effectively with colleagues, students, acquaintances or even the members of one's family. That it was not always so is a truism which attests to the reality of social change. One of the markers of such change, or of changes in social expectation, will be the realignment of relationships between the formal and the informal and of perceptions which govern interpretation of such relationships. In an age of revolution, or revolutionary aspiration, we might expect such realignments to be particularly dynamic or, more radically, for the categories of informal and formal themselves to be called in question.

This paper attempts to identify a discourse challenging formality in religious and thereby in political life in what might be regarded as more of a period of revolutionary aspiration than of revolutionary transformation, the period of the English Revolution.[1] It argues the centrality of that discourse for understanding the nature of revolutionary aspiration in the 1640s and 1650s as well as the nature of that aspiration's outcome. How, in religious terms, formality was identified, what the issues relating to it were perceived to be, and what underlay the sense of a crisis of formalism in the aftermath of military triumph, are questions to which answers will be attempted in the first half of the paper. Antiformalism takes up its second half: its case against formality; its political and social implications and, finally, its relationship with providence and apocalypse at the crisis of the revolution. The boundaries between formal and informal, as we know from our own experience, are treacherous, elusive and unstable. Nevertheless, as the nature

---

[1] By which is meant here the late 1640s and the 1650s. For one example amongst many which illustrate a revolutionary aspiration towards formalities (and its lack of fulfilment), one might take the proposals before the Nominated Assembly in August 1653 to cancel all titles and denominations in religion ('for God's people should be under one name viz. Christians') and in civil life to substitute 'Freemen of England' for all titles of honour and rank. See J. T. Cliffe, *Puritans in Conflict: The Puritan Gentry During and After the Civil Wars* (1988), 182.

of much social legitimation, order and ritual—not to mention embarrassment and amusement—bear witness, they are important. Similarly, in exploring a discourse of formality, informality and antiformalism we shall encounter a certain slipperiness, a capacity for unconscious, as well as conscious, paradox, and for confusion which make negotiating the territory difficult but not, as I hope to show unworthwhile. In particular, I shall suggest that understanding antiformalism[2] will throw considerable light on two distinctive aspects of England's revolutionary experience. First, it will help us to explain how the prospect of revolution opened up in the late 1640s while the possibilities of the revolutionary moment were simultaneously narrowed down. Secondly, it will help us to a better understanding of why, of all the crises of seventeenth-century Europe, it is England's troubles which gave rise to a seminal debate on liberty and authority.[3]

Formality was no marginal issue but one never far from the central concerns of England's mid-seventeenth-century crisis. In the Grand Remonstrance, for example, second, after 'Jesuited Papists', in a list of promoters of a design to subvert the fundamental laws and principles of government, came 'The Bishops, and the corrupt part of the clergy, who cherish formality and superstition ...'[4] Just over a week after the presentation of the Remonstrance, the king proclaimed his concern that divisions over liturgical forms 'may endanger the subversion of the very essence and substance of true religion'.[5] Later, Edward Hyde was to argue that God punished 'too much Formality in Religion' by visiting religious anarchy upon England in the 1640s and 50s.[6]

---

[2] There is a manifest danger, in developing the theme of 'antiformalism', of substituting another piece of 'manic abstraction' for those from which we are seeking to escape. But since abstraction, generalisation of some kind is the historian's inescapable obligation we must journey on in the hope of arriving at a city of less manic abstraction and more substance. Attention was drawn to manic abstraction in C. H. George, 'Puritanism as history and historiography', *Past and Present*, XLI (1968), 77–104. Salutary remarks on the issue are to be found in William Lamont's seminal essay, 'Pamphleteering, the Protestant consensus and the English Revolution', in *Freedom in the English Revolution: Essays in history and literature*, ed. R. C. Richardson and G. M. Ridden (Manchester, 1986), 72–92.

[3] A full and proper justification of these claims will require more space than is available here, where I attempt to give some illustration of the theme and some grounds for faith in its significance. But for some anticipation of the connections, see J. C. Davis, 'Religion and the Struggle for Freedom in the English Revolution', *The Historical Journal*, XXXV, 3 (1992), 507–30.

[4] *The Constitutional Documents of the Puritan Revolution 1625–1660*, ed. Samuel Rawson Gardiner (Oxford, 1906), 206.

[5] *Ibid.*,232.

[6] Edward Hyde, Earl of Clarendon, *Contemplations and Reflections upon the Psalms* quoted in Michael Finlayson, 'Clarendon, Providence and the Historical Revolution', *Albion*, XXII (1990), 627.

Both sides of the civil war divide claimed to be against formality. In this respect, as others, parliament's victory was seen to be pyrrhic. The covenanted struggle 'against Popery, Prelacy, Superstition, Schisme, Heresie, Prophaness and Formality' had somehow ended in the proliferation of what it had sought to vanquish.[7] In 1650 formality became subject to legislation. The Rump's Blasphemy Act of 9 August bracketed it with blasphemy, atheism and immorality. But Abiezer Coppe, putative object of that Act also saw his own *A Fiery Flying Roll* (January 1650) as 'a terrible threat to the Formalists'. In the same year Cromwell's campaign against Scots protestants in arms was represented as a war against formality.[8] Thus, in 1650, the repressive legislation of the Rump, the religious attitudes of the man who overthrew that institution, and one of the least acceptable radicals of his generation, shared a common antiformalism. All shades of the godly had a particular detestation of formality precisely because it characterised 'the seeming saint', rather than the godless, the impious or the papist. It was, in other words, a symptom of hypocrisy amongst God's chosen, of division and conflict within the saintly vanguard.

To identify formality was, then, one of the central concerns of revolutionary endeavour. What were the marks by which it might be known?

First, while atheism, blasphemy and immorality could be identified by their ungodliness, formality deceived precisely because it bore the face of godliness, piety and even of 'outward reformation'.[9] Formalists professed faith, holiness and reformation but their reforming piety was perverted into a preoccupation with externals; the pharisaism deplored by Jesus. Thomas Hooker identified 'Formall righteousness' with 'the practice of the outward duties of the first Table, joyned with a neglect of the duties of the second Table ...' There were saints and there were

---

[7]John Stalham, *Vindiciae Redemptionis* (1647), To My Beloved Brethren and Neighbours in Terling; quoted in K.Wrightson and D. Levine, *Poverty and Piety in an English Village: Terling, 1525–1700* (1979), 162. Cf. The Solemn League and Covenant, Clause II in *Constitutional Documents*, ed. Gardiner, 268–9.

[8]For the Blasphemy Ordinance see *Acts and Ordinances of the Interregnum 1642–1660*, ed. C. H. Firth and R. S. Rait (1911), II, 409–10. *Abiezer Coppe: Selected Writings* ed. Andrew Hopton (1987), 20; *A Collection of Ranter Writings*, ed. Nigel Smith (1983), 85. For Coppe's antiformalism see J. C. Davis, 'Fear, Myth and Furore: Reappraising the Ranters', *Past and Present*, CXXIX (1990), 98–103.

[9]Cf. Christopher Hill, *A Turbulent, Seditious and Factious People: John Bunyan and his Church 1628–1688* (Oxford, 1988), 72, citing Bunyan.

seeming saints and their coexistence was a source of pain and anxiety.[10]
'... meer formal profession', as Henry Robinson called it; outward
expression unrelated to either inner commitment or practical performance undermined the sense of godly brotherhood.[11] 'When I see
Prayers, Sermons, Fasts, Thanksgivings directed to this God in words
and shews', lamented Winstanley, 'and when I come to look for actions
of obedience to the Righteous Law, suitable to such a profession, I find
them men of another Nation, saying, and not doing; like an old courtier
saying *Your Servant*, when he was an Enemy. I will say no more, but
groan and waite for a restoration.'[12] Saying but not doing linked
formality with hypocrisy.[13] But it was a Janus-like link; both non-
performance—saying but not doing—and empty performance could
be identified with formality. If Christian liberty was the wholehearted
pursuit of God's purpose, its contrary might be hypocrisy—performance
without the whole heart. Hypocrisy came close to formality—the raising
of forms above substance. So for John Milton, 'Sacred things not
performed sincerely ... are no was acceptable to God in their outward
formality.'[14] 'If we grieve,' Peter Sterry told the House of Commons in
1647, 'and not in Christ, our Greife is Hypocrisie, or at best but
Formality.'[15] John Owen, likewise, saw an emphasis on forms over
substance as leading into 'the confines of self-righteousness if not
hypocrisy.'[16]

[10] R. T. Kendall, *Calvin and English Calvinism to 1649* (Oxford, 1979), 130. Compare John
Everard's identification of formality with those who 'champ the Letter between their
Teeth' but show no virtue in their lives by the pursuit of the 'Spiritual, Practical and
Experimental Life'. John Everard, *The Gospel Treasury Opened* (1657), I, 416; cited in Nigel
Smith, *Perfection Proclaimed: Language and Literature in English Radical Religion 1640–1660*
(Oxford, 1989), 132.

[11] Henry Robinson, *Liberty of Conscience* (1643), 18.

[12] Gerrard Winstanley, *The Law of Freedom* (1652) in *The Works of Gerrard Winstanley* ed.
George H. Sabine (New York, 1965), 509. Lest it be thought that such remarks are
confined to radicals, we should note similar statements by William Strong and Stephen
Marshall at about the same time. See Tai Liu, *Discord in Zion: The Puritan Divines and the
Puritan Revolution* (The Hague, 1973), 122, 146–7. The divisiveness of the pursuit of externals
instead of 'the economy of God' is also a theme of Jeremy Taylor's *The Liberty of Prophesying*
(1647). See Frank Livingstone Huntley, *Jeremy Taylor and the Great Rebellion: A Study of His
Mind and Temper in Controversy* (Ann Arbor, 1970), 40, 55.

[13] For Laurence Chaderton's linking of hypocrisy and the purely formal profession of
many English protestants in the 1560s see Peter Lake, *Moderate Puritans and the Elizabethan
Church* (Cambridge, 1982), 25, 32–3. One of the functions of preaching was to overcome
formality by awakening zeal and a lively faith. For John Bunyan's linking of formality
and hypocrisy a century later see Hill, *Turbulent, Seditious and Factious People*, 304–307; U.
Milo Kaufmann, 'Spiritual Discerning: Bunyan and the Mysteries of the Divine Will', in
John Bunyan: Conventicle and Parnassus: Tercentenary Essays, ed. N. H. Keeble (Oxford, 1988),
172–3.

[14] John Milton, *Eikonoklastes* (1649), xxvii.

[15] Peter Sterry, *The Clouds in Which Christ Comes* (1647), 30.

[16] John Owen, *A Complete Collection of Sermons* (1721), 73.

The challenge of true reformation had always been to get beyond outward conformity, formality, to inner conviction, the reformation of the heart, mind and will, and thence to conscientious action.[17] By the 1640s, profession of the truth hypocritically, for form's sake was coming to seem worse than 'honest error'.[18] Formality, overvaluing that 'which every intelligent man values but as forms, or inventions, or modes, or artifices', led, according to Matthew Hale, to doctrinal bitterness, clerical conflict, and confessional dogmatism, and thence by disgusted reaction to atheism.[19] 'Zealous professors, that live without the spirit' were observed by Winstanley to become, 'the most bitter enemies to Christ ... treacherous, self-seeking, self-loving, ful of subtil policy to waste and wear out every one that seeks to advance Christ, by their bitternesse and oppression.'[20]

Bearing the appearance of true religion, formality threatened to rob reformation of achievement in substance. It was the enemy within the gates, a cancer more insidious and potentially destructive than outward enemies. Hence anxiety to identify it and to overcome it.[21] Pilgrim's pursuit of the substance of true religion involved a continuing struggle with and avoidance of hypocrisy and formality.[22] The church might have the word, sacramental purity, credal uniformity and yet be, according to John Robinson, dead.[23] '... the substance of Christian Religion doth not stand in notions, but in contrition, charity and devotion.' So that by 1654 it would even be suggested to the godly that in such things the cavaliers might come closer to Christ than the formally disputing clerics who claimed to lead the people of God.[24]

[17] For two examples of this concern: 'Instructions given by the King's Highness to ... the archbishop of York and such other as shall be named hereafter, whom his Majesty has appointed to be of his Council resident in the North parts ...' (1544) in *The Tudor Constitution: Documents and Commentary*, ed. G.R. Elton (Cambridge, 1965), 206; Cf. *A Remonstrance: or the Declaration of the Lords and Commons now assembled in Parliament: 26 May 1642* where the King's wicked counsellors are identified as those 'more earnest in the Protestant Profession, than in the Protestant Religion'. John Rushworth, *Historical Collections* (1691), III.i, 586; Conrad Russell, *Causes of the English Civil War* (Oxford, 1990), 77.

[18] Jeremy Taylor, *The Liberty of Prophesying* (1647), 163. Cf. Blair Worden, 'Toleration and the Cromwellian Protectorate', in *Persecution and Toleration: Studies in Church History 21*, ed. W.J. Shiels (Oxford, 1984), 207.

[19] Worden, *ibid.*, 233 and quoting Matthew Hale, *Of the Nature of True Religion* (1684), 16, 37, 39.

[20] Winstanley, *The New Law of Righteousnes* (1649) in *Works of Winstanley*, ed. Sabine, 226.

[21] For examples from the 1650s see John Goodwin, *A Fresh Discovery of the High Presbyterian Spirit* (1654); John Hall, *The True Cavalier Examined* (1656).

[22] For Bunyan's depiction of this see *The Pilgrim's Progress* (Ware, 1987), 38–40, 201 and Valentine Cunningham, 'Glossing and Glozing: Bunyan and Allegory' in *Bunyan: Conventicle and Parnassus*, ed. Keeble, 223–4; Kaufmann, 'Spiritual Discerning' in *ibid.*, 172–4.

[23] Geoffrey F. Nuttall, *The Puritan Spirit: Essays and Addresses* (London, 1967), 97.

[24] Arise Evans, *The Voice of Michael the Archangel, To his Highness the Lord Protector* (1654), 16.

At best forms were childish things,[25] at worse, insistence on them was unchristian. Submission to form, for form's sake, was an Egyptian bondage.[26] Or, like a golden calf, it led away from the living God. 'There is a great deal of idolatry yet in England,' John Rogers complained in 1653, 'as when your Formalists set up any forme, or thing in the room of God, which is not God ...'[27] 'I am persuaded', Anna Trapnel warned those who called themselves saints, 'that bare Professors are the greatest Papists in the world; spirituall idolatry is the worst.'[28] The 'carnal mock-holiness' of formality[29] pitted the letter against the spirit, form against substance, the law against grace; in short, fleshly invention, imaginings and contrivances against the things of God.[30]

Formalists invaded both divine and magisterial authority. In the later seventeenth century, latitudinarians like Stillingfleet condemned formalists, whether of a high church or a nonconformist persuasion, for requiring the Church to insist on more than Christ did.[31] To put it another way, antiformalists gave human authority more scope by widening the range of things indifferent; formalists did the reverse. It was commonly accepted that in things indifferent, the *adiaphora*, the magistrate might have a determining authority. Consequently, formalists were seen as circumscribing the state's role in matters ecclesiastical, while antiformalists were frequently accused of Erastianism or, later in the century, of Hobbism. The most radical antiformalists denied the validity of the widest range of forms—including liturgies and set prayers—by whatsoever authority introduced. Ultimately, they reached the point, the paradox of which moderates reminded them, at which their antiformalism became so obsessively antipathetic to forms and so scrupulous about them as to become formality.[32]

Formality, then, was identified with the enemy within, the idol in

[25] The depiction of an excessively formal youth was almost a convention of spiritual autobiography. For examples see Edward Rogers, *Some Account of the Life and Opinions of a Fifth-Monarchy-Man* (1867), 7–17; Anna Trapnel, *A Legacy for Saints* (1654), 1–7; Laurence Clarkson, *The Lost Sheep Found* (1660), 1–7.

[26] Cf. Peter Sterry: 'to be subject to ... the Church in the outward forme for the outward forme's sake is a bondage.' Cited in Tai Liu, *Discord in Zion*, 49.

[27] John Rogers, *Dod, or Chatham* (1653), 341, 346.

[28] Trapnel, *Legacy for Saints*, 4.

[29] Abiezer Coppe, *A Remonstrance* (1651) in *Ranter Writings*, ed. Smith, 121, 119 margin.

[30] For a setting out of these contraries enmeshed with issues of social and political authority see Gerrard Winstanley, *Truth Lifting Up Its Head Above Scandals* (1649) in *Works of Gerrard Winstanley*, ed. Sabine, 99–101, 101, 105.

[31] John Marshall, 'The Ecclesiology of the Latitude-men 1660–1689: Stillingfleet, Tillotson and Hobbism', *Journal of Ecclesiastical History*, 36 (1985), 408, 410.

[32] For a general treatment of the theme and some exemplification see Geoffrey F. Nuttall, *The Holy Spirit in Puritan Faith and Experience* (Oxford, 1946), Ch. IV and 91, 97, 108, 114.

the temple, with hypocrisy, non-performance, lack of substance, a challenge to both divine and civil authority. But the issues it evoked ran deep into contemporary perceptions of reformation and so touched all those on the Protestant side of the Reformation divide.

Anxieties about the capacity of formality to stall the saints in their pursuit of godliness and the godly community were not confined to particular individuals or groups. Rather, they were inherent in contemporary perceptions of the Reformation, of the godly community, and of the direction and authority of godly rule.[33] Formality was an issue which embraced the reformed mainstream and its tributaries. The Reformation intensified antiformalist concerns, frequently confirming a sense of common purpose amongst the piously christian, but a decade of frustrated reformation endeavour—the 1640s—was to bring those concerns to a point of crisis. In that decade a great, perhaps *the* central, struggle in England was that between defending or reforming the reformation.[34] Episcopacy or presbytery, church courts, deans and chapters, convocation, the Book of Common Prayer, the thirty-nine articles, the Psalter, cathedrals, ordination, church furnishings and decoration, baptism, admission to the sacrament, a confession of faith, a directory of worship, a new catechism, the nature and function of the parish, the financial support of clerical and pastoral activity, the religious calendar and festivals: all of these and many more issues of church polity, liturgy and discipline absorbed great energy and generated intense and enormously detailed debate.[35] Considerable dis-

---

[33] The works of William Lamont are essential here in particular 'Pamphleteering, the Protestant Consensus and the English Revolution', and *Godly Rule: Politics and Religion 1603–1660* (1969).

[34] For John Morrill's view of the origins of the civil war in this light see his, 'The religious context of the English Civil War', these *Transactions*, 5th ser., XXXIV (1984), 155–78; 'The attack on the Church of England in the Long Parliament, 1640–2', in *History, Society and the Churches*, ed. D. Beales and G. Best (1985), 105–24; 'Sir William Brereton and England's Wars of Religion', *Journal of British Studies*, XXIV (1985), 311–32; *The Nature of the English Revolution* (1993) See also Conrad Russell, *Causes of the English Civil War; idem.*, 'Issues in the House of Commons 1621–9: Predictors of Civil War Allegiance', *Albion*, XXIII (1991), 23–39.

[35] We lack an adequate modern history of these debates. For divergence on the central issue of the Prayer Book amongst a discrete group of wealthy, puritan gentry see J. T. Cliffe, *Puritans in Conflict: The Puritan Gentry During and After the Civil Wars* (1988), 27–8. For the Harleys' attitude to the Prayer Book see Jacqueline Eales, *Puritans and Roundheads: The Harleys of Brampton Bryan and the Outbreak of the English Civil War* (Cambridge, 1990). On the significance of the Prayer Book in the 1640s see John Morrill, 'The Church of England 1642–9' in Morrill (ed.) *Reactions to the English Civil War* (1982), 89–114. For some parallel issues of forms see R. L. Greaves, 'The Ordination Controversy and the Spirit of Reform in Puritan England', *Journal of Ecclesiastical History* XXI (1970), 225–41; David S. Katz, *Sabbath and Sectarianism in Seventeenth Century England* (Leiden, 1988); Kenneth L.

illusion in the late 1640s related to the perception that the formalism of the pre-civil war church had been replaced by the formalistic demands of a new church order and the formalistic preoccupations of the gathered churches.[36] To reshape, or bring down and replace old forms meant that attention and priority had to be given to matters of formality.[37] Neglecting them meant disorder or the continuation of unacceptable, ungodly practices; addressing them meant diversion from christian substance, from the true marrow of divinity, and the confusion of godly reformation with narrowly conceived matters of ecclesiastical polity, liturgy and discipline.[38] At the antiformalist end of the spectrum, one response to this paradox was to play down the significance of formal distinctions and to reduce the criteria for Christian fellowship to the minimal fundamentals in expression of the faith. As the 1650s wore on and with the demise of the Cromwellian Protectorate this too proved elusive.[39]

The 1640s and 50s—decades of reformation crisis—were also witness to an associated crisis of formalism, which, while directed against the focal points of sectarian divisions, had little to do with their alignments and loyalties. There was a struggle *against* formality but also *for* the forms of godly order, a bifurcation reflective of the ambiguities of

---

Parker, *The English Sabbath: A Study of Doctrine and Discipline from the Reformation to the Civil War* (Cambridge, 1988).

[36] For Winstanley as epitomising this disillusion see *Fire in the Bush* in *Works of Winstanley*, ed. Sabine, 445–6; *Truth Lifting Up its Head*, in *ibid.*, 140–5; *The New Law of Righteousnes*, in *ibid.*, 174. There is an obvious comparison with Coppe's attack on the formalism of the gathered churches in *A Fiery Flying Roll*. See also *A Christian Caveat to the Old and New Sabbatarians* (1650).

[37] An example of such 'radical' formalists might be found in the Chidley family with their campaigns on church bells, cathedrals, Christmas and adult baptism. Ian Gentles, 'London Levellers and the English Revolution: The Chidleys and their Circle', *The Journal of Ecclesiastical History*, XXIX (1978), 281–309.

[38] For an early warning to this effect see [Henry Burton], *The Protestation Protested* (1641).

[39] For the difficulties inherent in this exercise see Guibon Goddard, 'Journal of the Parliament of 1654–5' in J. T. Rutt (ed.), *Diary of Thomas Burton, Esq., 1656–9*, 4 vols. (1828), I, xvii–cxxx. See also J. C. Davis, 'Cromwell's Religion', in John Morrill (ed.), *Oliver Cromwell and the English Revolution* (1990), 194–5. Thomas Hobbes' ecclesiology may perhaps be more illuminatingly seen in these terms rather than under the heading of Erastianism. Glenn Burgess, 'Liberty in the English Revolution: Hobbes and Some Contemporaries' (unpublished typescript). I am grateful to Dr Burgess for the opportunity to read this ahead of publication. See also Johann P. Sommerville, *Thomas Hobbes: Political Ideas in Historical Context* (1992).

protestant, reforming Christianity.[40] While popery could in its formal expression be identified with idolatrous superstition, literal protestantism had as one terminus a judaizing tendency which went back, beyond the grace of Christ, to the legal formalities of the Old Testament.[41] Between these extremes the problem of the formal expression of a *reformed* godly community was being worked at in proliferating forms. That itself appeared both to onlookers and participants, to be a frightening denial of Christian unity, so that fear of disunity and the longing for godly community without formalistic barriers held congregations and individuals back from the final identification and declaration of a distinctive ecclesiological identity.[42] As Joseph Salmon observed in 1651, 'The formall world is much affrighted, and every form is up in Arms to proclaim open wars *against it selfe*.'[43]

Even those most anxious about the extreme forms of sectarian proliferation had to wrestle with the formalist dilemma. In 1655 the faithful of the East Riding of Yorkshire were warned of a quaker led attempt 'to lay waste Scriptures, Churches, Faith, Hope, etc. and establish Paganism in ENGLAND'. The antiformalism of the quakers, and its implications were perceived to lie at the bottom of that threat. 'Surely the Doctrines of these men which we oppose, are levelled to subvert all Order, Churches, in whatsoever is done outwardly: for they say its Babylon, and all the worship, and teachers without, are of the Beast and AntiChrist.' By extension, it was argued, such doctrines threatened the overthrow of property and the enforcement of a 'Law of Community'. But what is interesting in this context is that, while warning against the quakers as subverters of forms, this tract also called for a revival of true spirituality as against the arid formalism which weakened the Church and gave appeal to quakerism.[44] The threat of what was seen as extreme antiformalism, the crisis of formality, should not be met by a reversion to formality.

---

[40] For Hugh Peter's vision of himself as campaigning against 'Formalists' in 1643 see Raymond Phineas Stearns, *The Strenuous Puritan: Hugh Peter 1598–1660* (Urbana, Illinois, 1954), 213. For the tension about forms at the heart of protestantism see Hill, *Turbulent, Seditious and Factious People*, 188; for its presence at the heart of 'puritanism' see Worden, 'Toleration and the Cromwellian Protectorate', 207–8.

[41] Katz, *Sabbath and Sectarianism*; idem., *Philo-Semitism and the Readmission of the Jews to England 1603–1655* (Oxford, 1982). For examples of contemporary anxiety about judaizing tendencies, see Zachary Crofton, *Bethshemesh Clouded or some Animadversions on the Rabbinical Talmud of Rabbi John Rogers* (1653); *Ludlow: A Voyce*, ed. Worden, 7.

[42] For example, John Gifford's congregation at Bedford. See White, 'Fellowship of Believers' in Bunyan: *Conventicle and Parnassus*, ed. Keeble, 8, 11–12, 17; Hill, *Turbulent, Seditious and Factious People*, 90.

[43] Joseph Salmon, *Heights in Depths* (1651), An Apologeticall Hint, (My emphasis); See also 4–5; also in *Ranter Writings*, ed. Smith, 206, 208.

[44] Joseph Kellet, John Pomroy and Paul Glisson, *A Faithful Discovery of a treacherous Design*

One of the most articulate and distinguished depictors of the crisis of formalism in the 1640s and 50s was Peter Sterry, fellow of Emmanuel College, Cambridge, chaplain to Lady Brooke in early 1640s, nominated for the Westminster Assembly by the House of Lords,and chaplain to the Commonwealth's Council of State from February 1649. Sterry's interest in form and formality may have been coloured by his Platonism but its direction and force accords well with the context we have been recovering. Late in 1645, in a Fast Sermon to the House of Commons, Sterry was already pointing to a post-war crisis which could only be resolved by moving beyond human invention to spiritual substance.[45] Two years later, preaching to a Commons struggling to impose a presbyterian settlement on the country, Sterry depicted 'Formality' as central to the crisis.

> Formes are sweet Helpes, but too severe Lords over our Faith. They may be Ornaments to our Face and Neck, serving the Beauty of Christ's Appearances to us and His union with us. But then they must be of Gold or Precious stone, taken out of the Mine of Treasury of the Spirit. So worne, they may become the Heires at age, the Spirit-borne Princes. But if they be of Iron or Brasse, loud upon our Feet or Hands; that is Grosse in Fleshly Darknesse, binding up the Activity and Motion of our Spirits towards God; then are they sad Marks of the Bondwoman's Children.

Forms should always be regarded as at best a means to an end, at worst a distracting constraint, a trap. "Tis in vain to attempt to shut up Christ in anything.'[46] Preaching on scribes and pharisees to the House of Lords, Sterry warned of the hypocrisy of 'Imposalls' upon men in Christ's name but without his spirit. In this respect, he saw four competitors for mastery over the human spirit: reason, which was corrupt and depraved; the authority of the Church, itself no more than the reason of a combination of men; miracles, which would only be distinguished through 'the Eye of God in the Soul of Man'; the scriptures, which must be reverenced because only the spirit excelled them in authority but the letter yet remained dead, killing, outward, a shadow.[47] In the aftermath of Cromwell's triumphant campaign in Ireland, Sterry reminded parliament of the uselessness of human ordinances and performance without the substance of sanctification. God's breath opened up the inadequacy of men's doings; 'the Letter,

---

(1655), title page, 27, 39–40, 50, 52. The tract was recommended by Christopher Feake, John Simpson and George Cokayn.

[45] Peter Sterry, *The Spirits Conviction of Sinne* (1645).

[46] Sterry, *The Clouds in Which Christ Comes* (1648), 30, 40–1, 46, 47–8.

[47] Sterry, *The Teachings of Christ in the Soule* (1648), 2–3, 23–36.

the Law, Formality, Hypocrisy, Profaneness, Atheism, the World, the Devill'. Despite present victory, Sterry advised the Rump, 'Fatnesse of Heart', 'Luxury' and 'Blindnesse of Minde' could lead to satisfaction with the deadness of ordinances and legality rather than the whole-hearted pursuit of the promptings of 'Free Grace and the Spirit of God'.[48] For Sterry victory over the Scots in 1650 and 1651 was more clear cut. He instructed parliament in the proposition that the formalism which presbyterianism shared with the Roman Papacy would bring about the downfall of both.

> ... that Presbytery, which I compare with the Papacy, is such, as appropriateth to the outward Forme, those things which pertain only to the Power of the Spirit: such as by vertue of an Outward, Church-form, assumes a Spiritual and Civil power to it self; such as out of the Golden cup of a glorious Profession, makes it self drunk with the wine of Fornications, with Earthly powers and interests; such as takes to it self the Iron Mace of fleshy force and fury, to break in pieces at pleasure Commonwealths, Crownes, Consciences, Estates, and Hearts of men.

After a decade of reformation, of the pursuit of a godly community, and despite England's triumph over its neighbours, the hard lesson had yet to be learned that these ends could not be reached by 'Annexing the Spirit to outward Formalities'.[49]

Whatever the achievements of republican imperialism, to such observers the 1650s disclosed a wasteland of blasted hopes: on the one hand, a prospective collapse of all forms in surrender to spiritual intuition; on the other, the fear that formality, like a shirt of Nessus, clung to the body politic of an aspirant godly nation even as that nation triumphed over its papistical and presbyterian neighbours. This was the crisis of formality which went to the heart of revolutionary concerns. What could antiformalists offer towards its resolution?

There were two levels on which the case against formality was articu-lated. As Sterry's sermons illustrate, the case against the undue priority given to forms could be a situational one: look at the mess which preoccupation with forms has landed us in. The second level of argument consisted of a series of observations on the implications of formality. Four of them will be considered more closely here.

Out of the dichotomy between form and substance arose, first, the argument that preoccupation with form distracted from the substance

---

[48] Sterry, *The Comings forth of Christ in the Power of his Death* (1650), 33–4, 43–4, 48–9.
[49] Sterry, *England's Deliverance from the Northern Presbytery* (1652), 6–7, 15, 18.

of true religion. In 1650 William Dell reproved those 'who are so Jewish, and so zealous of the honour of the Law, that they will by no means indure to hear, that the Gospel of the Son of God comes to abolish it ...'[50] The 'Vanitie of the Present Churches' in William Walwyn's view was that their energies were 'spent in talking upon some hard texts of Scripture ... or in disputes & contests, upon some nice & difficult questions' rather than upon the work of practical Christian charity 'without respect of persons, Opinions, Societies or Churches'.[51] Walter Cradock believed that the passion for correctness in church order had diverted men from more essential things: while they 'learn Church-discipline, they forget godliness'.[52] To get back to substance and away from form in religion what were needed were ministers of reconciliation—such as Walwyn considered himself to be—and the elimination of inventions which obscured the gospel message.[53]

The antidote to such distraction from the substance of religion was a proper approach to form. John Rogers in 1653 urged the saints to live not in, but through form. He engaged himself 'against the fearful Formality, and urged uniformity of many (yea of most) Churches in England and Ireland'. '... the Saints that are spiritual know how to handle formalities and such like things, viz. to do as

[50] William Dell, *The Crucified and Quickened Christian* (1650?) 4–5; see also 33. Dell had been secretary to William Laud, attended Fairfax in 1645–6, officiated at the marriage of Henry Ireton and Bridget Cromwell in 1646 and became a reforming Master of Caius College in May 1649.

[51] William Walwyn, *The Vanitie of the Present Churches* (1649), 22–3, 43. See also *Walwyn's Just Defence* (1649), 32. Cf. John Lilburne on the 'Carnal Professours' satisfied with forms only: Lilburne, *An Answer to Nine Arguments* (1644), To the Reader. R. B. Seaberg has shown that the Levellers viewed the Norman conquest as a disruption of form but not of legal substance, in the sense of Anglo-Saxon liberties or Englishmen's birthrights. In this respect it might be argued that the Levellers were traditionalists of substance concerned in the 1640s to see that substance protected by appropriate constitutional forms. R. B. Seaberg, 'The Norman Conquest and the Common Law: The Levellers and the Argument from Continuity', *The Historical Journal*, XXIV (1981), 791–806. There was, of course, room for variation on what the substance of Christianity amounted to. At one end of the spectrum, William Prynne saw too exclusive an attitude to the sacraments, too great an emphasis on the purity of ordinances, as jeopardising the work of moral reformation, the establishment of godly community. At the other, Abiezer Coppe condemned the gathered churches' formalistic hair-splitting as a diversion from the rigours of practical Christianity. In either case, however, substance involved the active reshaping of community. For Prynne see Lamont, *Godly Rule*, 120. For Coppe see J. C. Davis, *Fear, Myth and History: The Ranters and the Historians* (Cambridge, 1986), 48–58; 'Fear, Myth and Furore: Reassessing the Ranters', *Past and Present*, CXXIX (1990), 95–102.

[52] Geoffrey F. Nuttall, *The Welsh Saints 1640–1660: Walter Cradock, Vavasor Powell, Morgan Llwyd* (Cardiff, 1957), 28.

[53] William Walwyn, *The Power of Love* (1643), 27, 7–8. For the concession by his enemies that Walwyn consistently urged a shift of priorities from form to substance see [James Price], *Walwins Wiles* (1649), 7.

much good as they may, but to hurt or hinder none, with, or by them'. The proper, 'indifferent use of Formes' was the only path to a good church society for the saints and for the well being of the community as a whole. Amongst the hallmarks of such a society were harmony, charity, christian liberty; 'where they live more in the Spirit than on the Forms'; humility, self-denial and mutual aid; order and 'Gospel-decency'; 'where their unity consists not in the unity of the form, but in the unity of the Spirit'.[54]

If formality distracted *from* the substance of religion, it could only divert attention from God *to* some substitute; that is to say, secondly, that it was in essence idolatrous. 'There is a great deal of Idolatry yet in England; as when your Formalists set up any forme, or thing, in the room of God, which is not God ...'[55] In 1581, the 'Tudor anthropologist', George Gifford had identified such formality and the purely conventional observation of established forms which followed it as an invitation to atheism. 'They be those which we call Atheists of no religion: but look, whatsoever any prince doth set forth, that they will professe.'[56] Like all forms of idolatry, formality usurped the throne of a true, living and retributive God. For this reason, John Owen urged MPs assembling for the second protectoral parliament in 1656 not to be too hasty in settling religion, establishing discipline and eliminating error. God would achieve all of these things in his own time and his own way. In the mean time, 'Liberty and Protection of the people of God' was a priority, as were mutual love and the elimination of profanity, selfishness, pride and 'formality'. MPs should beware of allowing their wills and judgements to run before the will of God.[57] Yet

[54] Rogers, *Dod*, 40–1, 65, 67, 212. For an attempt by an individual congregation to achieve this shift of emphasis see John Gifford's Bedford congregation set up in 1650 'without respect to this or that circumstance or opinion in outward or circumstantiall things'. New members, identifying the distinction between substance and form, were to solemnly agree that 'union with Christ is the foundation of all Sainte's Communion, and not any ordinances of Christ, or any judgement about externals'. B. R. White, 'The Fellowship of Believers: Bunyan and Puritanism', in *John Bunyan*, ed. Keeble, 8, 11–12, 17–18. However, for the paradox whereby the testing for substance could result in the emergence of forms see Richard L. Greaves, 'Conscience, Liberty and the Spirit: Bunyan and Nonconformity', in *ibid.*, 24.

[55] Rogers, *Dod*, 346; see also 454. Cf. Trapnel, *A Legacy*, 4; on the Grindletonians, Smith, *Perfection Proclaimed*, f2. For Baptist concern at the idolisation of ordinances see B. R. White, 'Henry Jessey in the Great Rebellion', in *Reformation, Conformity and Dissent: Essays in honour of Geoffrey Nuttall*, ed. R. Buick Knox (1977), 143, 151.

[56] George Gifford, A Briefe discourse of ... Countrie Divinite (1581) fol., 22; cited in Patrick Collinson, *The Religion of Protestants: The Church in English Society 1559–1625* (Oxford, 1982), 200. Alan Macfarlane, 'A Tudor Anthropologist: George Gifford's *Discourse* and *Dialogue*' in *The Damned Art: Essays in the Literature of Witchcraft*, ed. Sydney Anglo (1977), 140–55.

[57] John Owen, *Gods Work in Founding Zion* (1656), 41–3, 30–31.

again formality's idolatrous, even atheistic, quality was to be observed in its distraction of the godly from the struggle against the enemies of religion, especially the Papists. James Ussher's antiformalism, his willingness to avoid controversy over forms, to encourage a Protestant irenicism, the better to fight Popery in unity, was frequently seen in this light.[58]

A third association of formalism was with immaturity, in life and in the faith, with the first, misdirected steps of youth to come to terms with religion.[59] In her teens, Anna Trapnel, like Sarah Wright, was chided by her mother for excessive formalism.[60] 'And from the age of 13 and so forward, I began to take and keep a dayly Register of my Sins, and set them down in a Book.' This was but a part of the adolescent Abiezer Coppe's religious regime which also included solitary confession at evening prayer; the study of nine, six or at least three chapters of scripture every day, as well as secret fasting. The point for the mature Coppe's recollection was that none of this misdirected scrupulosity assuaged his sense of sin.[61] John Rogers, whose father had been expelled from a prebendal position at Ely for his Laudian associations, also remembered his youth as a time of excessive formality. A schoolboy at Maldon in Essex he was influenced by the preaching of William Fennor and Stephen Marshall. Life became a round of memorising sermons, reading, praying, singing psalms and observing fast days. '... all this while I was labouring for life, exceeding formal ...' Beneath the rigorous piety lay fearfulness, dread of Hell, temptation of suicide, despair and torment, the fear of madness. A decade later, Rogers would see formalities as childish things, insistence on them as unchristian.[62]

Formality could invert religious priorities, divert pious effort into idolatry or atheism, and trap in immaturity those sincerely pursuing godliness, but, in terms of the struggle to set up a godly community in England, formalism's most hateful and damaging characteristic was its capacity to divide the saints. '... we think we love not God,' observed Jeremy Taylor, 'unless we hate our brother, and we have not the virtue

[58] R. Buick Knox, *James Ussher, Archbishop of Armagh* (Cardiff, 1967), 12, 22–3, 50, 72, 114–18, 130–3. For the argument that Ussher was not prepared to let his own moderation be exploited by radicals once Charles I had committed himself to unreformed episcopacy see William M. Abbott, 'James Ussher and "Ussherian" Episcopacy, 1640–56: The Primate and His *Reduction* Manuscript', *Albion*, XXII (1990), 237–59.

[59] For Bunyan's exemplification of this see Kaufmann, 'Spiritual Discerning', 174–5, 178–80; White, 'Fellowship of Believers', 4; Hill, *Turbulent, Seditious and Factious People*, 72.

[60] Trapnel, *A Legacy*, 1–9; Cf. Smith, *Perfection Proclaimed*, 49.

[61] Abiezer Coppe, *Copps Return to the Wayes of Truth* (1651), 3.

[62] Edward Rogers, *Some account of Life and Opinions of a Fifth-Monarchy-Man* (1867), 1–14, 19–20. See also Rogers, *Dod*, 341–2, 419–20.

of religion unless we persecute all religions but our own ...'[63] The formalist began by restricting charity to those of his or her form.[64] Once, Arise Evans recollected in 1655, the unity and order of family life was underwritten by their manner of church worship.

> ... the Master went before, the Mistress, Children and servants following with one consent; surely they were in the way of God ... but now the Master goeth one way, the Mistress another; the Children and Servants another: every one goeth several wayes; and when they come home Mum is best; for they can neither pray together nor speak anything of God; if they do, there is a hot house presently with their damning and confounding one another: God is not the author of such confusion, but of peace and concord ...

To restore that—somewhat idealised—order Evans had, ironically, no immediate prescription beyond that of a more formal observance of the sabbath.[65] Formality was, nevertheless, divisive in family, household and society. Joshua Sprigge was not alone in warning that the subversion of unity through formalistic division could provoke providential anger and the loss of apocalyptic status.[66]

If unity were to be preserved—and it was generally agreed that anything less would be catastrophic—there were only two approaches: to insist on uniformity, by persuasion or coercion,[67] or, alternatively, to minimise formal differences and stress unity of substance. Pursuing the second, or antiformalist, path Richard Baxter advocated unity within formal diversity. His appeal was to 'meer Catholicks; Men of no Faction, nor siding with any Party, but owning that which was good in all, as far as they could discern it; and upon a Concord in so much, laying out themselves for the great Ends of their Ministry, the Peoples Edification'. Such people, in Baxter's view, gave priority to substance over form, and, on that basis, were capable of uniting 'in things Necessary'. 'The Uniting of the Churches upon the Primitive Terms, and the tollerating (not of all, but) of tollerable Differences, is the way to Peace, which almost all men approve of, except those who are

[63] Frank Livingstone Huntley, *Jeremy Taylor and the Great Rebellion: A Study of His Mind and Temper in Controversy* (Ann Arbor, 1970), 40.

[64] Abiezer Coppe, *A Character of a True Christian* (1680); Rogers, *Dod*, 453–4.

[65] Arise Evans, *The Voice of King Charls the Father* (1655), 34–5. Less immediately Evans argued that godly order and authority in the family could only be restored if there were such in the commonwealth at large.

[66] Joshua Sprigge, *A Testimony of Approaching Glory* (1649), 127; quoted in Nuttall, *Puritan Spirit* (1967), 120–1. Cf. Rogers, *Dod*, 453.

[67] In an Augustinian frame of reference, coercion and persuasion were not seen as mutually exclusive. See Mark Goldie, 'The Theory of Religious Intolerance in Restoration England' in *From Persecution to Toleration: The Glorious Revolution and Religion in England*, ed. Ole Peter Grell, Jonathan Israel and Nicholas Tyacke (Oxford, 1991), 331–68.

uppermost, and think they have the Reins in their own hands.' Greater emphasis was to be placed on agreed fundamentals less on marginal controversies. Such judgement and charity led Baxter to lay even less stress on 'external Modes and Formes of Worship'.[68]

From the inception of the Westminster Assembly's attempt to formulate a new uniformity, the argument that God might have many ways to achieve the same substantial ends was reiterated.[69] If God's honour had 'been tied to any such precise outward form of worship', John Hall informed Oliver Cromwell, He would have made his intentions clearer. To scruple over 'the measure and manner of any outward Form' was to 'dis-serve him, when we break Charity and Order, and make Schism in our service to him'. God does not demand such a scrupulosity over the first table, as to make observance of the second table impossible.

> And therefore truly, if men could be once brought to put a greater rate upon things fundamental,and a less upon superstructures; considering that the not holding to the one brings on the loss of Heaven and the too strict holding to the other, brings on the loss of Charity, and thereby shrewdly endanger[s] the other also ... we should preserve the State in quiet also; and prevent all those mischiefs we now so much complain of through changes therein ...

From this perspective it was formality not diversity which was the cause of disunity and divisive conflict.[70]

Formality was, therefore, distracting, idolatrous, immature and divisive. But who were those who sustained and made powerful such a regrettable disposition? Who were the formalists?

At one level, contemporaries were in no doubt. They were the enemy within: not the immoral, blasphemous, atheistic; not the mockers and railers but from amongst the pious, zealously seeking a form of

---

[68] *Richard Baxter: Reliquiae Baxterianae*, ed. Matthew Sylvester, (1696), 97, 104, 126–7, 133. For the interregnum attempt to define fundamentals see William A. Shaw, *A History of the English Church during the Civil Wars and under the Commonwealth 1640–1660*, 2 vols. (1900), II, Ch. 3.

[69] For example: John Goodwin, *Theomachia or The Grand Imprudence of their running the hazard of Fighting against God in Suppressing any Way, Doctrine or Practice concerning which they know not certainly whether it be from God or no* (1644), 16, 52; *ΒΑΣΑΝΙΣΤΑΊL OR THE TRIERS [or Tormentors] TRIED AND CAST* (1657), 16, 18.

[70] John Hall, *The True Cavalier Examined by his Principles* (1656), 4, 5, 90. Hall was one of several in the 1650s urging a reconciliation between Cavaliers and Cromwellians. See also Huntley, *Jeremy Taylor*, 55. Also, William Walwyn, *The Compassionate Samaritan* (1644), 45: 'the diversity of mens judgements is not the occasion of division'. Cf. *The Vanitie of the Present Churches*, 8.

reformation—if a misdirected one. Indeed their piety, their assurance, their sanctification, coupled with their insistence not merely on forms but on uniformity, made them all the more menacing and objectionable. Theirs was an idolatry in which they insisted all others should share. To Abiezer Coppe they were the things that are—the reformation establishment—shortly to be set at naught.[71] But social inversion could be played many ways. 'Look into the gaols of England,' said Bunyan, 'and into the ale houses ... and I believe you will find those that plead for the spirit of prayer in the gaol, and those that look after the forms of men's inventions only—in the ale-house.'[72]

William Walwyn distinguished two social sources of formality. One was the sheer inertia of custom. Most people followed the religion they were brought up in, assuming its superiority and their right to impose it on others. '... it is in them traditionall, and they are not truly religious; but meere morall Christians: utterly ignorant of the cleare Heavenly brightnesse, inherent in pure and undefiled Religion.' The second source of formality was insecurity, in particular, that which arose in people who mistook superstition for true religion.[73] By 1649 Walwyn, like Coppe, was becoming more harshly critical of these 'seeming Saints'. He wished that they could be identified by a striking badge worn on their hats or tunics. 'A man that looks upon these seeming Saints, no mervail if they take them for such indeed, they are so solemn in their countenances, so frequent and so formall in their devotions, so sad at others cheerfulness, so watchful over others tripping, so censorious over others failings, having a kind of disdainfulness at others, bespeaking them in effect to stand farther off, I am holyer than thou ...'[74] John Rogers, unfortunate to begin his clerical career in the late 1640s, found himself anathema to Anabaptists of Dublin for refusing to ban infant baptism; attacked by 'the very formal and prelatic proud sort of Independents' for his views on the rights of women to speak, vote, ask, answer, consent and object in church affairs; condemned by the conservative for his opposition to tithes, and despised by all for his tolerance of religious diversity. Rogers came to see his ministry as a struggle against formality which he increasingly identified with the clerical and legal professions and—after Oliver's apostasy—with Cromwell.[75]

[71] This is the principal theme of Coppe's, *A Fiery Flying Roll*.
[72] Bunyan, *I will Pray with the Spirit* (1662?) quoted in Hill, *Turbulent, Seditious and Factious People*, 126.
[73] Walwyn, *A Still and Soft Voice* (1647), 2–3, 7–8.
[74] Walwyn, *Walwyn's Just Defence* (1649), 31–2.
[75] Rogers, *Some Account*, 29–30, 33–4, 58, 68. Cf. John Lilburne's argument that three sorts of men gained from the twin social evils of 'living on other men's lights' and self-love—the clergy, lawyers and formalists. Lilburne, *An Answer to Nine Arguments* (1644), To the Reader.

Forms were about regularity and thereby about predictability. This was the principal way in which they induced and confirmed a sense of order. Constitutional convention, due process, the rule of law—in all their formality—reconciled liberty and authority, constraining the former from the excesses of licence and the latter from the arbitrariness of tyranny. But a significant version of God in the seventeenth century was distinguished not so much by orderliness and restraint as by a dynamic wilfulness, by seemingly arbitrary and continuous interventions and by apocalyptic innovation. Where did a God, whose most immediately apparent characteristics might be the vagaries of particular providence, or a millennial overturning, fit into the undifferentiated amalgam of seventeenth century civil and religious concerns?

There can be no doubt that attitudes to particular providence were one of the major underpinnings of antiformalism. It was the work of providence, John Bond reminded parliament in 1648 to sift, rinse and resift, finally 'separating between the faithfull and the formalist'.[76] The forms of the ancient constitution, including monarchy, were swept away not because men intended such things to happen but because they were acting as blind instruments of providence.[77] Setting up such a modest form of ecclesiastical control as the Cromwellian Triers in 1654 was, according to John Goodwin, a usurpation of God's 'golden Scepter' and providence would surely cast them down.[78] 'Kings and Priests are Jewish ceremonies' declared the author of *Tyranipocrit*. They belonged to the formalities of a dispensation under the Law but under Christ's dispensation of Grace providence decreed their fall.[79] In 1659 it was, William Sprigge pointed out to its members, God's providence which had recalled parliament and put the nation 'like wax into your hands'.[80] Forms, because they were fleshly contrivances, frequently stirred providence into action. Sir Henry Yelverton, speaking of church discipline and ceremonies, insisted that 'Inventions of men provoked the wrath of God.'[81] Since the Protectorate usurped God's sovereignty, the assassination of Cromwell, it was argued in 1657, could be seen as tyrannicide, the removal of a usurper, not murder.[82] Submission to such a God

---

[76] John Bond, *Eschol* (1648), 1, cited in Worden, 'Providence and Politics in Cromwellian England', 95. Worden's essay remains the best introduction to providentialism in the period.

[77] For one expression of these views see Arise Evans, *The Voice of King Charls* (1655), To the most glorious King CHARLS.

[78] John Goodwin, *The Triers Tried* (1657), To the Reader.

[79] *Tyranipocrit* (1649), 3.

[80] [William Sprigge], *A Modest Plea* (1659), To the Right Honourable, The High Court of PARLIAMENT.

[81] Quoted in J. T. Cliffe, *The Puritan Gentry: The Great Puritan Families of Early Stuart England* (1984), 27.

[82] [Edward Sexby and Silius Titus], *Killing Noe Murder* (1657). Both this, and the reply

involved seeing all forms as transitory, transitional arrangements.

In April 1656 Major General Haynes warned the Lord Protector that it was always dangerous to attempt to place limitations on God's providence.[83] What such providence required were flexible human instruments not the regularity of formal contrivances.[84] In late 1648 or early 1649 the godly of Norfolk petitioned Fairfax and the General Council of the New Model Army not to set up a merely natural or worldly form of government. God's design was 'the falls and overthrows of worldly powers'.[85] By the mid-1650s, William Sedgewick was recalling the previous decade and a half as a struggle between traditional and invented forms, on the one hand, and, on the other, those who were the instruments of God prepared to be led by God wherever he went. The apostasy of the mid-1650s was that, fertile in forms, Cromwell and the nation had come to neglect the 'power of godliness'. '... in outward things, as matters of the Government' the nation, Sedgewick claimed, was still entangled in the manners and customs of Egypt, still seeking 'for a way or form of Government of our own that is proper for a godly people'. But such a search and its divisiveness was, in the longer term, irrelevant because men's intentions, however pure, were not what would determine the outcome. '... this Work begun amongst us, is not so much carried on by an inward *Spring of Grace*, but upon the *Wheels of Providence*; drawing or driving men on into ways and paths, that their own light neither did nor could direct them into.'[86]

What Geoffrey Nuttall calls the 'principle of mutability', the willingness to be flexible about doctrine, polity and discipline because it was necessary to be open to God's redirection, underlay a pragmatism about forms or an antiformalism which was reinforced further by contemporary eschatology.[87] The centripetal quality of

---

to it, were based on the premise that it was inconceivable that God 'had left the world to be governed by Fortune'. See *Killing is Murder* (1657), 7.

[83] Haynes to Cromwell, 9 April 1656, *A Collection of the State Papers of John Thurloe*, ed. T. Birch, 7 vols. (1742), IV, 688.

[84] Cf. *ibid.*, II, 113–14 for one example amongst many of Cromwell as such an instrument. Sterry, *The Clouds in Which*, 40–1, 46, 47–8; Owen, *God's work in Founding Zion*, 41.

[85] *Certain Quaeres Humbly Presented in Way of PETITION by many Christian People dispersed abroad throughout the County of Norfolk and City of Norwich* (1649), 3–4. Cf. Rogers, *Dod*, 13–14.

[86] [Sedgewick], *Animadversions*, 52–4, 62, 65, 66, 78. For contemporary perceptions of Cromwell's apostasy see Blair Worden, 'Oliver Cromwell and the Sin of Achan', in *History, Society and the Churches*, eds. Derek Beales and Geoffrey Best (Cambridge, 1985), 125–45. For its links with his abandonment of instrumentality for formality see Davis, 'Cromwell's Religion', 201.

[87] Nuttall, *Holy Spirit*, 107, 111–12.

what William Lamont has called the 'centripetal millenarianism' of the period has much to do with the desire to avoid formal distinctions in order to pursue God's climactic work in unity.[88] It was an age in which laws and ordinances based on human will must be disposable in favour of the Law from Sion and Jerusalem.[89]

It is not surprising that the professional in-fighting of the clergy should lead to their identification with formality.[90] But the attitude to formality and law, as to lawyers, the engineers of legal formalism, is perhaps more ambiguous and complex. If we accept that in the seventeenth century, liberty and authority were seen not as antithetical but as complementary, then it is important to recognise the significance of formality for that relationship. Liberty in the common parlance of the seventeenth century was expressed in submission to an appropriate authority operating in a duly regulated way.[91] The formalities of due process and constitutional propriety, of lawfulness, were critical in reconciling liberty and authority. What happened when antiformalists began to loosen those links was the inauguration of a process whereby liberty and authority moved from being complementary to becoming antithetical and so began to take on their modern meanings. Between the letter and the spirit, the equity and the rigour of the law, between the form and the substance a shadow of confusion began to fall. In civil matters, Winstanley insisted on the application of the 'bare Letter of the Law' but he also associated the 'bare letter' of Scripture with a hireling and corrupt clergy.[92] Sticklers for procedural forms, the Levellers yet insisted on the distinction between substance and form with respect to civil justice while depicting England's birthright as a fusion of

[88] William Lamont, 'Puritanism as History and Historiography: some Further Thoughts', *Past and Present*, XLIV (1969), 145. Cf. *Certain Quaeres*, 7.

[89] John Camm and Francis Howgill, *This Was the Word of the Lord* (1654). Cf. Abiezer Coppe's insistence that the forms of levelling having been tried the 'substantiality of levelling' was to come from God's hands. The strange postures of formality were the obstacle which was to be swept away. Coppe, *Some Sweet Sips* in *Ranter Writings*, ed. Smith, 43, 44, 46, 53, 54, 63, 76–7; *A Fiery Flying Roll* in *ibid.*, 86–7, 90, 103–4.

[90] In this respect, interregnum antiformalism may have had some role as a generator of the detestation of popery, priestcraft and ideology which Mark Goldie has shown to be such an influential feature of post-Restoratian *mentalité*. Mark Goldie, 'Ideology', in *Political Innovation and Conceptual Change*, eds. Terence Ball, James Farr and Russell L. Hanson (Cambridge, 1989) 266–291.

[91] Davis, 'Religion and the Struggle for Freedom in the English Revolution'. John Locke's formulation; 'Freedom of men, under Government, is, to have a standing Rule to live by common to everyone of that Society, and made by the Legislative Power erected in it ...' expressed a seventeenth century commonplace. *Locke's Two Treatises of Government*, ed. Peter Laslett, (Cambridge, 1970), 302.

[92] Winstanley, *Law of Freedom*, 554–5, 591; *The Mysterie of God* (1648) in *Works*, 82; *The Saints Paradice* (1648?) in *ibid.*, 94, 96.

'Equitie, Law, Justice and Conscience'.[93] John Warr in 1649 would have none of this. 'This formality of our English law in that to an oppressed man which school-divinity is to a wounded spirit, when the conscience of a sinner is pierced with remorse.' 'Why are so many men destroyed for want of a formality and punctilio in law.'[94] Very few interregnum commentators, however radical, would go as far as Warr in seeing civil formality as oppressive rather than protective. There were, nevertheless, doubts concerning the role of formality in civil as well as religious institutional life and the two predictably merged in ways which were to be critical for the outcome of the revolution.

The most dramatic illustration of this comes at the height of the revolutionary crisis in the Whitehall debates of December 1648, on the eve of regicide and republic. Central to those discussions was a set of constitutional proposals, the second Agreement of People, presented by the Levellers. After their withdrawal from the debates the so-called 'Officers Agreement' was presented to the Rump on 20 January 1649, ten days before the king was executed. It was never taken up by the Rump and no new constitution was adopted until December 1653.[95]

Two arguments run through the debates at Whitehall, intertwining with each other and finally producing deadlock.[96] The better known issue is that of religious liberty but more critical for the nature of the English revolution was the debate about the appropriateness of any form of constitutional provision. Faced with the Agreement of the People, Joshua Sprigge argued that any form of constitutional provision was entirely inappropriate. 'God will bringe forth a New Heaven and a New Earth. In the meantime you're work is to restraine, indeed to restraine the magistrate from such a power.'[97] Philip Nye, enmeshed in the same language, was caught in a paralysis of indecision. God would punish them if they thwarted his purpose by the erection of new formalities but retribution would also follow if they allowed impiety in

[93] Cf. [Overton], *Commoners Complaint* (1647), 8, 12; [Lilburne], *England's Birthright* (1645), 8, 12.

[94] John Warr, *The Corruption and Deficiency of the Lawes of England Soberly Discovered* (1649) in *Divine Right to Democracy* ed. David Wootton (Harmondsworth, 1986), 157, 159.

[95] Barbara Taft, 'The Council of Officers' Agreement of the People 1648/9', *The Historical Journal*, XXVIII (1985), 169–85; David Underdown, *Pride's Purge: Politics in the Puritan Revolution* (Oxford, 1971); Blair Worden, *The Rump Parliament 1648–1653* (Cambridge, 1974).

[96] The debates, arguably much more important than Putney in terms of the outcome of the revolution, have been strangely neglected. The most accessible edition of them remains *Selections from the papers of William Clarke, Secretary to the Council of the Army*, ed. C. H. Firth, 4 vols. (Camden Society, 1891–1901), II. Also available in a new edition with an introduction by Austin Woolrych (Royal Historical Society, 1992).

[97] *Ibid.*, 84–7. Note also comments by Peter and Clarke.

a relaxation of forms.[98] Harrison summed up a powerful theme in the debate when he argued the setting aside of the Levellers' proposals because the true Agreement would come from God not from men.[99] It was the argument which won the day. Forms were impieties in an apocalyptic moment. No constitution was formally adopted to replace that overthrown in 1648–9. When at last, in December 1653, Cromwell adopted the Instrument of Government, it was greeted by the saints as his great apostasy. Gideon had lost his way. The Lord Protector by placing his trust in fleshly instruments and carnal forms could no longer enjoy status as an instrument of providence.[100]

Space and lack of art have prevented me from giving more than a sketch of the conceptual framework which I have been trying to recover. In coming to terms with a society which could legislate against formality as a social evil comparable to blasphemy or atheism, that framework is worthy of further exploration. Such an exploration would uncover the terrible tensions evoked by the convergence of fears of formality and fears of formlessness: the desire for authentic, unfettered spirituality and the need for constraints against carnal self—and collective—deception; the desire to respect diversity of religious experience and the fear that unity could not be maintained without some formal insistence on fundamentals, some uniformity. In all these respects, formality could be seen as obstruction, barrier, diversion but also as inescapable necessity. Equally, the types and sources of antiformalist attitudes are worthy of more sophisticated portrayal. There are clearly broad links with traditions of thinking about adiaphora which reach deep into Reformation history and beyond. But there are also more immediate sources in the experience of a society fractured and frightened by the proliferating formalisms unleashed by the collapse of formal control and the emergence of sectarianism. Providence, apocalypse, the priority of practical Christianity all contribute to impatience with constraints on fluidity and action. It would be misleading, however, to make any close identification of antiformalism with antinomianism. As I hope I have indicated, anxiety about forms was too ubiquitous a phenomenon for that. The radical willingness to contemplate the disintegration of all forms was quantitatively insignificant (as was pure, intentional antinomianism). More moderate positions, where the need for forms, ordinances and rules was acknowledged but the concern was

---

[98] *Ibid.*, 119–20.
[99] *Ibid.*, 184–6. Cf. *Walwins Wiles*, To the Noble and Successful Englands Army, where the New Model is urged to leave matters to God not to Agreements.
[100] For example, 'A Word for God' in *State Papers of John Thurloe*, ed. Birch, IV, 381.

to deny them priority, were much more common. The confusions and divisions which disturbed that consensus had more to do with how that lower priority was interpreted; as an acceptance of the magistrates' right to determine matters indifferent; as a willingness to accept diversity of scruple with regard to forms; as a concern to 'settle' forms and so drop them from the agenda; or as a matter to be disposed of pragmatically by political means but not necessarily those of the centre.[101]

Antiformalists held that there were no *iure divino* forms. How then were forms and the ordinances underpinning them to be authorised? It is here, I believe, and not as contrasting authorities have suggested in the rise of antinomianism[102] that we might find the seedbed of the classic debate on authority which grips some of the finest minds of the seventeenth century. Three aspects of this are perhaps worth ending with. Formality reconciled liberty and authority. Antiformalism threatened to subvert that linkage. This is one of the critical contexts for the debate on the proper signification of liberty as of authority. It is one of the preconditions of the emergence of a modern language of both. Secondly, antiformalist attitudes free people for a radical approach to the institutions of their society and simultaneously limit the radical outcome of those approaches. In diminishing forms, antiformalism drew attention to them. The priority and legitimacy of old forms was downplayed. Reform became a contemplatable possibility. On the other hand, antiformalism set brakes on reformulation. As at Whitehall, the impact of antiformalism in the revolutionary moment was to reject alternative constitutions in favour of handing God a blank sheet of paper. When God failed to act, the revolution ultimately faltered and collapsed.

The third aspect relates to the way in which unity and substance were integral to the aspiration to a godly society in mid-seventeenth-century England. Formality impeded both by its divisive and diverting qualities. Antiformalism was both centripetal and demanding. As William Sancroft observed in 1652, 'The Politician must have the shadow of Religion, but the substance hurts.'[103] After disillusion with the godly prince, godly bishop, godly magistrate came disillusion with the godly politician. At the Restoration a process began whereby public

---

[101] Perhaps the Cromwellian Protectorate came closest to holding these responses in some sort of coexistence. See Anthony Fletcher, 'Oliver Cromwell and the godly nation', in *Oliver Cromwell and the English Revolution* ed. John Morrill (1990), 209–33; Davis, 'Cromwell's Religion' in *ibid.*, 196–99.

[102] Both Christopher Hill and John Pocock, in one of the few points of agreement between them, have seen the origins of the debate on authority in reaction to the rise of antinomianism. The rise of antinomianism is as spectral as the rise of the middle class.

[103] William Sancroft, *Modern Policies taken from Machiavel, Borgia and other choice Authors* (1652), B3. This work had gone through seven editions by 1657.

religion settled for forms as it settled for uniformity. All else—including the pursuit of substance—was to be derogated as 'enthusiasm', bundled into nonconformity, packed and labelled for ostracisation or exile. Here lie the origins of that distrust of public religiosity which has been such a persistent feature of English social and political culture.

THE ROYAL HISTORICAL SOCIETY
REPORT OF COUNCIL, SESSION 1992–1993

THE Council of the Royal Historical Society has the honour to present the following report to the Anniversary Meeting.

1. Review of the Society

This year Council has undertaken a fundamental review of the Society and its activities. The purpose of this review is to ensure that the Society continues, into the twenty-first century, to meet the needs of its members and the wider community of historians. The review was supported by the outgoing President, Professor F.M.L. Thompson, and has been actively implemented by the incoming President, Professor R.R. Davies. In December 1992 Council established four Working Groups, each under the chairmanship of a Vice-President, to consider Membership, Finance, Publications and 'The Public Face of the Society'. These Working Groups have all reported to Council, which is now engaged in the task of drafting concrete proposals to be submitted to the Fellowship at the Anniversary Meeting in November 1993.

2. Establishment of R.Hist.S.–B.N.C. link

The Society has also taken advantage of an opportunity to increase its direct contacts with historians in other countries. In November 1992 Council accepted responsibility for the general administration of the British National Committee of the International Congress of Historical Sciences for a three year period starting in April 1993. The move was prompted by the decision of the British Academy to discontinue its direct funding of the B.N.C. The Society now has a large representation on the reconstituted B.N.C. which will organize future conferences.

3. Issues of concern to historians

As in past years, the Society has kept a close eye on public and professional developments of concern to historians. Strong representations were made to the Government on the need for both adequate funding of The Victoria County History and proper protection of the buildings in the custody of English Heritage. Council also discussed the outcome of the Research Assessment Exercise in History and the nature of the Quality Assessment of History teaching in universities which is now being undertaken by the Higher Education Funding Councils.

4. The Society's Newsletter

The introduction of a Newsletter, circulated twice a year, has enabled members to receive more detailed and up to date information about the Society's activities. The Newsletter includes reports from the President and Officers, together with information about the Society's forthcoming books and conferences. It also provides a forum for advertising the Society's various research support funds. As in past years, the Society has continued to fund a Research Fellowship at the Institute of Historical Research, to provide prizes for outstanding A-level students and to contribute to the Young Historian scheme of the Historical Association.

5. Meetings of the Society

The Society held four meetings of Council and six paper readings in London. Two further Council meetings and paper readings were held at the University of Birmingham and the University of Wales College of Cardiff. A further meeting of Council and the annual one day conference were held at the University of Liverpool. All events were well attended and were followed by receptions which enabled Council to meet local members. As in 1991–92, the success of these meetings owed much to the hospitality provided by resident members of the Society. The Society has arranged to meet at Nottingham and Glasgow during the 1993–94 session. A two day conference will be held in Oxford in January 1994 to commemorate the bicentenary of the death of Edward Gibbon, and a one day conference in London in September 1994 on social change in medieval England.

An evening party was held for members and guests in the Upper Hall at University College London on Wednesday, 1 July 1992. 182 acceptances to invitations were received, and it was well attended.

6. Prizes

(i) The Whitfield Prize for 1992 was awarded to Dr. Christine Carpenter for her book *Locality and polity: A study of Warwickshire landed society, 1401–1499*, (Cambridge University Press). The assessors also declared Dr. Eugenio Biagini *proxime accessit* for his book *Liberty, Retrenchment and Reform: Popular Liberalism in the Age of Gladstone, 1860–1880*, (Cambridge University Press).

(ii) The Alexander Prize for 1993 was awarded to Mr. Clifford J. Rogers, from Ohio State University, for his essay *Edward III and the*

Dialectics of Strategy, 1327–1360, which was read to the Society on 28 May 1993.

7. Publications

Transactions, Sixth Series, Volume 3; *The Journal of William Schellinks' travels in England, 1661–1663,* ed. H. Lehmann and M. Exwood, (Camden, Fifth Series, Volume 1) and *Calendar of the Cartularies of Adam Fraunceys and John Pyel, mayors and merchants of London,* ed. S. O'Connor, (Camden, Fifth Series, Volume 2), went to press during the session and are due to be published in 1993.

The Society's *Annual Bibliography of British and Irish History, Publications of 1991,* was published by Oxford University Press.

The following three volumes in the STUDIES IN HISTORY series were published during the session: *Religion and Urban Change: Croydon, 1840–1914,* Jeremy Morris, (Volume 65), *Factional Politics and the English Reformation, 1520–1540,* Joseph S. Block, (Volume 66) and *Tyrone's Rebellion: the Outbreak of the Nine Years War in Tudor Ireland,* Hiram Morgan, (Volume 67).

8. Papers Read

At the ordinary meetings of the Society the following papers were read:

'The Thirty Years' War, 1914–1945: the Two World Wars in Historical Perspective' by Professor Sir Michael Howard (1 July 1992: Prothero lecture).
'Economic Depression and the Making of "Traditional" Indian Society, 1825–1855' by Dr. David Washbrook (16 October 1992).
'Against Formality: One Aspect of the English Revolution' by Professor Colin Davis (11 December 1992).
'General Franco as Military Leader' by Professor Paul Preston (22 January 1993).
'Symbolic meanings of hair in the Middle Ages' by Professor Robert Bartlett (5 March 1993).
'Men's Dilemma: the future of Patriarchy in England, 1560–1660' by Professor Anthony Fletcher (30 April 1993).

At the Anniversary Meeting on 20 November 1992, the President, Professor F.M.L. Thompson, delivered an address on 'English Landed Society in the Twentieth Century: IV, Prestige without Power?'.

A one day conference entitled 'The Eighteenth-Century Atlantic' was held at the University of Liverpool on 19 September 1992 at which the following papers were read:

'Conspiracy of Commerce: Colonial Perceptions of Empire on the Eve of the American Revolution' by Professor Tim Breen;

'Bristol West India Merchants in the Eighteenth Century' by Dr. Kenneth Morgan; and
'The Atlantic in the Eighteenth Century: A Need to Return to the "Big" Picture' by Professor Kenneth Maxwell.

9. Finance

The Honorary Treasurer had been working for some time to establish the full implications of the new charities legislation for the Society. This was surprisingly difficult but it was now almost complete. When it was completed she would circulate full details to Members of Council, in particular to inform them of their personal responsibilities under the new Act. She was confident that no major changes in the Society's methods of operation would be required. The Society was already soundly run.

The Society's investment income has fallen. However, we feel there is no immediate cause for concern about this and are satisfied with the management of our investments. Subscription income increased in 1992–93 over 1991–92 by £2,103. There was a small deficit this year. The finances of the Society still provide no cause for immediate concern, but in view of the above, the Council is considering a rise in the subscription rate. However, the decision on the timing and amount of the rise awaits the outcome of the current Review of the Society's activities. It does not seem wise to fix a new subscription rate until we are clear about the range of the Society's activities the subscription will assist in funding.

Council records with gratitude the following benefactions to the Society:

Mr. L.C. Alexander
The Reverend David Berry
Professor Andrew Browning
Professor C.D. Chandaman
Professor G. Donaldson
Mrs. W.M. Frampton
Mr. E.L.C. Mullins
Sir George Prothero
Professor T.F. Reddaway
Miss E.M. Robinson
Professor A.S. Whitfield

10. Membership

Council records with regret the deaths of 30 Fellows, 1 Associate and 2 Corresponding Fellows. They included Honorary Vice-President— Professor G. Donaldson, Fellows—Mr. E.L.C. Mullins, a former Honorary Librarian and Professor A.J. Taylor, a former Member of Council, and Corresponding Fellows—Professor B. Bischoff and Professor L. Hanke.

The resignations of 8 Fellows, 2 Associates and 19 Subscribing Libraries were received. 56 Fellows and 5 Associates were elected and 2 Libraries were admitted. Professor P. Contamine accepted Council's invitation to become a Corresponding Fellow. 21 Fellows transferred to the category of Retired Fellow. The membership of the Society on 30 June 1993 comprised 1942 Fellows (including 40 Life Fellows and 292 Retired Fellows), 39 Corresponding Fellows, 144 Associates and 666 Subscribing Libraries. The Society exchanged publications with 14 Societies, British and foreign.

11. Officers and Council

At the Anniversary Meeting on 20 November 1992, Professor R.R. Davies succeeded Professor F.M.L. Thompson as President from December 1 1992. The remaining Officers of the Society were re-elected.

The Vice-Presidents retiring under By-law XVII were Professor R.R. Davies and Professor W.A. Speck. Professor R.A. Griffiths and Dr. J.S. Morrill were elected to replace them.

The members of Council retiring under By-law XX were Professor M.D. Biddiss, Professor M.C. Cross, Professor D.K. Fieldhouse and Dr. J.S. Morrill. Following a ballot of Fellows, Dr. G.W. Bernard, Dr. K. Burk, Professor A.J. Fletcher and Dr. F. Heal were elected in their place.

Messrs. Davies Watson were appointed auditors for the year 1992–93 under By-law XXXIX.

12. Representatives of the Society

The representation of the Society upon various bodies was as follows:
Mr. M. Roper, Professor P.H. Sawyer and Mr. C.P. Wormald on the Joint Committee of the Society and the British Academy established to prepare an edition of Anglo-Saxon charters;
Professor H.R. Loyn on a committee to promote the publication of photographic records of the more significant collections of British Coins;
Professor G.H. Martin on the Council of the British Records Association;
Mr. M.R.D. Foot on the Committee to advise the publishers of *The Annual Register*;
Dr. R.C. Mettam on the History at the Universities Defence Group;
Professor C.J. Holdsworth on the Court at the University of Exeter;
Professor A.G. Watson on the Anthony Panizzi Foundation;

Professor M.C. Cross on the Council of the British Association for Local History;

Professor J. Sayers on the National Council on Archives;

Miss V. Cromwell on the Advisory Board of the Computers in Teaching Initiative Centre for History;

Professor Glanmor Williams on the Court of Governors of the University College of Swansea; Professor A.L. Brown on the University of Stirling Conference; and

Professor W. Davies on the Court at the University of Birmingham.

Council received reports from its representatives.

Professor E.B. Fryde represents the Society on a committee to regulate British co-operation in the preparation of a new repertory of medieval sources to replace Potthast's *Bibliotheca Historica Medii Aevi*; Professor C.N.L. Brooke on the British Sub-Commission of the Commission International d'Histoire Ecclesiastique Comparee;

During the year, Dr. A.M.S. Prochaska agreed to succeed Professor P.E. Lasko on the Advisory Council of the reviewing committee on the Export of Works of Art.

THE ROYAL HISTORICAL SOCIETY

BALANCE SHEET AS AT 30TH JUNE 1993

	Note	1993 £	1993 £	1992 £	1992 £
FIXED ASSETS					
Tangible assets	2		2,051		3,181
Investments	3		1,653,640		892,838
			1,655,691		896,019
CURRENT ASSETS					
Stocks	1(c)	7,803		812	
Debtors	4	21,836		15,779	
Cash at bank and in hand	5	17,449		27,013	
		47,088		43,604	
LESS: CREDITORS					
Amounts falling due within one year . . .	6	97,921		68,676	
NET CURRENT (LIABILITIES)			(50,833)		(25,072)
NET TOTAL ASSETS			1,604,858		870,947
REPRESENTED BY:					
General Fund			1,510,817		826,296
Miss E.M. Robinson Bequest			60,252		23,321
A.S. Whitfield Prize Fund			30,904		16,153
Studies in History			2,885		5,177
			1,604,858		870,947

THE ROYAL HISTORICAL SOCIETY

Income and Expenditure Account for the Year Ended 30th June 1993

GENERAL FUND

	Note	1993 £	1993 £	1992 £	1992 £
INCOME					
Subscriptions	7		60,899		58,796
Investment Income			67,291		83,612
Royalties and reproduction fees			5,360		5,696
Donations and sundry income			3,021		3,874
			136,571		151,978
EXPENDITURE					
SECRETARIAL AND ADMINISTRATIVE					
Salaries, pensions and social security		23,115		21,373	
Printing and stationery		3,144		4,534	
Postage and telephone		2,063		1,559	
Bank charges		2,073		1,998	
Audit and accountancy		3,231		3,114	
Insurance		536		475	
Meetings and travel		10,905		7,852	
Repairs and renewals		741		656	
Depreciation	1(b)	1,130		1,131	
(Profit)/loss on disposal of fixed tangible assets		—		(570)	
			46,938		42,122
PUBLICATIONS					
Publishing costs	8(a)	16,782		34,274	
Provision for publications in progress	8(b)	67,900		50,600	
Other publication costs	8(c)	4,277		(384)	
Sales of publications		—		(205)	
			88,959		84,285
			135,897		126,407
LIBRARY AND ARCHIVES	1(d)				
Purchase of books and publications		918		110	
Binding		2,457		1,143	
			3,375		1,253
OTHER CHARGES					
Centenary fellowship		5,658		5,498	
Alexander prize		297		418	
Prothero lecture		(100)		350	
Grants		4,125		3,000	
Research support grants		11,680		4,155	
Donations and sundry expenses		1,241		2,016	
A-level prizes		900		720	
Young Historian Scheme		1,993		1,993	
British Bibliography		2,000		3,000	
			27,794		21,150
			167,066		148,810
(Deficit)/surplus for the year			(30,495)		3,168
Surplus on sale of Investments			11,348		58,588
Surplus on revaluation of quoted investments			703,668		—
			684,521		61,756
Balance brought forward at 1.7.92			826,296		764,540
Balance carried forward at 30.6.93			1,510,817		826,296

THE ROYAL HISTORICAL SOCIETY

INCOME AND EXPENDITURE ACCOUNT FOR THE YEAR ENDED 30TH JUNE 1993

SPECIAL FUNDS

	1993 £	1993 £	1992 £	1992 £
MISS E.M. ROBINSON BEQUEST				
INCOME				
Investment income		3,782		2,376
EXPENDITURE				
Grant to Dulwich Picture Gallery	3,000		2,000	
Other expenses	24		23	
		(3,024)		(2,023)
Surplus/(deficit) for the year		758		353
Surplus/(deficit) on disposal of investments		4,000		—
Surplus on revaluation of quoted investments		32,173		—
		36,931		353
Balance carried forward at 1.7.92		23,321		22,968
Balance carried forward at 30.6.93		60,252		23,321
A.S. WHITFIELD PRIZE FUND				
INCOME				
Investment income		1,322		1,809
EXPENDITURE				
Prize awarded	1,000		1,000	
Surplus for the year		322		809
Surplus/(Deficit) on disposal of investments		3,519		(9)
Surplus on revaluation of quoted investments		10,910		—
		14,751		800
Balance brought forward at 1.7.92		16,153		15,353
Balance carried forward at 30.6.93		30,904		16,153
STUDIES IN HISTORY				
INCOME				
Royalties		1,583		1,498
Investment income		690		886
		2,273		2,384
EXPENDITURE				
Honorarium	3,500		3,500	
Editor's expenses	967		909	
Ex gratia royalties and sundry expenses	98		18	
Bank charges	—		5	
		(4,565)		(4,432)
(Deficit) for the year		(2,292)		(2,048)
Balance brought forward		5,177		7,225
Balance carried forward		2,885		5,177

THE ROYAL HISTORICAL SOCIETY

Notes to the Accounts for the Year Ended 30th June 1993

1. Accounting Policies
   (a) *Basis of accounting*
      The accounts have been prepared under the historical cost convention as modified by the revaluation of quoted investments to market value.
   (b) *Depreciation*
      Depreciation is calculated by reference to the cost of fixed assets using a straight line basis at rates considered appropriate having regard to the expected lives of the fixed assets.
      The annual rates of depreciation in use are:

   Furniture and equipment   10%
   Computer equipment   25%

   Prior to 1st July 1987 the full cost of fixed assets was written off to General Fund in the year of purchase.
   (c) *Stocks*
      Stock is valued at the lower of cost and net realisable value.
   (d) *Library and archives*
      The cost of additions to the library and archives is written off in the year of purchase.

2. Tangible Fixed Assets

	Computer Equipment	Furniture and Equipment	Total
	£	£	£
Cost			
At 1st July 1992	8,681	620	9,301
Additions during year	—	—	
At 30th June 1993	8,681	620	9,301
Depreciation:			
At 1st July 1992	5,810	310	6,120
Charge for the year	1,068	62	1,130
At 30th June 1993	6,878	372	7,250
Net book value			
At 30th June 1993	1,803	248	2,051
At 30th June 1992	2,871	310	3,181

The cost of additions to the library and archives is written off in the year of purchase.
Prior to 1st July 1987 the cost of furniture and equipment was written off in the year of purchase. Items acquired before that date are not reflected in the above figures.

3. Investments

	1993 £	1992 £
Quoted Securities at cost	824,670	826,421
Surplus on revaluation	746,751	—
Quoted Securities at market value	1,571,421	826,421
Money invested at call	82,219	66,417
	1,653,640	892,838

Quoted Investments are stated at market value in the Balance Sheet as at 30th June 1993. At 30th June 1992 and in previous years, Quoted Investments were carried in the Balance Sheet at cost.
The surplus arising on re-valuation plus profits (less losses) realised on disposals of investments is credited to Income and Expenditure Account in the case of investments held on General Fund and to the relevant fund accounts where investments are held for specific funds.

Movements in quoted investments during year were:

	£
Cost at beginning of year	826,421
Additions during year	100,562
Disposals during year	(102,313)
Cost at end of year	824,670
Market value at 30th June 1992	1,339,434
Market value at 30th June 1993	1,571,421

4. DEBTORS

	1993 £	1992 £
Sundry debtors	12,917	12,724
Prepayments	8,919	3,055
	21,836	15,779

5. CASH AT BANK AND IN HAND

	1993 £	1992 £
Deposit accounts	13,656	25,043
Current accounts	3,793	1,970
	17,449	27,013

6. CREDITORS

	1993 £	1992 £
Sundry creditors	1,000	1,350
Subscriptions received in advance	12,532	13,250
Accruals	16,489	3,476
Provision for publications in progress	67,900	50,600
	97,921	68,676

7. SUBSCRIPTIONS

	1993 £	1992 £
Current subscriptions	56,134	55,422
Subscription arrears received	2,149	1,465
Income tax on covenants	2,616	1,909
	60,899	58,796

8. PUBLICATIONS

	1993 £	1992 £
(a) Publishing costs for the year		
Transactions, sixth series Vol. 1	—	15,870
Camden, fourth series Vol. 41	—	19,962
Camden, fourth series Vol. 42	—	6,745
Guides and Handbooks No. 17	—	18,895
Reresby	—	2,882
List of Fellows	—	4,809
Clarke Papers	—	5,315
Transactions, sixth series Vol. 2	17,172	—
Camden, fourth series Vol. 43	22,262	—
Camden, fourth series Vol. 44	16,708	—
Camden, fifth series Vol. 1	151	—
Indirect costs, paper storage and usage and insurance	8,608	6,823
Printing costs for circulation to members	2,481	1,973
	(67,382)	(83,274)
Less: Provision b/fwd	(50,600)	(49,000)
	16,782	34,274

(b) Provision for publication in progress

Transactions, sixth series Vol. 3	18,300	—
Camden, fifth series Vol. 1	18,550	—
Camden, fifth series Vol. 2	18,550	—
List of Fellows	2,500	—
Guides and Handbooks No. 18	10,000	—
Transactions, sixth series Vol. 2	—	16,700
Camden, fourth series Vol. 43	—	16,950
Camden, fourth series Vol. 44	—	16,950
	67,900	50,600

(c) Other publication costs

Annual Bibliography	6,586	3,089
Less: royalties received	(2,309)	(3,473)
	4,277	(384)

R. R. DAVIES, *President*
P. M. THANE, *Treasurer*

We have audited the accounts on pages 295 to 300 in accordance with Auditing Standards.

In our opinion the accounts give a true and fair view of the Society's affairs at 30th June 1993 and of its result for the year then ended.

118 SOUTH STREET, DORKING
24th September, 1993

DAVIES, WATSON & CO
Chartered Accountant
Registered Auditor.

ROYAL HISTORICAL SOCIETY
DAVID BERRY ESSAY TRUST

ACCOUNTS
FOR THE YEAR
ENDED
30TH JUNE 1993

DAVIES, WATSON & CO.
CHARTERED ACCOUNTANTS
DORKING

	1993 £	£	1992 £	£
FIXED ASSETS				
1117.63 units in the Charities Official Investment Fund				
(Market Value £6,709: 1992 £5,610)		1,530		1,530
CURRENT ASSETS				
Bank Deposit Account	9,404		8,698	
LESS: **CREDITORS**				
Amounts falling due within one year	4,076		3,992	
NET **CURRENT ASSETS**		5,328		4,706
NET **TOTAL ASSETS**		6,858		6,236
Represented by:				
Capital fund		1,000		1,000
Accumulated Income Account		5,858		5,236
		6,858		6,236

ROYAL HISTORICAL SOCIETY THE DAVID BERRY ESSAY TRUST

INCOME AND EXPENDITURE ACCOUNT FOR THE YEAR ENDED 30TH JUNE 1993

	£	1993 £	£	1992 £
INCOME				
Dividends		334		332
Bank Interest Receivable		372		315
		706		647
		—		—
EXPENDITURE				
Prize		—	150	
Adjudicators Fee	84			
		84		150
Excess of income over expenditure for the year		622		497
Balance brought forward		5,236		4,739
Balance carried forward		5,858		5,236

The late David Berry, by his Will dated 23rd April 1926, left £1,000 to provide in every three years a gold medal and prize money for the best essay on the Earl of Bothwell or, at the discretion of the Trustees, on Scottish History of the James Stuarts I to VI, in memory of his father the late Rev. David Berry.

The Trust is regulated by a scheme sanctioned by the Chancery Division of the High Court of Justice dated 23rd January 1930, and made in action 1927 A 1233 David Anderson Berry deceased, Hunter and Another v Robertson and Another and since modified by an order of the Charity Commissioners made on 11 January 1974 removing the necessity to provide a medal.

The Royal Historical Society is now the Trustee. The investment consists of 1117.63 Charities Official Investment Fund Income units.

The Trustee will in every second year of the three year period advertise inviting essays.

We have audited the accounts on pages 301 and 302 in accordance with Auditing Standards.

In our opinion the accounts give a true and fair view of the Trust's affairs at 30th June 1993 and of its surplus for the year then ended and have been properly prepared in accordance with the provisions of the Trust deed.

118 SOUTH STREET, DORKING
24th September, 1993

DAVIES, WATSON & CO
Chartered Accountant
Registered Auditor

ALEXANDER PRIZE

The Alexander Prize was established in 1897 by L. C. Alexander, F.R.Hist.S. The prize is awarded annually for an essay on a historical subject, which has been previously approved by the Literary Director. The essay must be a genuine work of original research, not hitherto published, and not previously awarded any other prize. It must not exceed 8,000 words, including footnotes, and must be sent in by 1 November. Further details may be obtained from the Executive Secretary. Candidates must *either* be under the age of 35 *or* be registered for a higher degree *or* have been registered for a higher degree within the last three years. The winner of the prize is awarded a silver medal and £250.

1993 PRIZE WINNER

Clifford J. Rogers, BA, MA
'Edward III and the Dialectics of Strategy, 1327–1360'

Proxime Accessit

Benjamin J. Thompson, MA, PhD
'Monasteries and their Patrons at Foundation and Dissolution'

DAVID BERRY PRIZE

The David Berry Prize was established in 1929 by David Anderson-Berry in memory of his father, the Reverend David Berry. The prize is awarded every three years for an essay on Scottish history, within the reigns of James I to James VI inclusive. The subject of each essay must be submitted in advance and approved by the Council of The Royal Historical Society. The essay must be a genuine work of research based on original material. The essay should be between 6,000 and 10,000 words excluding footnotes and appendices. Further details may be obtained from the Executive Secretary.

1991 PRIZE WINNER

M. H. Brown
' "That Old Serpent and Ancient of Evil Days"
Walter, earl of Atholl and the Murder of James I'

WHITFIELD PRIZE

The Whitfield Prize was established by Council in 1976 out of the bequest of the late Professor Archibald Stenton Whitfield. The prize is currently awarded to the best work on a subject of British history published in the United Kingdom during the calendar year. It must be the first solely authored history book published by the candidate and an original and scholarly work of research. Authors or publishers should send three copies (non-returnable) of a book eligible for the competition to the Executive Secretary before the end of the year in which the book is published. The award will be made by Council and announced at the Society's annual reception in the following July. The current value of the prize is £1,000.

1992 PRIZE WINNER

Christine Carpenter, MA, PhD
'Locality and Polity:
A Study of Warwickshire Landed Society, 1401–1499'

Through the medium of the local study, this book presents a portrait of a ruling class, the gentry of late-medieval England, and an analysis of how the business of rule in this period – a co-operative venture between centre and locality – was carried on. The lesser landowners of Warwickshire, from meanest gentleman to knight, are examined as a group in the first, thematic, section. This study of their fortunes, values and aspirations is the essential foundation for the second section, a chronological exploration of politics in fifteenth-century Warwickshire. The structures of rule, from centre to locality, and the attitudes of the ruling class, both of which, in the reaction against 'Whig constitutionalism' in late-medieval historiography, have been somewhat neglected, are integral to this analytical narrative. This is a view of governance from the shires. Thus, at the heart of the book lies the elucidation of the meaning and implications of 'good' and 'bad' rule for late-medieval political society.

THE ROYAL HISTORICAL SOCIETY

(INCORPORATED BY ROYAL CHARTER)

Patron
HER MAJESTY THE QUEEN

OFFICERS AND COUNCIL

DECEMBER 1992–NOVEMBER 1993

President
Professor R. R. DAVIES, BA, DPhil, FBA

Honorary Secretary
R. E. Quinault, MA, DPhil

Literary Directors
J. A. Ramsden, MA, DPhil
Professor M. C. E. Jones, MA. DPhil, FSA

Honorary Treasurer
P. M. Thane, MA, PhD

Honorary Librarian
D. A. L. Morgan, MA

Vice-Presidents
M. Roper, MA, Dlitt
Professor C. S. R. Russell, MA, FBA
Professor J. Gooch, BA, PhD
Professor C. J. Holdsworth, MA, PhD, FSA
Professor O. Anderson, MA, BLitt
Professor H. T. Dickinson, BA, DipEd, MA, PhD, DLitt
Professor R. A. Griffiths, BA, PhD, DLitt
J. S. Morrill, MA, DPhil